JOHN NEWTON
AND THE
ENGLISH EVANGELICAL TRADITION

John Newton
and the
English Evangelical Tradition

Between the Conversions of
Wesley and Wilberforce

D. Bruce Hindmarsh

WILLIAM B. EERDMANS PUBLISHING COMPANY
GRAND RAPIDS MICHIGAN / CAMBRIDGE, U.K.

To my parents
(I think John Newton would have liked them)

First published in 1996 by Oxford University Press Inc.

This edition published in 2001 by
Wm. B. Eerdmans Publishing Co.
255 Jefferson Ave. S.E., Grand Rapids, Michigan 49503 /
P.O. Box 163, Cambridge CB3 9PU U.K.

Printed in the United States of America

06 05 04 03 02 01   7 6 5 4 3 2 1

Library of Congress Cataloging in Publication Data

Hindmarsh, D. Bruce.
John Newton and the English evangelical tradition / D. Bruce Hindmarsh.
p.   cm.
Originally published: Oxford : Clarendon Press ; New York : Oxford
University Press, 1996, in series : Oxford theological monographs.
Includes bibliographical references and index.
ISBN 0-8028-4741-2 (pbk. : alk. paper)
1. Newton, John, 1725-1807. 2. Church of England – England –
Clergy – Biography. 3. Evangelicalism – Church of England –
History of doctrines – 18th century. 4. Evangelicalism – England –
History of doctrines – 18th century. 5. Anglican Communion
– England – History – 18th century. 6. England –
Church history – 18th century. I. Title.
BX5199.N55 H54 2000
283′.092 – dc21
[B]

00-045320

www.eerdmans.com

PREFACE TO THE PAPERBACK EDITION

In 1970 the pop singer Judy Collins recorded her album *Whales and Nightingales* and the last song she chose to include was "Amazing Grace." A few weeks after the album was released "Amazing Grace" was playing on the radio and quickly went to the top of the charts. At countless concerts and gatherings folksingers would end the evening by leading everyone in "Amazing Grace" as a kind of prayer. Judy Collins even went to an encounter group that ended its sessions with the song. Then in 1989 "Amazing Grace" was again in the media spotlight when Bill Moyers hosted a PBS television special that traced the history of the song and included a wide range of renditions. More poignant is a story surrounding the September 2, 1998, Swissair flight 111 crash into the Atlantic ocean off the coast of Nova Scotia, in which all 229 people on board were killed. The grief of the family members who gathered at the small village of Peggy's Cove and looked out over the rocks toward the waves where their loved ones had died was unspeakable. Then in the midst of all this sorrow, a family spontaneously began to sing "Amazing Grace," and everyone at the water's edge, including the firemen and rescue workers, were transfixed until the hymn was finished. These are but three examples of how in modern-day America, as in Scotland where the song is traditionally performed on bagpipes, "Amazing Grace" has become firmly embedded in popular consciousness.

The hymn was originally written by the subject of this book, John Newton (1725-1807), a converted slave-trader who felt keenly that God's mercy to him was an amazing experience of divine grace. Newton went on to become one of the leading evangelical ministers of the Church of England during the eighteenth-century Evangelical Revival. Although a few of his hymns live on, Newton is now largely forgotten, even among his evangelical descendants. I wrote this book because I thought Newton was a subject worthy of scholarly study, not only for the interest of his life's story, but also for his contribution as a pastoral theologian and for the way his life sheds light on the evangelical tradition in the eighteenth century. The original hardback

v

edition of this book was priced for research libraries and scholars with a generous professional allowance for books. That edition is now out of print. I am pleased that this book will now be available in an affordable edition for a wider audience, since John Newton's life and times are of significance not only for research academics but also for ministers, students, and educated lay people. The continued popularity of the hymn "Amazing Grace" is but one indication of that wider relevance of Newton and English evangelicalism.

Some readers of the first edition expressed a desire for more information about Newton's friend, the poet William Cowper. As I reread the text, however, I decided to leave it largely as it was. In my original preface I referred to the need for a fresh source-critical approach to the study of Newton and Cowper that would press beyond the question of Cowper's madness to ask something of how the self-understanding of these two men differed in their writings. The reader who is interested may find some help in my article, "The Olney Autobiographers: English Conversion Narrative in the Mid-Eighteenth Century," *Journal of Ecclesiastical History* 49 (January 1998): 61-84.

I am grateful to Charles Van Hof and the editorial staff at Eerdmans for their interest in republishing this book, and to Hilary O'Shea at Oxford University Press for her oversight of the original edition and her continued advice and assistance as I have called on her with various questions. My wife Carolyn is still my best friend and critic in my scholarly endeavors, and my children, though older, still hear a lot of eighteenth-century hymns at bedtime.

PREFACE

JOHN NEWTON (1725–1807) is one of those figures in the history of Christianity whose life has been familiar, even hackneyed, within certain religious circles, while at the same time being largely overlooked by modern historians interested in the eighteenth century. It may be that his remarkable maritime experiences and crisis conversion, reiterated every generation in pious biography, made commonplace through sermon illustrations and hymn introductions, have actually put off some scholars from giving him more than a passing look. This book seeks to save Newton both from evangelical hagiography and from academic neglect by treating his life and religious thought as a serious subject for scholarly consideration. Set in context, Newton's life helps to illuminate the religious self-understanding of a whole generation who knew themselves as 'evangelical' in a sense much different from those who later sometimes adopted the term as a badge of merely partisan loyalty. For some, the value of this book will be the way in which Newton's theology and piety is related to other contemporary Church of England evangelicals, Methodists, and various Dissenting bodies. For others, it will be the way in which Newton's life sheds light on several little-explored aspects of the eighteenth-century Evangelical Revival and how this enhances our understanding of the church in general during this period. The scope of this book is wider, however, than simply Newton and eighteenth-century evangelicalism. Life in the eighteenth century, as now, does not break down into sealed compartments, and so a real effort has been made here to relate Newton to developments in eighteenth-century culture, drawing at various points on wider primary sources and secondary discussions of the literature, ideas, social history, and theology of the century. The result, I hope, is a well-rounded picture of Newton, a sharper interpretation of the evangelical tradition, and a better understanding of aspects of eighteenth-century religion and culture as a whole.

The organization of this book is roughly chronological and

many important episodes in Newton's biography are re-
constructed from a thorough review of the archival sources,
but my aim has not been strictly biographical in the sense of
providing a comprehensive, connected narrative of all periods
of his life. The method I have followed here is rather that of
exposition: to expound a number of themes of central
importance to Newton in his life and writings, to relate these
to their context, and to draw out the implications for a general
understanding of Newton and the contemporary evangelical
tradition. The subjects I seek to address in this way include
conversion narrative, theological formation, ordination,
Calvinism, pastoralia and devotion, hymnody, religious topography (Midlands and London), and ecclesiology.

There are two issues which have sometimes clouded
Newton's biography and produced reactions ranging from
condemnation to defensive apologetic. These are, first, the
question of the hypocrisy of his continuing involvement in the
slave trade even after his evangelical conversion, and, second,
the question of whether his influence aggravated the dementia
of the poet William Cowper. As these issues are not a primary
concern of this study, a few words may be said about them
here. With respect to the first, it must be said that the full evil
of chattel slavery and of the exploitation of African peoples
was something which Newton, like most contemporary
Europeans, came to realize only gradually during the last
third of the eighteenth century. He came late in life to repent
of his involvement in the trade and to support Wilberforce in
the abolition crusade. Even in the earlier period, however, it is
wrong to picture Newton, as some have done, as *simultaneously*
a slave trader and a representative or leading evangelical. The
chronology of Newton's spiritual formation which I trace in
the opening chapters of this book demonstrates quite clearly
that Newton's introduction to evangelicalism begins only as
his slave trading career ends. His understanding of evangelical
theology comes later. While Newton must never be excused
for his participation in the slave trade, it would be wrong to see
his evangelicalism as peculiarly hypocritical on that account.

The related subject of Newton's involvement in the
abolition movement I discuss only in passing, since the main
events of the protracted British abolition campaign occur, for

the most part, in the period following that with which I am concerned here. The range of social, economic, and political issues is complex, and for an introduction to some of these the reader is referred to Roger Anstey, *The Atlantic Slave Trade and British Abolition, 1760–1810* (London, 1975).

The second question of Newton's influence upon Cowper was much debated in the nineteenth century and continues to influence twentieth-century attitudes towards the lives of both men. I review the history of this controversy briefly in the Introduction but do not attempt in this book to enter significantly into the debate itself. As others have argued, the debate has grown stale and has diverted attention away from the careful interpretation of sources to the expression, more often than not, of simple *parti pris*. My own feeling is that there are very promising areas of research, obscured by this debate, which have yet to be explored. I hope to demonstrate elsewhere, for example, how a comparison of the use each figure made of the genres of spiritual autobiography and hymnody yields much more sophisticated insights into the similarities and differences between these men than the frequently evoked caricatures of 'lusty, forthright sailor' and 'highly-strung, sensitive poet'. In any case, I expect that this study of Newton may contribute indirectly to the assessment of his influence upon Cowper by treating his life and religious thought as a subject in its own right, rather than merely as an episode in the history of Cowper's melancholy.

A few notes should be made about usage. In most cases when quoting manuscript sources I have emended spelling to correspond to modern usage. Except where noted, dates within the text are given as New Style, with the year beginning 1 January. The word 'evangelical', with the lower-case initial, is used throughout the text without distinguishing between those within and without the Established Church. In part this is an interpretative decision, since one of the points argued here relates to partisan consciousness, which in lexical terms defines the point at which 'evangelical' becomes 'Evangelical'. Quotations from the Bible are taken from the Authorized Version, since the majority of these references are to texts as used and understood in the eighteenth-century context. Unless otherwise stated, London is the place of publication for all works cited. And, finally, references to Newton's *Works*, cited by volume and page number, appear in parentheses in the text following quotations. The chief exception to this is with respect to the hymns, where parenthetical references are to the first edition of the *Olney Hymns* (*OH*), by book and hymn number.

It is a pleasure to acknowledge my debt to the many individuals who have contributed in various ways to this book. I am grateful to the Rt. Revd Geoffrey Rowell for supervising my work on this project while I was a D.Phil. student at Oxford, and for his continued friendship and interest in my work. I am thankful likewise to have had the sage advice and criticism of John Walsh, from whose fund of knowledge about evangelicalism and the eighteenth-century church I have benefited along with so many others. Among the scholars who have helpfully critiqued my work or provided insight or assistance in other ways, I should mention in particular David Bebbington, Henry Rack, Andrew Goddard, Paul Schaefer, Norm Klassen, Timothy Underhill, Richard Heitzenrater, Daniel Howe, Isabel Rivers, Michael Haykin, Grant Gordon, Ray Stephanson, and Jim King. I am particularly grateful to David Scroggie, who was a sensitive and meticulous proof-reader. Among those who were especially helpful with my extensive archival searches were the late Catherine Bull of Newport Pagnell and Liz Knight, archivist of the Cowper–Newton Museum at Olney. The depositories listed in my Bibliography will give some indication of how indebted I am to the staff of many other libraries and archives which are too numerous to mention by name. While obliged to all these individuals for their assistance, the errors which remain in the text reflect not on them, but on me. Finally, I am thankful for the support which I received for this project through a grant from the Social Sciences and Humanities Research Council of Canada. Above all, however, it is my wife Carolyn whom I must acknowledge as my best and most severe critic, while also being a constant friend. My children too have shared in this book, not least by patiently learning at bedtime to distinguish some of the finer points of theology in eighteenth-century evangelical hymns.

Oxford, Trinity 1995   D.B.H.

CONTENTS

FIGURES

TABLE

xii

ABBREVIATIONS

ALS	Autograph letter signed
AM	*Arminian Magazine*
AMS	Autograph manuscript signed
ANS	Autograph note signed
BBC	Bristol Baptist College
Bodl.	Bodleian Library, Oxford
Bull, *Bull*	Josiah Bull, *Memorials of the Rev. William Bull* (1864)
Bull, *Newton*	Josiah Bull, *John Newton of Olney and St. Mary Woolnoth* (1868)
Cecil, *Newton*	Richard Cecil, *Memoirs of the Rev. John Newton*, 3rd edn. (1808)
CNM	Cowper and Newton Museum, Olney, Buckinghamshire
CUL	University Library, Cambridge
Diary (1751–6)	John Newton, MS Diary, 1751–1756, Firestone Library, Princeton, NJ
Diary (1758)	John Newton, 'Miscellaneous Thoughts & Enquiries on an Important Subject', MS Diary, June 1758, Lambeth Palace Library, London
Diary (1767)	John Newton's autograph diary for 1767, written in *The Complete Pocket-Book . . . for the Year of our Lord 1767*, Lambeth Palace Library, London
Diary (1773–1805)	John Newton, MS Diary, 1773–1805, Firestone Library, Princeton, NJ
Diary (1793–1803)	John Newton's autograph diary, 1793–1803, written in an interleaved copy of his *Letters to a Wife*, 2 vols. (London, 1793), Cowper and Newton Museum, Olney, Buckinghamshire
DNB	*Dictionary of National Biography*
DWL	Dr Williams's Library, London

EM	*Evangelical Magazine*
FLP	Firestone Library, Princeton, NJ
GM	*Gospel Magazine*
JWJ	*Journal of the Rev. John Wesley*, 8 vols., ed. Nehemiah Curnock (1909–16)
JWL	*Letters of the Rev. John Wesley*, 8 vols., ed. John Telford (1931)
Letters (Barlass)	*The Original Letters of the Reverend John Newton, A.M. [sic] to the Rev. W. Barlass* (1819)
Letters (Bull)	*One Hundred and Twenty Nine Letters from the Rev. John Newton to the Rev. William Bull* (1847)
Letters (Bull, ed.)	*Letters by the Rev. John Newton . . . with Biographical Sketches*, ed. Josiah Bull (1869)
Letters (Campbell)	*Letters and Conversational Remarks of the Rev. John Newton*, ed. John Campbell (1808)
Letters (Clunie)	*The Christian Correspondent . . . Letters Written by the Rev. John Newton to Captain Alexr. Clunie* (Hull, 1790)
Letters (Coffin)	*Sixty-Eight Letters from the Rev. John Newton to a Clergyman* [James Coffin] *and his Family* (1845)
Letters (Dartmouth)	*Historical Manuscripts Commission. XV Report, Appendix, Part I, The Manuscripts of the Earl of Dartmouth*, vol. 3 (1896)
Letters (Jones)	*Twenty-Five Letters of the Rev. John Newton* [to Robert and Josiah Jones] (Edinburgh, 1840)
Letters (Palmer)	*Correspondence of the late Rev. John Newton with a Dissenting Minister* [Samuel Palmer] *on Various Subjects and Occasions* (1809)
Letters (Taylor)	*The Aged Pilgrim's Triumph over Sin and the Grave . . . a Series of Letters by the Rev. John Newton to some of his most Intimate Friends* [Walter Taylor, William Cadogan, et al.] (1825)

LPL	Lambeth Palace Library, London
LyH	A. C. H. Seymour, *Life and Times of Selina Countess of Huntingdon*, 2 vols. (1840)
OH	*Olney Hymns* (1779)
PMLA	*Publications of the Modern Language Association*
PWHS	*Proceedings of the Wesley Historical Society*
Works	*The Works of the Rev. John Newton*, 6 vols. (1808–9)

CHRONOLOGY OF NEWTON'S LIFE

24 July 1725 (os)	John Newton born in London, son of John and Elizabeth Newton.
26 July 1725 (os)	Baptized, Independent Meeting in Old Gravel Lane, Wapping; pastor, David Jennings.
11 July 1732 (os)	Death of mother; father remarries shortly afterwards.
c.1733–5	At boarding school in Stratford, Essex.
1736–42	Novice in the merchant marine. Five Mediterranean voyages with father; intervals at Aveley.
Dec. 1742	First visit to Catlett home at Chatham in Kent.
c.1742–3	Voyage to Venice; portentous dream.
Dec. 1743	Second visit to Catlett home.
4 Mar. 1744 (os)	Impressed on board HMS *Harwich*.
Apr. 1745	Whipped and degraded to rank of ordinary seaman for attempted desertion at Plymouth.
9 May 1745 (os)	Transferred at Madeira to a Guinea slave-trading ship.
c.1746–7	Apprenticed to slave factors on Guinea Coast.
Feb. 1747	Embarked on board the *Greyhound*.
10 Mar. 1748 (os)	Near shipwreck of the *Greyhound* in North Atlantic storm provokes spiritual crisis.
8 Apr. 1748 (os)	*Greyhound* arrives safely in Ireland.
Aug. 1748–Dec. 1749	First Mate on board the *Brownlow* on slave-trading voyage to Guinea Coast and West Indies.
1 Feb. 1750 (os)	Marriage to Mary, daughter of George and Elizabeth Catlett.
11 Aug. 1750–	First slave-trading voyage as captain.
17 Oct. 1751 (os)	Master of the *Duke of Argyle*.
c.June 1751	Death of father.
30 June 1752 (os)– 29 Aug. 1753	Second voyage. Master of the *African*.

21 Oct. 1753–7 Aug. 1754	Third voyage. Master of the *African*.
May 1754	First acquaintance with Alexander Clunie.
Nov. 1754	Epileptic seizure causes him to leave the slave trade.
*c.*1754–5	Unemployed. Resides alternately at Chatham and London.
June 1755	First acquaintance with George Whitefield.
Aug. 1755	Commences as tide surveyor at Liverpool.
Apr. 1757	First acquaintance with John Wesley.
Dec. 1758	Refused holy orders on first application.
29 Apr. 1764	Ordained deacon by Bishop of Lincoln.
17 June 1764	Priested and instituted to the living of Olney.
Aug. 1764	Publication of the *Authentic Narrative*.
14 Sept. 1767	Arrival of William Cowper and Mrs Unwin at Olney.
1768	First acquaintance with John Ryland, Jun.
1774	Publication of Omicron's *Letters*.
May 1775	Beginning of correspondence with Thomas Scott.
Oct. 1777	Fire at Olney.
1779	Publication of *Olney Hymns*.
8 Dec. 1779	Inducted, St Mary Woolnoth; John Thornton, patron.
1780	Publication of *Cardiphonia*.
Jan. 1783	First meeting of Eclectic Society.
6 Dec. 1785	Wilberforce calls on him for spiritual counsel.
15 Dec. 1790	Death of wife. He preaches her funeral sermon eight days later.
25 Apr. 1800	Death of Cowper.
21 Dec. 1807	Death of Newton.
31 Dec. 1807	Buried in chancel of St Mary Woolnoth. Service read by Henry Foster. Funeral sermon the following Sunday by Richard Cecil.

INTRODUCTION
John Newton and the Evangelical Tradition

> . . . this much-misunderstood man.
>
> J. H. Overton

JOHN NEWTON (1725–1807) came to maturity during the period which followed the remarkable conversions and field-preaching of the late 1730s and early 1740s, events which signalled the beginning of the Evangelical Revival. By the 1790s, important changes were coming over the religious and political world, and Newton, though revered within his circle, was an old man whose influence was giving way to a younger generation of evangelical leaders. Between these two periods—for which the conversions of John Wesley in 1738 and William Wilberforce in 1785 may stand as symbols—lies approximately half a century during which John Newton's religious convictions were formed and expressed. During these years Newton also emerged as a significant figure with a wide public within the evangelical movement.

For the purposes of this study Newton is set chiefly in the context of developments within the evangelical tradition. Newton and his contemporaries did not use the word 'evangelical' very often, but they used the word 'Gospel' (usually with the capitalized initial) to the same effect as a ubiquitous prefix of approval. Thus there were 'Gospel clergy' and 'Gospel sermons'; believers could delight in a 'Gospel ministry' or a 'Gospel conversation', and sinners rejoice to see 'Gospel light'. One of the central questions which recurs throughout this book concerns, therefore, the extent of consensus between Newton and his contemporaries about the meaning and implications of the evangel, and the nature of the religious consciousness formed by loyalty to it. By viewing Newton's life and religious thought as an episode in the larger story of English evangelical theology and piety, several

I

conclusions are drawn about what it meant to Newton and his contemporaries to be 'of the Gospel'.

It is the particular character of Newton's biography that makes it possible to extrapolate from his experience some of the general characteristics of the evangelical milieu in which he flourished. Newton understood himself from very early days as a 'non-aligned' evangelical and saw his role to be that of a kind of middleman between the partisans of the Revival. He was in touch with large and varied numbers of evangelical clergy and laymen in the course of his life, and he felt he shared something in common with them all. Although it would be a mistake to universalize his sentiments as at all points the absolute centre or lowest common denominator of evangelical self-understanding, Newton's life and thought nevertheless afford an important perspective on what were evangelical essentials for a wide cross-section of people during his lifetime. Observing how he sustained religious intimacy with large numbers of individuals, particularly with those from whom he differed on various matters, illuminates some of the core beliefs around which evangelical identity coalesced.

The life of John Newton has been studied to date principally by three classes of writers: sympathetic biographers, biographers and critics interested in William Cowper, and historians. Newton was himself the first to provide an interpretation of his life. Writing an autobiography at age 39, he argued that his life was a symbol of divine grace to hardened sinners, designed to display the extent of God's mercy to all who should take notice. This perspective was largely shared in the biographies which followed after his death, such as Richard Cecil's *Memoirs of the Rev. John Newton* (1808). The predominant use of Newton's life was emblematic, and the intent was less to explain, than to receive his life as a matter for religious instruction and devotional reflection. Despite the limitations of filiopietistic biography, many of these sympathetic biographers readily understood and elucidated Newton's religious motivation, and such writings continue to form the chief repository of information and anecdotes about him. The lives of Newton's contemporaries have supplied additional facts, and often from a unique perspective. Especially noteworthy in this respect are John

Scott's *Life of Thomas Scott* (1822) and Josiah Bull's *Memorials of the Rev. William Bull* (1864). Josiah Bull also wrote the first research biography of Newton, *John Newton of Olney and St. Mary Woolnoth* (1868). Collating knowledgeably a wide range of original materials, this remains the most important primary source for Newton's life. Inspirational biography, deriving from these standard sources, sometimes incorporating new research, has appeared in every generation since Newton's death, often published in inexpensive editions for mass distribution. The most important twentieth-century life of Newton is Bernard Martin's *John Newton: A Biography* (1950), but this book falls short of anything like a standard biography. Here, as in many more pious biographies, it is unfortunately sometimes difficult to separate factual narrative from imaginative embellishment.[1]

The second context in which Newton's life has been studied is with reference to the biography of the poet William Cowper (1731–1800). Soon after Cowper's death, a long and often acrimonious debate commenced over the causes of his dementia. Lodwick Hartley has summarized the lines of argument that were soon established.[2] On the one hand, it was argued that Cowper's madness derived from natural causes or from some form of sin; on the other, it was insisted that the emotionalism and eschatology of evangelicalism were to blame. Among evangelicals, some Arminians were prepared to refine this second argument, assigning the cause of Cowper's troubles specifically to Calvinism. Because Newton had been so closely connected to Cowper for many years, he quickly became the focus of arguments hostile to evangelicalism and Calvinism. The belief that Newton's influence had helped to undermine Cowper's sanity was long perpetuated by Robert Southey's influential biography of the poet in 1835. For more than a century controversy raged over the influence of Newton upon Cowper. But, as Hartley comments, this

---

[1] More recently, Newton's story has been retold, with additional research, by Brian Edwards, *Through Many Dangers* (Welwyn, 1975), and John Pollock, *Amazing Grace* (1981).

[2] 'Cowper and the Evangelicals: Notes on Early Biographical Interpretations', *PMLA*, 65 (1950), 719–31; id., *William Cowper: The Continuing Evaluation* (Chapel Hill, NC, 1960), 16–32.

whole biographical tradition became inbred, with interpretations of Cowper's religion and psychological condition being imposed on a relatively static body of factual material. Although a more source-critical approach since the 1950s has drawn attention to new problems in Cowper's biography and opened up fresh lines of enquiry and interpretation, Newton continues frequently to be presented as an unsympathetic foil to Cowper.[3] Indeed, the assessment of Newton's influence upon Cowper demands a more sophisticated understanding of Newton and the evangelical tradition than has typically been the case.

Historians, whether writing of the eighteenth century in general, of particular denominations, or of the Evangelical Revival, have also taken notice of Newton. Most who took some account of him in the nineteenth century wrote with a sense of responsibility towards the ongoing Christian tradition, even if they did not necessarily share the perspective of early evangelical historiographers such as Joseph Milner, Thomas Haweis, or John White Middelton who saw the Evangelical Revival in continuity with the hidden operation of God's grace in all generations.[4] Among the latter, for whom evangelical piety itself was seen as an organizing principle for the selection and interpretation of church history, Newton was portrayed appreciatively as a warm, moderate evangelical with 'the sweetness of Melanchthon'. While this was to be expected, the prevailing view of Newton among other historians was much the same, and the contrast with those literary writers who detested his influence upon Cowper is striking. Newton was regarded not only as a founding father of the Evangelical Party in the Church of England, but also as a 'singularly genial man', a devoted and exemplary Christian

---

[3] See e.g. James King, *William Cowper* (Durham, NC, 1986), 65–71. George M. Ella, *William Cowper: Poet of Paradise* (Darlington, 1993), 22–7, 141–3, reviews some of the harshest criticisms of Newton, and rejects these, but charges him with being excessively possessive of Cowper's friendship and indiscreet in speaking of the details of his derangement.

[4] Joseph Milner, *History of the Church of Christ*, 5 vols. (1794–7); Thomas Haweis, *An Impartial and Succinct History of the Rise, Declension and Revival of the Church of Christ, from the Birth of Our Saviour to the Present Time* (1800); John White Middelton, *Ecclesiastical Memoir of the First Four Decades of the Reign of George the Third* (1822).

minister, a theological moderate, and a skilled spiritual director. Sir James Stephen's article on the 'Evangelical Succession' in the *Edinburgh Review* (1838) might have contributed to the caricature of Newton as a 'manly' and rugged individual who never had a doubt, but 'manly' was an adjective Stephen, like many of his contemporaries, used as a term of approbation. More importantly, Stephen described Newton and his contemporaries as representing an ideal of earnest piety and theological purity from which evangelicalism in his own generation had sadly deteriorated.[5] Marked by the industry and thoroughness characteristic of the late nineteenth century, Charles Abbey and John Overton's *English Church in the Eighteenth Century* (1878), and William Lecky's *History of England in the Eighteenth Century* (1897–9), became standard ecclesiastical and general histories for many years.[6] In these works Newton was seen as one of a number of evangelical clergy who helped to raise the spiritual tone of the Church of England in a century during which the church in general was at a low ebb and badly in need of reform. While this view of the eighteenth-century church has since been contested, Newton's place within that church has been examined little further.[7] The discussion here of Newton's ordination, the detailed round of his parish work at Olney, and the infrastructure of Anglican evangelicalism in London when he arrived in the 1780s, along with other concerns, should serve to update this discussion and to assist in understanding how he and other evangelicals related to the wider church and its formal hierarchy.

Newton has routinely appeared in other denominational histories, and these sources remain crucial to the task of historically reconstructing certain phases in his biography. He

[5] Stephen's essay was incorporated in his later *Essays in Ecclesiastical Biography* (1849).

[6] See also John Overton, *Evangelical Revival in the Eighteenth Century* (1886).

[7] For a review of recent scholarship on the 18th-c. church, see John Walsh and Stephen Taylor, 'Introduction: The Church and Anglicanism in the "Long" Eighteenth Century', in John Walsh, Colin Haydon, and Stephen Taylor (eds.), *The Church of England, c.1689–c.1833: From Toleration to Tractarianism* (Cambridge, 1993), 1–64. For an analysis of the interpretative perspectives of Victorian writers such as Abbey and Overton, and Lecky, see B. W. Young, 'Knock-Kneed Giants: Victorian Representations of Eighteenth-Century Thought', in Jane Garnett and Colin Matthew (eds.), *Revival and Religion since 1700: Essays for John Walsh* (1993), 79–93.

had connections with numerous religious bodies, especially in his early years, and, consequently, several episodes from his biography have appeared in works such as John Waddington's *Congregational History, 1700–1800* (1876), or Luke Tyerman's lives of John Wesley (1871) and George Whitefield (1876). More recent articles have probed Newton's links with Baptists also.[8] The value of these studies to an understanding of Newton and the evangelical tradition has been to correct the teleological view of Newton as simply a founder of the nineteenth-century evangelical party in the Church of England. Otherwise, James Stephen's essay, like the work of later authors such as G. R. Balleine, *History of the Evangelical Party in the Church of England* (1908) and L. E. Elliot-Binns, *The Early Evangelicals* (1953), could lead to an underestimation of Newton's broad inheritance in Dissent and of the fluidity of evangelicalism generally during his lifetime.

Denominational histories and works which are explicitly concerned to gather religious insights from Newton and eighteenth-century evangelicalism continue to be written, but since the middle of this century authors of scholarly studies of eighteenth-century religion have tended to bracket out and make private their own beliefs in order to devote attention to questions germane to historical-critical research. Most often these questions have had to do with explaining the origins of a religious movement or idea, identifying the relationship between these and other historical phenomena, or accounting for the distinctive character of a religious body. As the Evangelical Revival has become the subject both of specialized studies and more synoptic interpretation, Newton has figured, if only infrequently, as one source of evidence among many for answering these kinds of questions. The picture of Newton has not, however, altered significantly since the nineteenth century. He has recurred primarily as an illustration of the moderate character of Anglican evangelicalism.[9]

[8] See e.g. R. W. Thomson, 'John Newton and His Baptist Friends', *Baptist Quarterly*, 9 (1939), 368–71; G. F. Nuttall, 'Baptists and Independents in Olney to the Time of John Newton', ibid. 30 (1983), 26–37; Michael Haykin, 'Anglican and Baptist: A View from the Eighteenth Century', *Prolegomena*, 2 (1990), 21–8.
[9] See e.g. Charles Smyth, *Simeon and Church Order: A Study of the Origins of the Evangelical Revival in Cambridge in the Eighteenth Century* (Cambridge, 1940), 266; id.,

In contrast, the picture of the Evangelical Revival has changed and enlarged considerably, and since this is the context in which Newton will be examined in the pages which follow, it is worth reviewing here briefly. One of the first questions to engage modern scholarship, and one which has continued to fascinate scholars, has been the question of the origins of the Revival itself. Most eighteenth-century evangelicals, and many since, saw the surprising and seemingly inexplicable character of the Revival as evidence itself of its divine origins, but as Gordon Rupp once wrote, 'it will not help if good Christians, like bad scientists, bring in the Holy Spirit to plug the gaps in our historical knowledge'.[10] John Walsh succinctly described some of the historical 'gaps' in 1966: 'First, why did a number of Anglicans, especially between about 1735 and about 1760, pass through a parallel conversion experience? Secondly, how were they then drawn into the leadership of a campaign for the conversion of the nation . . . ? Thirdly, why did this campaign garner such a remarkably large harvest of converts?'[11] Some of the early sociological, psychological, and historical explanations of the Revival have been reviewed in an excursus buried in Michael Watts's important survey, *The Dissenters, i. From the Reformation to the French Revolution* (1978), 406–28. As Watts concludes, however, the most satisfactory explanation of the origins of the Revival is still one which many of the early evangelicals would have recognized themselves:

The Evangelical revival, like the Antinomian and Quaker movements of the previous century, was a reaction against legalistic religious systems which made impossible demands on the moral and spiritual resources of the ordinary believer, and the Methodist

'The Evangelical Movement in Perspective', *Cambridge Historical Journal*, 7 (1943), 163; John Walsh, 'Methodism at the End of the Eighteenth Century', in Rupert Davies and Gordon Rupp (eds.), *A History of the Methodist Church in Great Britain*, i (1965), 290; id., 'The Anglican Evangelicals in the Eighteenth Century', in Marcel Simon (ed.), *Aspects de L'Anglicanisme* (Paris, 1974), 94, 97; David Bebbington, *Evangelicalism in Modern Britain: A History from the 1730s to the 1980s* (1989), 63.

[10] 'Introductory Essay', in Davies and Rupp (eds.), *History of the Methodist Church*, i. p. xvii.

[11] 'Origins of the Evangelical Revival', in G. V. Bennet and John Walsh (eds.), *Essays in Modern English Church History* (1966), 133.

preachers, like the Antinomians and early Friends, brought relief and joy to men and women whose consciences were tormented by the memory of unforgiven sins and whose lives were burdened by the over-scrupulous performance of religious duties.[12]

While this explanation does not account for why the Revival happened when and where it did, and among whom (Anglicans) it did, nor for the form it took, it does relate general conditions to the responses of individuals in a convincing way, and without anachronism. Other explanations, which have put the Revival in a larger cultural context, have helped to fill in this picture. In particular, a number of studies have appeared in the last decade which have used the methods of comparative history to grapple with the question of origins in a larger international context, including both transatlantic perspectives and European antecedents.[13] In this study, an effort has been made to understand Newton's religious conversion and theological formation, along with his ministry at Olney and elsewhere, in a way which will contribute to the general question of origins. Above all, Newton's biography demonstrates how Old Dissent was a key link between Puritanism and the Evangelical Revival, and the extent to which the Anglican matrix of the Revival did not exclude ideas and influences from the Anglo-Calvinist tradition.

A related question, treated in many of these same studies of the origins of the Revival, has been the question of the character of evangelicalism. While some historians have sought to describe an 'essential' evangelicalism and to account for this, others have been content to describe the traits of

---

[12] Michael R. Watts, *The Dissenters* (Oxford, 1978), i. 427–8.
[13] See e.g. Susan O'Brien, 'A Transatlantic Community of Saints: The Great Awakening and the First Evangelical Network, 1735–1755', *American Historical Review*, 91 (1986), 811–32; Marilyn J. Westerkamp, *The Triumph of the Laity: Scots–Irish Piety and the Great Awakening, 1625–1760* (New York, 1988); Keith Robbins (ed.), *Protestant Evangelicalism: Britain, Ireland, Germany, and America, c.1750–c.1950: Essays in Honour of W. R. Ward* (Oxford, 1990); Michael Crawford, *Seasons of Grace: Colonial New England's Revival Tradition in Its British Context* (New York, 1991); W. R. Ward, *The Protestant Evangelical Awakening* (Cambridge, 1992); George Rawlyk and Mark Noll (eds.), *Amazing Grace: Evangelicalism in Australia, Britain, Canada, and the United States* (Montreal, 1994); Mark Noll, David Bebbington, and George Rawlyk (eds.), *Evangelicalism: Comparative Studies of Popular Protestantism in North America, the British Isles, and Beyond, 1700–1990* (New York, 1994).

various strands of evangelicalism and to relate these to earlier
and contemporary expressions of religion and culture. The
most important 'essentialist' survey of evangelicalism is David
Bebbington's *Evangelicalism in Modern Britain* (1989), in which
an emphasis upon conversion, the Bible, the atonement, and
activism is seen to have been characteristic of evangelicals
throughout their history, even while the movement has
in other respects modulated significantly with respect to
intellectual and popular culture. With few exceptions,
however, most studies of English evangelicalism in the
eighteenth century have tended to isolate certain aspects
of the Revival for specialized attention. Geoffrey Nuttall's
articles on the relationship of the Evangelical Revival to Old
Dissent, or John Walsh's on subjects from the Evangelical
Revival, Methodism, and the structure and theology of
Anglican Evangelicalism may be taken as illustrations of this
research.[14] Still, however, there are many aspects of the
Evangelical Revival which remain to be explored, such as
the history of Calvinism in the eighteenth century, evangelical
pastoralia and ecclesiology, and the relationship between
evangelical spirituality and contemporary cultural sensibilities. In these and other areas, Newton's life helps to shed light
on the character of early evangelicalism.

Thus, while this book aims to provide a detailed treatment
of John Newton as a religious figure, exploiting untapped but
extensive archival and antiquarian sources for his biography,
it also aims to contribute to the quest to understand the
origins and character of the Evangelical Revival in England
by using Newton as not just a subject, but a 'site'.[15] By
analysing texts and contexts, religious ideas and the ways in
which they were communicated, something may be learned
about the movement in which he played such a large part. In

---

[14] For references, see further the Bibliography at the close of this book.

[15] Two theses have examined aspects of Newton's career as a minister. His
preaching and hymnody are the subject of Donald E. Demaray's Ph.D. thesis
(Edinburgh, 1952), published as *The Innovation of John Newton*, Texts and Studies in
Religion, 36 (Lewiston, NY, 1988); Newton's letters of spiritual direction are treated
by Grant Gordon, 'John Newton: A Study of a Pastoral Correspondent', unpublished
Th.M. thesis (Princeton Theological Seminary, 1987).

the end, it is hoped that Newton and the evangelical tradition are subjects which mutually enlighten each other.

Note on Sources

The archival sources for the life of Newton run into thousands of folios of manuscript and are scattered in record offices across Britain and the United States. The chief collections are listed in the Bibliography at the end of this book. Some more detailed description is required, however, of Newton's diaries.

Newton began keeping a confessional diary in 1751 and he maintained the practice until shortly before his death in 1807. There are three principal diaries: 1751–6, 1756–73, and 1773–1805. Newton's friend, William Bull of Newport Pagnell, came into possession of most of Newton's papers after his death, and the first and the third of these diaries were for many years in the possession of his descendants, until acquired by Princeton University Library some time before 1982. (Princeton accessioned the diaries in 1982 but have no records of when or how they acquired them.) These diaries are substantial folio volumes of more than 300 pages each. In 1868 Josiah Bull, grandson of William, wrote in the preface to his biography of Newton, 'Our best thanks are especially due to Mrs. Janson for the use of the missing volume of the diary.' Evidently, then, the middle volume of the diary (1756–73) was separated from the bulk of the archive from a very early date.

Extensive researches by the present writer have failed to locate this missing diary or to identify Mrs Janson with certainty. This lacuna in Newton's archive may be restored in part from the frequent, lengthy quotations included by Josiah Bull in his biography. While other biographers since Bull have certainly had reference to Newton's diaries, none quotes directly from the missing diary; all subsequent references follow Bull's extracts. According to Bull, for four of the sixteen years covered by the missing diary, Newton did not write in it; it appears that Newton instead recorded diary entries in small notebooks. For one of the years, 1767, Newton used an octavo pocketbook, now preserved at Lambeth Palace Library in London. There are likewise two handsewn octavo notebooks, with entries for portions of 1768 and 1769, preserved at the Cowper and Newton Museum at Olney. These entries were recorded by Newton in shorthand, using the system taught by John Byrom.[16] Consequently, sections of this study treating the period covered in the missing diary have relied primarily upon the notebooks, Bull's biography, and Newton's correspondence, to reconstruct his activities.

[16] I am grateful to Timothy Underhill, an expert on the subject of Byrom and shorthand, for identifying and translating passages of shorthand from Newton's diaries for me.

1

'I know of no case more extraordinary than my own'
The *Authentic Narrative* (1764)

> Then I turned to myself and asked, 'Who are you?'
>
> St Augustine

IN his eightieth year John Newton recorded in a shaky hand the last entry in his diary: '21 March 1805. Not well able to write. But I endeavour to observe the return of this day with Humiliation, Prayer and Praise.'[1] For more than half a century he had kept this day as an anniversary, noting it in his diary with appropriate reflections and whenever possible devoting the greater part of the day to prayer and fasting. More than once he used the event commemorated as the subject of his preaching. For it was from this day in 1748 that Newton dated the first workings of grace in his soul when, in a ship foundering in a violent North Atlantic storm, he muttered a faint prayer for mercy after years of unbelief and moral recklessness. As through the 1750s he became more religiously observant, and particularly as after 1754 his acquaintance with evangelicals enlarged, he reflected upon the meaning of his past life in religious terms. Increasingly he came to trace, in events like this near-shipwreck, the hand of God working out a high drama of salvation in his soul. This self-understanding became more pronounced the longer he lived. It was literally engraved in stone after he died, for he had left his executors with a letter stating the exact text he wished to have inscribed on his monument:

---

[1] Diary (1773–1805).

13

JOHN NEWTON,

CLERK,

ONCE AN INFIDEL AND LIBERTINE,

A SERVANT OF SLAVES IN AFRICA,

WAS,

BY THE RICH MERCY OF OUR LORD AND SAVIOUR

JESUS CHRIST,

PRESERVED, RESTORED, PARDONED,

AND APPOINTED TO PREACH THE FAITH

HE HAD LONG LABOURED TO DESTROY.

The distorted hour-glass shape of the text is itself significant (it was the shape of the drama) just as the sentiment could be given no more symbolic permanence than as an epitaph. This was fitting for one who often described his life figuratively as a 'monument' of God's almighty power. A very similar sentence was also included in the exordium to his last will and testament.[2] Here evidently is what he most passionately believed his life had meant.

The representation he gave of his life is so complete that it does not at first occur that it could have been constructed otherwise; that there could have been another way of selecting, arranging, and interpreting his experiences which might have suggested a different self-understanding. There was, however, a wide body of contemporary travel literature which included tales of maritime adventure no less remarkable than Newton's but which did not necessarily compel his particular evangelical reading of divine salvation from sin, though providence of some sort was usually acknowledged where Christian piety existed. There was, for example, the widely known story of the Scottish sailor Alexander Selkirk who was rescued in 1709 after enduring four years as a castaway on the uninhabited island of Juan Fernández. Through Captain Woodes Rogers's *Cruising Voyage Round the World* (1712), and other popular accounts, Selkirk's adventures

[2] See Cecil, *Newton*, 211–14; Bull, *Newton*, 359–60.

14

captured the imaginations of many in the eighteenth century, including Daniel Defoe and William Cowper.[3] But Selkirk's story was not Newton's particular kind of an adventure-cum-conversion narrative. Behind Newton's own autobiography lay a process in which biographical facts and current beliefs were only gradually fused in a coherent concept of an evangelical self. The climax of this process came just after his thirty-ninth birthday with the publication of his first book of any consequence, *An Authentic Narrative of Some Remarkable and Interesting Particulars in the Life of* ******** (1764), in which he told the story of his varied experiences as a drama of religious conversion. Once having discovered and declared this as the underlying meaning of his life, he would try, in a long dénouement of self-reflection during his remaining years, simply to understand and live out its implications.

The term 'evangelical' has been defined in a myriad of ways. In David Bebbington's judgement, however, the first characteristic to emerge and sustain evangelical identity in the popular Protestant movement of the 1730s was an emphasis upon conversion, the belief that the gospel called men and women to a fundamental change of life.[4] This central stress was apparent not only in summaries of theological essentials such as the Methodists' three cardinal doctrines of original sin, justification by faith, and the new birth, with its concomitant holiness of life, but also in the testimonies of laymen and clergymen alike, spoken extempore in society meetings or written up for pious edification. John Newton's *Authentic Narrative* is a lucid example of the latter and provides a detailed illustration of how an evangelical version of the self was shaped by the central theme of personal conversion.

In addition to reflecting the eighteenth-century evangelical ethos, the *Authentic Narrative* helped to form it, for it quickly became a popular piece of literature. It went through ten

---

[3] Cf. also 'The True Travels, Adventures and Observations of Captain John Smith', in Awnsham and John Churchill (eds.), *A Collection of Voyages and Travels*, 6 vols. (1732), ii. 327–66. Smith was sold into slavery and like Newton called himself the 'slave of slaves to them all' (pp. 342–8), but while he acknowledged divine providence in his preservation and escape, he did not interpret his experiences as having any salvific significance.

[4] Bebbington, *Evangelicalism in Modern Britain*, 2–10.

British and eight American editions before the end of the century and was quickly translated into several other languages. It was published in a Dutch edition within three years of its first appearance in England. Its popularity in Scotland may be gauged by the remarks of William Barlass, an Anti-Burgher who lived near Aberdeen: 'I had one copy of my own, which I lent to some friends; from one it passed to another, so that I could scarcely get it back. It wandered almost half a year that way, but at length I have given it to a printer.'[5] Barlass hoped to publish the rest of Newton's works this same way, but he felt the *Authentic Narrative* was his best. It was the *Authentic Narrative* above all that made Newton a public and international figure within the evangelical movement.

NEWTON'S STORY: A SUMMARY OF THE *AUTHENTIC NARRATIVE*

In recent studies, literary critics have stressed that the expository element of autobiography is not simply dross to be refined, but the legitimate articulation of principles governing the autobiographer's self-interpretation.[6] Certainly, Newton's own narrative was strongly governed by his didactic intentions, and highly interpretative commentary was interwoven into his story. Rather than edit this out, it will be helpful to retain his perspective and something of his idiom in reviewing the *Authentic Narrative*. It will be the burden of the last half of this chapter to analyse just how he arrived at this perspective.

Born in London in 1725, Newton was an only child, and he was raised and educated conscientiously by a Dissenting mother who intended him for the ministry. He shared her quiet temperament, delighted in her attentions, and advanced rapidly in learning and piety under her care. His father, a captain in the merchant marine, though a good man, was too distant to take the place of his mother when she died before Newton was 7. After his father remarried, his education

---

[5] *Letters* (Barlass), 73.
[6] See e.g. Linda Peterson, 'Newman's *Apologia pro vita sua* and the Traditions of English Spiritual Autobiography', *PMLA* 100 (1985), 311.

therefore passed into other hands. He soon mixed with 'profane' children, and two years of grammar school seemed if anything only to set him back, despite his evident facility in Latin. Though his father took him on several voyages during his adolescence and sought to watch over his behaviour, Newton recalls how he oscillated between sin and conscience. Affected by religious books and near-death encounters on the one hand, he was tempted on the other to curse and act wickedly when out of his parents' observation. Amidst repeated moral failures and renewed attempts at a devout life, he remained religiously observant, though in his heart he wished only to escape damnation. His last adolescent reform lasted two years, during which he put on an especially self-righteous, dour asceticism that left him, notwithstanding his efforts, unable to refrain from wrongdoing. In this state of mind he came across Lord Shaftesbury's *Characteristics*, and this book, he says, acted like a 'slow poison' on him, preparing the way for all that followed.

Upon a journey to Kent, he visited distant relations, close friends of his late mother, and fell immediately in love with their eldest daughter Mary Catlett. Being, as he recalled, of a dreamy and romantic turn of mind, he found this all the encouragement he needed to prolong his visit, and thereby evade his father's plans to send him to Jamaica to be set up in business. On a subsequent voyage to Venice he began his long decline into 'apostasy', relaxing the sobriety he had observed for two years past; even a remarkable cautionary dream had no lasting effect. When he returned to England at the close of 1743, he again upset his father's plans for him by a protracted visit to the Catlett family. Then, before another business opportunity could be found, he was captured by a naval gang and impressed upon a man-of-war off the Kentish coast. This was only months before France formally declared war on England (at the height of the War of the Austrian Succession, 1739–48), and the French fleet was hovering off the coast in preparation for the intended Franco-Spanish invasion of England.

Promoted to midshipman by his father's influence, Newton went absent without leave because of his passion for Mary Catlett. When he was later caught attempting to desert altogether he was put in irons, whipped, degraded from office, alienated from his friends, and cast among the lowest rank of sailors on the ship. Earlier a companion on board had confirmed him in the 'Free-Thinking' scheme, destroying what remained of his Christian principles. Now, left in shame, fear, and indignation, he had little to comfort or restrain him. With the prospect of a five-year voyage of unimaginable misery ahead of him, it was only, he says, the secret hand of God which kept him from attempting to murder the captain or commit suicide.

The day before the ship was to leave Madeira, a number of unexpected circumstances concurred to allow him to be transferred to a ship in the African trade. Entering among strangers on this ship, he found he could now be as abandoned as he pleased, sinning and seducing others to do so. After six months trading on the Guinea coast, he determined to stay in Africa in the service of a rich slave factor, hoping to become likewise wealthy by dealing in slaves. But during the next two years he suffered illness, starvation, exposure, and ridicule as his master's black mistress used him poorly, and as he lost his master's trust. He notes that divine grace had not yet entered his soul, and that it was therefore a mercy that he was banished to a region where his wickedness was restrained by relative isolation and tempered by suffering.

Hearing from him of his desperation, his father arranged for a captain to look for him on his next voyage to the Guinea coast. But meanwhile Newton had found a new master under whom his prospects had improved considerably, so that when, against all odds, the captain located him, he could persuade him to come aboard and leave Africa only by claiming falsely that a legacy had been left him in England. The ship, the *Greyhound*, continued a long trading voyage south down the coast of Africa, during which Newton amused himself by studying mathematics and inventing blasphemies that shocked even coarse men. In a drinking party he was nearly lost overboard; hunting on shore, he was nearly lost in dangerous swamps and woods. But neither these deliverances nor near-death illness gave him any checks of conscience at the time. He observed that he seemed to have every mark of final impenitence. The crew proceeded on the long voyage home via Brazil and Newfoundland in a vessel out of repair. Early in March Newton casually picked up a copy of Thomas à Kempis's *Imitation of Christ*, reading carelessly at first, but then becoming troubled with the possibility that it might be true. He put it out of his mind. But when 'the Lord's time was come', this momentary conviction was lastingly impressed on his conscience by the terrifying dispensation of a severe storm. Awakened in the middle of the night on 10 March 1748 (os) to find the ship breaking apart and filling fast with water, and a man already swept overboard, he breathed his first prayer for mercy for many years. He was left wondering whether there were any hope of mercy for him and whether the Scriptures might after all be true.

Tied to the ship to prevent being washed away, he pumped and bailed all night until he was called upon to steer the ship. All the while he reviewed his life: his former professions of religion, the extraordinary twists of past events, the warnings and deliverances he had met with, his licentious conversation, and his mockery of the Gospels. He felt at first that his sin was too great for forgiveness, but when some faint hope arose that he might survive the storm, spiritual hope began to revive as well. During the several uncertain weeks before the ship reached Ireland, when all on board yet feared they would perish from thirst or starvation, he prayed and read the Scriptures, *The Imitation*, and some sermons by Bishop Beveridge; accordingly, by the time they reached port he was fully convinced of the truth of the gospel, no longer an 'infidel'. Yet he was not a believer 'in the full sense of the word' until a considerable time after, and though he had some right notions he was, Newton recalls from his later perspective, still unaware of many important truths. It would be another six years before he would come across any evangelical preaching.

On shore he was now a 'serious professor', went to prayers twice a day, and made solemn vows of surrender to God at the sacrament. To all appearance safe after having endured such an ordeal at sea, he narrowly escaped death yet again when a gun went off near his face in a hunting accident. He corresponded with his father, who had given him up for dead because of his long absence, but was delayed too long to be able to join him on a three-year voyage to Hudson Bay (a voyage on which, as it turned out, his father died). But before leaving, his father had visited Kent and consented to his marrying Mary Catlett. An intimate friend of his father's at Liverpool, a leading merchant, became like a second father to Newton, providing for him to go on another voyage as mate, with the prospect of becoming a captain after that. Before he left he gained hopes from Mary Catlett that she would await the outcome of this voyage and consider proposals of marriage when he returned.

Newton recollects that though he had been a great sinner, the beginnings of his religious course were surprisingly faint and moderate. On this new voyage his sense of religion faded quickly and he was soon almost as bad as before, finding himself in bondage to sin. Only a violent fever finally broke the fatal chain and brought him to himself. Weak and delirious, he crept to an isolated spot and cast himself before God in utter surrender, with his only hope being Christ's atonement, and from that hour, he claims, his peace and his health were restored and the power of sin in his life destroyed. As the voyage continued he began to teach himself Latin, becoming proficient after a few years' practice. One example he recalls of 'particular providences' during this period was that the captain quite casually asked him on one occasion to stay behind from a long-boat voyage which, in the issue, proved fatal to those who went.

Newton reflects that though God was caring for him at this time, God was also leaving him largely to his own experience and reflection, so that he only slowly broke from the world: his Christian conduct was yet inconsistent. Upon his return to England, seven years of waiting were finally rewarded when he and Mary Catlett were married, and his happiness at this moment seemed in stark contrast to his misery just a few years earlier. He describes how all too soon, however, he found himself resting in his temporal well-being as he made his wife his idol and forgot God. It was only the summons to prepare for his next voyage, with the attendant anxiety over separation from his wife, which returned him to earnest prayer. Peace was restored to his conscience again by trusting in Christ's atonement. He was preserved in safety and avoided indulging in worldly company on this, his first voyage as a captain. He treated his sailors well, established public worship on board, and proceeded with his Latin studies.

Newton recalls that in the interval before his next voyage he once more rested too much in his temporal comforts, though he gained some ground too by reading authors such as James Hervey, Henry Scougal, and Philip Doddridge. Still, he heard only 'common' preaching, had no Christian friends, and was cowardly about his Christian profession, even with his wife. On his second voyage as captain he enjoyed many scenes of solitude and prayer. He also found he was remarkably protected by God from a threatened mutiny, from an attempted insurrection by the slaves, and from a plot against his life by other traders. His 'idolatrous' heart was, however, severely punished in the West Indies when, his wife's letters having miscarried, he was left in sharp anxiety over her welfare.

Back at Liverpool, Newton met a former maritime acquaintance whose moral and religious principles he had earlier corrupted and whom he sought now to restore. Taking him along on his next voyage, he found the man grew only more intractable, horrifically announcing his own damnation even as he suffered a fatal fever. This could have been his own case, he realized, had he not been granted 'distinguishing mercy'. When Newton himself suffered from a terrible fever a little later, during the middle passage, he describes his faith, weak though it was, as fixed on Christ. A full assurance of faith, however, he did not yet have. Recovering, he met at the West Indies another Christian captain who helped him in his faith as they spent every opportunity together. Thus far he says he had been led by God in a hidden way; now his mind and heart were expanded as he was challenged to social prayer, Christian conversation, and a bold, public profession of faith. He recalls of this period that his views became clearer and more evangelical, for he was introduced to the security of the covenant of grace and recovered from the fear of falling away from God. He learned about the controversies of the times, and where to go in London for further instruction.

After returning to England Newton suffered an alarming convulsive fit which prevented him from going on the next

proposed voyage, an undertaking which he later learned was
dogged by death and misfortune. He had at this time no
scruples about the slave trade, widely regarded as a genteel
occupation, but he disliked the role of gaoler, the separation
from his wife, and the lack of religious opportunities. So he
was thankful to be out of the trade, though he worried
throughout the next year about his future settlement and his
wife's poor health, while he alternated living with friends and
family in Kent and London. In London he made many
religious friends, benefiting most from the public ministry and
acquaintance of the Dissenters Samuel Brewer and Samuel
Hayward. He met George Whitefield and thrived under his
preaching, and he profited from religious societies and private
Christian conversation. He credited Providence with successfully furnishing him with a civil service job as a tide surveyor
at Liverpool the following year and thanked God for restoring
his wife's health.

Since settling at Liverpool, his trials seemed light and few
except for the daily struggle with sin in a town where the
gospel was little known or respected. He now learned from
experience and from reviewing the truths he had learned in
London. He made many friends in Yorkshire, where the
gospel flourished, and he gained a wide acquaintance and
correspondence with many godly ministers; he learned from
all parties but strove to maintain the golden mean between
them. With a house of his own and much leisure, he
abandoned classics and endeavoured instead to know only
Christ, teaching himself Greek, Hebrew, and Syriac, and
keeping up a course of reading in the best writers in divinity.
The example of St Paul, who was made useful to Christ after
having opposed the faith, now prompted him to think of the
ministry himself. Strongly encouraged by some friends to go
forward, he took time to consider it more seriously. He then
thought of joining the Dissenters, supposing that he would not
be able in good conscience to make the necessary subscriptions in the Established Church. But a clerical friend in
Yorkshire later moderated his scruples and even provided a
title to a curacy. He was not, however, able to achieve
episcopal ordination either from the Archbishop of York or
from anyone else. At the close of the *Authentic Narrative*, he

describes himself as waiting on God to fulfil his desire of entering the ministry.

SOURCES, FORM, AND LITERARY CONVENTIONS

When Newton devoted three weeks early in 1763 to write up the story thus recounted, he was not without literary models ready to hand. While his account was drawn chiefly from his own immediate recollections, written in relative haste, and presented in a discursive, episodic manner, a few explicit analogues were clearly identified in the text itself. These, together with other literary types and traditions with which Newton was familiar, illustrate how, by allusion and convention, he linked his own story with a cluster of others. By doing so he made his own narrative both more universal and more distinct, since at various points it echoed sacred and familiar associations, while at others it departed from general and expected patterns.

Use of Scripture

The most obvious source from which Newton drew inspiration was the Scriptures. He began most sections of his autobiography with a quotation from the Bible, and then introduced the ensuing narrative with appropriate comments on the text. His diction, like that of most evangelicals, was dominated by biblical idiom, and his prose was put together in a style at times reaching almost to anthology, in which favourite scriptural phrases and tropes recurred at intervals. Often it was a matter of dropping a biblical text directly into the running narrative in a kind of cut-and-paste fashion, using the borrowed words as part of his own first-person vocabulary. Thus, for example, when describing his voyage to Venice in 1743, he wrote that if his eyes could have been opened to see the import of the cautionary dream he had had on that occasion, he would have seen a contest in heaven: 'I should perhaps have seen likewise, that Jesus, whom I had persecuted and defied, rebuking the adversary, challenging me for his own, as a brand plucked out of the fire, and saying, "Deliver him from going down to the pit; I have found a ransom".' (i. 26). Here one whole sentence was constructed as a collocation of indirect and direct scriptural references: an allusion to St Paul's conversion ('I should perhaps have seen . . . Jesus, whom I had persecuted,' Acts 9); an allusion to Zechariah's vision ('rebuking the adversary . . . brand plucked out of the fire,' Zechariah 3: 1–2); and a quotation from the book of Job ('Deliver him . . . I have found a ransom,' Job 33: 24). Yet these extracts functioned in a new semantic context and were made to bear the internal weight (and in this sentence, the full weight) of Newton's own narrative. Even when he was not describing, as here, the spiritual reality behind his experience, he would often use words drawn from the Bible to tell his story or make a point along the way. While there was a real danger that such a habit of mind could deteriorate into sectarian jargon ('Methodistical cant'), the impulse to speak and write in the words of Scripture has been present in many Christian traditions whose piety has centred around the Bible.[7] It was a devotional mode of expression which at its highest strove to see present experience transfigured in an aureole of sacred associations, but at its worst could become simply self-referential.

Beyond vocabulary, however, the Scriptures offered biographical *exempla*. Of the immense inventory of potential analogues to his own personal experience available in the Bible, the one sacred narrative which he, like other evangelicals, most often laid side-by-side with his own history, was the life of St Paul. In the preamble to his own narrative he made the identification with Paul central and explicit, excepting only that he was worse in wickedness before conversion, and Paul was superior in usefulness after. He quarried almost every line of Pauline testimony for phrases with which to describe himself at various stages of life in the *Authentic Narrative*: he was, for example, one of those who served 'divers lust . . . hateful, and hating one another', 'the chief of sinners', chosen 'to shew forth all longsuffering, for a pattern to them which should hereafter believe', being 'in

[7] See further with respect to 18th-c. biblical diction, Thomas R. Preston, 'Biblical Criticism, Literature, and the Eighteenth-Century Reader', in I. Rivers (ed.), *Books and their Readers in Eighteenth-Century England* (Leicester, 1982), 97–126.

deaths oft' and hoping one day to 'preach the faith which once he destroyed'.[8] More than any other source, the life of St Paul provided Newton with the overall narrative structure of his autobiography.

Yet, while the life of St Paul must be given hermeneutical priority in the *Authentic Narrative*, Newton was also struck by the way his case resembled the account in the Gospels of the man delivered of an unclean spirit, as well as the parables of the prodigal son and the spared fig tree.[9] Allusions were also made at certain key dramatic points in Newton's story to the lives of Old Testament saints: like Jacob he had occasion to reflect on his increased prosperity when revisiting a site of his former destitution; like Joseph he had experienced the concurrence of seemingly fortuitous circumstances, which were later understood as crucial providences upon which his life turned; like Sampson he found his strength fail him in his hour of need; like David he was delivered from on high out of deep waters; and, of course, like Jonah he endangered all on board his ship when in rebellion against God.[10]

But the two loftiest analogues that Newton identified were the history of Israel as a whole, and the life of Christ himself. He began his autobiography by referring to the scene in Deuteronomy 8: 2 where Moses had prophesied to the Israelite nation in the wilderness that there would come a happy day when their journey and their warfare would be over, and when they would look back with pleasure on their present troubles. Newton commented that these words could be taken in a spiritual sense as addressed to all who by faith must pass through the world (wilderness) to heaven (Canaan), and who may therefore likewise expect a future time when present difficulties would be seen as having been instrumental of greater glory. Even now believers could anticipate, in large measure, such a perspective by reviewing past dispensations

---

[8] Titus 3: 3 cf. *Works*, i. 46; 1 Tim. 1: 15 cf. *Works*, i. 94: 2 Cor. 11: 23 cf. *Works*, i. 89; 1 Tim. 1: 16 cf. *Works*, i. 9, 104; Gal. 1: 23 cf. *Works*, i. 104.

[9] Mark 5: 1–20 cf. *Works*, i. 7; Luke 13, 15 cf. *Works*, i. 7.

[10] Gen. 32: 10 cf. *Works*, i. 45; Gen. 37–50 *passim* cf. *Works*, i. 51; Judg. 16: 20 cf. *Works*, i. 75; Ps. 18: 16 cf. *Works*, i. 59; Jonah 1: 7–16 cf. *Works*, i. 53, 64.

in the light of Scripture. This was, he claimed, what he was seeking to do in his present memoir. The important point here is the way in which the history of Israel was drawn into the very centre of a bundle of associations with which Newton crowded his narrative. To describe himself as 'an outcast lying in my blood' (the metaphorical representation of Israel in Ezekiel 16), while at the nadir of his spiritual declension in Africa, was a natural extension into the narrative of the symbolic use of Israel already made explicit in his introduction.

Much more allusively did Newton imply that Christ's own life was typical of his. The key phrase was from John 2: 4 where Christ says to his mother, 'Mine hour is not yet come.' This was used by Newton to dramatic effect, though he was careful not to 'indwell' the language of Christ as immediately as he had in the case of Israel. He did not incorporate the clause into his own vocabulary but, remarking that these words of Christ had great import, he associated them with his two years in Africa (again the low point of his narrative) during which 'the Lord's hour of grace was not yet come' (i. 38). Internally, this gave his story a dramatic tension which could mount for another nineteen pages before the fore-shadowed crucial moment came when he announced, in describing the storm of March 1748, 'now *the Lord's time was come*' (i. 57, italics his). Externally, the allusion acted as a symbolic link, however slight, between Christ's passion and Newton's unjust suffering in Guinea (his servitude was largely due, he claimed, to having been falsely accused of dishonesty and stealing), adding a Messianic motif to the fugue of biblical tropes already set resonating in the text. It also established the storm as the climax of his story.

Newton's use of Scripture thus created an essentially figural interpretative structure for his autobiography. When he stated on the first page of his narrative that the history of Israel might be applied in a 'spiritual sense' to all who were journeying from this world to eternity, he was not, however, invoking some sort of *sensus allegoricus*, recalling medieval and patristic exegesis. (Dante, for example, had explained that the tropological meaning of Israel's history was 'the conversion of the soul from the sorrow and misery of sin to a state of grace'.)[11] Newton elsewhere made explicit his commitment to the Reformation tradition of literal exegesis, allowing for typological interpretation only in cases where the New Testament set an explicit precedent.[12] Divine revelation was understood in the context of Reformed theology as a historical phenomenon of promise and fulfilment, not an allegorical phenomenon of the abstract extrapolated from the particular.[13] Rejecting allegory as such, Newton described his own practice of figuration as one of 'accommodating' certain biblical texts to illustrate doctrines made clear elsewhere in Scripture (iv. 260–2). This concession, however, proved licence enough to mine a multitude of sacred symbols for his autobiography. The final effect was that his own life read as an episode in salvation history, one small story embedded in the larger sequence of God's saving acts.[14]

Philip Doddridge's Life of Colonel Gardiner *(1747)*

If the epistles of St Paul were the principal source of sacred inspiration, Philip Doddridge's *Some remarkable passages in the life of Colonel James Gardiner* (1747) provided the modern narrative which stirred Newton most deeply. Newton believed that while all Christians could gather evidence from their lives of divine grace and providence, some were particularly selected by God to show the riches of his grace for the encouragement of others. In these lives the divine work proceeded not secretly and gradually, but openly and powerfully, as God convinced, pardoned, and changed them beyond all expectation. It was a kinship of the latter sort of life that Newton felt with Gardiner.

James Gardiner (1687/8–1745) was an officer who served

---

[11] Quoted in Mason I. Lowance, Jr., *The Language of Canaan* (Cambridge, Mass., 1980), 18.　　　　　　　　　　　　　　　　　[12] Bull, *Newton*, 231–2.

[13] Harriet Guest, *A Form of Sound Words: The Religious Poetry of Christopher Smart* (Oxford, 1989), 136–7, 222–7, argues that Smart's *Jubilate Agno* is grounded in a typological hermeneutic similar to Newton's, which stood in contrast to the growing tendency of the period to interpret especially the Old Testament chiefly as a sequential chronological narrative to be explicated by antiquarian research.

[14] For a study of this pattern among the Puritans, see Lowance, *Language of Canaan*. Cf. also Bunyan's use of the Israel typology in a way similar to Newton's in *Grace Abounding to the Chief of Sinners* (Oxford, 1962), 2.

various commissions in the British military before dying of wounds incurred in the battle at Prestonpans in 1745, when the English forces were routed by an army of Highlanders loyal to the Young Pretender. The spiritual saga described by Doddridge was of Gardiner's decline from the early pious influence of his mother to the life of a dissolute young rake in Paris, whose moral degeneracy was arrested suddenly by a startling vision of the crucified Christ reproaching him for impiety. Though at first Gardiner felt certain he should be damned, he soon gained more sanguine hopes of divine mercy, experienced exquisite spiritual joys, and proved himself an exemplary Christian in private devotion, self-denial, and public profession, sealing his Christian character in the end by his bravery in the face of death.

Newton's diary and letters corroborate the evidence of the *Authentic Narrative* that this biography was, after the Bible, the most formative literary influence upon his own autobiography. While still at sea in 1752/3 Newton found that Gardiner's story moved him to tears several times. Again in 1754 he wrote to his childhood pastor that the book had affected him 'more frequently and sensibly than all the books I ever read', and at home in 1755 he recorded having promoted the tract among his friends, sending his copy to London for a minister to read.[15] The mention of Gardiner in diary and letters prompted some of his earliest and longest written reflections on his own life. On 19 July 1752 Newton recorded in his diary that among the books he was reading he could not but take particular note of Doddridge's *Life of Gardiner*, for despite Gardiner's higher social station, his experience was remarkably like his own. Both had similar secular callings, both were distinguished from common sinners by the degree and arrogance of their impieties, and both were arrested in the course of their profaneness by a remarkable divine call, brought in a moment to cry out to God for mercy. When Newton came to write his own narrative more than ten years later, he would single out for treatment other details with parallels in Gardiner's biography, such as the piety of his

[15] *Works*, i. 8, 9; Diary (1751–6), 19 July 1752, 17 May 1753, and 20 May 1755; Newton to David Jennings, [Jan.] 1754, ALS, DWL.

mother (a theme which echoed Doddridge with especial closeness), unheeded deliverances from near-death experiences, the hardening of his heart in youthful sins, a remarkable dream, and a casual look into a religious book on the eve of his conversion. Reading Gardiner's life revealed to Newton the pattern of his own experience.

But while Gardiner's life helped thus to provide a principle of selection for his autobiography, Newton also established his own individuality by tracing deviation from, as well as conformity with, the curve of Gardiner's narrative. Thus, in his diary, as in the *Authentic Narrative*, Newton went on to record how dissimilar his progress had been from Gardiner's after conversion: where Gardiner manifested humility and perseverance from the first day, Newton had sinned in an aggravated way against the one who had forgiven him so much. The bottom curve of Newton's spiritual course was flatter than Gardiner's, more U-shaped than V-shaped. So he remarked in the *Authentic Narrative* how he had never had that period of 'first love' and how faint were the beginnings of grace in his life. But his diary indicates he continued strongly to uphold Gardiner as a suitable pattern for his future behaviour.

Personal Papers

In December 1751 Newton began a diary which, together with his letters to his wife, would supplement his own recollections not only for the last fifth of his narrative (1751–63) but also for the earlier period, since he had often reviewed his past in this diary by the time he came to write his autobiography. These were primary documentary sources for his narrative, in a more obvious sense than Scripture or collateral biography, because the diary and letters were records that supplied the content, not simply the form, of his story. But they nevertheless made a contribution to form as well, for the shape in which Newton's autobiography appeared as a printed book evolved naturally out of his diary and letters.

Even before commencing his diary, Newton had been accustomed, in the manner of his profession, to keep a nautical journal, recording minute details of weather,

location, activities of the crew, sightings of other ships, and
transactions in trade. Traversing the Atlantic during the years
before an accurate way of plotting longitude had been
discovered, he and his crew depended on many of the
observations recorded in his journal for their own safety and
for the commercial success of their voyages.[16] It was natural
then that this practice should inform his contemporaneous
habit of keeping a spiritual diary and that metaphors were
drawn from his daily outward life to describe his inward state.
He charted the progress of his soul just as he did the motions
of his ship. The spiritual diary had, of course, Puritan
precedents, and Newton's principal motivation for keeping
one was as an aid to faith: a stimulus to pious resolve, self-
examination, and praise. It was a practice which looked back
to his Dissenting roots, and he had even kept a spiritual diary
of sorts as a young adolescent (i. 15). But when he began his
habit of closing each week with a serious review of mercies
received and sins committed, he resorted easily to the
language of commerce: 'By thus frequently posting my
accounts with my Maker (if I may use such an expression) I
should be always calm and prepared against attacks of
sickness or accidents.'[17] Likewise, he began his practice of
New Year's Day meditations by writing: 'It is customary with
traders at this time to settle their accounts and examine more
particularly into the state of their affairs, and a man should be
counted an ill Oeconomist who should wholly omit it. The like
scrutiny is methinks equally necessary or at least no less
expedient in spirituals.'[18] Such commercial metaphors were
frequent in Puritan confessional diaries as well.[19]

The tendency to think of the spiritual life in specifically
maritime symbols was also confessed in the *Authentic Narrative*:
'My connections with sea-affairs have often led me to think,
that the varieties observable in Christian experience may be
properly illustrated from the circumstances of a voyage'

[16] These nautical journals are abridged in *Journal of a Slave Trader (John Newton): 1750–1754*, ed. Bernard Martin and Mark Spurrell (1962).
[17] Diary (1751–6), 11 Jan. 1752.   [18] Ibid., 1 Jan. 1753.
[19] Owen C. Watkins, *The Puritan Experience* (1972), 20–1.

(i. 72–3).[20] Storms, compass, port, rules of navigation, shipwreck, enemy ships—all these and more served as Bunyanesque images of his Christian experience. In such ways as these his diary proved a key instrument for working out an incipient autobiography as he related outward events to his inward condition, reviewed his past history in the light of present resolves, and tested available metaphors for their capacity to explain the state of his soul. That he reread his diary carefully, reviewing what he had written of his experiences, is evident from the way he cross-referenced passages at several points.

Like his diary, many of his letters were at hand when he came to write his autobiography, for he was from an early date an avid correspondent. While away from home he made a regular practice of writing to his wife two or three times a week; consequently, he had some 200 sheets of paper lying in his bureau when he wrote the *Authentic Narrative*, comprising letters to his wife from their time of courtship to the present. And like the diary, this correspondence made a formal contribution to his autobiography, since the published account was written and presented as an epistolary narrative. A quick look through his œuvre shows how thoroughly the familiar letter became his most typical literary form: he seems virtually to have thought in quarto sheets folded once. As his distinctive form of public expression, it evolved naturally and progressively out of his private life. Thus, looking over his correspondence with his wife on one occasion, he observed in it his increasing seriousness as he gained more religious knowledge, his growing capacity to think and write on a variety of subjects, and his advancing ability to express himself readily in prose.

When a friend asked him in 1762 for a written account of his conversion, it was natural therefore for Newton to respond in a series of eight letters.[21] When these letters were seen by

---

[20] Here too Newton had Puritan precedent in e.g. John Flavel, *Navigation Spiritualized* (1682). He mentioned having seen Flavel's book and others like it in a letter to David Jennings, 29 Aug. 1752, ALS, DWL.

[21] The friend was a man named Fawcett, probably the Baptist John Fawcett (1740–1817) from Bradford.

Thomas Haweis (1734–1820), the recently ejected curate of St Mary Magdalene in Oxford who was now a chaplain at the Lock Hospital in London, Haweis asked Newton in January 1763 for an expanded account, including additional details he had heard from Newton in conversation.[22] Newton responded in fourteen letters. For the next eighteen months copies of the letters were passed around ever more widely, until Newton and Haweis decided to go to press to forestall the publication of an unauthorized edition. At first the idea of a subscription was floated, and Newton even solicited permission from Martin Madan, Andrew Gifford, and Samuel Brewer to mention their names in the pre-publication advertisement, but in the end it was decided to publish Newton's *Authentic Narrative* on the strength of anticipated sales. The line between the manuscript culture of the familiar letter and the print culture of the commercial book was crossed almost imperceptibly.[23]

Standing midway between the subjectivity of the confessional diary and the objectivity of the literary essay, the genius of the familiar letter in the eighteenth century was its combination of spontaneous expression with the treatment of a substantial subject. Because the personal letter was still a form of polite conversation and to receive one still something of an event, the writer was generally aware, as Newton was, that his letter might be read aloud to the recipient's friends, and kept for rereading or for posterity. Existing thus ambiguously somewhere between the private and public document, it was quite readily taken up by writers of fiction who saw it as a convenient literary device to achieve verisimilitude in novels.[24] In like fashion Newton used the

---

[22] For the relationship between Haweis and Newton, see further, A. Skevington Wood, 'The Influence of Thomas Haweis on John Newton', *Journal of Ecclesiastical History*, 4 (1953), 187–202.

[23] *Works*, i. 3; Newton to Thomas Haweis, 7 Jan. 1763, ALS, FLP; *Letters* (Clunie), 44–5, 48, 52, 62; Bull, *Newton*, 116–17.

[24] See further, Herbert Davis, 'Correspondence of the Augustans', in Howard Anderson *et al.* (eds.), *Familiar Letter in the Eighteenth Century* (Lawrence, Kan., 1966), 1–13; Howard Anderson and Irvin Ehrenpreis, 'The Familiar Letter in the Eighteenth Century: Some Generalizations', ibid. 269–82; Natascha Würzbach, *The Novel in Letters* (1969); Patricia Meyer Spacks, 'Forgotten Genres', *Modern Language Studies*, 18: 1 (1988), 47–57.

epistolary form in the *Authentic Narrative* to achieve all the
immediacy of personal address while in the full knowledge
that his letters would have a large readership. It was like the
skilled public speaker who knows that establishing effective
eye contact with one person makes everyone in the room feel
directly addressed. Thus Newton wrote in the first letter:

Though you [Thomas Haweis] have signified your intentions of
communicating what I send you to others, I must not on this
account affect a conciseness or correctness, which is not my natural
talent, lest the whole should appear dry and constrained. I shall,
therefore, if possible, think only of you, and write with that freedom
and confidence which your friendship and candour deserve.   (i. 11)

Newton was seeking to maintain for himself as much as for his
readers the fiction that he was only writing personal letters to
a close friend.

   This had many implications, given that Newton was
writing his own life. Between the writer and the reader stood
the subject-matter, but how was the subject to be handled if it
were one's own self? Newton was keenly aware of 'the great
difficulty of writing properly when *Self* is concerned' and of the
possibility that he would be charged with self-conceit (i. 10,
96). From the beginning he was genuinely reticent to write
about his own spiritual experiences. He explained to Haweis,

Something of this sort might now and again occur in a familiar letter
to a friend, that could pity and conceal my weakness—but when you
tell me beforehand, that the letters you expect from me are to be
transmitted I know not where—you make me exceedingly fearful of
writing too much in the detail! Alas you know not my heart, & how
hard I find it to fight against that accursed principle of *Self*.[25]

In the event, the private-cum-public letter was well suited to
overcome all objections. By writing to Haweis, and only over
his shoulder, so to speak, to the general reader, he could
readily excuse whatever might seem egotistical with the
apology that he was only disclosing himself as might
reasonably be expected in a personal letter to a friend. So, for
example, Newton could appeal to Haweis's request for more
information about his courtship as warrant for making public

---

[25] Newton to Haweis, 7 Jan. 1763.

details of his life which would be thought too private by some
readers (i. 32). But this device only partially succeeded, as the
remarks of John Wesley bore witness. Shortly after the book
was published, Wesley wrote to Newton, 'The objection
current here, that you talk too much of Mrs Newton, seems to
me of no force at all. I cannot apprehend that you could well
have spoken less or any otherwise than you do.'[26] At least
Newton won Wesley. But more importantly, the form allowed
Newton to explore his own identity outside the solipsism of the
diary. The progression from diary through familiar letter to
autobiography was as natural as it was important to his
emergence as a visible figure in the wider evangelical
community.

Related Literary Types and Traditions

In addition to the documentary sources and inspirational
examples which Newton explicitly acknowledged in the
Authentic Narrative, there were wider classes of contemporary
literature with which his narrative had further affinities as a
genre.

One of the first indications of genre is the title of a work.
Newton's title points in two directions which relate respectively to the outward and the inward aspects of his story. As
regards the outward aspect, the key words *Authentic Narrative*
and *remarkable experiences,* or their close synonyms, were often
used in sensational tracts such as the sordid lives (and
executions) of criminals, tales of travellers in strange lands, or
accounts of current catastrophes, all of which were in popular
demand at the time of Newton's writing. There was, for
example, *The remarkable life of James Smith, a famous young
highwayman, who was executed at Surbiton-Common . . . for a robbery
in Surrey. Containing a true and faithful narrative of all robberies that
he has, within a few years, committed . . . written by himself* [1756],
or, more spectacularly, *News from the dead, or a faithful and
genuine narrative of an extraordinary combat between life and death,
exemplified in the case of William Duell . . . who was executed at
Tyburn . . . and who soon return'd to life . . . the whole taken from his
own mouth in Newgate* (1740). Examples could be multiplied,

[26] *JWL* iv. 292.

but in all cases the special pleading of the word group 'authentic/genuine/true/faithful', with the accompanying attestation of autobiographical veracity, is in proportion to the 'sensational/remarkable/disputed/surprising' content of the narratives. Given its inherent drama and adventure and its sworn truthfulness, Newton's own *Authentic narrative . . . of some remarkable and interesting particulars* . . . would no doubt have gratified the same kind of curiosity, pious or profane, which fuelled demand for such literature. A standard twentieth-century study of biography in this period picks up this strand in Newton's work and treats it with other contemporary lives under the heading, 'Lives of soldiers of fortune'.[27]

Newton's title also points in another direction, however, linking his autobiography in its religious aspect to contemporary conversion narratives and providence literature. Famously, there was Jonathan Edwards's *Faithful narrative of the surprising work of God in the conversion of many hundred souls in Northampton, and the neighbouring towns* (1737), or James Robe's *Faithful narrative of the extraordinary work of the Spirit of God, at Kilsyth, and other congregations in the neighbourhood* (Glasgow, 1742). At the level of individual biography there was the *Faithful narrative of the life and character of the Reverend Mr. Whitefield* (1739), or the reprint of the Puritan John Flavel's *A Saint indeed: or, the great work of a Christian. . . . To which is added, a faithful and succinct narrative of some late and wonderful sea-deliverances* (Glasgow, 1754). Although it presumably owed something to Newton's precedent, there was also Thomas Scott's *Force of Truth: An Authentic Narrative* (1779). Because of the conventional use of 'faithful narrative' or 'authentic narrative' in this kind of religious literature, the astute evangelical reader would have been alerted by Newton's title page to the fact that his story was of an inward as well as an outward odyssey.[28]

[27] Donald A. Stauffer, *The Art of Biography in Eighteenth-Century England* (Princeton, 1941), 218–19.
[28] The analysis in the two paragraphs above is based upon a survey of approximately 200 titles in the *Eighteenth-Century Short Title Catalogue* (1991) which contain the words 'faithful [or] genuine [or] authentic narrative'.

For all its adventure, it was this latter link to the evangelical conversion narrative and its Puritan antecedents that was most important. Here was a native lives-of-the-saints tradition with which Newton was thoroughly acquainted, the soil in which his own narrative germinated. Owen Watkins in *The Puritan Experience* (1972) has traced the genesis of spiritual autobiography as a popular genre in England from the second half of the seventeenth century, and has shown how it emerged as the result of specific characteristics in the Puritan way of life. Persistent emphasis from pulpit and press on the application of doctrine to experience, on the internal spiritual warfare of the soul, and on the importance of self-examination, all within the context of well-defined schemata of regeneration, fostered widespread religious concern at a personal level. The typical literary expression of this concern was at first principally the confessional diary. This passed over into actual autobiography with the rise to prominence of the radical Puritans during the Commonwealth period, when a growing interest in biographies of pious men, an upsurge in religious innovation, and a stress on personal testimony in the reception of new members by the gathered churches, all contributed to the emergence of the personal conversion narrative. Thus, Puritan culture provided a basis in theory, technique, and language for spiritual autobiography to flourish for several generations.[29]

Newton was the distant heir of this Puritan tradition which, after the Great Ejection of 1662 and the sanction of orthodox Dissent in 1689, was sustained into the eighteenth century in Nonconformist chapels such as the one in Old Gravel Lane, Wapping, in which he was baptized as an infant. Even by the time of writing the *Authentic Narrative*, when he was hoping to be ordained in the Church of England, his friendships among evangelical Dissenters were numerous and varied. By then he

---

[29] Watkins, *Puritan Experience*, 66. See further, Paul Delany, *British Autobiography in the Seventeenth Century* (1969); Patricia Caldwell, *The Puritan Conversion Narrative* (Cambridge, 1983). For a discussion of 18th-c. spiritual autobiography and its antecedents, with special reference to the contribution of Pietism and Moravianism, see Reginald Ward's Introduction to *Journals and Diaries I*, ed. W. Reginald Ward and Richard P. Heitzenrater, vol. xviii in *The Works of John Wesley*, ed. Richard P. Heitzenrater and Frank Baker (Nashville, 1988), 1–119 (esp. 1–36).

would have heard many times the public testimonies of candidates for membership of an Independent Meeting—the important 'Congregationalist church relation'—oral conversion narratives which anticipated his own.[30] His reading through the 1750s drew him further into the Anglo-Calvinist tradition as he studied the writings of many famous Puritans.[31] The *Life of Colonel Gardiner*, though the sole literary model mentioned explicitly in the *Authentic Narrative*, should be taken only as the most influential representative of a whole culture in which Newton was immersed.

Given the common cultural inheritance which Newton shared with Puritanism, the *Authentic Narrative* could be expected to exhibit some of the characteristics of seventeenth-century spiritual autobiography. The Covenanter James Fraser touched what was the central thread of scarlet for all these writers when he wrote in his own memoirs, 'A Man's whole Life is but a Conversion.'[32] This most basic theme upon which endless changes could be rung figured prominently in Newton as well: peace, distress, and then peace again; conviction, compunction, and submission; ruin, redemption, and regeneration.[33] Of the many incidents which typically recurred in the Puritan narratives (many which were also in the *Life of Colonel Gardiner*), several were singled out by Newton. He gave attention to details from his past such as childhood piety, falling-away in youth, a dream, self-righteous behaviour, feelings of excessive sorrow, temptation to suicide, conviction of damnation, recollection of Scripture texts, and providential deliverances. He described some of the latter occasions at one point and commented, 'I seemed to have every mark of final impenitence and rejection; neither judgements nor mercies made the least impression on me'

---

[30] e.g. Diary (1751–6), 2 May 1755. Nuttall, 'Methodism and the Older Dissent', *United Reformed Church Historical Society Journal*, 2 (1981), 265–8, describes the journals, memoirs, and autobiographies which flourished in the early 18th c. among Dissenters ('evangelicals before the revival'), and comments, 'The Revival encouraged . . . declarations of experience, which had been common form in independent and Baptist churches.' [31] See further, the Appendix.

[32] Quoted in Watkins, *Puritan Experience*, 40.

[33] Ibid. 37; Caldwell, *Puritan Conversion Narrative*, 2; Bebbington, *Evangelicalism in Britain*, 3.

(i. 55). Bunyan had earlier recounted a comparable train of close calls with death and had written in the same vernacular, 'Here as I said, were judgements and mercy, but neither of them did awaken my soul to righteousness.'[34] There were common features of style as well, such as a similar use of scriptural idiom and vogue expressions (Bunyan was a chief of sinners before Newton), and of technique, such as the use of the passive voice as a subtle way of identifying a lonely soul at the mercy of mighty spiritual forces. And Newton was not the first to make the claim of reluctant authorship or to have this claim endorsed by a respected clergyman in an added preface. More important were the didactic aims which Newton shared with his forebears. 'If God may be glorified on my behalf,' he wrote, 'and his children in any measure comforted or instructed by what I have to declare of his goodness, I shall be satisfied' (i. 10–11).[35] These were motives which Watkins identifies in the Puritans as the evangelical, pastoral, and prophetic voices of spiritual autobiography.[36] In some respects the *Authentic Narrative* could as easily have been written in the seventeenth century as in the eighteenth.

The morphology of conversion was elaborated and debated at great length by the sort of Puritan writers read by Newton, but reduced to its most basic elements it involved (except among Antinomians) a progression from a 'legal call' to an 'evangelical call', which was understood to reflect in experience the important dialectic between law and gospel in theology. This twofold structure is evident in Newton's narrative. He carefully circumscribed his description of his initial change of heart on board the *Greyhound* after the storm in 1748. After acknowledging that he was no longer a Deist, had some right notions, and had given over the habit of swearing, Newton began the next paragraph with 'But', and added all the concessions demonstrating this to have been only a legal repentance: he still did not know the innate evils of his heart, he still did not understand the spirituality and

---

[34] John Bunyan, *Grace Abounding to the Chief of Sinners* (1st edn. 1666; repr., Welwyn, 1983), 12.   [35] Cf. *Letters* (Clunie), 63.
[36] Watkins, *Puritan Experience*, 227.

extent of the law, and he still did not comprehend a life of continual dependence upon and communion with God. In short, he was still self-righteous. It is another eight pages until his evangelical repentance is described. This came when, within six months, he was back on the Guinea coast and had broken all his sacramental vows of holy living. He was then prompted by a severe fever to make a wholehearted surrender to God in which he acknowledged his own moral impotence. From that moment he claimed to have been delivered from the power of sin, if not wholly from its effects.

Newton did not consciously think of his conversion in generic terms. He wrote, 'We must not therefore make the experience of others, in all respects, a rule to ourselves, nor our own a rule to others ... As to myself, every part of my case has been extraordinary.—I have hardly met a single instance resembling it' (i. 74). Yet this implied that he allowed the experience of others to be normative in *some* respects. Moreover, the assumption that his case was extraordinary demanded that he possess a strong and clear sense of what was in fact ordinary. Newton wrote of his evangelical call: 'I do not remember that any particular text, or remarkable discovery, was presented to my mind; but in general I was enabled to hope and believe in a crucified Saviour' (i. 76). This caveat shows that he recognized how his case deviated at this point from typical experience (a Scripture text leaping to mind, a vision, an overwhelming supernatural presence, and so on) but that he still felt the overall pattern ('in general') applied to his conversion. Other exceptions which he noted help also to prove the presence of some sort of conscious rule: he noted, for instance, that he was turned to God without having heard much evangelical preaching, the normal means of converting grace. An earlier aside, when describing the period of his legal call, likewise implied teleological aware-ness. He confessed, 'You will please to observe, Sir, that I collect the strain of the reasonings and exercises of my mind in one view; but I do not say that all this passed at one time' (i. 61). He had telescoped the account. In view of his statement elsewhere that grace dawned unusually slowly in his soul (distinguishing his own from the usual pattern), it seems that he wished here still to describe his legal phase as conforming as closely as possible to common expectations, without actually falsifying the account.

It is possible to go one step further in establishing the presence in Newton's narrative of conscious design and structure deriving from his evangelical cultural experience. For the ethical failure in Africa which figured so largely in the *Authentic Narrative* as the occasion of his surrender to God was not only omitted, but even sanguinely glossed in an earlier letter to his wife. In this letter he reflected on the voyage during which (as he later wrote) he had fallen into an unthinkable course of evil. He wrote to her in 1751 saying this voyage, 'though troublesome enough, yet, enlivened by the hopes you had given me, was to me light and easy. And as it pleased God to enable me, in some measure, to act up to my new resolutions, I was, for the most part, at peace in every way' (v. 370). However, this acting up to his new resolutions 'in some measure' was in 1764 described as a 'black declension'. Something must have occurred between 1751 and 1764 to overcome his reticence to disclose fully to his wife the 'train of temptations' and 'course of evil' to which he succumbed in Africa, or, at least, to single out this episode as significant for his autobiography. The most plausible explanation is that, through the 1750s, his renewed acquaintance with orthodox Dissent, his introduction to contemporary evangelicalism, his growing familiarity with the Puritan literary tradition, and his strengthening commitment to Calvinism, all reinforced the most basic morphology of conversion as comprising a legal and an evangelical phase.[37] With this pattern at hand, he was able to see clearly the importance of the surrender he had made to God in Africa following the breaking of his religious vows.

NARRATIVE STRUCTURE, THEME, AND IMAGERY

The drama of the *Authentic Narrative* comprised the three interwoven plots of Newton's vocation, his courtship, and his evangelical conversion. In the first instance it was a rags-to-riches story of a young man who squandered all the greatest

---

[37] Cf. *Works*, i. 320.

advantages and opportunities in commerce, who was consequently reduced to extremities of misery and want, but who then, beyond all expectation, was raised to respectable social status and given more than he could desire of the good things of life. It was also a tale of romance in which love at first sight was followed by years of unrequited passion, crowned at long last by the happiness of marriage when all obstacles were finally overcome. And lastly, it was an evangelical narrative in which common grace in childhood was spurned, resulting in a course of hardened unbelief and wilful sin from which the protagonist recovered only through an act of divine mercy, leading in time to a new season of religious usefulness. Because the three plots concurred in shape and corresponded in chronological sequence, there is a continual narrative echo which recurs through the work as a whole. Thinking of the Puritans, Owen Watkins writes, 'It is the ability to set up this kind of resonance between the inward and the outward that does the most to give significance to the private events of a spiritual autobiography,' and he isolates several notable seventeenth-century examples of such genius.[38] Newton recognized these two sides of conversion narrative. To Haweis he wrote, when summoned to provide his account, 'The Lord's dealings towards his people may be perhaps reduced to two heads. *Providence* and *Experiences*. The case of some are more remarkable for their providential dispensations, of others for the variety of their inward experience.'[39] While this inward and outward concurrence did not make Newton's autobiography a great work of literature, it did heighten its intrinsic value and interest as a story.[40]

What unified the three-layered narrative was the central

---

[38] Watkins, *Puritan Experience*, 66.   [39] Newton to Haweis, 7 Jan. 1763.
[40] In contrast, the autobiography of the Methodist preacher Silas Told—though its outward story includes sea-deliverances, disease, mutiny, storms and hurricanes, shipwrecks, torture, pirates, poisoning, starvation, desertion, and tales of maritime exotica which strain credulity—manifests no such narrative coherence, nor any correlation of inward spiritual experience with outward events. On the contrary, Told seems simply to indulge in the story for its own sake, and then, having told of his adventures, he starts over again halfway through, saying, 'Here my readers will permit me to enter upon my religious life . . .' *An Account of the Life, and Dealings of God with Silas Told, Late Preacher of the Gospel . . . Written by Himself* (1786), 73.

theme of a benign providence working out the salvation of the elect. Newton gave a concise statement of this in his introduction where, after recalling Israel's hope of Canaan while still in the wilderness, he claimed that, by reviewing past events in the light of Scripture, Christians too may

collect indisputable proof that the wise and good providence of God watches over his people from the earliest moment of their life, over-rules and guards them through all their wanderings in a state of ignorance, leads them in a way that they know not, till at length his providence and grace concur in those events and impressions which bring them to the knowledge of him and themselves. (i. 7)[41]

Thus a proleptic knowledge of the ultimate meaning of one's past life was attainable by viewing Scripture and biographical facts in a kind of stereoscopy. Providence and grace concur: outward and inward experience come into focus. As literature, this gave his autobiography the structure of 'comic irony', in which past and present perspectives were juxtaposed and bad events were narrated in terms of appearance and reality—to all appearances bad, but in reality a means of good. As theology, this made his autobiography a kind of emblematic literature dramatizing the predestinarian order of salvation: effectual calling, justification, sanctification, and glorification. Hence Newton's language described his life as an exhibit, monument, proof, warning, and encouragement: always pointing to, and representing, a meaning beyond itself. This persistent pointing beyond himself, and the related cluster of allusions which linked his story with so many others, allowed his narrative, in a sense, to glow under borrowed light. Archetypal patterns were evoked: what Northrop Frye calls

---

[41] The exodus motif was prominent in Puritan autobiography, and Bunyan had an almost identical typological prolegomenon in his preface to *Grace Abounding*. Ward, *Protestant Evangelical Awakening*, 7–8, notes the dominance of the exodus theme in the 18th c. itself, a time during which there were great population movements in Europe. Isabel Rivers, 'Strangers and Pilgrims: Sources and Patterns of Methodist Narrative', in J. D. Hilson, M. M. B. Jones, and J. R. Watson (eds.), *Augustan Worlds* (Leicester, 1978 189–203, describes a different pilgrimage motif among Methodists, shaped by Wesley's Arminianism and the itinerant experience of his preachers, in which the life of the autobiographer was an unfinished journey from this life to the next. The proleptic element which Newton stressed—knowing how the story will end—was absent, or at least less pronounced.

'not the horizontal line of precedent and prudence, but the U-shaped progression of original prosperity, descent into humiliation, and return', which is the pattern of the Bible and the dominant pattern of most Western literature since.[42]

Recurring dialectical imagery in Newton's narrative reiterated the central theme or pattern of conversion in another mode. Repeated pairs of contrasting images emphasized how crucial was the notion of conversion to his religious identity. In these metaphors can also be seen a linking of outward sensory experience and inward spiritual reality typical of the period, for empiricism was ascendant in religion as much as in philosophy.[43] For example, he thought of his experience in images of darkness and light from an early date. In 1752 he recorded words in his diary which would later be echoed in his famous hymn 'Amazing Grace'. After lamenting his sin and wondering that God should show him mercy, he wrote, 'The reason is unknown to me, but one thing I know, that whereas I was blind, now I see . . .'.[44] In the *Authentic Narrative* those who could not see the workings of providence were likewise 'blind'; those who could were 'enlightened'. The beginnings of his religious course were 'faint' rather than 'bright' like those of others. When he returned to a habit of sin he was 'lulled to sleep' and suffered a 'black declension'; when recovered, 'awakened' in conscience. Likewise, he often wrote of his experience in terms of bondage and freedom. In his moral decline he was 'fast bound in chains', and only illness could 'break the fatal chain'; he was 'delivered' from the dominion of sin and gradually set at 'liberty' from compliance in worldly diversions; in retired moments of prayer he sought 'enlargement'. Several other similar contrasting sets of metaphors could be added. Word groups associated with distance–proximity, depth–height, violence–peace, storm–calm, hardness–softness, illness/insanity–health—all of these were

[42] Northrop Frye, *The Great Code* (1982), 198.
[43] See further, R. E. Brantley, *Locke, Wesley, and the Method of English Romanticism* (Gainesville, Fla. 1984); F. D. Dreyer, 'Faith and Experience in the Thought of John Wesley', *American Historical Review*, 87 (1983), 12–30.
[44] Diary (1751–6), 9 Aug. 1752.

repeated in the *Authentic Narrative*, at some times as descriptions of outward reality, and at others as symbols of inward experience. That some recur as dead metaphors or in clichés does not mean that conversion was any less dominant a theme in his self-understanding; on the contrary, that it was these particular metaphors which had sunk below immediate consciousness belies how habitual such a frame of reference had become.

The most disturbing aspect of Newton's typical imagery, drawn as so much of it was from daily life, was the correlation of blackness and bondage with alienation from God while, at the same time, these ideas were so closely associated with the enslaved African peoples, to whose suffering he remained largely unsympathetic throughout his narrative. These images were laden with many associations, and drew as much on biblical precedent in Newton's usage as on his experience of the slave trade, but the correlation was nevertheless evident. In describing his state during his two years in Africa, he recounted how, after some success in business under a new master, he desired perhaps to stay there, adding, 'There is a significant phrase frequently used in those parts, That such a white man is grown *black*. It does not intend an alteration of complexion, but disposition. . . . I entered into closer engagements with the inhabitants; and should have lived and died a wretch amongst them, if the Lord had not watched over me for good' (i. 48). His spiritual deliverance was thus aligned with his emancipation from the presence of Africans themselves. He would later repent of his participation in and compliance with the slave trade, and would contribute significantly to the abolition movement by giving evidence to the Privy Council, and by writing a popular tract against the trade, but at this point he seemed, at best, indifferent.

CONVERSION AND IDENTITY

Newton's life may be divided roughly in two at the year 1764. The thirty-nine years to 1764 which made up the first period of his life were tumultuous in the extreme, and the contemporary observer would have been hard pressed at most points to predict what manner of man he would become. The

early death of his mother, adolescent passion, seizure by a
naval press gang, servitude in Africa, disaster and deliverance
at sea, religious conversion, marriage, civil preferment,
disappointed attempts to enter the ministry—such experiences
made it an uncertain period of failures and successes. Being
the years in which he came to maturity, it was also the time
when he was most malleable and receptive to new ideas. The
forty-three years from 1764 until his death in 1807 appeared,
however, as the reverse image of the earlier period. They were
not without trying times, or events which would modify his
opinions, but comparatively it was a period of stability and
conservatism. Unlike the turbulence and unpredictability of
the first half of his life, the trajectory of the second half could
be taken almost entirely from the events of 1764.

The significant events of that year were two. The first was
the publication of the *Authentic Narrative*. It was sixteen years
after the central crisis of near-shipwreck upon which the story
turned, and he now saw most clearly the providential, salvific
interpretation of his life which he had contemplated for some
time, and saw it with sufficient conviction to proclaim it at
large. This first important book therefore helped to mark a
transition in his life from the experience of a private individual
to that of public person, from a period of impression and
formation to one of expression and conviction. So also did the
second event of 1764, his ordination to a curacy in the Church
of England. In this too there was an element of public
accountability, to sustain unblemished the character not
merely of a professor, but also of a minister, of the gospel. It
was a conservative profession, and he felt strongly the social
significance of his state-supported and divinely ordained role
as spiritual guide and moral monitor of the people of his
parish, and by extension of the wider nation as well. With his
ministerial vocation came obligations not only to his vows but
also to his patrons, his ecclesiastical superiors, his evangelical
colleagues, and his parishioners, all of which would bind him
more strictly to the course of life he had chosen.

There was, however, an important symbolic hiatus between
the writing of the autobiography and the ordination, for the
former was in a sense left unfinished when it was sent to
the press. It ended on the plaintive note of his as yet

unfulfilled desire to enter the ministry. Most of the parallel narratives which Newton had folded into his account by direct and indirect allusion were of converts who had gone on to become special instruments of divine grace, such as St Paul, who went on to preach the faith which once he had destroyed. This was a pattern underlying countless contemporary funeral sermons and clerical biographies.[45] He acknowledged this when, years later, he asked in his memoirs of William Grimshaw of Haworth:

May we not consider every person whom the Lord is pleased to qualify and send forth to preach the word of life to sinners, as thus set apart from his birth; and that the dispensations he meets with, and the steps he is permitted to take during his time of ignorance, are directed and overruled to promote his future competency and usefulness?[46]

The question here was rhetorical, but taken as a matter of earnest concern it could as well have closed the *Authentic Narrative*. Newton's story had a curve which projected beyond his last page and seemed to prophesy that the dramatic call of God to salvation which he had experienced should be reflected in no less divine a call to the ministry. The incompleteness of the narrative was observed by one correspondent who later wrote to Newton to suggest that he add a further letter about his entry into ministry.[47] Already four years earlier he had written, in a diary of private thoughts about the ministry, that many had heard his testimony and given praise to God on his behalf; and he had added the hopeful prayer, 'Will it please thee O Lord to give them matter for farther praise?'[48] But he was still waiting.

He did not have to wait long, however, for before the ink was dry on the last copy of the *Authentic Narrative*, Newton was successfully ordained to a curacy at Olney in Buckinghamshire. His story had helped to fulfil the very pattern it

[45] This was so much the case that in 1822 Thomas Scott's son and biographer felt he had to warn young persons not to think (on the basis of such models as Newton, Cecil, Buchanan, and Scott) that they could allow themselves a season of 'youthful depravity' in the expectation of a later experience of sudden grace and Christian usefulness. John Scott, *Life of the Rev. Thomas Scott*, 6th edn. (1824), 14.
[46] Newton, *Memoirs of the Life of the Late Rev. William Grimshaw* (1799; 1825), 4.
[47] *Letters* (Barlass), 73.   [48] Diary (1758).

proclaimed, for Newton's conversion narrative was, in fact, a kind of curriculum vitae. In the same correspondence in which Haweis had called for Newton to write up his story at greater length, Haweis had urged him to consider ordination in the Church. Haweis then brought Newton's case to the notice of the Lord Dartmouth, a regular hearer at Haweis's chapel, who asked for a copy of Newton's narrative while it was still circulating in manuscript.[49] In consequence, Dartmouth later exerted his influence and patronage to secure for Newton a place in the Church of England. In a different sense from the North Atlantic storm of 1748, the writing itself of the *Authentic Narrative* in 1763–4 was the fulcrum upon which Newton's life turned, the point at which years of private reflection passed over into public commitment. For it encapsulated a self-understanding which gave him sufficient confidence for the spreading of his evangelical message from pulpit and press throughout his long adult career. Launching his career with a religious autobiography at age 39, he was to have many years to fulfil the public self he had created.

Modern theoretical and critical studies concerned with autobiography have stressed the way such writing is at once a discovery, a creation, and an imitation of the self.[50] If even straightforward discursive writing conceals a high degree of conscious artistry, then the interaction of author and subject-matter is all the more complex when that subject-matter is the author's own life (as St Augustine discovered in his discussion of memory and time in the *Confessions*). This is true despite the prima-facie plausibility of autobiography as self-authenticating history. Difficult issues of interpretation and identity are raised as one contemplates in the process of writing how the present self (the *autos*) relates to the life lived in the past (the *bios*). How, for example, are the child, the adolescent, the grown man, and the author at once different and identical? Autobiography involves a particularly radical act of self-discovery and self-definition as the genre implicitly forces an

---

[49] Newton to Haweis, 7 and 23 Jan. 1763, ALS, FLP; Bull, *Newton*, 116–17.
[50] The literature is surveyed in James Olney, 'Autobiography and the Cultural Moment', in id. (ed.), *Autobiography: Essays Theoretical and Critical* (Princeton, 1980).

answer to questions such as this.[51] Unlike St Augustine, John Newton did not consider at a high intellectual level the process of self-reflection in which he was engaged. These kind of critical issues remained largely transparent to him, and in this sense his personal narrative reads simply as naïve factual history. Yet, like all writing about oneself, his narrative was fundamentally a response to the imponderable question, 'Who am I?' Newton's answer was unequivocal. In 1764 he wanted the world to know that he was above all a converted person. It was the sacred narrative of the Old and the New Man. This was the centre of his evangelical consciousness. In a funeral sermon for Newton, Richard Cecil quoted him late in life, 'Whatever I may doubt on other points, I cannot doubt whether there has been a certain gracious transaction between God and *my* soul.'[52]

---

[51] Cf. Peterson, 'Newman and English Spiritual Autobiography', 311, who describes the genre as 'essentially hermeneutic[al], a category that supersedes the label of fiction or nonfiction'.
[52] *Works of Richard Cecil*, 3rd edn., 2 vols. (1827), i. 73–89.

2

'My own experiences are as good as mathematical demonstrations to me'
Newton's Theological Formation, 1725–1756

> Thus he was prepared to receive the fundamental doctrines of that system which is called Calvinistic.
>
> John Venn, *Memoir of Henry Venn*

By 1764 it was clear that Newton understood his life fundamentally as the story of a climactic religious conversion. It is possible, however, to distinguish further in his life an important doctrinal conversion which provided him with the theological perspective from which he wrote his autobiography. Brought up as an orthodox Dissenter, impressed by Deism as a late adolescent, he returned to serious religious profession several years before he embraced the Calvinistic beliefs which marked the balance of his life. When he accepted Calvinism is relatively easy to determine: it was in the last half of 1754. It was then, he claimed, that he really 'began to understand the security of the covenant of grace'; and over the next two years that he discovered 'much encrease of light, with respect to the nature and properties of [the] covenant of grace, especially its immutability'.[1] This covenantal language signalled his reception of ideas from the Reformed tradition. The more difficult question of how and why he came to Calvinistic convictions, at a time when such beliefs were widely despised in polite circles, is the subject of this chapter.

John Walsh has described the prejudice against Calvinism in the eighteenth century: 'Calvinism had acquired deep psychological associations with the Civil War and Commonwealth, the antinomianism of sectaries, the dismemberment of the Church, the killing of the king. These folk memories

---

[1] *Works*, i. 96; Newton to David Jennings, 31 Oct. 1756, ALS, DWL.

dogged it like a kind of political original sin.'[2] The Great Ejection of 1662 had moved Calvinism from the centre to the margins of public life, and it remained the property largely of Dissent until rediscovered in the middle third of the eighteenth century by a number of evangelical Anglican divines. While Calvinism never recovered the prominence it had had in public and religious discourse during the seventeenth century, there was nevertheless a significant return to Reformed theology in the context of the Evangelical Revival. Although in a few important points Newton's experience differed from that of his theological peers, his journey to Calvinistic convictions provides a useful case study of some of the influences which contributed more widely to the contemporary resurgence of predestinarian theology.[3]

THEOLOGICAL FORMATION

Becoming and remaining a Calvinist was for Newton not solely, or even principally, an intellectual affair, though he allowed a place to reason ('when enlightened') in the attestation of correct doctrine. After Scripture, it was experience itself that bulked largest in his theological method. When Newton learned that James Stillingfleet of Hotham was challenged by a younger Yorkshire minister about his views on election, and chose not to engage in controversy, he wrote in 1775 to reassure him: 'I believe most persons who are truly alive to God, sooner or later meet with some pinches in their experience which constrain them to flee to those doctrines for relief, which perhaps they had formerly dreaded, if not abhorred . . . In this way I was made a Calvinist myself' (vi. 279). Thus, Newton felt that Calvinism was usually adopted by his contemporaries after, not before, an evangelical conversion, and that its tenets were arrived at by reasoning a

[2] Walsh, 'Anglican Evangelicals in the Eighteenth Century', 87.
[3] Except where specifically qualified, the term Calvinism is used broadly in this chapter to designate the native theological tradition associated with the Reformation articles of the Church of England and the Calvinistic confessions of the 17th c., without distinguishing the differences within that tradition which arose out of various controversies. Ch. 4 will be concerned to distinguish more sharply the nature of Newton's beliefs.

posteriori from immediate experience to theological rationale. This had indeed been the route he travelled to theological certitude, and it was the same for many others as well. John Berridge of Everton became a Calvinist after several years as a rigid Arminian, largely because of a long period of illness and mental distress which prevented him from preaching.[4] Once a similarly zealous Arminian, Henry Venn was led to accept Calvinism after suffering unexpected poverty at Huddersfield.[5] Perhaps the most intellectual conversion to Calvinism was that of the famous commentator Thomas Scott. Yet in his autobiography, *The Force of Truth* (1779), he too indicated the importance of certain experiences, such as his crisis of conscience over subscription to the Thirty-Nine Articles, in his decision to accept Calvinism. For all evangelicals, experience counted for much. For Newton this was particularly true: he saw his life as the story not of 'books-I-have-read', but of how 'providence and grace concur'. A number of factors, then, account for his acceptance of Calvinism as a coherent theological system.

Early Childhood Impressions

It has been observed that Newton's very early formation occurred not in fact within Established Church circles, but among that small religious minority that had most conscientiously preserved Anglo-Calvinist traditions: he was baptized and raised an Independent by his mother. The best estimates place the numbers of Independents in London in the early eighteenth century at approximately 1 per cent of the population. Even adding the Presbyterians (whose Calvinistic orthodoxy was in general less strict than that of the Independents) and the Particular Baptists (with whom Independents had less to do than with Presbyterians), the residual Puritan culture was embraced in all by less than 4 per cent of Londoners.[6] Those living in this Dissenting milieu in

---

[4] *Works of the Rev. John Berridge*, ed. Richard Whittingham (1838), 14–15.

[5] John Venn, *Life and . . . Letters of the Late Rev. Henry Venn*, 2nd edn. (1835), 29–32.

[6] These estimates are based upon information from the Evans List, 1715–18, analysed in Watts, *The Dissenters*, i. 267–89, 509. The proportion of Independents may have increased between the period of the Evans List and that of Newton's childhood, particularly in the wake of the Salters' Hall subscription debate.

the eighteenth century were proud of their theological pedigree and understood themselves as the faithful remnant within England of a bygone Puritan glory. This perspective differed sharply from the Anglican Calvinists of the Evangelical Revival, who came fresh to Reformed theology from contrary predispositions. Newton's early religious education within Dissent gave him, like Richard Cecil later, a head start over contemporaries such as William Grimshaw, John Berridge, Henry Venn, or Thomas Scott, all of whom were beneficed clergymen in the Church of England for some years before undergoing evangelical conversion, and subsequently appropriating Calvinism as a lapsed Puritan inheritance.

But the question remains to what degree Newton's childhood experience of Dissent contributed to his theological formation as a whole, since this early influence was arrested by his mother's death when he was not quite 7 years old. How significant were those first seven years? When he encountered Calvinism after his religious conversion, did it appear an entirely new revelation, coming as it did after a period of strident unbelief? Or was it rather a revolution, in the older sense of the term of a wheel coming round to where it began?

It was probably a little of each, since Newton lost touch with his theological heritage for a time, only to recover it again under the changed conditions of popular evangelicalism. Because Newton's recollections were informed by late Calvinistic hindsight into original sin, he stressed the regulative more than the educative value of his early religious experience. He considered his early impressions as of value to him only after conversion, when contemplated afresh with regenerate insight. Yet he stressed at many points that the influences of his first seven years were durable enough to be felt throughout his adolescence. 'I could not at once forget the religious impressions I had received in my childhood, they often returned upon me, but still fainter and fainter,' he wrote, and again, 'it was very long before I could wholly shake them off'.[7] From 7 to 19 years of age he was often discouraged by temptation, but he sought to live a religious life, coming back again and again conscientiously to disciplines of prayer,

---

[7] Newton, *Memoirs of Grimshaw* (1799; 1825), 98–9; *Works*, i. 13.

reading Scripture, diary-keeping, and edifying reading. These practices looked back to the example and teaching of his mother. The two books he explicitly mentioned having read were both from the Dissenting tradition: Benjamin Bennet's *Christian Oratory: or, the Devotion of the Closet Display'd* (1725) and Daniel Defoe's popular *Family-Instructor* (1715). After his crisis at sea in 1748, it was, significantly, to his childhood pastor he turned for advice, and to Dissenters in London he at first attached himself. Evidently, those first years were important.

For Newton memories of Old Dissent were inseparable from those of his mother. It was at her knee that he learned by heart the whole of the Shorter Catechism with its scriptural proofs and all of Isaac Watts's smaller catechisms and children's hymns; from her that he learned to read Scripture, with her that he attended the Independent Meeting in Old Gravel Lane, Wapping.[8] When he renewed his contact with Dissenters in London more than twenty years after her death, her piety was still spoken of highly by many. In his autobiography and throughout his writings he spoke of his mother with manifest affection and devotion: she was 'a pious and experienced Christian', 'my dear mother', 'this excellent parent', 'a pious woman', 'my good Mother', and so on. This kind of filial piety went far towards making Newton well-disposed towards Calvinism. He simply could not have the same prejudices against Calvinism as one raised solely within Established Church circles. Her early spiritual encouragement was, if not theologically decisive given Newton's young age, still psychologically formative.

There was a counterpoint to this as well. Upon his mother's death his religious education was largely abandoned, since neither his father nor his stepmother (both Anglican) were 'under the impressions of religion'. And he felt alienated from them both. Of his father he wrote, '[He] could not take my mother's part . . . he always observed an air of distance and severity in his carriage, which overawed and discouraged my

---

[8] Newton's childhood reading may have originated in the Catechetical Lecture scheme established by William Coward's trustees in 1740. See further, John Waddington, *Congregational History, 1700–1800* (1876), 269–73.

spirit. I was always in fear when before him' (i. 14). Likewise, of living with his stepmother's family while his father was away at sea he recalled, 'the loss of my mother's instructions was not repaired' (i. 13). Though his stepmother seemed willing to adopt him, she had a son of her own after two or three years who absorbed the attentions of the family. The consequence of all this for Newton's theological formation was that he would later associate Calvinism with genial memories of his Dissenting mother, in contrast to more dissatisfying memories of his Anglican father and stepmother.

When as a young man he first consulted David Jennings, his mother's former pastor, he was prompted, he wrote, 'by having often heard that my Mother was favoured with a share of your regard when living, and that you have often made obliging mention of her Memory since her death'.[9] He was writing in 1750, only two years after his momentous crisis at sea, asking for spiritual counsel to help him live up to his new-found religious seriousness. It was thus from this Independent quarter that Newton had initially encountered Calvinism as an impressionable child, and to this quarter he most naturally returned when 'awakened' as a young man. It was only later that he associated with Calvinists from the Church of England.

Danger and Deliverance

Some historians have argued that the presence of widespread anxiety is a cultural condition which has made evangelical piety in general and Calvinism in particular more plausible at different times and places in history. Thus, for example, emotional conversion and the intimacy of the small religious group on the one hand and concepts of sovereign grace and providential order on the other are supposed to have been especially appealing at times when social, political, or economic order has been in chaos.[10] John Walsh and Michael Watts have each cautioned, however, that such hypotheses,

---

[9] Newton to David Jennings, 6 July 1750, ALS, DWL.

[10] See e.g. on evangelicalism and anomie, Alan Gilbert, *Religion and Society in Industrial England* (1976); and on religion and social change in American history, William McLoughlin, *Revivals, Awakenings, and Reform* (Chicago, 1978).

relating religious sensibility to large-scale social change, can be difficult to prove from particular cases in eighteenth-century evangelicalism. The mental strain which preceded individual evangelical conversions can most often be traced to factors within the personal context. More often than not it was guilt rather than anxiety, and the fear of death, judgement, and damnation rather than anomie, which precipitated conversion. Here the moralistic tone of much early eighteenth-century devotional literature went hand in hand with the largely unquestioned belief in a literal hell.[11] Thus, Thomas Scott described the contemplation of eternal misery as an 'awakening reflection, God's sword in the conscience'.[12] At Northampton, Massachusetts, where Jonathan Edwards did not shrink from preaching about sin and damnation, the untimely deaths of two young people preceded the famous community revival in 1734/5. Less famously, at Northampton in England, where John Collett Ryland had a school, the death of a boarder prompted three boys brought up under evangelical preaching to become concerned for their souls and begin a secret religious society in 1766.[13] In mid-century James Hervey's widely read writings reflected a solemn concern with death, as did Richard Burnham's popular *Pious Memorials* (1753), containing the death-bed sayings and last hours of more than a hundred religious persons. A large number of Methodist converts came from occupations with significantly high mortality rates, such as the Cornish tinners or the Kingswood colliers, and converts included many condemned criminals or soldiers. Moreover, the picture of Henry Venn in his pre-conversion days at Cambridge walking round the cloisters of Trinity college while the great bell of St Mary's tolled nine o'clock, meditating in the stillness and the darkness upon the awful facts of Death and Judgement,

---

[11] Walsh, 'Origins of the Evangelical Revival', 142–4; id., 'Moderate Calvinism', unpublished essay; Watts, *Dissenters*, i. 406–21.

[12] Thomas Scott, *The Force of Truth: An Authentic Narrative* (1779; repr., Edinburgh, 1984), 25.

[13] John Ryland, Jun., 'An Account of the Rise and Progress of the Two Society's at Mr. Rylands and at Mrs. Trinder's Boarding School in Northampton', 1768–70, AMS, Angus Library, Regent's Park College, Oxford. See also *The Life and Writings of Mrs. Dawson* [née Flower] (Kirkby Lonsdale, 1828).

Heaven and Hell, demonstrates how, even far from scenes where death was ubiquitous, conscience and thoughts of eternity ran together in the eighteenth century.[14]

In John Newton's case it was toward the end of a maritime career, which had exposed him to remarkable extremities of danger and recovery, that his childhood and adolescent concerns with sin and judgement recurred, prompting spiritual distress and sober theological reflection. Of his adolescence he wrote, 'struggles between sin and conscience were often repeated'. After describing a dangerous fall from a horse, he noted, 'My conscience suggested to me the dreadful consequences, if in such a state I had been summoned to appear before God' (i. 15). One source of this concern may be found in his attempt to maintain at this time the life of piety described in Bennet's *Christian Oratory*. Bennet's chief aim was to enlarge upon typical manuals of devotion, by carrying his description of the life of spiritual discipline into more minute detail than was usual, and the result was an almost impossible ideal of private reading, meditation, self-examination, and prayer. The bulk of the book was taken up with more than twenty specimen meditations on eschatological themes such as death, the immortality of the soul, the resurrection of the just, and so on. These meditations were, in the style of Richard Baxter, designed to move concepts from the mind to the heart, so that the reader felt his or her affections deeply moved by the subject. In one meditation on death the reader is taken through sections on what it is, its certainty, some of its circumstances, how to apply the meditation to oneself, and then on through a further process of personal lamentation, resolution, and aspiration—all in the first person. Newton claimed, after trying to keep up the pattern of spiritual practice advocated in Bennet's manual, 'I was soon weary, gradually gave it up, and became worse than before' (i. 15). But he continued to be haunted all the more by his failure and by the prospect of eternal damnation.

After recounting his later humiliation on board the *Harwich* in 1744, he remarked that these guilty feelings faded as to all appearance the Lord had now given him up to 'judicial

[14] Venn, *Life of Venn*, 14–15.

hardness': 'I had not the least fear of God before my eyes, nor (so far as I remember) the least sensibility of conscience' (i. 33). The special pleading of 'so far as I remember' suggests the past may not have been wholly forgotten, though for the next four years he claimed he was largely untroubled by thoughts of sin and divine retribution as he adopted as thoroughgoing a Deistic frame of reference for life as he could. In 1748, however, suddenly faced with the imminent prospect of dying in a violent storm, a fissure opened in this hardened free-thinking exterior and all the repressed agonies of his religious conscience erupted in full force. 'I dreaded death *now*', he wrote (italics his), 'and my heart foreboded the worst, if the Scriptures, which I had long since opposed, were indeed true' (i. 59). 'I waited with fear and impatience to receive my inevitable doom' (i. 60). Any pretence of virtue as a matter of Shaftesburian disinterestedness was shattered. As he reflected in 1753, 'When the Holy Spirit first rais'd me to look up to a crucified Saviour, Justification from the punishment I had incurr'd was my principal motive,' and again a few months later, on the anniversary of the storm, 'I who . . . was then brought to the very brink of eternity, with hell in my own breast, was at length . . . delivered from the punishment, I then dreaded as much as I had formerly Dar'd.'[15]

What was the nature of the sins which caused Newton to fear he would be cast into hell? Heaviest upon his conscience weighed his offences against God himself, particularly his habit of blasphemy and his ridicule of the Scriptures. He claimed that at his worst his impieties had made even his coarse, unbelieving shipmates cringe. In later life he often called himself the 'African blasphemer', wanting not to forget what he had once been or the extent of God's mercy to him. The fact that he had actually opposed the gospel and ruined the lives of others as he proselytized for Deism was to him like the way the apostle Paul had persecuted the early Christians before his conversion. Newton appears also to have been ashamed of past sexual profligacy. At Madeira, where prostitution was rife, he claimed to have been as abandoned as he pleased and that his state was that of 2 Peter 2: 14 ('having

[15] Diary (1751–6), 1 Jan. and 21 Mar. 1753.

eyes full of adultery, and that cannot cease from sin'). When he described the evils of the slave trade in a later abolitionist tract, he reported also that the practice of sailors using female Africans for their own sexual gratification was widespread (vi. 532). The extent to which his own conscience may have been stricken by past sexual immorality of this kind was, however, undeclared to the general reader.

That blasphemy headed the list of his sins, while participation in the cruelty of the slave trade did not yet seem even to trouble his conscience, appears almost incredible now. His naïve complicity in a commerce which systematically devastated innumerable African families and communities is today readily seen as contradicting the egalitarian implications of the gospel by which he was converted; as, indeed, the whole trade is now recognized as the blind spot of an age of supposed enlightenment and universal reason. It took Newton longer to come to this realization than some Quakers or Methodists who had spoken out earlier against slavery. It would not be until many years after his conversion that Newton would realize the slave trade was not just distasteful, but immoral, and repent of his earlier career. The depth of Newton's remorse over his former blasphemies, a sin which to all appearances has no social consequences, stands out in contrast therefore as peculiar to the modern reader, since blasphemy has figured little in the concerns of later generations affected by secularization. Yet his remorse helps to establish how thoroughly religious Newton's mind and conscience had remained, despite his period as a Deist.

The immediate impact of renewed pangs of conscience and spiritual concern after the danger of the *Greyhound* voyage was that Newton became religiously observant in private disciplines and corporate worship. That he lived to tell the tale also prompted theological reflection. 'I thought I saw the hand of God displayed in our favour: I began to pray' (i. 60). He began to realize that this was only the most dramatic of many preservations and escapes he had experienced. In 1750 he wrote to his wife, 'I endeavour, in every scene of distress, to recollect the seasons in my past life, in which, when I have given myself up for lost, I have been unexpectedly relieved. Instances of this kind have been very frequent with me, some of them perhaps as remarkable as any that have been recorded' (v. 329–30). This sense that God somehow had peculiar designs upon his life provided the impetus that later carried him over into a full predestinarian theology. Aware that he had been inexplicably delivered from repeated crises, he found it plausible that God could have been mysteriously involved in his salvation before he actually came to faith. Perhaps it took only a shift of perspective to view what were, in classical terms, matters of fate and fortune as, in a more theological light, matters of providence and grace; to view what were, in Deistic terms, matters subject to inexorable natural law as, in Calvinistic light, matters subject to an inexorable decree. Certainly, this was how Newton saw his deliverances in retrospect. The idea of predestination had tremendous explanatory power.

Contingency and Conscience

It was not only this sense of divine providence interposing in the external affairs of his life that opened Newton to the concept of predestination; it was also the inward sense of his own finiteness and moral inability. This was similar to the case of the sixteenth-century Swiss reformer Huldrych Zwingli, whose near-death experiences under the plague contributed to his understanding of the stark contrast between human impotence and divine omnipotence. More than a dozen comparable episodes, in which Newton was confronted with his own mortality, were recorded in the *Authentic Narrative*. Many of them, to be sure, were gleaned from memory after the fact as evidence for his thesis that providence preserved him for the display of extraordinary mercy, but several of them, likewise, gave him from the beginning a sense that his inconsiderable life was at the mercy of an alien power.

To this sense of contingency must be added an even more significant, long-standing pattern in his life of being utterly unable to do the good he wished. Other evangelicals quipped that they were led from 'Law' to Gospel, by which they meant that the high standards of moral and devotional purity stressed by the non-juror William Law (1686–1761) in his *Christian Perfection* (1726) and *Serious Call to a Devout and Holy Life* (1729) led them to discover their own inadequacy to live a moral life, and that this in turn prepared them to accept the message of justification by grace alone. This was the case for Wesley, Whitefield, Venn, Scott, Thomas Adam, and James Stillingfleet, and certainly Newton himself was for a period a great admirer of Law (vi. 246–7).[16] For Newton, however, this 'preparatory' work was chiefly done much earlier by such works as Bennet's *Christian Oratory*. That he could therefore identify so thoroughly with St Paul's experience in the seventh chapter of Romans made him all the more ready to see his need for the unconditional grace spoken of by the apostle in chapter 8 (i. 573). The tension of his adolescent cycle of ethical resolution, moral failure, and rededication reached its climax in 1748 when he returned to religious profession as a young adult, only to experience a momentous moral collapse six months later. As described in the last chapter, it took a severe fever to bring him to himself. Physically shattered, he crawled to an isolated spot: 'Here I found a renewed liberty to pray. I durst make no more resolves, but cast myself before the Lord, to do with me as he should please. The burden was removed from my conscience, and . . . my health was restored' (i. 76).

This moral desperation and the relief which followed it was arguably the psychological crisis which most prepared him to receive Calvinistic ideas. Within a year he wrote, 'I have been foiled too often, to dare say anything positively of myself. I was going to say that my principal strength is the knowledge I have gain'd of my own weakness, but even this if I was left alone, I should soon forget.'[17] Like boxes within boxes, he found only an endless regress of spiritual inadequacy within himself: it would be weakness even to rely upon his own weakness. The more readily therefore, he confessed, did he concur 'with so interesting a thought' as the doctrine of final perseverance—what hope had he else? Once having shuddered back from the revelation of his own innate sinfulness and abject misery, he was the more ready to credit his deliverance wholly to a gracious and indefectible supernatural power, and to trust therein for the future. Newton's evangelical repentance predated by perhaps a year his first reintroduction to ideas

[16] John Overton, *William Law . . . A Sketch of His Life, Character, and Opinions* (1881), 109–11.   [17] Newton to David Jennings, 16 Aug. 1750, ALS, DWL.

from the Calvinistic milieu, but once reintroduced he increasingly recognized that such concepts had for him remarkable explicative and assuasive force. John Walsh suggests that this was in fact a general principle for many Calvinistic evangelicals:

As they passed through the mysterious 'great change' of the New Birth, many converts felt themselves to be in the grasp of a power totally beyond themselves, carried inexorably along against any wish or desire of their own. . . . The first stages in regeneration—the intense feeling of personal insufficiency ('the conviction of sin') and the renunciation of self-righteousness that followed it ('evangelical repentance')—could both be more easily explained in Calvinistic terms than Arminian.[18]

Newton put it thus in his diary, 'My experience joins in with the Word to teach me, that all my good is from free sovereign grace.'[19]

The pattern of tension and release—failure to live up to vows, relieved by an overwhelming sense of divine forgiveness—though having reached a crisis in 1748, continued as the tenor of the spirituality recorded in his diary throughout his life. The tension was reduced as he discovered slowly an assurance of his salvation, but from 1751 to 1756 it continued to dominate his devotional disciplines of sabbath and sacramental preparation. The pattern harked back to his adolescence: self-examination, lamentation, consolation, resolution, and aspiration. He summed it up tersely and pessimistically one day at Liverpool: 'I resolve and fall off every day.'[20] Drawing on examples from his reading he had, like Dissenters and the early Methodists, made several personal written covenants in which he solemnly vowed to God that he would keep a number of rules.[21] Dominated by a concern with self-denial, his covenant of 15 October 1752 was reviewed

---

[18] Walsh, 'Moderate Calvinism', unpublished essay.
[19] Diary (1751–6), 29 May 1755.   [20] Ibid., 7 Nov. 1755.
[21] The drawing up of a personal covenant with God was a common practice among Dissenters in the first third of the 18th c., as it was also in New England where Jonathan Edwards's 'Resolutions' of 1722–3 provides perhaps the most famous example of the practice. Geoffrey Nuttall, 'Methodism and the Older Dissent', 262, traces the practice to Joseph Alleine's covenant, preserved in the *Vindiciae Pietatis* of Richard Alleine. These were sources with which Newton himself was very familiar.

frequently, if not daily, as a part of his private devotion. Although on appearance this could seem a moralism in conflict with concepts of predestinarian grace, in reality it aggravated the need to continue to 'fly to those doctrines for relief'. A sense of moral impotence continued to drive him to Calvinism.

Conjoined to his feelings of spiritual weakness was the anxiety he felt about separation from his new wife when he was called back to the sea six months after they were married on 12 February 1750. Mary Catlett was the daughter of friends of Newton's late mother; she had been light-heartedly spoken of as a match for him by them both; and she was courted by him in the house where his mother died. Perhaps at some level he associated her with the memory of his mother and feared that his childhood grief would be repeated. In any case, as he worried for her well-being, concerns of sexuality and spirituality converged. Because it was the desire to marry her that had sustained him through much of the hardship he suffered before his conversion, he had come to describe her as something of a spiritual mediatrix, 'the appointed instrument and mean, of my recovery'. Yet, paradoxically, he worried that he idolized her and that God might on that account take her from him. Such a fear was shared by other evangelicals. Henry Venn wrote to his wife in 1759 that they must love God as though they were unmarried: 'By this means we shall be most likely to continue together, and not provoke the stroke of separation by an idolatrous love to one another.'[22] After Newton married, he and Mary had only their clothes and seventy pounds in debt to their names. Consequently, he was distressed about whether he could provide for her. In his letters to her from this period there was often the sense of a consummate happiness which at the same time cast a threatening shadow of imagined separation or loss. His first forced absence from his wife was, he said, 'bitter as death': 'When I was forced from her . . . serious thoughts, which had been almost smothered, began to revive. And my anxiety with respect to what might possibly happen while I was abroad, induced me to offer up many prayers for her . . . In a word, I

[22] Venn, *Life of Venn*, 73.

soon felt the need of that support which only religion can give' (v. 307–8). This then became the direct occasion of his consulting with David Jennings, who subsequently reintroduced him to Calvinistic tenets in the pastoral context of his sharp anxiety.

Need for Assurance of Salvation

For the six years from 1748 to 1754—the period between his religious and his doctrinal conversions—Newton's sense of peace before God varied considerably. A recurring strain in his letters and diary was the characteristic Puritan preoccupation with assurance: how could he set his conscience at rest before a holy God? And how be sure he would persevere until the end? In April 1754, on the middle passage from the Guinea coast to the West Indies, Newton was troubled, almost to the point of distraction, by his failure to make the proper returns to God for the grace he had received. As in the case of Colonel Gardiner, surely, he felt, extraordinary grace deserved extraordinary service. He bitterly lamented his own inconstancy and lukewarmness, and a fever left him almost delirious with worries that, if he should die, God might overlook him amongst so many already departed souls. To Jennings he described an interminable, downward spiral of introspection which left him in despair over the evils of his heart. He went on,

Alas, Sir, I am not half so much affected with a sense of my unworthiness as you will charitably suppose. I cannot realize these thoughts as I ought to do. Sincerity is all I dare pretend to & that not of myself . . . [but] I trust having this seal, that He who has begun, he who alone could begin anything good in me, will perfect it unto the day of Christ Jesus.[23]

Sincerity was, at bottom, his only indissoluble sign of divine grace.[24] Yet he described his affections and understanding as divided, and he had little peace. He mourned for 'pleasure in communion with [God], & zeal & ability to serve him'. In his

---

[23] Newton to David Jennings, [Jan.] 1754.

[24] As Newton put it later in a hymn, 'Should I grieve for what I feel, | If I did not love at all?' (*OH* 3. 438).

diary he recorded the lament, 'Must this be the result of my enquiry into the state of my soul; to find myself going backwards instead of forwards?' Knowing that a true principle of grace in the soul ought necessarily to increase, he feared that his own situation did not bear this out. Wearily, he prayed, '[T]each me to act agreeable to Thy commands, that I may have a comfortable evidence in myself that I am Thy real disciple.'[25] This interior struggle, which was gradually ameliorated during the years 1754–6, indicates that Newton was already acting as a Calvinist, albeit a restive one. The struggle itself led him deeper into the ethos of Calvinistic thought and Puritan spirituality, as he found how predestination could both stimulate and satisfy his need for assurance; its finality either reducing or heightening his fears depending on whether he was, or was not, content that he was numbered among the elect.

Within Puritanism the predestinarian *ordo salutis* led almost invariably to a concern with the attainment of what Max Weber called the 'certitudo salutis'. John von Rohr has recently discussed this Puritan preoccupation with assurance and the several means to achieve it.[26] The search for subjective evidences of conversion as testimony of God's favour could be pursued on the basis of the 'practical syllogism': The elect will do good works (or manifest certain graces or affections, etc.), I do good works, I am therefore of the elect. Because, however, it was always possible to doubt that one's good works were up to standard, it was common enough to retreat, like Newton, to the position of sincerity; namely, that one at least desired to do the good one ought. The need for assurance could also lead to simple trust in the objective, unconditional promises of the covenant, and to contemplating Christ directly as the mirror of one's election. But here too one could be driven back to the introspective question of whether one had faith in the promises, whether one trusted adequately in Christ. Cowper put it with a simple, almost naïve, poignancy in his hymn, 'The Contrite Heart':

---

[25] Diary (1751–6), 13 Jan. and 8 Feb. 1754.
[26] John von Rohr, *Covenant of Grace in Puritan Thought* (Atlanta, 1986), 155–91.

> The Lord will happiness divine
>   On contrite hearts bestow:
> Then tell me, gracious God, is mine
>   A contrite heart, or no?   (*OH* 1. 64. st. 1)

Thus, in both its subjective and objective dimensions, the quest for assurance among the Puritans stimulated a radical interiority, a penetrating examination of the heart for the sincerity of one's spiritual motives. In this vein Thomas Shepard once commented on the question of covenant conditions, simply, 'Sincerity is a very witnessing grace.'[27] Once having found even only this, however, one could fairly claim all the promises of God to the elect in Christ. Von Rohr concludes with respect to the Puritans,

Without question the major emphasis in Puritan theology and practice was upon the conditional. This was the direction of Gospel piety, leading to the introspective search for evidence of covenant partnership with a faithfully responding God. But as the doctrinal heritage of predestination was united with these concerns of piety, the search for certainty needed to recognize another kind of faithfulness, that which carried the promise actually to supply the conditions upon which one's covenant partnership was based.[28]

There was thus both an absolute and a conditional understanding of grace in Puritan spirituality.

This kind of theology framed the quest for assurance in which Newton was involved during the winter of 1754. Concern for his own salvation was made at first more anxious by his self-examination, but then he was drawn on through soul-searching to a contented hope that he had a saving interest in Christ. Once satisfied that he was within the covenant, predestination became a doctrine of great comfort as the guarantor of his final obedience. By June 1754 he was largely delivered from the fear that he would relapse into his former unbelief. By 1756 he arrived at a position he would maintain throughout life, realizing that there must be two levels of assurance: there was the peace which proceeded from a hope of acceptance before God through the efficacy of

[27] Quoted ibid. 184.   [28] Ibid. 190–1.

65

Christ's atonement, of which he could be assured at all times; and then there was also the more variable peace arising from a sense of communion with God in the duties of life and the divinely appointed ordinances, of which he could be assured only during gracious seasons of divine communication. As he put it, one could be safe without necessarily being comfortable.

David Bebbington has argued that eighteenth-century English evangelicalism involved a fundamental shift in the received Puritan doctrine of assurance: 'Whereas the Puritans had held that assurance is rare, late and the fruit of struggle in the experience of believers, the Evangelicals believed it to be general, normally given at conversion and the result of simple acceptance of the gift of God.'[29] It would perhaps be well to add that there was a spectrum of opinion on assurance among evangelicals as surely as there was among Puritans. While James Hervey and Whitefield might have argued that assurance was a corollary of saving faith, Newton wrote in his diary in 1756 that assurance must be 'in some respects' of the essence of faith, 'yet so as not to exclude a possible mixture of much doubting and fears at times'.[30] Moreover, in a later exposition he modified his position further, explaining that he saw assurance as belonging to appropriating faith not to saving faith, and that assurance belonged not in fact to the essence but rather to the establishment of faith (i. 178–9).[31] As Simeon put it, 'Assurance is a privilege, but not a duty.'[32] Newton's spirituality may have been brighter and more cheerful in some respects than that of many of the Puritans, but it was to their thought on the subject he was most indebted.[33]

---

[29] *Evangelicalism in Britain,* 43.   [30] Diary (1751–6), 8 Mar. 1756.

[31] Cf. Newton's later remarks concerning his parishioners at Olney: 'It is usually a good while before they obtain a firm assurance, though I bless God they do obtain it gradually. Dear Mary Lambert ... was 14 years in much grievous exercise and temptation, before the Lord turned her mourning to joy, though she was an earnest seeker, and an exemplary walker, from her first awakening. Something like this is the experience of most of them.' Newton to John Thornton, 15 Dec. 1775, ALS, Ridley Hall, Cambridge.

[32] William Carus, *Memoirs of the Life of the Rev. Charles Simeon,* 3rd edn. (1848), 20.

[33] See also Newton's use of something like the Puritan 'practical syllogism' in *Letters* (Coffin), 118.

Timely Contact with Calvinistic Dissenters

At the right psychological moment, when all these previous factors had made him ripe for Calvinism, Newton came under the influence of several individuals, in positions of respect, who were themselves adherents of Calvinistic theological traditions: in 1750, David Jennings, in 1754, first Alexander Clunie, then Samuel Brewer, and then finally a host of others.

When Newton struck up his correspondence with Jennings in 1750, he wrote with deference to the pastor from his childhood who was thirty-four years his senior. He described himself as young and inexperienced, needing help in 'difficult points', and he begged Jennings's guidance and advice through the busy life upon which he was entering as a master mariner in sole command of his ship. David Jennings (1691–1762) was a staunch Calvinist. Ordained pastor of the Independent congregation at Gravel Lane, Wapping, in 1718, he sided with the non-subscribers the following year at the Salters' Hall debates on whether subscription to a Trinitarian credal statement should be required of ministers. Yet, while favouring a simple scriptural standard for belief, he was himself a robust Trinitarian and part of that conservative coterie of Independents, financed by William Coward, who sought in the aftermath of Salters' Hall to defend Calvinism by every available means. He was, under the Coward Trust, one of the respected lecturers at St Mary Axe and Little St Helen's and a divinity tutor at the Wellclose Square Academy from 1744 until his death. Obliged by Coward's will to teach the doctrines of the Westminster Assembly's Catechism, he conscientiously insisted upon high orthodox standards. Despite his early position as a non-subscriber and his association with moderates such as Isaac Watts and Philip Doddridge, Jennings was remembered for his 'solicitude to preserve the reputation of orthodoxy at his seminary'.[34]

It was to Wellclose Square Newton addressed his letters of

---

[34] Joshua Toulmin, 'A Review of the Life and Writings of the Rev. David Jennings, D.D.', *Protestant Dissenters Magazine* (Mar. 1798), 81–9; (Apr. 1798), 121–7; *DNB;* R. T. Jones, *Congregationalism in England, 1662–1962* (1962), 140; Waddington, *Congregational History,* 269–73.

spiritual inquiry in 1750. After only two letters from Jennings, he was already considering elements of Reformed orthodoxy: 'The doctrine of final Perseverance, which you touch upon I was a stranger to till very lately, but my reason soon closed in with so interesting a thought, when I first considered it, especially as I find it rather encouraged by Scripture.'[35] A year and a half later Newton submitted a book of occasional thoughts to Jennings, which he had filled from his Sunday meditations on the previous voyage, seeking an 'agreeable confirmation' that his opinions were right in the main. He pleaded 'a sincere desire of better information where amiss'. But Newton's progress towards settled Calvinistic beliefs was slow. On 31 October 1756 he offered a rough periodization of his growth to theological conviction, saying, 'I think within these two years or there abouts the Lord has favoured me with much encrease of light, with respect to the nature and properties of his covenant of grace, especially its immutability; tho my believing in Christ was (I trust) of 3 or 4 years longer standing.'[36] From what quarter did this 'encrease of light' come in 1754? It was then, in fact, that Jennings's solitary voice, encouraging Newton toward Calvinistic convictions, was joined by a chorus of other London Dissenters. After his winter of self-doubt and spiritual anxiety during the middle passage that year, Newton met fellow captain and Independent Alexander Clunie ('whose acquaintance I esteem beyond any temporal advantage'). Through Clunie he 'began to understand the security of the covenant of grace' and the 'state of religion, with the errors and controversies of the times' (i. 96). Thus, by him Newton was introduced to Calvinism *vis-à-vis* the contemporary theological and religious landscape. Newton wrote to Clunie from Liverpool in 1761: 'By you the Lord was pleased to bring me to know his people; your conversation was much blessed to me at St Kitt's, and the little knowledge I have of men and things, took its first rise from thence.'[37] Newton and Clunie both soon quit the maritime trade, but they corresponded frequently and exchanged visits until Clunie's death sometime after 1770.

---

[35] Newton to Jennings, 16 Aug. 1750.
[36] Newton to Jennings, 31 Oct. 1756.   [37] *Letters* (Clunie), 6.

Importantly, this friendship was the conduit by which Newton passed into the wider evangelical community.

From August 1754 until the same month in 1755, Newton lived with his wife and her parents at Chatham in Kent but spent as much of his time as he could in London ('the fountain-head ... for spiritual advantages'). Following Clunie's advice, he sought out his fellow-captain's pastor Samuel Brewer. Although largely unnoticed in modern scholarship, Samuel Brewer (1723-96) was an important figure in Dissent and in early evangelicalism. Only two years older than Newton, he had been educated in part under Jennings and was in 1746 ordained pastor of the Independent meeting at Stepney. Under his ministry the church grew from thirty-two members to between two and three hundred, 'one of the most flourishing and important churches in the *Dissenting Interest*'.[38] David Bogue and James Bennett remarked that Brewer's became in fact the largest congregation among Dissenters in all of London.[39] Brewer had many seafaring people in his congregation, and he was remembered to have often prayed publicly for individual crew members before a voyage. Newton attended Brewer's preaching more than any other when in London, claimed that of all his many friends he was most indebted to Brewer, and enrolled himself as an occasional member in the religious society which met on Monday evenings under Brewer's oversight. Whereas Jennings was something of a spiritual father, Clunie and Brewer were more like brothers in age and influence. Brewer added to Clunie's lay spirituality the legitimacy and authority of an ordained minister.

With Brewer's introduction, Newton circulated widely among Independents and Presbyterians in London, taking in sermon after sermon. He did not write in his diary for the last half of 1754, but during the first half of 1755 he recorded five visits to London comprising more than thirteen weeks in all. Having been so long at sea and unable to attend church, he now devoured all he heard with insatiable appetite. Judging from his sermon reports, it was a steady Calvinistic diet.

---

[38] 'Life of the Rev. Samuel Brewer', *EM* 5 (1797), 5-18.
[39] *History of Dissenters*, 4 vols. (1812), iv. 455-9.

Although he would sometimes vary the pattern, he would typically rise well before dawn on Sundays to hear Thomas Adams or one of George Whitefield's other assistants at the Tabernacle in Moorfields; after breakfast he would attend the Independent meeting at Stepney to hear Brewer; in the afternoon he would venture out again to hear David Jennings at the Independent meeting in Wapping where he grew up; and then in the evening he would listen to one of the preachers at the Presbyterian meeting in Shakespeare's Walk in Upper Shadwell. He still, however, resorted to the Church of England monthly to communicate, usually exchanging the morning service at Stepney for one at the parish church at Barking where an evangelical named Murden was lecturer. During the week he attended the Pinners' Hall lecture in Old Broad Street on Tuesdays where Richard Rawlins, John Guyse, Thomas Bradbury, and other Dissenting worthies expounded on themes such as the covenant of grace; on Wednesdays he went to the casuistical lecture on cases of conscience at the Presbyterian meeting in Little St Helen's, Bishopsgate, where Samuel Hayward and Samuel Pike preached on alternate weeks; and on Fridays he would often venture out to hear John Guyse or David Jennings again at Little St Helen's on subjects such as effectual calling or imputed righteousness.[40] If there was a Puritan tradition in London which survived into the eighteenth century, this was it. All this preaching fortified Newton's lately recovered Calvinistic convictions. Newton would later look back on these heady days in London, when he walked in a cloud of wonder from sermon to sermon, from Church to Chapel to religious society, as the turning point in the settlement of his religious principles.

Whitefield and Calvinistic Methodism

Surprisingly, Newton seemed to be in large measure ignorant until the winter of 1754/5 of the popular revival of evangelical religion under Methodism. When at sea in 1749,

---

[40] Brief descriptions of the careers of these ministers may be found in Bogue and Bennett, *History of Dissenters*, and Walter Wilson, *History and Antiquities of Dissenting Churches and Meeting Houses*, 4 vols. (1808–14).

between his conversion and his marriage, he visited Charleston in South Carolina, and could find little difference between preachers in the city, and little particularly to distinguish Josiah Smith, the Independent minister whom he heard on several occasions. This is remarkable, considering the fact that Smith was one of George Whitefield's key supporters in the Awakening in the American colonies. Smith had stood by Whitefield in the row that erupted when Alexander Garden, the Church of England Commissary at Charlestown, created a sensation some years earlier by attempting to defrock Whitefield.[41] Newton seems also to have been unaware of the spectacular field-preaching in London, the controversial paroxysms which were accompanying Methodist preaching, and the fractious debates which had splintered the English Revival into several divisions. But then, immersed in a flurry of religious activity upon returning to England, he encountered Methodist activity at Chatham and learned more of the reputation of the Wesleys and Whitefield in London. He was at first wary. After reading a journal and an apologetic tract by Wesley in January 1755, he expressed his approval of Wesley's sincerity and zeal for the gospel, but lamented nevertheless what appeared to him a certain mixture of weakness and error in the Methodist evangelist and his followers. A few days later he read some letters of Whitefield and others, and was only a little less ambivalent: 'Tho I have no cause to subscribe myself their followers, yet I cannot but admire and respect many of them.' Yet he continued to frequent the preaching of Calvinistic Methodists at Chatham and London and confessed by the end of June, 'If I mistake not, these have been more own'd and blessed to me, for the little time I have known them than any,' and he hoped he would have the courage to bear the reproach which could follow his identifying with them.[42]

What overcame Newton's prejudices? And what was the consequence of this closer affiliation with Methodism? It was, above all, his association with younger Congregationalist

---

[41] *Works*, i. 79–80; cf. Arnold Dallimore, *George Whitefield*, 2 vols. (Edinburgh, 1970), i. 511–25; L. Tyerman, *Life of the Rev. George Whitefield*, 2 vols. (1876), i. 357–400.   [42] Diary (1751–6), 21 and 25 Jan. and 29 June 1755.

Dissenters in London which first brought him into the
Calvinistic milieu of the revival, for links between Whitefield
and the Independents were 'numerous and close'.[43] Brewer's
congregation, for instance, included 'serious Christians of all
denominations . . . being composed of persons converted to
God under the preaching of Churchmen and Methodists, as
well as Dissenters.'[44] While training for the ministry under the
independent Abraham Taylor of Deptford, Brewer himself
(only perhaps 16 years old at the time) used to join the
thousands who flocked to hear the 24-year-old Whitefield
preach in the open air at Kennington Common a few miles
away. Brewer was 'zealously attached to the Methodists' and
began an intimacy with Whitefield which lasted until the
evangelist's death. The difference between generations of
Dissenters here was significant. Taylor severely resented
Brewer's attachment to Whitefield and once, on his return
from Kennington, inflicted 'disgraceful corporal punishment'
upon him and sent him fasting to his room. This is all the
more remarkable when it is considered that Taylor, author of
The Modern Question (1742), took an evangelical position in the
controversy with John Gill over 'duty faith' and was a strong
voice among Dissenters in insisting on the obligations of
ministers to preach to the unconverted.[45] For the younger
generation, who were even further removed than their elders
from living memories of the suffering of Dissenters before the
Act of Toleration in 1689, Whitefield's popular evangelicalism
made the barrier between Church and Chapel seem perme-
able. It was Newton's contemporaries, Brewer and Samuel
Hayward, who introduced him to Whitefield in June 1755.
Although Newton was an occasional conformist from the
beginning of his return to religious seriousness, ironically, his
friendships with these younger Dissenters actually facilitated,
in time, the strengthening of his ties to the Church of England.

Whitefield fast became Newton's supreme ideal. At the
Tabernacle for a three-hour communion service at dawn one

---

[43] Jones, *Congregationalism*, 149.   [44] 'Life of Brewer', 16.
[45] Ibid. 6; Geoffrey Nuttall, 'Northamptonshire and the *Modern Question*: A
Turning-Point in Eighteenth-Century Dissent', *Journal of Theological Studies*, NS 16
(1965), 101–23.

Sunday, he was captivated by Whitefield: 'Never before had I such an idea and foretaste of ye business of heaven.'[46] To share the sacrament and hear Whitefield's charismatic oratory with 1,000 people in the morning, and to return again in a crowd of 5,000 to hear him in the evening, was to participate in a social phenomenon of proportions unimaginable to one of Newton's experience. It was through observing the popular success of Whitefield, a Calvinist and an ordained clergyman in the Established Church, that Newton was given the confidence of his Calvinistic convictions. Already he had heard William Romaine and other evangelicals from the Church, and he was eagerly following the reports of the Revival in Cornwall under Walker of Truro. He thrilled to hear of the increase of all such clergymen preaching 'free grace'. 'Especially as a member of the Established Church', he wrote in his diary, 'I ought to pray that the number of such faithful labourers may be increased.'[47] His principal concern was for national revival. But he was perhaps also aware of the social disadvantages of being tied too closely to Dissent. That he could be a Calvinist without giving up the perquisites of conformity was important at a time when he was unemployed and needing to secure influence and patronage to get a job. As it turned out, he was indeed required to take a sacramental test at Liverpool in order to hold office as tide surveyor, a position in the patronage of the town corporation.

Newton's attachment to Whitefield was only strengthened after he moved to Liverpool. Whitefield attracted an audience of some 4,000 when he visited there for a week in the autumn of 1755, shortly after Newton's arrival. Newton saw more of him than he could have hoped for in a year at London: 'I heard him preach nine times, supped with him three times, and dined with him once . . . and on Sunday he dined with me. I cannot say how much I esteem him' (v. 503). Because of this time together, he rejoiced to his wife, 'So we are now very great [intimate]' (v. 503). While critical of Wesley and his followers, Newton extolled Whitefield's work, claimed his own faith was invigorated by Whitefield, and confessed that he was himself called 'young Whitefield' around Liverpool. The

---

[46] Diary (1751–6), 13 June 1755.   [47] Ibid., 28 Mar. 175.

contact with Whitefield during these years, in person and by letter, deepened the impact of their London acquaintance and made Newton feel again—even in a provincial town—that he was a part of an exciting movement sweeping the country. The next spring Newton recorded in his diary: 'I particularly prayed for the town of Liverpool, in which I reside, that, if it please the Lord, we may partake of that great enlightening which is breaking forth in different places on the Church of England side.'[48] Whitefield, as the orator *par excellence* of this movement, was Newton's Calvinist hero. As Harry Stout has remarked, Whitefield was an 'actor–preacher', taking the gospel into the market-place of a growing consumer society, as opposed to the traditional 'scholar–preacher', who presumed upon a monopolistic religious hegemony over his hearers.[49] The sheer exhilaration of this was captured by Newton in a vivid reminiscence of his winter in London:

I bless God that I have lived in his time; many were the winter mornings I have got up at four, to attend his Tabernacle discourses at five: and I have seen Moorfields as full of lanterns at these times as I suppose the Haymarket is full of flambeaux on an Opera night. As a preacher, if any man were to ask me who was the second I ever had heard, I should be at some loss, but in regard to the first, Mr. Whitfield exceeded so far every other man of my time, that I should be at none. He was the original of popular preaching, and all our popular ministers are only his copies.[50]

If Old Dissent grounded Newton in Reformed orthodoxy, Whitefield and his Methodist followers showed Newton that Calvinism could be an exciting part of the forward current of life, the creed of progressives.

Camaraderie among Calvinists

For some six years after his conversion Newton was led, as he put it, in a 'secret way' with but few Christian friends. Meeting Clunie in 1754 ended his religious solitude; their intimacy was immediate and they stayed up most of the night talking about spiritual experience. 'I was all ears,' wrote

---

[48] Diary (1751–6), 28 Mar. 1756.
[49] *The Divine Dramatist* (Grand Rapids, Mich., 1991), 30–48.
[50] Quoted in *LyH*, i. 92.

Newton later. Clunie pressed on Newton the benefits of seeking out further Christian conversation. Consequently, in contrast to his predominantly solitary experience at sea, his religious acquaintance expanded exponentially once back in England. After spending two hours with Mr Woodgate at Chatham, 'communicating experiences and discoursing of the great truths and glories of the kingdom of grace', he reflected, 'Every fresh acquaintance I make of this kind, is a new confirmation of my faith and hope, and I bless God for the many witnesses I have been of late brought to the knowledge of.'[51] After James Webb preached at the Methodist Meeting at Chatham, Newton mulled over the sermon and remarked similarly, 'He treated of the benefit of Christian conference, and communicating of experience, which so far as I have been enabled to attempt, I can thankfully witness to, with him.'[52] Newton's chief reason for making so many protracted journeys to London was not only to hear preaching but also to enjoy 'religious conference', and his visits to the metropolis read like one long conversation on theological subjects, interrupted only by sermons.

When there was no one at hand to speak with, the conversation spilled over into a correspondence which increased significantly from this period. Newton urged Clunie in 1762 not to be backward in writing 'fulsome' letters, but to speak 'largely and warmly of what God has done for your soul', for, he added personally, 'I find no reading or writing so profitable and refreshing to me, as a correspondence with my Christian friends. I get more warmth and light sometimes by a letter from a plain person who loves the Lord Jesus, though perhaps a servant maid, than from some whole volumes, put forth by learned Doctors.'[53] In addition to this kind of informal discourse in conversation and letters, Newton also participated in at least one religious society from time to time. That he felt obliged to speak up and urge charity toward those, not of their number, who might not be enlightened about 'Election, Assurance, Perseverance, etc.,' suggests that it was a robustly Calvinistic assembly. Within this group he

---

[51] Diary (1751–6), 28 May 1755.   [52] Ibid., 15 Feb. 1755.
[53] *Letters* (Clunie), 9–10.

found his spiritual loneliness removed as he spoke of his own
case and commiserated with the others: 'I have the encouragement to find I am not alone in my complaints of indwelling
sin, and hardness of heart.'[54] The importance of this kind of
religious society in the history of the Evangelical Revival has
been often remarked. Gordon Rupp writes, for example,
'Certainly the cell, the *koinonia*, the society, was at the heart of
the Revival.'[55] The importance of this for Newton's theological
formation was noted by him in retrospect: 'As I received
benefit and pleasure from my intercourse with my new
friends, it is no wonder that, while my heart was warm, and
my experience and judgement unformed, I should enter with
readiness into all their views' (v. 18–19). It is significant
therefore that Newton's initiation to 'Christian conference'
was among Calvinists, for companionship experienced within
this fraternity went far to bolster his own theological
convictions.

At Liverpool too Newton participated in religious societies.
Disappointed in the spiritual life of the Established churches
and Dissenters' congregations in town, Newton was happy to
make the acquaintance of some Calvinistic Baptists of whom
he had not previously heard. Although he continued to take
the sacrament in the Established Church and remained
strongly paedobaptist, he nevertheless found the preaching
and the friends he made among the Baptists more congenial to
his faith. He therefore participated with them as much as he
could without entering into full membership. He was at first
attached to the eccentric John Johnson (1706–91), whose
theology has been described as an eclectic mix of modalist
ideas concerning the Trinity, millenarianism, highly
separatistic ecclesiology, and high Calvinism.[56] Later, with
Whitefield's introduction, he became more closely connected
with the less exclusive John Oulton, minister of the original
Baptist congregation from which Johnson had led a secession

---

[54] Diary (1751–6), 14 Apr. 1755.
[55] *Religion in England, 1688–1791* (Oxford, 1986), 330; see also Walsh, 'Origins',
145–8.
[56] Raymond Brown, *English Baptists of the Eighteenth Century* (1986), 86. A
Johnsonian Baptist sect survived into the 19th c. See Robert Dawbarn (ed.), *History of
a Forgotten Sect of Baptized Believers heretofore Known as 'Johnsonians'* (n.d.).

seven years earlier. The tone of the two Baptist congregations can be taken from the fact that Oulton's reorganized along traditional lines after the secession, ratifying together the Particular Baptist Confession of 1677 and joining the Yorkshire and Lancashire Association of Particular Baptists in 1757, while Johnson's affiliated with the more high Calvinist Northern Association and moved eventually in a sectarian direction.[57] Newton usually attended both their meetings at least once on Sundays, sometimes also visiting the Methodists, but after a few visits to Johnson's Wednesday evening conference, he became instead a regular participant at Oulton's weekly society. However, Newton acknowledged to Whitefield that he thought neither Baptist congregation was 'calculated for general usefulness'; he also earned a certain amount of social opprobrium from his wife's family and his fellow townsmen for these connections. So it indicates something of his adherence to Calvinism at this point that he would remain so closely affiliated with the Baptist meetings.

The round of sermons, religious conversations, and society meetings taken in at London was thus continued at Liverpool except in a more baptistic and, if anything, more doggedly Calvinistic context. He had learned the value of 'Christian conference' and he would continue to seek it out. He even considered in 1756 starting his own religious society and during the last three years in town held a meeting in his own home for a few select friends on Sunday evenings. His first literary venture at Liverpool was a small tract which has not survived, but its title was, significantly, *Thoughts on Religious Associations*. The experience of spiritual camaraderie itself at London and at Liverpool was important for his theological formation.

In his famous study of the ethical basis of modern capitalism, Max Weber wrote: 'As a substitute for the double decree Pietism worked out ideas which, in a way essentially similar to Calvinism, though milder, established an aristocracy of the elect resting on God's especial grace.'[58] This

[57] W. T. Whitley, *Baptists of North-west England, 1649–1913* (1913), 66–7, 135.
[58] *The Protestant Ethic and the Spirit of Capitalism*, trans. Talcott Parsons (New York, 1958), 133.

analogy between Calvinism and Pietism may be reversed in Newton's case to demonstrate simply how the distinction between real and nominal, implicit in his experience of the pietistic *ecclesiola*, could readily be interpreted in the light of the distinction between elect and non-elect explicit in the Reformed *ordo*. Moreover, the spiritual intimacy, which he discovered through casual friendship and religious society, meant that Calvinism for him could no longer be a matter merely of intellectual speculation. He was caught up in a web of committed relationships where it was the assumed frame of reference.

Personal Study of Divinity

It was important to Newton not only that his theology could be co-ordinated with his experience, but also that it was rational and biblical. He had neither a university education nor any training at a Dissenting academy; even his grammar school instruction was poor and incomplete. But having worked hard while at sea to give himself a competent classical education, he thought he would try to do the same for theology once settled at Liverpool in the autumn of 1755. When in 1757 he began to have thoughts of seeking ordination, his programme of theological self-education picked up in intensity accordingly. Writing to a younger minister in Scotland in 1778, in response to a request for recommended books, Newton provided several titles but confessed, 'Most of my reading was before my admission into the ministry,' since the incumbent calls of ministry gave him little time afterwards.[59]

What did he read? First and most important was Scripture itself. He seems after his conversion to have followed the Prayer Book lectionary for a time. Now at Liverpool he taught himself to read the Old and New Testaments in the original languages, even compiling extensive lexical notes from his Greek Testament in hopes of publishing a work of criticism someday. Overstating his case, he later claimed that his 'leading sentiments concerning the grand peculiarities of the Gospel' were formed while he had scarcely any religious book

[59] *Letters* (Barlass), 80.

78

but the Bible within his reach and before he had any
knowledge of the divisions and controversies which subsisted
among Christians (iv. p. vi). While he acknowledged some
'writers and ministers eminent for genuine piety and sound
learning . . . who assisted him in his early inquiries after
truth', he was so thoroughly imbued with the Protestant
principle of *sola scriptura* that he tended to play down the
importance of wider theological study (i. 210–11).

Although he eschewed theological tradition as a source of
authority, he manifestly unlocked the meaning of the sacred
text with the hermeneutical key provided by the Calvinism
implicit in the numerous sermons, books, and conversations
already taken in. When circumstances demanded, he was
ready to acknowledge with satisfaction the pedigree of his
doctrine. Thus, in 1775, when Thomas Scott was still
unconverted and sceptical about Calvinism, Newton wrote to
him: 'My divinity is unfashionable enough at present, but it
was not so always; you will find few books written from the era
of the Reformation, till a little before Laud's time, that set
forth any other. There were few pulpits till after the
Restoration from which any other was heard' (i. 561). It was
to an Anglo-Calvinist tradition that he appealed. This
apologetic dart hit its mark and unnerved Scott who had
subscribed to the Thirty-Nine Articles carelessly and was
presently suffering from a guilty conscience. For Newton
himself, it was through the reading of largely Calvinistic
writers during his Liverpool period that he became convinced
that Calvinism could be defended for its scriptural, intellectual,
and historical fidelity.

The Appendix at the end of this book provides a catalogue
of the reading which Newton recorded up to 1756 in his diary
or, retrospectively, in his autobiography. Although the reading he noted can only have been a portion of the whole, his
specifying and remarking upon these books suggests that they
were regarded as particularly important for his own development. The first observation prompted by this catalogue is how
remarkably eclectic Newton's reading was. He read literature
written by Puritan Nonconformists such as John Owen and
later Dissenters such as Isaac Watts; High Churchmen such
as William Beveridge and Latitudinarians such as Gilbert

79

Burnet; Scottish Episcopalians such as Robert Leighton, Scottish Presbyterians such as Thomas Halyburton, and Scottish Secessionists such as Ebenezer Erskine; regular Anglican evangelicals such as Samuel Walker and itinerant Methodists such as John Wesley, and so on. Still, the traditions from which he drew varied within larger confines which were for the most part Protestant and British. His later writings indicate a familiarity with the works of Continental Reformers, Moravians, the Port-Royalists, and the Quietists, but more insular traditions continued throughout his life to predominate in his theological outlook.[60]

The eclectic nature of his reading was reflected not only in the traditions upon which he drew but also in the way he read with equal pleasure writers who themselves had disagreed in earlier theological controversies. Coming to Reformed theology more than two centuries after Calvin's *Institutes* first appeared in the middle decades of the sixteenth century, he was inevitably heir to a tradition which had feathered out over the years in increasing complexity. Six generations of Calvinism in England under varying social and political conditions had produced many distinct religious groupings and doctrinal factions, and modern scholarship has been particularly keen to classify writers accordingly from the beginning of the Arminian controversies in the Jacobean church through the Socinian controversies which haunted religious discussion in the first third of the eighteenth century. Newton read not only such of these writers as differed on matters of polity and the sacraments (v. 30–42) but also writers from across the Calvinistic theological spectrum who have been described variously as antinomian, high Calvinist, orthodox, or moderate. So, for example, besides John Calvin's *Institutes*, Newton read with equal pleasure during 1755/6 the controversial *Marrow of Modern Divinity*; the sermons of the allegedly antinomian Tobias Crisp; John Owen's *Christologia*; and the writings of Isaac Watts and Philip Doddridge, inheritors of Richard Baxter's 'middle-way' Calvinism.

Again, however, more narrow patterns may be discerned

---

[60] Some of Newton's most esteemed authors were mentioned in his *Plan of Academical Preparation for the Ministry* (1784), in *Works,* v. 82–98.

within the variety apparent here, particularly when Newton's reading is broken down into the contemporary categories of speculative (or doctrinal), controversial, and practical divinity.[61] His reading included relatively little of the middle category of disputative writings, except perhaps for some of the literature from the Methodist 'Free Grace' controversy of 1739 and a tract against the Moravians. His reading of doctrine was a little more extensive, but it was restricted chiefly to writers within the confines of Calvinistic orthodoxy. It was his reading of practical divinity that was the most catholic.[62] This distinction was clear in some later comments he made about John Owen and Richard Baxter. Owen was, he felt, among the foremost teachers of theology but suffered from a style 'something obscure'; in contrast Baxter had 'rather cloudy' sentiments in divinity but was a superb pastor and a man of deep spirituality (ii. 101; cf. i. 628–9). Owen was a doctrinal authority; Baxter was read for spiritual inspiration. Moderate Calvinists, Arminians, Roman Catholics—writers from these and other traditions were read not for formal theology, but for help with the spiritual life that would be 'experimental', 'affectionate', and 'practical'. Such writings on the devotional life predominated in the books mentioned in his diary. Works such as Henry Scougal's *Life of God in the Soul of Man* and Philip Doddridge's *Rise and Progress of Religion in the Soul,* which meant so much to other evangelicals, figured largely. High Calvinist writers were not absent from his reading, but these too he claimed to like best when they were writing in a spiritual vein, emphasizing piety rather than speculative theology.

In the period from his birth in 1725 until the time when he was doing most of this reading, the number of printing presses in England had doubled, and the annual output of books had quadrupled. Newton was able to enjoy the wealth of popular religious works which were in vogue and ever more accessible

[61] Cf. Isabel Rivers, 'Dissenting and Methodist Books of Practical Divinity', in id. (ed.), *Books and their Readers,* 127.

[62] This was similar to Wesley's *Christian Library,* and to his approach to Dissenters generally. See further, Frank Baker, *John Wesley and the Church of England* (1970), 133.

in inexpensive octavo and duodecimo editions.[63] These he sometimes purchased, or sometimes borrowed from friends such as John Oulton at Liverpool or Alexander Clunie in London. In his typical reading, easily digested histories, biographies, sermons, devotional handbooks, poetry, or other such forms of 'middle-brow' theological literature, out-numbered more tightly argued and sophisticated treatises of high doctrine. Simply to tally up the books Newton read in different categories would not, however, establish his dependence upon certain authors, since reading does not imply agreement or indicate the direction of influence. Indeed, Newton read Voltaire only as a kind of object lesson of human depravity. It is possible, however, to make some preliminary observations on his reading as a whole, especially since he usually recorded what were his motives for reading, or how a given book affected him. Broadly speaking, the two directions in which his reading pointed were, on the one hand, toward scholastic orthodoxy and high Calvinistic doctrine, and on the other, toward affective devotion and evangelical piety. His task remained to work out in practice the difficult relationship between predestination and piety.

[63] See Thomas Preston on the variety and popularity of religious literature in Rivers (ed.), *Books and their Readers,* 98–102.

3

'I cannot, I will not give up the desire'
Newton's Ordination Crisis, 1757–1764

Do you trust that you are inwardly moved by the Holy
Ghost to take upon you this Office and Ministration, to
serve God for the promoting of his glory, and the edifying
of his people?

'The Ordering of Deacons,' *Book of Common Prayer*

THERE were three significant religious turning points in
Newton's early manhood: his evangelical conversion in 1748,
his acceptance of Calvinism in 1754, and his ordination in
1764. It was only with difficulty, however, that Newton was
able to accomplish this last change. Seven years of disappointed hopes and frustrated expectations elapsed from his
first thoughts of entering the ministry in 1757 until he was
finally admitted to holy orders.

FROM LAYMAN TO CLERGYMAN

Becoming a minister in 1764 was the beginning of Newton's
third career. Through his adolescence and during his twenties,
he worked his way up in the merchant marine, and for most of
his thirties he was a tide surveyor at Liverpool, a senior post in
the Customs service. Finally, a few months shy of his thirty-
ninth birthday, he was ordained in the Church of England
and took up a curacy at Olney in Buckinghamshire, moving in
later years to become rector of a notable church in the city of
London. The protracted series of events leading up to
Newton's ordination may be analysed in five phases.

*Initial Sense of Vocation and Hopes of Episcopal Ordination,
1757/8*

It was in conversation with friends in the autumn of 1757 that
the idea of entering the ministry first occurred to Newton.

Slowly it took hold of his mind and found a place in his prayers. Already, he had found ample opportunity as a layman to discover his capacity for ministry and to feel the satisfaction of having been of help to fellow believers. Not long before his move to Liverpool, Newton was in London and remarked in his diary, 'Spoke up at society meeting this evg. Called upon to pray. Spoke 2 or 3 times on cases that offered.'[1] At Oulton's weekly conference at Liverpool, he was likewise asked to pray or comment on the experiences described by members. By the time he was thinking seriously about the ministry he had also written a few edifying tracts, distributed Bibles and other books among the poor, recounted the story of his conversion to unbelievers on occasion, and started his own society for young persons for religious conversation.

This last initiative he had had in mind since at least the spring of 1756, and by August 1758 it had come to fruition and he could write: 'We have had three meetings & I have found much enlargement & comfort in speaking to & with them, particular[ly] last night when tho I had nothing considerable prepared for the purpose, I found a pleasing liberty & enlargement both in thought & expression.'[2] In 1756 he had also begun the practice of conducting family worship. From what he wrote a few years later, it appears that this would have included an extempore prayer before the assembled household at least once a day, with the usual addition of a Bible reading and the singing of a hymn or a psalm (i. 128–34). However, in November 1757 Newton took the further step of also 'expounding in the family'. No doubt he had been inspired in this by his intimate acquaintance with many evangelical ministers and by his close reading of Philip Doddridge's *Family Expositor*, published the previous year with the express aim of promoting just such a practice.[3] In a variety of ways, therefore, inside and outside the home, he moved from the passive role of 'attending and hearing' to the more active role of 'praying and speaking', and he was pleased with the results that seemed to follow from his efforts to do

---

[1] Diary (1751–6), 21 Apr. 1755.   [2] Diary (1758).
[3] On the practice of family worship among evangelicals, see Smyth, *Simeon and Church Order*, 1–43.

good. This period of religious activism as a layman became a kind of unofficial noviciate for evangelical ministry in which his desire to be spiritually useful was heightened as his abilities were tested and developed. The times when he could usefully speak and pray extempore were particularly noted by Newton and associated with a sense of 'enlargement' and warmth of spiritual emotion.

Throughout the period in which he was considering and seeking ordination, he also found his desire to be of spiritual service quickened by his contact with several Yorkshire evangelicals. In June 1758 he made the first of many visits to the West Riding to see for himself the progress of the Revival of which he had heard so much. He visited James Scott of Heckmondwike (1710–83), an Independent itinerant with his own connexion of congregations, who also supervised an academy for the training of evangelical ministers; John Edwards of Leeds (1714–85), an Independent minister who had seceded from the Manchester round of Wesley's connexion in 1754; Henry Crooke of Hunslet (1708–70), a loyal minister of the Church of England who none the less supported irregular evangelism; and William Grimshaw of Haworth (1708–63), the colourful 'apostle of the North' who laboured tirelessly both as a parish minister in the Established Church and as an itinerant in connexion with Wesley. On subsequent journeys Newton enlarged this acquaintance to include, among many others, Henry Venn of Huddersfield (1725–97), perhaps the leading Anglican evangelical among Newton's contemporaries; and several Moravians, such as Benjamin Ingham (1712–72), the former Oxford Methodist who had established a large number of societies in the North. After one journey into Yorkshire, Newton wrote to Clunie in London and could only describe the region in metaphors of paradise:

That is a flourishing country indeed, like Eden the garden of the Lord, watered on every side by the streams of the Gospel. . . . I do not mean that the truth is preached in every church and meeting through the country; but in many, perhaps in more proportionably than in any other part of the land, and with greater effect both as to numbers, and as to the depth of the work in particular persons.[4]

[4] *Letters* (Clunie), 19.

This description of the Yorkshire revival led Newton to rhapsodize about how much more wonderful yet would be the state of believers in eternity. His letters from 1760 to 1769 to a group of women he had met in a religious society at Kippax near Leeds, including especially Miss Medhurst (the niece of Lady Huntingdon), exhibit further the ardent lay spirituality sustained by his journeys into Yorkshire. Of all Newton's voluminous correspondence, these letters contain some of the most spontaneous outpourings of his heart and maintain perhaps the highest pitch of spiritual emotion. In them he repeatedly breaks off in apostrophe or doxology from passages of description and exhortation, remembering how his 'heart burned within' him when in Yorkshire and the 'joy unspeakable' he had then felt (vi. 3–53). During the winter of 1754/5 Newton had been inspired spiritually by his contact with believers in London; from 1758 to 1764 he looked even more to the West Riding for religious invigoration. Over the entire seven-year period of his unfulfilled desire to enter the ministry, he repeatedly found encouragement in his sense of vocation among his Yorkshire friends.

It was immediately after his first visit to Yorkshire—only eight months after his first consideration of entering the ministry—that he began a notebook in which over the next six weeks he filled sixty octavo sheets with 'Miscellaneous Thoughts & Enquiries on an Important Subject'. In a series of meditations on various Scripture texts treating the character and calling of a minister, he confided to this diary his fears and hopes about entering the ministry. The content of this diary is discussed below, but at its conclusion Newton recorded, on his birthday in 1758, his entire submission to God to make himself available for the work of the ministry. After eleven hours of prayer and fasting, he wrote, 'I now enter upon and give myself up to a new view of life. From this time I only wait for light and direction, when and where to move and begin.'[5] Once having made this solemn surrender Newton never seriously considered remaining simply a layman, despite the many obstacles which he encountered.

At the end of September 1758 Newton was back in

---

[5] Diary (1758).

Yorkshire, and John Edwards persuaded him to make his first attempt at public preaching to his congregation at White Chapel in Leeds. Newton was nervous. In the middle of his sermon he was left speechless and unable to continue since he had refused to depend upon any written notes. To Newton's embarrassment Edwards had to come into the pulpit to finish the discourse.[6] While this shook his confidence considerably, he was encouraged afterwards by a conversation with Henry Crooke. Crooke reassured him that it might take time to learn to preach without notes. Even more importantly, he pressed Newton to consider applying for ordination in the Church of England.

Until now Newton had assumed that he would need to join the Dissenters because he would not be able to make the subscriptions required in the Established Church. One of the Canons of 1604 remained troublesome to consciences within the Church throughout the eighteenth century (as it did through much of the nineteenth century until revised in 1865). Canon 36 required that all candidates for the ministry subscribe to three statements, affirming respectively that the Sovereign was supreme in Church and State, that the Book of Common Prayer with the Ordinal contained 'nothing in it contrary to the Word of God', and that 'all and every' of the Thirty-Nine Articles were agreeable to Scripture. The form of subscription was strict:

To these three Articles whosoever will subscribe, he shall, for the avoiding of all Ambiguities, subscribe in this Order and Form of Words . . . *viz.*, *I* N. N. *do willingly and* ex animo *subscribe to these three Articles above mentioned, and to all things that are contained in them.*[7]

There was pressure throughout the century from various quarters for this form of subscription to be relaxed. Famously, there were those who wished to accommodate clergy with Socinian sympathies, but more widely there was concern to accommodate those who did not like the Calvinistic tone of

---

[6] *LyH* 271.
[7] Edmund Gibson, *Codex Juris Ecclesiastici Anglicani*, 2nd edn. (Oxford, 1761), 148; cf. the 19th-c. revision in *Constitutions and Canons Ecclesiastical, 1604*, with notes by J. V. Bullard (1934).

some of the Thirty-Nine Articles dealing with the doctrines of original sin and predestination.[8] For evangelicals, however, the crisis of conscience was over the second statement, affirming that the Prayer Book was perfectly consistent with Scripture. Like Samuel Walker of Truro (whose friends had worried that he might leave the Church on this account), Newton objected to expressions in the Baptismal office and the Catechism which suggested baptismal regeneration, and in the Burial office which stated that all those buried had a 'sure and certain hope of the Resurrection'.[9] Could he really subscribe *ex animo* that there were not a line contrary to the word of God? Crucially, Crooke moderated his scruples, and Newton was prepared thereafter to consider subscribing. He took the position that he could affirm the Prayer Book as the most satisfactory writing of its kind, being of a merely human authority; therefore, he could publicly assent to it as a whole, while differing on two or three small points as matters of private judgement. Years later Newton had to rehearse these arguments for a clerical correspondent whose conscience was troubling him about the liturgy. Newton wrote,

I have subscribed my assent and consent to the common prayer, as well as you; but not in the same manner as I would to the truth of the Bible. If the liturgy, or any other human composition, in some parts contradicts itself, I do not accede to both parts of the contradiction. I expound the baptismal office and catechism by the homilies, to which I have likewise assented.[10]

When Newton returned to Liverpool in 1758 he began reading Hooker's *Ecclesiastical Polity*. Despite fears that he was choosing the easier path by seeking a place in the Established Church, he satisfied himself that he could honestly proceed with an application for episcopal ordination.

Shortly after returning from Yorkshire, Newton received a letter from Crooke offering him title to a country curacy. In addition to being Perpetual Curate of Hunslet, Crooke had also recently become Vicar of Kippax and wished Newton to

---

[8] Charles Abbey and John Overton, *English Church in the Eighteenth Century*, 2 vols. (1878), ii. 437–42; Walsh and Taylor, 'The Church and Anglicanism', 48–9.
[9] On Walker, see G. C. B. Davies, *Early Cornish Evangelicals* (1951), 193–6.
[10] *Letters* (Coffin), 131, cf. 45–6.

provide for the cure of souls there in his stead. At Kippax Newton would be among intimate friends, and at the centre of that part of the country he already thought of as a religious paradise. Although the curacy was to be only £30 or £40 per annum, much less than he could earn as tide surveyor at Liverpool, he accepted the title joyfully.

Unsuccessful First Attempts to Enter Orders, 1758–9

Thus far Newton's way had been unimpeded and he had high hopes of continued success. One serious obstacle had been overcome with his possession of a suitable title, however meagre the income, for by long precedent one could not be admitted to holy orders without some such certain prospect in view. However, he soon discovered other difficulties. The same Canons of 1604 which required strict subscription also specified, under Canon 34, that a candidate for orders should have a university education or, if not, should prove his knowledge of Latin and of Scripture. The non-graduate was also to 'exhibit Letters Testimonial of his good Life and Conversation, under the seal of . . . three of four grave Ministers', together with similar testimony of other reputable persons who had known him for at least the past three years.[11] Newton was able to obtain these testimonials eventually, but not without three clergymen refusing him because they did not want to be associated with a 'suspected Methodist'. Then, upon proceeding to London in December, he was turned down by Edmund Keene, the Bishop of Chester (his present diocese), and John Gilbert, the Archbishop of York (the diocese to which his title belonged). The former simply countersigned his testimonials and referred him to the latter as a matter of jurisdiction. But Newton was able to gain an audience only with the Archbishop's chaplain and secretary. After his case was relayed to the Archbishop, the answer came back that his Grace felt he must support the 'rules and canons of the Church, etc.'. Ostensibly, Newton was rejected for not having the usual university degree. A little more than a year later Wesley recorded in his journal his disgust at this decision:

[11] Gibson, *Codex*, 146.

I had a good deal of conversation with Mr. N[ewto]n. His case is very peculiar. Our Church requires that clergymen should be men of learning, and, to this end, have a university education. But how many have a university education, and yet no learning at all? Yet these men are ordained! Meantime, one eminent in learning, as well as unblameable behaviour, cannot be ordained *because he was not at the University*! What a mere farce is this! Who would believe that any Christian bishop would stoop to so poor an evasion?[12]

Like Wesley, many suspected that the underlying reason of Newton's refusal was that he was tainted with the charge of Methodism and 'enthusiasm'.

Newton persisted through much of 1759 with his application for orders. So not unduly to prejudice his application, he decided for a time to associate less with the Methodists, even forgoing the opportunity to hear Wesley and Whitefield on different occasions, and he determined to attend steadily the worship of the Established Church. Then, in February he made a second enquiry to the Archbishop of York with the necessary papers but received a flat refusal, without any explanation except to say, 'His Grace thinks it best for you to continue in that station which Providence has placed you in.'[13] In April he applied again to the Bishop of Chester, only to receive a further letter of rejection because of the precedent set by the Archbishop's decision. In May he was about to make a final appeal to Thomas Secker, the Archbishop of Canterbury, when he thought it might be best first to ask Lord Dartmouth to intercede on his behalf, for he realized that the primate's refusal would surely prevent any further hopes from any other quarter. First he confided to Lord Dartmouth what he felt were the true causes of his previous rebuff by the Archbishop of York:

One was on the part of Mr. Crook who appeared to his Grace to be so obnoxious a person that he was determined never to ordain anyone whom he should recommend. Against me, there was no direct proof of enthusiasm, but strongly presumptive [evidence] in two respects; the one, that I had accepted a title from Mr. Crook, the

[12] *JWJ* iv. 373.
[13] Richard Chapman [Archbishop's Notary] to Newton, 10 Feb. 1759, in *Letters* (Dartmouth), 173.

other, that I was willing to resign a post under the Government which was for life, and as was supposed, worth more than 100*li per annum* to qualify myself for an uncertain curacy of 30*li* or 40*li per annum*.[14]

Newton had hoped this last sacrifice would have testified to his disinterested motivation, but it appeared instead that it was considered a mark of unsound judgement.

There is no record of Lord Dartmouth's response to this request, but in August Newton recorded his intention to proceed with the appeal to the Archbishop of Canterbury. Still, he was pessimistic and wondered if William Romaine were right to conclude already that it was manifestly not the will of God for him to receive ordination in the Church of England. Evidently he got no further with Secker. Already within the past year Secker had counselled Gilbert to reject an application for priest's orders from the Moravian and former Methodist lay preacher Francis Okely, and he had been displeased that certain other Methodists were being ordained by a 'pretended' Greek bishop.[15] In a letter to David Jennings the following January Newton confessed finally to accepting his fate after having experienced so thorough a rejection by the episcopate:

It is likely you have heard of the event of my application for Orders. I pursued it as far, & raised as much interest as I could, from York to Chester to Canterbury, but it has pleased the Lord to overrule my design & I have given it up. I have not been able to purge myself from a suspicion of Enthusiasm & am rejected as an improper if not a dangerous person. I have been charged by some & represented to others as having formed a design to foment disturbance & confusion in the Church.[16]

These allegations of 'enthusiasm' and 'disturbance' point to how potent remained the fears of bishops that the excesses which had in the preceding century brought down the

[14] Ibid. 172.
[15] Thomas Secker, Abp. of Cant., to John Gilbert, Abp. of York, 28 July 1758, ALS, Bishop Thorpe Papers, Borthwick Institute of Historical Research, York. About the same time, Secker rejected an appeal from Thomas Haweis, who was threatened with expulsion from St Mary Magdalene in Oxford.
[16] Newton to David Jennings, 26 Jan. 1760, ALS, DWL.

monarchy and the episcopate might yet revive and threaten the Church.[17] The political climate was much more insecure than it would be four years later when Newton applied again for orders. In 1759 George III had not yet ascended the throne, and the tide had only just begun to turn in England's favour in the Seven Years War (1756–63); there had been militia riots, and the fear that England might be invaded by the French was widespread. Newton could only comment plaintively on his own case to Jennings, saying that his intentions had been honest and peaceable. His aim would have been rather 'to unite than to divide'. But it was not to be. After five applications for orders, involving one bishop and two archbishops, he had no other recourse. His hopes of ministry in the Church of England were relinquished.

Frustrated Desires and Uncertain Exploration of Alternatives, 1760–2

One consequence of Newton's failure to achieve orders was a painful sense of personal embarrassment in Liverpool. In his last appeal to the Bishop of Chester in 1759 he had written, 'The affair is become public and even the reversion of my place [as tide surveyor] secured. The refusal I have met with has been a pretty general subject of conversation, and perhaps some who know me not, may judge hardly of my moral character, because I could not succeed.'[18] Now, early in 1760, he published a series of six specimen sermons which he had originally drawn up to be preached at Liverpool after his ordination. His motive for publishing them was to satisfy or silence, once and for all, those who were speculating about what kind of views could possibly have disqualified him from ministry in the Church (ii. 257). Seeking to put his disappointment behind him, he returned to his job as tide surveyor and resumed his familiar pattern of involvement in lay ministry. Consequently, when Wesley visited Liverpool in January, Newton no longer held back from hearing him and talking with him on every available occasion.

However, having given up hopes of episcopal ordination,

---

[17] Cf. C. J. Abbey, *English Church and its Bishops, 1700–1800*, 2 vols. (1887), i. 391–8. [18] *Letters* (Dartmouth), 173.

Newton was almost immediately confronted with a number of invitations from other quarters. Earlier he had turned down the offer of an Independent charge in Yorkshire in connection with James Scott ('one of the most considerable in those parts', he told Lord Dartmouth) because he had determined to pursue his application for holy orders to the last resort. Now he received an invitation from an Independent congregation with a new chapel in Cow Lane at Warwick. The church was dependent on temporary preachers, and Samuel Brewer advised them to invite Newton to settle among them permanently. Newton recorded that his desire, Providence, the advice of friends, his private surrender to God for ministry—all of these seemed to unite to urge him forward. In May he obtained leave from his job and visited the church to preach on probation for three months. He was well-received by the people and enjoyed the opportunity to be their minister. Afterwards he took time to consider whether he should accept a permanent call, and he visited Yorkshire to consult with his friends.[19] While there he received another pressing invitation from Warwick and was on the point of accepting when, as Josiah Bull put it, 'unexpected circumstances arose which threw the whole matter into doubt'.[20]

It is not possible to determine with certainty what these 'unexpected circumstances' were, but some later remarks, in a funeral sermon by the Dissenter Samuel Palmer of Hackney (1741–1813), suggest the most probable occasion of Newton's hesitation. Palmer had wanted to correct the impression left by a misleading comment in a memoir of Newton from the *Evangelical Magazine* in 1808. The memoir cryptically stated that a sermon by the Baptist minister Benjamin Beddome of Bourton (1717–95) had occasioned Newton's conformity.[21] Palmer provided more detail, explaining that while at Warwick Newton had desired that he and his congregation would shut up their meeting-house temporarily

---

[19] He also visited London and Oxford in July to consult with friends about this opportunity, and even promised Samuel Brewer that he would not immediately accept the call but would keep the people 'in suspense'. Newton to his wife, 9, 16, and 28 July 1760, ALS, LPL.   [20] Bull, *Newton*, 107.
[21] *EM* (1808), 98.

to go and hear Beddome, who was the visiting preacher at the Baptist chapel. Some of the congregation were so offended at this that they made bitter comments about Newton and those who wished to go. The background, which Palmer did not explain, was that the Independent meeting had only recently been formed through a paedobaptist secession from the open communion Baptist church. Palmer claimed that, because of this whole episode, Newton had developed an opinion of Dissenters as a 'litigious people' and had turned his thoughts toward the Established Church where he might enjoy more peace and quietness.[22]

If Newton had heard news of the bitterness at Warwick while he was still in Yorkshire in August 1760, this would explain not only why he was suddenly reticent about accepting their invitation, but also what lay behind allusions in his diary to a letter from one Mr Vennor of Warwick, 'full of resentment and provocation'.[23] While he received letters from others in the congregation which compensated for Vennor's unkindness, it was not until another seven years had passed that Newton recorded, upon a visit to Warwick during which he called on Vennor, how happy he was to have 'that long breach healed'.[24] In any case, Newton rejected the invitation sometime in the autumn of 1760. In January 1761 he wrote to his unbelieving brother-in-law that he was not mad to have considered going to Warwick but that he had nevertheless determined not to go.[25] One more avenue of potential ministry had been explored and exhausted.

On his Yorkshire journeys in 1760 Newton continued to have opportunities to test and develop his gifts for ministry. In April he sought to make amends for his previous embarrassment in the pulpit by sticking closely to a prepared text when

---

[22] *Letters* (Palmer), 19; *EM* (1808), 97. Another possible explanation of the 'unexpected circumstances' that prevented Newton from going to Warwick is found in John Byrom's *Journal* for 20 Apr. 1762, where it was noted that the differences between Newton and the Warwick congregation were 'not about doctrine but maintenance'. Given the date of this journal entry, this may refer to a second, later invitation to Newton from the congregation. *Private Journals and Literary Remains of John Byrom*, ed. Richard Parkinson, 2 vols. (Manchester, 1854–7), ii. 636.

[23] Bull, *Newton*, 111.

[24] Diary (1767), 11–17 May and 3–9 Aug.; cf. Diary (1773–1805), 13 Aug. 1778.

[25] Bull, *Newton*, 108.

invited again to preach. But he found that he simply erred in
the opposite extreme and appeared fixed like a statue, as he
huddled over his notes like a young boy learning to read,
barely looking up until he was finished. In August, after the
Warwick locum, he had more success. He wrote to Wesley in
November, 'I forgot to tell you in my last that I had the
honour to appear as a Methodist preacher.' At William
Grimshaw's urging, Newton had preached at Haworth to a
congregation of 150, comprised about equally of Methodists
and Baptists. From Newton's letter, it is clear that he had
been previously invited by Wesley to become a Methodist
preacher himself. After his Haworth venture, he felt he should
defend to Wesley his unwillingness to continue in the same
way. He raised three principal objections. First, he did not
have the strength of body or mind for itinerancy, since his
physical constitution had been broken for some years already.
Then again, he did not feel he could expose his wife or his
dependent orphan sister to the potential poverty and difficulties involved, especially when Providence had provided for
them as they were. And most importantly, too many
preachers were, he claimed, very different from Grimshaw—
how could he wish to 'live in the fire'? Although he did not
elaborate upon this last objection, he presumably meant that
he was not willing to live with the doctrinal contention, the
opposition, and the charges of 'enthusiasm' that would be
involved in joining Wesley's connexion.[26] While he expressed
his own impatience to be employed in the ministry, he also
acknowledged that he was reticent to thrust himself forward
without something 'more determining'. Lay preaching as a
Methodist, a second alternative to episcopal ordination, was
thus considered and ruled out by Newton in 1760.

Whatever ideas Newton had of finding another avenue of
ministry, Samuel Brewer persuaded him early in 1761 'to lay
aside all thoughts of making a stir at the present' until God's
will in his situation should become more clear.[27] In April he
nevertheless took the bold step of inviting a few friends to join
him regularly on Sunday evenings while he expounded the
Scriptures in his home. In a subsequent letter to Thomas

[26] *AM* (1780), 441–4.   [27] *Letters* (Clunie), 5.

95

Haweis, Newton confessed to having had this 'little lecture in my own house' for over two years, with a regular congregation of anywhere from a dozen to twenty persons.[28] Coming from someone whose frustrated attempts to enter the ministry were well known, this looked suspiciously like a conventicle to many of Newton's friends. Technically, he was in violation of the Second Conventicle Act of 1670 and liable to be prosecuted and fined, for the Act of Toleration of 1689 only exempted from the penalties of the Conventicle Act those who registered their places of worship as Dissenters' Meetings. This would become a serious issue for Methodists after the precedent-setting case of Lady Huntingdon's Spa Field's Chapel in London in the early 1780s. In 1787 Wesley realized 'that execrable Act called the Conventicle Act' would eventually compel him to register all his chapels, and licence all his preachers, under the terms of the Act of Toleration, even if he would still try to keep the term 'Dissenter' itself out of the legal deed. Newton did not seem in 1761 to be in any immediate danger of prosecution, though it soon became clear that he had more in mind than simply enlarging his family worship to include a few friends. By June he felt the 'lecture' was well-established but wished for something more. To Miss Medhurst he admitted that his desire to enter more formally into ministry continued unabated: 'My heart is led that way, but the Lord's hand keeps me in' (vi. 17).

Things continued much the same until the following June when Thomas Jones of St Saviour's, Southwark, died at only 33 years of age. Newton was four years older than Jones, and he could not but think of the shortness of life and of how little he had been able to do in the way of ministry in return for all that God had done for him. He chafed under the restraints which kept him from his sense of vocation. Within a fortnight of Jones's death, Newton put some of his thoughts down in a letter for his wife (v. 531–6).

The letter is of some importance and may be summarized briefly. Newton thanked his wife for the sacrifices she had made over the past three years while he had been seeking to enter the ministry, but he confessed that he was still trying

---

[28] Newton to Thomas Haweis, 7 Feb. 1763.

to suppress thoughts of an undertaking which did not have her approval. She would, he knew, suffer in silence if his conscience demanded he proceed, but he was writing to try to persuade her to a more wholehearted concurrence with his designs. He stated his intention plainly: 'I much desire to enlarge my little attempts in the way of preaching, or expounding (call it what you please), in Liverpool' (v. 533). It seemed to him that the advice of all his friends was united on one side, and only Samuel Brewer's sentiments and her own weighed on the other. He could see only two objections: that he might encounter scorn, or that he might lose his job. The former he would want willingly to suffer for the gospel, but in fact he thought that opposition would be negligible. After all, his Sunday evening gatherings had been publicly known for over a year and there had been no disturbances at the house, nor had he met any disrespect in the town. Surely if he were to procure a larger place, he might go on as quietly. Regarding the latter objection, about the insecurity of his job, he promised that he would in prudence only choose times of preaching that would not interfere with his responsibilities. He had consulted his superiors upon the point and was satisfied that he should not hazard his place if he were thus careful. He tried to mollify her by suggesting that success in such a venture could even bring him more respect and estimation in town. And were there not much nobler motives as well? He would not proceed with only her dutiful acquiescence: he wanted her sincere approval. While he remained in suspense, he concluded, 'I feel, at times, a burden which I can hardly bear, and cannot possibly shake off' (v. 535).

Both Alexander Clunie and Samuel Brewer had, like his wife, expressed concern about Newton setting himself up as a preacher at Liverpool. They had recently heard of someone having been dismissed from the Custom House for such a cause. The job of tide surveyor was a Crown appointment and subject to a sacramental test, so there were just grounds for their concerns. But Newton reassured them that they were mistaken about the individual who had left the Custom House, and that he would not jeopardize his place by preaching. Yet, he wrote to Clunie, 'other circumstances are not likely to be favourable'. By this he could have meant simply that his wife was not yet agreed, but he did not elaborate any further. Even at this extremity, however, his resolve was not shaken: 'As to laying aside all thoughts of the Ministry, it is quite out of my power: I cannot, I will not give up the desire; though I hope I shall not run before I am sent.'[29] He felt he had an inward call. It simply remained to wait for God's providence to place him in the work. This third alternative to episcopal ordination, to set himself up as an independent at Liverpool, remained long on Newton's mind as the most attractive of his options.

Vacillation Between a Succession of Invitations, 1762–4

After being refused holy orders, Newton had considered, but held back from, three different opportunities to enter the ministry: as an Independent pastor at Warwick; as a Methodist preacher; and as the minister of an Independent congregation which he thought he might raise at Liverpool. About the time Newton was first considering entering the ministry, he had been involved in unsuccessful efforts to try to settle John Whitford at Liverpool. Whitford (*fl.* 1745–82) was a lay preacher who had left the Manchester Round of Wesley's connexion. Newton wanted him at Liverpool because there were so few of the town's inhabitants who would go to hear the gospel under John Oulton, simply because he was a Baptist. But instead of settling at Liverpool Whitford became an Independent minister nearby at Bolton, taking charge of a congregation that had seceded from a Methodist society. Now, five years later, Whitford accepted an invitation to Yorkshire, against Newton's advice, and left the young Bolton congregation without a pastor. During the summer of 1762 Newton went for a short while to take Whitford's place.[30]

By August Newton was himself, in fact, leaning toward

---

[29] *Letters* (Clunie), 12–14.

[30] On Whitford, see Bull, *Newton*, 113; *Letters* (Jones), 35–6; F. M. Parkinson, 'Notes on Methodism in Liverpool [part 2]', in *Proceedings of the Wesley Historical Society* (1899), 65; H. D. Rack, 'Survival and Revival: John Bennet, Methodism, and the Old Dissent', in *Protestant Evangelicalism*, 1–23; *Works*, ii. 61–79.

accepting a call in connection with a group of Independent ministers in the North-West of England who had links to the Bolton congregation, and with whom he was on terms of increasing intimacy. He had written to a friend at Hull a little earlier, 'I do give preference to that Church order which is generally called Independent.'[31] In April he had been to Manchester for the opening of the new Independent Chapel. Now he wrote to its minister, Caleb Warhurst, saying that things were not working out as he had hoped at Liverpool, and acknowledging that he had been too optimistic about the support he would find there for enlarging his 'little lecture' into something more substantial. He lamented to Warhurst, 'I have made all the overtures towards it that the situation of things will bear; but it will not do. There is not a person (one woman excepted) who is willing to concur in the necessary preliminaries.' Newton added, 'I have quite done with the Established Church . . . and I believe if the admission I once so earnestly sought was now freely offered, I could hardly, if at all, accept it.' He wanted to see James Scott because, Newton continued, 'I am disposed to accept a call within his connection.'[32]

By January 1763, however, Newton's position had swung round dramatically and he was hesitantly reconsidering the prospect of ordination in the Church of England. He and Thomas Haweis had been corresponding since Haweis had come across the manuscript account of Newton's remarkable conversion.[33] Haweis now asked Newton whether he would embrace again the opportunity of ordination if offered. Newton responded by enumerating five points of importance. First, his desire for the ministry was as warm as ever, but after what he had been through he was determined not to stir, unless God's leading was clear both to him and to his 'spiritual friends'. Secondly, he was unattached to any denomination and might be prepared to accept a call among

[31] *Letters* (Jones), 52.

[32] Newton to Caleb Warhurst, Aug. 1762, quoted in Waddington, *Congregational History*, 522–3; cf. Bull, *Newton*, 113–34.

[33] For Haweis and Newton see, Wood, 'Influence of Haweis on Newton'; and id., *Thomas Haweis* (1957).

the Dissenters, if one was offered first. Thirdly, he might encounter some difficulty with subscription, though he supposed he should probably be able to get over this scruple. Fourthly, he was afraid both that he might not have the courage to face what amounted to 'almost a national opposition' against faithful ministers and, conversely, that he might be tempted, if he were popular, to think more highly of himself as a minister in the Established Church than he would if he were among Dissenters. Lastly, despite all these concerns, he would nevertheless choose an appointment in the Church over any other. Fond of parochial order and of peace, he saw within the Church a greater field of usefulness, and it seemed to him as though God was singularly reviving his work through ministers in the Established Church. But he added the caveat that he would have to be accepted in good faith, without restrictions, and that he should feel it to be his general duty to be 'regular'. The case of an itinerant like Berridge was different, he noted, from that of a person 'whose eyes are open beforehand'.[34] Thus, although he had reservations, Newton retreated significantly here from the position he had declared just five months previously to Warhurst; namely, that he was through with the Established Church and could hardly accept an opportunity if offered.

By March, after 'solemn deliberation & prayer', his resolve had strengthened even further and he could write boldly to Haweis, 'I am willing & ready to accept any call or opportunity you shall recommend.' Haweis had evidently asked whether Newton would be content with as little as £40 per annum, for Newton answered that he would, and added, 'I therefore empower & entreat you, Sir, to answer for me, I am willing to accept ordination *bona fide* in the established church, in any place or character which the Lord shall point out, & upon any terms that will provide honest bread, its being brown will be no material objection.'[35] His only concern was that his intentions be kept secret to avoid embarrassment in the event that he was again unsuccessful. For the same reason, he did not want to solicit new

[34] Newton to Thomas Haweis, 7 Jan. 1763.
[35] Newton to Thomas Haweis, 19 Mar. 1763, ALS, FLP.

testimonials around Liverpool, knowing the affair would immediately become public. His Christian friends in particular might be offended at his continually changing his views.

This was not to be Newton's last turnabout. Although Haweis mentioned two potential opportunities in May, nothing seemed to come of them, and by the end of the year Newton was again open to all possibilities. He hinted to Haweis that some of his friends thought God had another place of service for him. Newton explained further that the proposal for him to set up as an Independent preacher at Liverpool had been resurrected:

Several ministers in Yorkshire, men who have been eminently useful & at the head of Independent congregations, tho some of them of the Methodist stock originally—such as Mr. Edwards of Leeds, Knight of Halifax, Warhurst of Manchester—these with others would be ready to come & break the ice, by keeping up a course of preaching for some months to raise a congregation, & then to open a way for my appearance.[36]

In time Newton felt he should be able to raise most of the funds for a building by canvassing his friends in London and around the country. He asked for Haweis's advice. For Newton's part, he thought the openings in the Church were so few that there would always be candidates more suitable than himself, coming either from the colleges or from those who had already suffered loss for the gospel. Conversely, he could think of nothing better than remaining in Liverpool in the way he had outlined and with a regular connection. 'I love the place,' he confessed plainly. Moreover, it seemed to him that there were thousands in the town grossly ignorant of the gospel. He lamented that 'that darkness which by a Catachresis is called The New light' abounded in town, for a lavish new chapel had just been erected whose ministers' beliefs were to Newton a refinement even upon the Socinians.[37] He hoped that by retaining his post at the Custom House he

---

[36] Newton to Thomas Haweis, 30 Dec. 1763, ALS, FLP.
[37] On the strength of Presbyterian 'new scheme preachers' at Liverpool, see Jeremy Goring, 'The Break-Up of the Old Dissent', in G. Bolam *et al. English Presbyterians*, (1968), 180–3.

could begin immediately, with minimum expense to his people, to counter the work of such as these. Haweis's response was unequivocal, as a note scrawled on the back of this letter bears witness: 'Newton wants to settle at Liverpool. I press him into the Church.'[38] Haweis also raised the question of whether Newton would still be able to fulfil the sacramental test for his position as tide surveyor. But Newton responded that he was not worried about this, since he was only obliged to take the sacrament upon the accession of a new king. George III having just been crowned as a young man, he was content to trust that a sacramental test would not be required again in his time.

However, even as Newton was writing this to Haweis about the Liverpool scheme, he received an unexpected letter from one Mr Spencer making fresh proposals which changed everything. He forwarded the letter to Haweis. Newton's references to this new development over the next month are cryptic, but it seems he was offered something in the Church, because, shortly thereafter, upon Haweis's advice, he wrote again to the Archbishop of York's Notary, Richard Chapman, to enquire about orders. In 1761 Hay Drummond had succeeded John Gilbert in the archiepiscopal see, so perhaps Newton thought he might have greater hopes of success with the new Archbishop. But after more than a month passed without a response from Chapman, Newton took this silence as a sign that he had displeased him, by hinting he would not be content to receive orders simply to read prayers. Nothing more was to come of this episode.

At the beginning of January 1764, while Newton was pursuing this opportunity, he was at the same time remaining open both to the possibility that Haweis might yet be able to offer something, and to the hope that the Liverpool proposal might still go forward. As if this were not enough, at the end of the month another opportunity offered, this time from a Presbyterian congregation on the borders of Yorkshire. The letter came from a minister, Mr Burgess, who had himself been invited by the congregation but was loath to leave his

---

[38] Newton to Haweis, 30 Dec. 1763.

present place of ministry.[39] Newton's initial reaction to this invitation was one of caution. 'There is little encouragement', he wrote to Haweis, 'to engage in the Presbyterian connexion, when the far greater & encreasing number of their ministers have openly departed from the Christian Faith.'[40] By February, however, Newton had received a second letter from Mr Burgess providing more detail about the situation. Although it was a country place, the meeting-house was large and the congregation comprised over 600 hearers. The previous pastor had indeed been given entirely to the 'New light Scheme', but he was for this reason disagreeable to the majority of the people. Not being able to reconcile the congregation, the pastor had resigned and proposed that they find a new minister of their own sentiments, from which had resulted the invitation to Burgess and thence to Newton. With this new information, Newton began to consider the opportunity seriously. He was concerned about the smallness of the stipend but was tempted by the location—'almost in the centre of the land of Goshen'—two miles from Halifax and half-way between Huddersfield and Haworth. He would have Christian friends in almost every town for miles around. At the same time though, he was wary of possible bitterness on the part of those church members influenced by the former Socinian teaching. Moreover, he wondered if the location in some ways actually told against him going, since the people could surely hear the gospel easily nearby. He told Haweis that he intended to visit the congregation in the first week of March and would value his advice before then.

Successful Second Attempt at Episcopal Ordination, 1764

Realizing that Newton was on the point of accepting the Yorkshire invitation, Haweis prevailed on Lord Dartmouth to give Newton the living of Olney in Buckinghamshire. Lord Dartmouth had offered it first to Haweis, but he had declined it. The Earl was only too happy to offer the presentation instead to Newton, since he had read the manuscript account

---

[39] Burgess is mentioned in Newton's letter to Warhurst, quoted in Waddington, *Congregational History*, 522.
[40] Newton to Thomas Haweis, 31 Jan. 1763, ALS, FLP.

of Newton's conversion and was suitably impressed by his remarkable career. In the event, Newton became curate-in-charge rather than vicar of Olney, for Moses Browne (the vicar since 1754) chose not to resign the living when he removed to Morden College.

The immediate problem in the spring of 1764 remained how to achieve Newton's ordination. Newton was instructed by Haweis in March to come to London with his testimonials for ordination. While in London he stayed with Haweis, frequented the Lock Chapel, and delighted in deepening his acquaintance with Lord Dartmouth and others likewise above his own station to whom the Earl introduced him. Early in April he wrote to his wife to caution her that his ordination was by no means certain, and that she should be prepared for a disappointment.[41] Lord Dartmouth's influence proved crucial in overcoming the obstacles which remained. He provided a letter of introduction which pacified the Bishop of Chester, Edmund Keene, when Newton needed the Bishop to authenticate his letters of testimonial. (Keene had earlier refused Newton twice.)[42] He also called upon John Green, the Bishop of Lincoln, in whose diocese Olney lay, to ensure his favourable response to Newton's application. In Newton's preliminary meeting with Green he was treated with 'civility and candour', and an examination date was set. But when Green learned that the Archbishop of York, Hay Drummond, was to hold a private ordination in London, he wrote to Lord Dartmouth that Newton ought simply to wait on the Archbishop's chaplain to be examined and his ordination would follow shortly.

However, Newton did not receive this message until an hour after the examination was scheduled to have taken place. He immediately ran all the way, a mile and a half, but arrived too late. A few hours later he was able to see the Archbishop's secretary but was dejected to discover that it was the same person (Richard Chapman) who had served as secretary

---

[41] Newton letters to his wife, 10 and 16 Apr. 1764, ALS, LPL, are the primary source for his interviews in London.

[42] Haweis had earlier had his own problems with testimonials in 1757. See Wood, *Thomas Haweis*, 53–6.

under Gilbert. When he was told that his Grace had heard of Newton's former refusals and wished to be excused from ordaining him, he was certain that the secretary had poisoned the Archbishop's opinion of him. He was referred again to the Bishop of Lincoln. Newton asked for a personal audience with the Archbishop but was refused. Not to be put off, he ran back to Lord Dartmouth's residence and returned with a letter from the Earl which at length gained him an interview with the Archbishop. But this was all to no avail. Though Drummond raised no objections, he 'thought it his duty to demur—he could not do it with propriety'. Newton left the Archbishop with a letter for Lord Dartmouth and the assurance, hard for him to believe after all he had been through, that the Bishop of Lincoln would doubtless ordain him.[43] Lord Dartmouth again exerted himself on Newton's behalf. He wrote and then called upon the Bishop of Lincoln, and afterwards sought to encourage Newton that he would be successful this time. On 16 April Newton was received with kindness by the Bishop. Although he dissented openly from him on some points of theology, he was not on this account disqualified. After an hour the Bishop had satisfied himself and promised to ordain Newton within a fortnight. So it proved. At long last, on 29 April 1764, Newton received deacon's orders, and on 17 June the same year he was priested.[44]

The conditions under which Newton successfully sought ordination in 1764 were different from those under which he had applied six years earlier. Politically, any residual fear that the Church constitution might be in danger was dissipated. The possibility of a dynastic crisis or any real Jacobite threat had been removed with the accession of the third Hanoverian in 1760 and the successful end to the Seven Years War. New bishops were involved in Newton's ordination and they had

[43] See further, Lord Dartmouth to Drummond, Abp. of York, 13 and 14 Apr. 1764, ANS, Bishop Thorpe Papers, Borthwick Institute of Historical Research, York.

[44] The details of Newton's ordination, licensing, and institution are recorded in Register 39, fos. 31 and 33, Episcopal Rolls and Registers, Lincolnshire Archive Office.

assurances about him from one of the peers of the realm. But still, his ordination had been fraught with difficulties to the end. When he finally found himself a Clerk in Holy Orders, Newton might fairly be said to have ended his own Seven Years War.

EVANGELICAL VOCATION IN THE MID-EIGHTEENTH CENTURY

Several questions are raised by Newton's arduous path from the ranks of the laity to those of the clergy. What prompted and sustained his desire to enter the ministry? Why was he so often refused by the episcopate? Given his serious consideration of a ministry in one of a number of denominations, what was his understanding of church order and how did this relate to a wider sense of evangelical identity? And how did his conception of the gospel relate to his understanding of ministry? Such questions call for a closer examination of the character of the mid-century evangelical milieu in which Newton's ordination crisis occurred.

Lay Activism

In hindsight it is all too easy to think of Newton's religious activity at Liverpool in the light of his later career as a minister, failing to notice what a striking figure he cut in the Evangelical Revival as a layman, pure and simple. It was as a layman that he cultivated a wide correspondence with clergymen up and down England, that he regularly entertained eminent evangelical clergy in his home, that he visited Yorkshire and other areas to observe and hasten the progress of the Revival, and that he began to expound the Scriptures informally at home and from the pulpit of various churches. Respectable, intelligent, and having a fascinating personal history, he quickly gained a wide acquaintance with evangelicals of many types.

He wrote from Liverpool in 1761 to his brother-in-law, a solicitor and a Deist, 'Though there are comparatively but few persons of fine parts and great accomplishments, humbled by the plain and artless power of the gospel, yet it is my encouragement that some are. We have some scholars, some wits; nay, what is more, some attorneys and lawyers amongst us, and therefore I must not quite despair of you.'[45]

Wryly poking fun at the irredeemability of lawyers, seeking not to put off his brother-in-law by coming across in too grave a tone, Newton was nevertheless trying to make a serious point after the manner of 1 Corinthians 1; namely, that the evangelical laity included few from among the cultural élite and few from the learned professions, and that conversion demanded a certain chastened humility on the part of such. Newton's own position and his religious principles did not give him access to the highest polite society at Liverpool, but it did not keep away either those 'sufficiently well-bred to be received as visitants anywhere', as he encouraged his wife when she (or perhaps her family) worried that Newton's evangelicalism would lead to her 'keeping company with washerwomen' (v. 510). For the job of tide surveyor, the Crown patronage was administered by the Member of Parliament for Chester, and Newton received the position through the influence of his former employer and Liverpool Town Councillor, Joseph Manestay. A responsible and senior post, it meant that Newton had fifty or sixty staff working under him—land-waiters, tidesmen, boatmen, and office staff—and he earned an official salary of £50 per annum, supplemented liberally by a share in contraband seizures and unofficial gratuities, though the latter he later forswore as a matter of conscience. He was an upstanding citizen and householder, on occasion waited upon the mayor at his house, and was of sufficient status to be called upon to join in an official public procession at Liverpool to celebrate the coronation of George III. Well beneath the nobility of Lord Dartmouth and the wealth of John Thornton, yet somewhere above the artisan lay preachers in Wesley's connexion, Newton at Liverpool was an evangelical layman who could relate to most evangelical clergy as a social equal without especial deference or condescension.[46]

[45] *Letters* (Bull, ed.), 30.
[46] For a recent analysis of the social composition of the clergy, based on statistics garnered from the metropolis, see Viviane Barrie-Curien, 'The Clergy in the Diocese of London in the Eighteenth Century', in Walsh, Haydon, and Taylor (eds.), *The Church of England*, 86–109.

Equally important was the leisure his post afforded. The way his responsibilities at first fell out he had to board incoming ships to check for smuggled goods one week but then had the next week largely to himself. With the onset of the Seven Years War traffic at the port dropped off drastically as French privateers patrolled the Irish Sea, and consequently he was free even more of the time to do as he liked. This meant that he could be virtually a 'full-time' layman, devoting himself almost exclusively to religious concerns. It was in this context that he began to consider entering the ministry.

The evangelical tradition in his generation was neither as clerical as it was among the Puritans, nor as indebted to lay leadership at it would be toward the end of the century with the rise of the home and foreign missionary societies. Yet there was great scope for the expression of lay zeal in a network of friendship and informal extra-institutional activity. As noted above, Newton's first thoughts of ordination arose out of a satisfying experience of lay ministry in which he found abundant opportunity to discover and develop his gifts. In this respect it was significant that he was in close proximity to areas of Yorkshire touched by revival. It was there he made his first essays in preaching publicly among Churchmen, Independents, Methodists, and Moravians. There the large rural parishes of evangelical ministers and the remote village Meetings of Dissenters were removed alike from close episcopal scrutiny and accountability to cosmopolitan clerical élites; there too he was away from the civic and social obligations of Liverpool. His growing number of intimate clerical friendships in Yorkshire, as elsewhere, drew him into a circle where it became increasingly plausible to imagine that he belonged more naturally and properly among them in the full character of a minister, than in Liverpool as a civil servant.

Newton's path to the ministry in the Established Church was decidedly not the familiar path of family precedent and influence and a university education. His was an alternative route. As an evangelical layman with moderate wealth, leisure, mobility, and social status, he was able to educate himself and to carve out his own informal apprenticeship to numbers of evangelical clergy, until able finally to gain the necessary influence of Lord Dartmouth to overcome episcopal prejudice and accomplish his ordination.

Newton's ordination crisis might be said to reflect a twist in what has been described by John Walsh as the case of the 'Eloquent Convert' in the Evangelical Revival. Walsh describes the typical scenario which recurred under the ministries of Henry Venn, William Grimshaw, Thomas Jones of Creaton, and many others:

An able young man would be converted by a powerful sermon in his parish church; he would feel a call to preach the Word; he would contemplate taking holy orders—but discover that his educational qualifications were too slender to impress a bishop already frightened off by his reputation as a 'Methodist'. And so he would accept a Dissenting pastorate.[47]

This repeated experience helps to explain Michael Watts's comment that although the Evangelical Revival occurred originally chiefly within an Anglican context, it was Dissent that reaped the ultimate benefit.[48] In Newton's case, however, his path ran in the opposite direction. Although he was an 'Eloquent Convert', it was among Dissenters such as Samuel Brewer that his evangelical fire was first kindled in 1754/5, and in an interdenominational context that it was kept aglow over the next decade. Only latterly was he was encouraged to enter the Church and did he succeed, against many obstacles, in achieving episcopal ordination.

Lord Dartmouth was nearly contemporary with Newton in age, and his evangelical conversion occurred at roughly the same time as Newton first began to consider ordination. His influence was another more obvious way in which a kind of lay activity, typical of the eighteenth-century Establishment, facilitated Newton's ordination. When in 1934 Norman Sykes referred to the 'steady and progressive laicisation of religion' as the keynote of ecclesiastical development in the eighteenth century, he was not describing principally the kind of popular religiosity and extra-institutional activity in which Newton

---

[47] Walsh, 'Methodism at the End of the Eighteenth Century', 294; cf. id., 'The Magdalene Evangelicals', *Church Quarterly Review*, 159 (1958), 499–500.
[48] Watts, *Dissenters*, 440.

engaged, so much as the kind of influence exerted in the Church by powerful laity such as Lord Dartmouth through patronage, interest, and legislation.[49] Lord Dartmouth's critical efforts on Newton's behalf were an instance of evangelicals using the unreformed structure of the Hanoverian Church to further their own agenda.

Denominational Pluralism

Newton's interdenominational credentials were certainly well-established by the fact that during the seven years before his ordination he contemplated at least three opportunities among the Independents, one among the Methodists, and one among the Presbyterians; and that he considered at least four prospects in the Established Church, taking his application for orders (in most cases at least twice) to the Bishops of Chester and Lincoln, to two Archbishops of York, and to the Archbishop of Canterbury. His case illustrates how easily denominational barriers could be surmounted by evangelicals of different communions during the mid-eighteenth century. At one stage he was in the ironic situation of finding that an Anglican (William Romaine) was counselling him that it was not God's will for him to enter the ministry of the Established Church, and that he should accept the invitation of an Independent congregation, while not much later an Independent (Samuel Brewer) was advising him, contrariwise, that it was not God's will for him to set up as an Independent preacher. That Newton himself could in good conscience contemplate ministering in any of number of denominational contexts demonstrates how 'low' was his ecclesiology, and how thoroughly matters of church order were subordinated to evangelical expediency. What chiefly mattered was that any given situation be suitable for advancing the gospel message.

Because of the prerogatives of the Established Church, Newton could write that its clergy had a 'fairer field for being useful'. Moreover, he claimed to see 'a double portion of the Lord's spirit reviving his work & assisting his ministers on

---

[49] Norman Sykes, *Church and State in the XVIIIth Century* (Cambridge, 1934), 379; cf. Rupp, *Religion in England*, 518–19.

that side'.[50] Newton later observed to a Dissenting layman from Hull,

[Dissenters] had been praying and wishing for a revival of the power of godliness; but, alas! they thought, when it should take place, it would be on their side of course. But, when the Lord was pleased to raise up and send forth labourers, unfurnished with their learning and unconnected with their *order*, many of them could not rejoice.[51]

He would later chide some Dissenting ministers in London with a similar apologetic for the Established Church based upon the success of the Revival. 'Unattached to any denomination', as Newton described himself before ordination, he was inclined to join where he saw the Revival progressing most strongly. Theologically, he felt the real threat to the gospel came from Deism and Socinianism, and for this reason he was wary of establishing a connection with Presbyterianism, and much more happy to think of being among the Independents, should he become a Dissenting minister. With the Baptists and Methodists his objections had more to do, it appears, with what he regarded as their lower social standing. He considered the Methodists at Liverpool as 'sour' and the Baptists as 'not calculated for general usefulness'. With regard to the Church of England the situation was the opposite. Although Newton saw the prerogatives and hegemony of the Established Church as something that could be exploited for the purpose of parish evangelism (the best boat from which to fish), there was also the inducement of enhanced social status and an income derived without dependence on a local congregation or a board of ministers.

Newton was worried that he might be seduced by these incentives into compromising his principles: 'The Character of a Clergyman is more generally respectable than that of a Dissenting teacher, & would probably open me a larger acquaintance especially with persons of rank; & how far this thought may interfere & make me more desirous of being one, I dare not say, for my heart is deceitful.'[52] Aware of this temptation, Newton searched his own heart for unworthy

[50] Newton to Haweis, 7 Jan. 1763.
[52] Newton to Thomas Haweis, 7 Feb. 1764, ALS, FLP.
[51] *Letters* (Jones), 100.

motives, and he felt himself on many occasions at least as happy at the thought of joining the Dissenters as with the prospect of ordination in the Church. But still, the pull was there. It was particularly from his wife and her family that he felt strong pressure to join the Established Church if he would insist upon becoming a minister. When Newton first considered episcopal ordination, his father-in-law was 'much griev'd' since he had wrongly thought that Newton was turning a Dissenting preacher; when he thought to settle at Warwick, his brother-in-law told him he was 'mad'; when he wondered about raising a congregation at Liverpool, his wife was reluctant. In contrast, when Newton was applying for holy orders, her family were 'well pleas'd' and only expressed a little concern over the smallness of the stipend. They even tried to obtain a more generous title for Newton near their home at Chatham in Kent. After Newton finally gained the confidence in 1764 that he would be ordained, he encouraged his wife by writing of all the 'persons of distinction' he had met. He wrote, 'There is nothing of the recluse, sour, self-tormenting spirit which has so often disgusted you among the Methodists,' and he added the reassurance that she could now anticipate leaving behind the 'barren, tedious Sabbaths' she had complained of at Liverpool. Newton's persevering in his efforts to be accepted in the Established Church was certainly motivated in part by a desire to appease his wife and his in-laws. Since he did not have strong ecclesiological principles, it was easy for the ideal of evangelical usefulness to merge with that of propriety.

The Primacy of the Gospel in Ministry

Chiefly, Newton was concerned to advance the gospel by all and every means. He clearly felt that it was the gospel itself, once experienced as the instrument of conversion, that created a vocation to ministry and established overwhelming motives for preaching. Newton confessed to Haweis that wherever he was finally to minister, 'Grace, free Grace must be the substance of my discourse—to tell the world from my own experience that there is mercy . . . for the most hardened.'[53]

---

[53] Newton to Haweis, 7 Jan. 1763.

From Liverpool he pleaded with Whitefield, Haweis, and other ministers to come and preach the good news to the spiritually destitute people of the town. In his diary he wrote with feeling as his thoughts turned to prayers,

I live in the midst of thoughtless sinners who abuse the tenders of thy mercy, & throng the downward road by thousands, my bowels yearn over them, my heart trembles for the ark of God, & my hearts desire & prayer is that thou wouldst be pleas'd to send me forth in thy strength to plead thy cause, & to publish the glad tidings of salvation by redeeming blood.[54]

Although his language here borrows heavily from Scripture in expressions which could easily deteriorate into evangelical clichés, Newton's earnestness is evident. His aspirations, as recorded often in this diary, were those called for in the Ordinal: 'to serve God for the promoting of his glory, and the edifying of his people'. Newton had more than once read the *Conclusion of Bishop Burnet's History of His Own Life and Times* (1734), which circulated widely, both as a part of the larger history and as a separate tract. Writing well before the beginnings of the Evangelical Revival, Burnet gave his parting views on the state of the Church and its needs, and he added his earnest proposals for reform. He made particular remarks on the necessary character of those who would desire to serve in the Church, addressing such candidates: 'Study to keep alive in you a Flame of exalted Devotion; be talking often to yourselves, and communing with your own Hearts . . . Above all Things, raise within yourselves a Zeal for doing good, and for gaining Souls; indeed I have lamented during my whole Life, that I saw so little true Zeal among our Clergy.'[55] While the famous Bishop would doubtless have taken exception to several aspects of Newton's doctrine and experience, he could not easily have faulted him on this account.

Manifestly, Newton understood ordination in terms not of symbol and sacrament, but of word and ministry. In his diary, 'Miscellaneous Thoughts on an Important Subject' (1758), he complained that he had not been able to find anything

---

[54] Diary (1758).
[55] *Conclusion of Bishop Burnet's History of His Own Life and Times* (1734), 9.

written on the nature of the ministerial call, and he set himself the task of ascertaining from Scripture what it was.[56] He did not pursue the project beyond recording a few thoughts that occurred from his reading, but it is evident that his concern was almost exclusively with how one might discern a special divine appointment to preach the gospel. He had an exalted concept of the office of a minister, but this was reflected in questions chiefly about what kind of person was either worthy or able to bear the gospel message itself.[57] Here he would have found familiar works like Richard Baxter's *Reformed Pastor* (1656) set the standard high. In Newton's first meditation he determined that the ministerial character required 'zeal, courage, diligence, faithfulness, tenderness, humility & self-denial', an extensive knowledge of Scripture, a large stock of 'divine experience', and discernment and prudence. To this must be added a thirst for God's glory and the salvation of souls; a ready ability to share what one has personally learned of God; a desire to wrestle in prayer privately, in assemblies, and in families; a willingness to converse with hearers upon what has been preached publicly; and a determination to use every opportunity to extend the gospel into adjacent, perhaps even distant places. No wonder then that he not only felt his own insufficiency for the ministry, but realized that anyone wishing to become a minister would have to depend on a divine calling and assistance.

How was one to determine this call and anointing? Newton recorded a number of what he felt were reasonable evidences of a calling to ministry, such as the possession of strong and appropriate desires for the work, a sense of its greatness, and a measure of suitable gifts. But he felt confronted by the two opposite dangers of presumption and cowardice as he attempted to assess his own vocation. He longed for 'sensible

[56] It is surprising that Newton does not mention Burnet here, since Burnet's *Conclusion* and his *Discourse of the Pastoral Care* (1692) were both well-known and treated the subject of the call to the ministry. Many of the characteristics of the worthy candidate which Newton identified were remarkably similar to those expounded by Burnet.

[57] Cf. Walsh and Taylor, 'Introduction', 14: 'What distinguished the self-consciously "serious" evangelical clergy towards the end of the century was less their definition of pastoral duties than their conception of what it was to be a Christian.'

manifestations' of God's call (this is in part why he waited in fasting and prayer for so long on his birthday), but these were not forthcoming. Concluding his written meditations, he resolved nevertheless to go forward, offering himself for the work of the ministry upon the strength of his sober reflections over the past months.[58] In all, his diary reads as a search for evidences of grace not unlike his recently resolved quest for assurance of salvation.

The Primacy of the Gospel in Corporate Christian Identity

Thus, the gospel was central to Newton's motivation for seeking ordination and his sense of calling to the ministry. From the events of his protracted ordination crisis it is also clear that a common experience and understanding of the gospel formed the basis for identifying those who were regarded as within or without the evangelical milieu (the 'Gospel world'), whether from the Established Church or Dissent. During the mid-century there were few of the structures of 'party' that would develop among Anglican evangelicals towards the end of the century—clerical societies, patronage trusts, Bible and mission societies, magazines, and so on; neither were there yet many structures by which to identify an interdenominational network of evangelicals.[59] Haddon Willmer has cautioned that it is easy to misunderstand the term 'evangelical' by reading the modern signification of the word as a party label back into this period for which an older, more theological understanding of the word is better applied, and that the concern of eighteenth-century evangelicals related to attitudes towards the evangel, not to adherence to a party.[60] It is in this sense that the word

[58] Cf. Newton's deliberations to those of the Methodist lay preacher Christopher Hopper (1772–1802) some years earlier (recorded in *AM* for 1781). Hopper, like Newton, wanted to ground his call to the ministry in a conscious theological method (Scripture, reason, and experience), and set aside time to pray and fast and examine himself, but he placed less importance generally on learning than did Newton. Both men struggled to reconcile 'gifts' and 'graces'.

[59] On the development of party consciousness among Anglican evangelicals, see John Walsh, 'The Yorkshire Evangelicals', unpublished doctoral thesis (Cambridge, 1956), 327; id., 'Anglican Evangelicals'. Interdenominational co-operation among evangelicals is discussed in Roger H. Martin, *Evangelicals United* (1983).

[60] Haddon Willmer, 'Evangelicalism, 1785–1835', unpublished Hulsean Prize Essay (Cambridge, 1962), 20.

'Gospel' was used as an adjective. None the less, the way that these and other terms ('awakened', 'serious', 'spiritual', etc.) were used by Newton and his acquaintances suggests that implicit criteria of belief and experience existed for identifying who was, and who was not, 'evangelical'. When Newton thanked Thomas Haweis for the addition that he had made to his list of 'awakened Clergy', or asked him for an account of all the new clergy who had been awakened since 1760, he was not troubled that the identity of those who were thus awakened should be in any doubt.

Different evangelicals provided different lists of beliefs essential to the gospel. Newton summed up his understanding of the gospel in a letter to Francis Okely, shortly after Okely had visited Liverpool with Wesley in 1759 (i. 618–22). It was a first letter inviting Okely to correspond with him on an ongoing basis. Newton explained that he had a wide acquaintance with truly spiritual persons who yet differed on some minor matters. This called forth an exposition of what Newton regarded as the essential points contained in the gospel. All men are by nature sinners, utterly unable to do as God commands and subject to his wrath. Jesus Christ made a propitiation for sin by his death and perfect obedience, and he is now exalted to give repentance and forgiveness to all that believe. The Holy Spirit is the only guide into all truth and through the influence of Scripture makes believers wise unto salvation and equips them for good works. Love of God and man is the essence of religion and of the law. Without holiness no one shall see God, but eternal life awaits those who persevere in well-doing though this reward is not of debt but of grace. This was Newton's creed. He chiefly emphasized human depravity, Christ's atonement, and sanctification by the Spirit and the Word—themes which likewise provided the principal subjects of the six specimen sermons he published in 1760. John Wesley offered a similar reduced creed of essentials in 1764: original sin, justification by faith, and holiness. These were evangelical basics.

If such beliefs constituted an evangelical in theology, what constituted an evangelical in experience? Although many characteristics could be identified, such as an emphasis upon practical and affective piety, a strong biblicism, and an

insistence upon self-denial and unworldliness, two distinguishing traits occur from this period in Newton's life. First and
foremost, it was necessary that one's belief was real and not
merely nominal—felt in the heart and not simply assented to
by the mind. In this sense, regeneration was normative in a
way that justification was not, for whereas the new birth could
be observed in the conversion of one whose conscience was
demonstrably awakened, and who then subsequently discovered faith though the quickening of the Holy Spirit,
justification was a largely inscrutable divine activity.[61] It was
here that Newton's conversion narrative played such a
significant role in his rise to prominence among evangelicals
in the years leading up to his ordination. His narrative
identified him clearly as having had an authentic evangelical
religious experience. But secondly, and particularly as a
matter of clerical concern, there was a distinctive evangelical
homiletic, characterized by a stress on the popular preaching
of a supernaturally revealed gospel. It was to be popular
because it was for all. Newton wrote emphatically in his diary
what was the common commitment of most evangelical
ministers: 'I resolve to express plain propositions in plain
words.' Although not all of the preachers with whom Newton
associated spoke extempore, their ideal was to attain much
more to the liveliness of Whitefield in the pulpit than to the
reputed dullness of James Hervey (whom Thomas Haweis
described as 'uncommonly whining'). An evangelical sermon
was certainly recognized as such for its theology, but Newton
was also quick to criticize a sermon as non-evangelical in its
style, particularly any sermon which seemed simply a show of
refined eloquence for polite auditors. A 'florid declamation,'
mere 'Ciceronian divinity', he would describe it in his diary.

How then did Newton recognize other evangelical ministers?
Chiefly, it seems, it was through their common belief in a
simple but supernatural gospel, their common experience of
climactic conversion, and their common commitment to a

---

[61] Even those, like Wesley, who fused justification and assurance ('I want that
faith which none can have without knowing that he hath it') and who could therefore
use the terms interchangeably, emphasized, by that very fusion, the importance of
real versus nominal belief.

style of preaching aimed at 'awakening' sinners to their need of the gospel. This basis for corporate identity would be strengthened in the nineteenth-century as evangelicals came to distinguish themselves sharply from Tractarians. But during the period of Newton's ordination crisis, they chose much more so to distinguish themselves from 'nominal' believers and 'time-serving' clerics. This polarization could very easily turn evangelical *esprit de corps* into something which appeared to threaten, or at least to be obnoxious to, established ecclesiastical authority and practice. Newton was more conservative than some evangelicals, whom even he charged with 'enthusiasm' and 'irregularity', but if these accusations appeared between evangelicals, it is little wonder that they recurred from the mouths of bishops when Newton sought ordination in the Church of England. Cheshire, York, and Lincoln were the three largest dioceses in England. The bishops of these dioceses had to rely on the uncertain testimony of unknown individuals to determine Newton's suitability. Once he was tainted with the charge of 'enthusiasm', from whatever source, it is not surprising that it took the influence of Lord Dartmouth to have him finally admitted to holy orders and settled upon a curacy.

4

'We need not be more consistent than the inspired writers'
The Defining of Newton's Evangelical Theology

Then, Sir, with your leave I will put up my dagger again; for this is all my Calvinism.

Charles Simeon

THE Calvinism to which Newton acceded in the 1750s continued in the 1760s and 1770s to be more clearly defined through his interaction with individuals from across a spectrum of Christian belief. It remains, therefore, to ask what precisely Newton came to believe as a Calvinist, how this compared with the beliefs of his contemporaries, and the extent to which his convictions shifted over the following years.

Because of the occasional nature of most of his writings and his dislike for controversy, his Calvinism does not distil easily or systematically from his writings. Newton's theology may be brought into sharper relief, however, by viewing it against the backdrop of two contemporary religious controversies in which he played a small but significant role. The first controversy relates to the perfectionist outbreaks among the followers of Wesley during the years 1758–63; the second, to the presence of high Calvinism in Particular Baptist circles in Northamptonshire during the 1770s. These disputes tested Newton's beliefs and brought to the fore those convictions which were of central importance to him. Wesley's stress upon general redemption and entire sanctification appeared to Newton to give too much scope to human initiative in salvation, establishing the limits of his theology in an Arminian direction. Conversely, the heightened emphasis of John Gill and John Brine upon predestination, and hence upon divine initiative in salvation, seemed to him to constrain evangelism and pulpit exhortation too severely, fixing the boundary of his theology in a high Calvinist direction. Newton once remarked significantly to Richard Cecil, 'I find I am considered as an Arminian among the high Calvinists, and as a Calvinist among the strenuous Arminians.'[1] He was not disturbed to be regarded in this way, however, for the balance between predestinarian grace and evangelical piety was one which he sought to maintain throughout his ministry and in his writings.

THE ANGLO-CALVINIST INHERITANCE

Before discussing Newton's theology in its contemporary context, it will be useful to survey briefly the broad tradition of English evangelical theology to which he was heir. The history of Reformed theology in England since the sixteenth century had been one of vigorous debate, and several distinct theological positions within the wider tradition were mapped out and defended. Newton's immediate theological inheritance in the Calvinistic orthodoxy of Old Dissent and the resurgent Calvinism of the Evangelical Revival reflected the embattled past of a theological movement which had struggled from the outset to contain internal tensions. Consequently, few of the theological issues which surfaced among evangelicals during Newton's lifetime were new.

Dewey Wallace has traced the vicissitudes of the doctrine of predestinarian grace in English theology from 1525 to 1695 in his study *Puritans and Predestination* (1982). He argues that a pattern of theology based upon a Swiss Reformed order of salvation was the outlook of England's earliest Protestant reformers and set the basic shape of almost all English Protestant theology during the Elizabethan period and well beyond. This pattern was significantly, if variously, refined as it was defended against sectarian and Roman Catholic opponents, expounded by Puritans in highly personal terms focusing on assurance, and hardened by university theologians into a more rigid scholasticism. The bitter Arminian controversies of the Jacobean and Caroline church and the

---

[1] Cecil, *Newton*, 227–8.

Antinomian movement of the Interregnum stimulated the division of Calvinists into parties whose theological differences figured largely in the self-definition of Dissenting groups late in the seventeenth century.

Peter Toon has followed the fortunes of predestinarian theology among Dissenters into the eighteenth century in his study, *The Emergence of Hyper-Calvinism* (1967). The Westminster Confession of 1647—shaped by the scholastic elaboration of Calvinism in the late sixteenth century, the articulation of the Federal theology by the Rhineland reformers during the same period, and the polemics of the Synod of Dort in 1619—continued in various forms to represent Calvinistic orthodoxy for most Independents and Particular Baptists and for many Presbyterians at the end of the seventeenth century. Baxterian Neonomianism, popular among Presbyterians after the Great Ejection and among Independents after 1700, drew on the hypothetical universalism of the Amyraldian school in France and moved away from the doctrine of a limited atonement affirmed at Dort. A fully Arminian position, which based election upon God's prescience, had been owned historically by the General Baptists but was increasingly accepted by other individual pastors and congregations as the eighteenth century unfolded. The advocates of strict Reformed orthodoxy pointed to a slippery slope from Neonomianism through Arminianism to Arianism, Socinianism, Unitarianism, and finally to complete infidelity. But as the orthodox faced these factions to the left, they were just as often forced to fight their own rearguard action against those who took the doctrine of sovereign grace to unwonted extremes to the right. Seeking to exalt God's grace, but sharply proscribing human agency, some of these 'high Calvinists' elaborated a doctrinal antinomianism which owed much to the republication of the works of Tobias Crisp in 1690. Among Particular Baptists and Independents were others in later years who followed the logic of predestination even further, to the point of denying the validity of the free offer of the gospel and saying that unbelievers did not have a duty to believe and repent. They marked out an extreme that in the nineteenth century would be described as hyper-Calvinist.

With the remarkable conversions and field-preaching of the 1730s and 1740s that signalled the beginning of Methodism, the Arminian–Calvinist debate was given new life within the matrix of the Evangelical Revival. Allan Coppedge has outlined three main phases.[2] First was the Free Grace controversy of 1739–41 in which, both privately and publicly, Wesley opposed and Whitefield defended the doctrine of predestination. Then followed an interim period, 1745–70, during which Wesley continued to write against predestination but maintained ties of friendship and co-operation with Whitefield and many other Calvinists. At the same time, however, he engaged in controversy over imputed righteousness with James Hervey, and over necessity and free-will with Augustus Toplady. Finally, the Minute controversy broke out after the publication of the proceedings of the Methodist Conference in 1770, when it was discovered that Wesley had made remarks which sounded as though he were advocating works-righteousness. John Fletcher was Wesley's chief literary defender in the ensuing dispute with Richard and Rowland Hill and Augustus Toplady over the place of human works in the economy of God's grace, a dispute in which the Arminians were charged with legalism and the Calvinists with antinomianism.

Among avowed Calvinists themselves in the mid-century there were variations which followed older lines of debate. Andrew Fuller, the leading Baptist theologian in the last half of the eighteenth century, identified three recurring types that he described as the *high*, the *moderate*, and the *strict* Calvinists. The first were 'more Calvinistic that Calvin himself; in other words, bordering on Antinomianism'; these he sometimes also called false Calvinists. The second were 'half Arminian, or, as they are called with us, Baxterians'. The last, in which category Fuller included himself, were those who really held 'the system of Calvin'.[3] Fuller sometimes also called himself an evangelical Calvinist. The terminology here is important for in the current secondary literature many of Fuller's

---

[2] 'John Wesley and the Doctrine of Predestination', unpublished doctoral thesis (Cambridge, 1976).

[3] John Ryland, Jun., *Life and Death of the Reverend Andrew Fuller* (1816), 566–7.

descriptive terms are used somewhat differently. What Fuller called 'high Calvinism' has come to be referred to as 'hyper-Calvinism', whereas 'high Calvinism' is used either to describe the confessional orthodoxy of the seventeenth century or the supralapsarian scheme of Theodore Beza, reproduced in England by William Perkins. In the discussion which follows, 'high Calvinism' is used in the eighteenth-century sense employed by Newton after the manner of Fuller above. Likewise Fuller's designation of 'moderate Calvinist' has been given a wider application in current scholarly discussion, not only to refer to Baxter's mediating theological position of hypothetical universalism, but also to describe individual Calvinists who took a conciliatory approach to theology, such as Bishop Hall at the time of the Dortian controversy. In this sense various eighteenth-century evangelicals whose Calvinism was unsystematic and subordinated to the preaching of the gospel are sometimes described as 'moderate Calvinists', though they may have disavowed Baxter's position on the atonement. Here it is important, therefore, to distinguish between a moderate tone and the moderation of a substantial theological position. In this chapter the latter kind of 'moderate Calvinism' is referred to as either hypothetical universalism or Baxterianism. Despite the equivocal application in modern scholarship of some of Fuller's terms, the categories themselves which he outlined remain useful as descriptions of distinctions in Calvinistic belief among Newton's contemporaries.

The Table below summarizes English evangelical theology in the mid-eighteenth century, distinguishing four positions along a spectrum ranging from a relative emphasis upon human agency (Evangelical Arminianism) to a relative emphasis upon divine agency (High Calvinism) in salvation. It should be stressed that these positions are presented more as functional types than as absolute categories. Despite their obvious association with certain contemporary figures—for example, Evangelical Arminianism with John Wesley, Hypothetical Universalism with Philip Doddridge, Strict Calvinism with Andrew Fuller, High Calvinism with John Gill—it is not suggested that these types can be applied narrowly to any one theologian without falsifying his thought through over-

TABLE: *English evangelical theology during the mid-eighteenth century*

Distinct theological positions maintained during the Evangelical Revival:

Evangelical Arminianism	Hypothetical Universalism
Election is conditional, based upon God's prescience; divine grace may be resisted	Election is unconditional, based upon God's secret will; divine grace is irresistible
Unlimited, universal atonement	Atonement unlimited in provision but limited in application; sufficient for all but efficient only for the elect
Justification based upon faith which is both volitional (active) and fiducial (passive); Christ's righteousness both imputed and imparted to the believer	Justification based upon faith and repentance conceived as obedience to a 'new law' made by God by virtue of Christ's death and satisfying the demands of his government
Final salvation contingent upon sustained faith and co-operation with divine sanctifying grace	Final perseverance a corollary of election, but sanctification necessary and guided by the law
Free offer of gospel based upon universal atonement for every person, original sin and disability having been removed by common grace	Free offer of gospel based upon universal atonement
Charged by Calvinists with legalism and Pelagianism	Charged by stricter Calvinists as being inconsistent and half-Arminian

simplification. The positions outlined here form only a provisional taxonomy of evangelical theology in the period.

It is evident, however, that the Calvinism which had first been refracted into a wide spectrum of partisan theologies in the polemics of the mid-seventeenth century was reconstituted

Strict Calvinism	High Calvinism
Election is unconditional, based on sublapsarian scheme of divine decrees; divine grace is irresistible	Election is unconditional, based on supralapsarian scheme of divine decrees; divine grace is irresistible
Limited, particular atonement	Limited, particular atonement
Justification based solely upon faith which is fiducial (passive) and Christ's righteousness imputed not imparted to believers	Eternal justification; Christ's righteousness imputed to the elect from eternity, before the actual exercise of faith
Final perseverance a corollary of election, but sanctification necessary and guided by the law	Final perseverance a corollary of election, doctrinal antinomianism sometimes implied
Free offer of gospel based upon general sufficiency of Christ's death for sinners whose duty it is to believe	Free offer of gospel constrained or even repudiated; faith is not properly the duty of unbelievers
Charged by Arminians as holding doctrines which imply high Calvinist conclusions	Charged by Arminians and other Calvinists as Antinomians

in a similar complexity under the conditions of Nonconformity and the Evangelical Revival in the eighteenth century. And it is the amorphous nature of this Anglo-Calvinist tradition that raises the question of the precise character of Newton's theology.

JOHN NEWTON, JOHN WESLEY, AND PERFECTIONISM

It is not surprising that Newton was a little wary of Wesley when he first made his acquaintance at Liverpool in the spring of 1757. While Newton had read some of Wesley's writings earlier, he had before meeting Wesley moved largely among Calvinistic Dissenters and the followers of Whitefield. Moreover, what impression he had received of Wesley's followers had not been positive. After removing to Liverpool from London in 1755, just missing Wesley's first recorded visit to the town, he discovered that Wesley's followers there were a despised people who met in the dirty part of town. Although they had just put up their own building, those attending services had to walk across a pool of water on stepping-stones to get to the door. One resident preacher a little later described the house as being located 'neither in hell nor purgatory, yet in a place of torment'.[4] The people themselves even Wesley described on one occasion as being like 'wild asses' colts'.[5] When a Mr M———y ('one of the chief of Mr Wesley's people') visited Newton at home, Newton confessed in his diary to having to get over his 'pride, prejudice and bigotry' to receive him freely as a follower of the Lord.[6] As noted earlier, Newton's in-laws worried that their daughter would be left keeping company with 'washerwomen' because of the contacts he kept up with Methodists and Baptists. Although Newton frequently attended the Methodist meeting early on Sunday mornings and often found his heart warmed by the proceedings, he was just as often disappointed in the 'confused' and 'rambling' discourses of the preachers. He wrote to Whitefield in 1756, begging him to return to Liverpool, saying of Wesley's chapel,

I have been quite pained & ashamed to see what empty ignorant pretenders have undertaken to speak to the people in the name of God at that place. . . . I think I have heard you say, you were cautious of introducing a division amongst the Methodists, but I beg you to consider who they are that bear that name amongst us, very

---

[4] Parkinson, 'Notes on Methodism in Liverpool [part 1]', *PWHS* (1898), 107–8.
[5] *JWJ* iv. 312.
[6] Diary (1751–6), 9 May 1756.

few in number, low for the most part in experience, still lower in knowledge, & chiefly distinguished by an imprudent & bigoted zeal & as they go on, there is no likelihood of their being either more numerous, or more exemplary; & shall 30 or 40 such, keep out an opportunity of declaring the grace of God to thousands?[7]

Newton also complained that the preachers sent by Wesley emphasized controversial points of doctrine. This feeling must have been reinforced when James Scofield, one of the lay preachers whom Newton heard on several occasions, later caused the first division in the Liverpool Methodist society and was expelled from the Manchester Round in 1757.[8]

When Newton finally met Wesley in 1757, however, his prejudices were almost immediately removed and they struck up a warm acquaintance. Wesley made Liverpool a regular part of his annual itinerancy, usually visiting for at least a few days each spring. In 1758 Newton requested that they might exchange letters occasionally as a means of strengthening his faith. Twenty-two years Wesley's junior and still new to evangelicalism, Newton wrote to Wesley with deference, and Wesley later remarked that Newton had at this time accounted him a 'father and a brother'. Despite acknowledged differences of theological opinion between them, this was the golden period of their relationship. That Wesley even asked Newton to become one of his itinerant preachers demonstrates this mutual regard.

Yet Newton's diary and letters reveal that he continued to harbour some doubts about Wesley and his followers. Sometime around 1762 Newton dropped his correspondence with Wesley entirely. Because Wesley did not visit Liverpool in 1763, and Newton moved to Olney in 1764, they had no further contact until Wesley broke the silence by writing to Newton in April 1765. A brief correspondence ensued of three or four letters each, in which they disputed several points upon which they differed. After 1766 there is record of very little further contact between them.[9] While the tone of their

[7] Newton to George Whitefield, 2 Jan. 1756, ALS, LPL; cf. Bull, *Newton*, 82–4.
[8] Parkinson, 'Methodism in Liverpool [part 2]', 67–8.
[9] For the relationship between Newton and Wesley, see further, Bull, *Newton*, 92–110, 146–7; *AM* (1780), 390–1, 441–4, and *AM* (1797), 355–7; *JWL* iv. 292–3,

letters during this dispute remained cordial, Newton's estrangement from Wesley and his followers was reflected in a letter to a friend at Hull in 1766. Newton remarked that while Wesley was not an enemy to the gospel and had sincere aims, he was 'very dark with respect to some of its glorious truths'. Newton continued, 'I account it a part of the happiness of my present situation that Mr Wesley has no society here [at Olney], nor for half a score miles round me.'[10]

The Epistolary Dispute and Its Background

The ostensible occasion of Wesley's first letter to Newton on 9 April 1765 was that he had just read the *Authentic Narrative* and wanted to write to encourage Newton that he saw it as remarkable proof of God's saving power. Wesley added that the calm and dispassionate way in which Newton spoke of Particular Redemption in the book should not offend reasonable men. In later years Newton claimed that Wesley, upon reading the *Authentic Narrative*, said that he did not wonder but that he should become a Calvinist himself.[11] This claim is hard to reconcile with the evidence of Wesley's letter, for after his opening remarks about Newton's narrative, he quickly turned to his primary reason for writing. Wesley accused Newton of having dropped their relationship because of the hideous portrait drawn of him in James Hervey's posthumous *Letters* (1765); he complained that Newton was afraid still to own him as his friend; and he suggested that Newton had fallen from his previous ideal of allowing others latitude in expression when it was plain they believed in Christ and strove after holiness. 'O beware of bigotry!' he urged Newton. Wesley asked Newton to disarm his friends against Wesley's teachings, even as he would seek to soften his own friends towards Newton's opinions. What if he were a Papist after all,

---

296–300; v. 4–6, 7–8. Of particular interest is the letter, Newton to John Wesley, 16 Apr. 1765, ALS, Southern Methodist University, Dallas, Texas. I am indebted to Prof. Frank Baker for his help locating this letter, which will appear in the forthcoming vol. xxviii of the *Bicentennial Edition of the Works of John Wesley*.

[10] *Letters* (Jones), 75.

[11] John Ryland, Jun., 'Remarks on the *Quarterly Review*, for April 1824, Relative to the Memoirs of Scott and Newton', in *Pastoral Memorials of the Rev. John Ryland*, 2 vols. (1826), ii. 352.

as Hervey's *Letters* alleged? Surely they could still unite on the one point of faith working by love?[12]

Newton responded seven days later saying that he still held Wesley in high regard and assuring him of his friendship. The reason for the interruption in their correspondence was, he wrote, that 'some things that had happened after I saw you last embarrassed me'. Newton added, 'I knew not how to write without either baulking the freedom of my own spirit, or assuming a part which from *Me* to *You*, I thought would appear Unbecoming & forward.'[13] He felt caught between, on the one hand, not wanting his letter-writing to be constrained because of unacknowledged grievances, and, on the other, not wanting to seem presumptuous by raising objections against a senior evangelical leader. But in the face of Wesley's accusations, Newton took the occasion to defend his Calvinistic principles and criticize Wesley's teaching at a number of points. This unpublished letter is crucial for reconstructing their relationship. Before examining the text of the letter, however, it is worth asking what were the unidentified 'some things' mentioned by Newton that had troubled him enough to cause him abruptly to drop his association with Wesley in 1762.

(*a*) *The occasion of their initial estrangement.* The last time Newton and Wesley had met was in 1761 on Wesley's annual visit to Liverpool. On at least one occasion during that nine-day visit Newton heard Wesley preach on perfection. He wrote in his diary of Wesley's doctrine that he would rather press towards it than dispute against it, though he still expected to be saved in the end as a sinner and not a saint. It seems that when Wesley left the town their relations were still cordial in every way. It was therefore sometime after this, during the period from April 1761 to April 1765, that 'some things' occurred to embarrass Newton. Their correspondence suggests three possibilities.

The first occurs from the charge made by Wesley that Hervey's *Letters* had alienated Newton from him. Hervey and Wesley had quarrelled over the former's *Theron and Aspasio* (1755), which included a strong emphasis upon 'imputed

---

[12] *JWL* iv. 292–3.   [13] Newton to Wesley, 16 Apr. 1765.

righteousness'. Wesley published in 1758 the text of a private letter that he had written to Hervey on the subject.[14] Then *Eleven Letters From the Late Rev. Mr. Hervey, to the Rev. Mr. John Wesley; Containing An Answer to That Gentleman's Remarks Upon Theron and Aspasio* (1765) was published after Hervey's death, containing sharp criticism of Wesley's views, his character, and his lack of theological consistency. Although Newton sympathized with Hervey, he denied that the *Letters* had in any way altered his theology or poisoned his attitude towards Wesley. Hervey's book could not in any case have accounted for the previous three or four years' silence between Newton and Wesley. Primarily, Wesley's accusation demonstrates his larger fear that the rift between himself and the evangelical clergy, based upon their theological differences, would be further widened by the controversy stirred up by the *Letters*.[15]

Another possible explanation of Newton's silence is offered by his increased involvement, during the period he was seeking ordination, with a circle of ex-Methodist, Calvinistic Independents near Liverpool. Through this circle Newton would have heard stories alleging that Wesley treated his preachers harshly when they took up predestinarian doctrines. For example, John Bennet, John Whitford, and John Edwards were all erstwhile followers of Wesley from the North-West who had seceded from his connexion in the early 1750s after they took up Calvinism. Their cases would have been well-known to Newton.[16]

That Newton was increasingly drawn into this group during his residence at Liverpool, while at the same time becoming acquainted with other Independent and Anglican Calvinists, must have contributed to the 'embarrassment' which led him to drop his correspondence with Wesley sometime after 1761. This was at least the context for Newton's accusing question to Wesley in 1765: 'How many of your best preachers have been thrust out & branded, because their consciences have compelled them to dissent with you in

---

[14] *JWL* iii. 371–88.

[15] See further, Coppedge, 'Wesley and Predestination', 155–70.

[16] See further, Rack, 'Survival and Revival'; and Parkinson, 'Methodism in Liverpool [parts 1 and 2]'.

these particulars [Particular Election and Final Persever-ance]?'[17] Newton may well have been thinking here of Bennet, Whitford, and Edwards. Newton's friendship with these men accounts more, however, for the way his attitude toward Wesley progressively hardened, than it supplies a specific occasion for Newton's abrupt silence, because the secessions of Bennet, Whitford, and Edwards occurred more than six years before the rupture with Wesley. The secessions can therefore only form part of the background to their estrange-ment. Newton's choice of words ('some things that happened after I saw you last embarrassed me') argues for something more recent and pointed. The most plausible explanation of what 'happened' relates rather to the perfectionism outbreaks among Wesley's Methodists in 1758–63.

One of the most spectacular outbreaks took place at Liverpool in the summer of 1762. Wesley recorded in his *Journal* for Wednesday, 4 August,

> I rode to Liverpool, where also was such a work of God as had never been known there before. . . . This, I found, had begun here likewise [as at Congleton in Cheshire] in the latter end of March, and from that time it had continually increased till a little before I came. Nine were justified in one hour. The next morning I spoke severally with those who believed they were sanctified. They were fifty-one in all.[18]

Wesley was informed two days later of 'the flame which had broken out at Bolton' among his people there. It was reported that seven had been justified, and six sanctified, at one meeting; that several at both places had been justified and sanctified together within the space of a few days; and that some others had been wrought upon in three minutes or less. Because this was going on at the same time that Newton was helping with the Independent congregation at Bolton, he would have been exposed to the outbreak both here and at Liverpool. He had long objected to Wesley's doctrine of instantaneous and entire sanctification but had subordinated his concerns in the interests of unity. Here, however, was the phenomenon itself occurring with dramatic effect among the poor and despised people about whom he had already

---

[17] Newton to Wesley, 16 Apr. 1765. [18] *JWJ* iv. 523.

entertained some doubts. Would he be able to continue to associate with them? This must surely have been the breaking point for Newton. The timing of the outbreak certainly coincides with the opening of the rift between him and Wesley.

In a letter to John Thornton in 1775 Newton recalled a Liverpool Methodist preacher as having been 'one of the most disagreeable persons I ever met with among professors': 'He . . . pretended to Sinless perfection, and supposing he ought to make good his claim by something extraordinary, he manifested the most disgusting affectation, labouring to set himself off in everything he did or said.'[19] No doubt Newton had also heard of the notorious millenarian and antinomian excesses which followed on the perfectionist preaching of Thomas Maxfield and George Bell at Wesley's Foundery society in 1762–3. The latter had caused a particular scandal with his prophecy that the world would end on 28 February 1763. Even after this date passed, the Maxfield–Bell crisis did not abate, and eventually it created another schism in Methodism. That Wesley was forced to give it his extended attention in 1763 accounts largely for his failure to visit Liverpool during that year. Although Wesley disassociated himself from the excesses of Maxfield and Bell, it was thought by many to show exactly where Wesley's teaching about perfection would end. Stephen Gunter writes, 'Many held John Wesley indirectly responsible; he had moved entirely too slowly in controlling the situation. Why? . . . Was Wesley sufficiently inclined towards enthusiasm to allow perfectionist claims to continue, so long as they did not go to 'unreasonable lengths'—such as absurdly predicting the end of the world?'[20] These sort of excesses go far towards explaining why in 1765 Newton wrote to Wesley that the main point between them was indeed perfection. Newton's growing confidence in Calvinism and his increasing association with ex-Methodist, Calvinistic Independents were the tinder to which the perfectionism revival set the spark.

(b) *Newton's letter of 16 April 1765.* While the perfectionism

---

[19] Newton to John Thornton, 29 Apr. 1775, ALS, CUL.
[20] *Limits of 'Love Divine'* (Nashville, 1989), 221.

outbreaks at Liverpool are the most plausible explanation of what occurred to cause Newton to drop his correspondence with Wesley in 1762, Newton's reply to Wesley's opening salvo in the 1765 correspondence demonstrates that there were significant underlying objections to Wesley's theology.

Wesley's letter had revolved around the principle, upon which he said their friendship was founded, that if a person believed in Christ and lived suitably to his profession, latitude ought to be allowed in matters of mere opinion. Assuming that Hervey's *Letters* had made Newton afraid of him, Wesley strove to win him back to this principle. Newton therefore prefaced his return letter by reviewing the development of his own beliefs, saying,

> When I first had the pleasure of seeing you, I had embraced the Calvinist principles (so called) & I have seen no sufficient reason since, to discard them. [Thus] far I am the same. Yet I hope the interval of 7 years has not been wholly lost, I think my judgment is something more enlarged & established by experience & observation [and] indeed I find by looking back, that I have altered my sentiments upon several points of a secondary importance.[21]

He added that one of the things that had changed was his position on the very issue raised by Wesley of opinions versus essential beliefs. Newton had come to believe that he ought not to reduce to the status of an indifferent opinion *any* truth revealed in Scripture, because while views may differ about a truth, that truth may itself still be highly significant. The context makes clear that Newton was thinking here of predestination, for this was a doctrine which he had come to believe was foundational to Christian experience, even when notionally rejected by a believer. For Newton, Particular Redemption was not therefore a mere opinion as Wesley had implied in his letter.

Turning the tables, Newton accused Wesley and his preachers of stressing precisely those matters which Wesley had previously identified as opinions. Newton made three charges: Wesley opposed election and perseverance, he emphasized perfection over repentance, and he elevated

---

[21] Newton to Wesley, 16 Apr. 1765.

Church over Chapel even in places where the gospel was preached only by Dissenters. Moreover, Newton noted that the pacific tone in Wesley's letter to him was conspicuously absent in Wesley's previous dealings with Hervey, who had just as certainly been a believer living agreeably to his profession. Surely, Newton remonstrated, the liberality in opinions that Wesley advocated could have prevented the whole acrimonious dispute which had followed in that case. Added Newton, 'Many of y[ou]r hearty friends as well as myself were grieved that you should break in such [a] manner with such a man.'[22]

Newton then proceeded to the heart of his objections. He did not really think that Hervey believed Wesley a Papist. Even so, it was readily apparent to Newton that Wesley had receded in some things from the doctrine of the Protestant divines on justification by faith. He acknowledged that Wesley despised the 'system of popery' as much as himself, but still, he stated plainly, 'I believe a difference of apprehension wth. regard to what Luther calls *Articulus stantis vel cadentis Ecclesiae*, is at the bottom of our differences.'[23] Newton was prepared to leave Methodists to their Arminian views, letting God and their own experience change their minds in due course. 'But with respect to the tenet of Perfection,' he wrote,

I confess I am not so indifferent. I should think it my duty to oppose it (if it had any prevalence in these parts) with my whole strength, not as an opinion, but as a dangerous mistake, which appears to me subversive of the very foundations of Christian experience—& which has in fact given occasion to the most grievous offences, & the wildest sallies of Enthusiasm.[24]

Having voiced his objections, Newton concluded the letter with cordial best wishes and the hope that he and Wesley would not need to exchange any more letters in this strain.

(*c*) *The aftermath.* Wesley responded on 14 May and treated the issues raised by Newton one by one. He claimed that he did not oppose those who held to Particular Election, that he did not discriminate against Dissenters, and that he believed

---

[22] Newton to Wesley, 16 Apr. 1765.   [23] Ibid.   [24] Ibid.

on justification 'just as I have done any time these seven-and-twenty years, and just as Mr. Calvin does'.[25] He acknowledged that their main dispute was over perfection, but stressed that he had once thought it his duty to oppose predestination just as Newton now felt it his to counter perfection. For his own part, however, he had come to recognize authentic Christian experience in those who were predestinarians and to accept that he was a bigot to remain implacably opposed to such men. 'I leave *you*,' he said to Newton, 'in your calm and retired moments to make the application.'[26] He then went on to describe how he had arrived at his views on perfection. Newton and Wesley exchanged at least two more letters after this, but only Wesley's survive. From these it is apparent that they continued to debate their views on imputed righteousness and sanctification, Wesley concluding that they differed chiefly in their expressions—Newton's expressions being a little less plain and scriptural than his.

Sometime in 1766 their correspondence lapsed once again, never to be revived. The perfectionism controversy had occasioned Newton's estrangement from Wesley, but several further factors maintained the distance between them. With Newton's move to Olney in 1764 he was no longer on one of Wesley's regular circuits and so was removed from routine contact with the evangelist. Charged with a cure of souls, Newton did not in any case want to appear to condone Wesley's teaching through continued co-operation, since there would now be wider pastoral implications of his friendship with Wesley. Wesley, for his part, gave up on most of the evangelical clergy after his circular of 1766, inviting their general co-operation, was overwhelmingly ignored. Famously, he said that they were no more than a 'rope of sand'. As a result, there was little further effort on Wesley's side to sustain an intimacy with regular clergymen such as Newton. Finally, the Minutes controversy of the 1770s revived smouldering resentments which remained from previous Calvinistic controversies and confirmed for all sides the futility of thinking of *rapprochement* or co-operation.

<hr>

[25] *JWL* iv. 298.   [26] Ibid.

Summary: Perfectionism and Newton's Calvinistic Theology

Newton and Wesley had long differed over predestination, the extent of the atonement, and the indefectibility of grace without finding these issues necessarily a rock of offence between them. The earlier Free Grace controversy between Wesley and Whitefield was some seventeen years old by the time Newton first met Wesley, and the strife caused by their dispute had by 1757 significantly abated. Wesley's practical concern had been that the doctrine of 'Particular Redemption' hindered evangelism and encouraged antinomian libertinism; Whitefield's concern had been that the doctrine of 'General Redemption' derogated from God's sovereignty and made salvation to depend on man's free-will. But though the Methodist movement had split over the controversy, there were still many cases of mutual affection and amicable relations between individuals of opposing views. Just so did Whitefield and Wesley continue for many years, despite the expressions of mutual distrust which occasionally found their way into private letters. If in the 1770s Toplady and Fletcher would pick up the cudgels once again, Whitefield and Wesley had earlier declared a truce. It was in this hiatus in the Calvinist–Arminian dispute that Newton was himself converted and introduced to evangelicalism. Thus, because he had not been party to the contention of the 1740s, he was able under the very different conditions of the late 1750s happily to co-operate with Wesley even while being most closely allied to Whitefield in doctrine.

That in 1765 Newton felt he needed to defend predestination to Wesley illustrates the way that perfectionism exacerbated Calvinist–Arminian tensions which had until 1762 remained, however uneasily, suppressed. Wesley's Arminianism was already suspect; perfection appeared as a further 'Arminian Delusion.'[27] With the outbreak of claims to entire sanctification, Newton worried, along with other evangelicals, that Wesley's theology was in danger of compromising the Reformation theology which stood at the heart of the Revival.

[27] Phrase from William Parker, *A Letter to the Rev. Mr. John Wesley, Concerning his Inconsistency with Himself* (1766), 22, quoted in Gunter, *Limits of 'Love Divine'*, 41.

Under the impetus of the perfectionism revival Wesley was gradually revising his theology to integrate more completely several strands from his own religious experience: the Protestant teaching of justification by grace through faith, the Moravian emphasis upon an instantaneous work of justification including assurance, and his long-standing High Church concern for holiness. Whereas during the period immediately following his Aldersgate experience he represented justification as marking a dramatic break with the past, during the 1760s he came increasingly to emphasize its role as simply a means to the end of holiness.[28] The locus of his theology had demonstrably shifted. Stephen Gunter argues that Wesley during these years felt his way to an enlarged concept of faith as *fides caritatem formata*, a formula which avoided fideism and antinomianism, included rational assent, affirmed personal inward certainty, maintained the priority of faith in the *ordo*, and sustained a strong experiential focus.[29] The so-called Catholic–Protestant synthesis of the ethic of grace with the ethic of holiness, and the expectation of two discrete stages of Christian experience, each initiated by an instantaneous work of grace, were emerging as distinctive Methodist doctrines.

Many evangelicals grew worried that these doctrines defined an alien sort of piety. Wesley's stress upon conduct (especially after the 1770 conference, but already in the 1760s) raised the spectre of popery and Pelagianism; his emphasis upon the attainability of instant perfection conjured up images of wild sectarian enthusiasm. Perfectionism was disputed between Wesley and Henry Venn just as it was between him and Newton. William Grimshaw stayed away from the conference at Leeds in 1761 because of perfectionism and was reconciled to the connexion only by the personal attentions of Wesley. When many were claiming perfection, Grimshaw wrote, 'I wish they know [*sic*] their own Hearts. My perfection is to see my own Imperfection. . . . I know no other, expecting to lay down my Life and my Sword

---

[28] On Wesley's theology, see H. D. Rack, *Reasonable Enthusiast: John Wesley and the Rise of Methodism* (1989), 381–409.
[29] Gunter, *Limits of 'Love Divine'*, 270–6.

together.'[30] William Romaine put it even more forcefully: 'A perfection out of Christ, call it grace, and say it is grace from him, yet with me it is all rank pride and damnable sin.'[31]

Why the notion of entire sanctification should so disturb Newton and other Calvinistic clergy is not at first clear. Did not Calvinists hold that believers would be made perfect at death by an act of God's grace destroying the remnants of indwelling sin? If then, why not sooner? And how Pelagian was Wesley if he was teaching that one could be sanctified by *faith*? It is not necessary to pursue the dispute through its entire course to see why perfectionism provoked the immediate opposition of the Calvinists. Key belligerents aside, many of the clergy were in large measure mollified by Wesley's careful rhetoric when he had personal dealings with them; it was the behaviour of Wesley's followers that set the Calvinists' teeth on edge. The claim to perfection, however hedged about by talk of grace, appeared in many cases to be simply 'enthusiastic' self-righteousness.[32] Romaine complained to Lady Huntingdon that Wesley's societies were all in an uproar of ranting, madness, and delusion. Repudiating perfectionism, he exclaimed, 'Oh! Madam, we should be careful of his glory, and not give it to another, least of all to ourselves.'[33] Here was the point precisely: subtracting from God's glory in salvation by pretending to an immediate revelation of one's own righteousness. That the Calvinist evangelicals had themselves to fend off charges of antinomianism and enthusiasm made them all the more sensitive to these excesses breaking out in the Arminian wing of the movement. But the crucial issue was that the perfectionism outbreaks seemed to give the lie once and for all to Wesley's claim to believe in original sin and justification by faith. Plainly many of the perfected were merely presumptuous; they did not take sin seriously, nor did they continue to feel a need to trust wholly in Christ's merits for their redemption. The whole ethos of Newton's Calvinistic spirituality was just the reverse of this. In his hymn, 'A Sick

[30] Grimshaw to Charles Wesley, Mar. 1760, quoted in F. Baker, *William Grimshaw* (1963), 74.　　[31] Quoted in *LyH* i. 330.
[32] See further on these excesses, Gunter, *Limits of 'Love Divine'*, 202–26.
[33] *LyH* i. 330.

Soul', for example, he used the common metaphor of sin as a consumptive disease to stress the very intractable nature of sin: 'It lies not in a single part, | But thro' my frame is spread' (*OH* 1. 83). Treating such a condition was not, for Newton, a matter of simple, out-patient surgery.

Newton had co-operated with Wesley for at least four years, seeing him as an evangelical who preached justification by grace through faith, but Wesley's Arminianism and his teaching on perfection seemed increasingly to compromise even this most basic evangel. Despite Wesley's avowals to the contrary, the perfectionist revival at Liverpool and Bolton in 1762 had emphatically demonstrated that the theological differences between him and Newton could not be treated any longer as opinions of little consequence. Here a difference in theology manifestly expressed and stimulated an unacceptable difference in piety. The controverted points between Newton and Wesley—predestination, justification, and perfection—reduced in the end to a concern on Newton's part that Wesley collapsed the dialectic in evangelical theology, between divine initiative and human response, unacceptably around the pole of human striving. The estrangement which began in 1762, and was completed in 1765, fixed the limit of Newton's theology in the direction of voluntarism.

Newton's theology was, however, also affected by his period of camaraderie with Wesley and his followers in constructive ways. Wesley's 'empiricism' has often been remarked by historians, since he included experience as a significant source of spiritual truth alongside, though subordinate to, Scripture.[34] Although there were many sources for this emphasis in Newton's own theology (not least the 'experimental divinity' of the Puritan divines and his own reading of John Locke and Jonathan Edwards), the similarity of his theological method to Wesley's is noteworthy. When Newton defended his Calvinism as being 'consonant to scripture, reason (when enlightened), and experience' (vi. 278), he was making a kind of appeal with which Wesley was already familiar.

Once again, Newton took seriously the criticisms of Calvinism made by the Arminian followers of Wesley. Newton

[34] See especially Dreyer, 'Faith and Experience in Wesley', 12–30.

steadfastly opposed doctrinal antinomianism and any reticence about evangelism among his Calvinist brethren. What is less known is that Newton also sought to integrate positive insights from the perfectionism controversy into his own theology. He wrote to Lord Dartmouth in 1772, 'Far, very far, am I from that unscriptural sentiment of sinless perfection in fallen man. . . . there will never be wanting causes of humiliation and self-abasement on the account of sin; yet there is a liberty and privilege attainable by the Gospel, beyond what is ordinarily thought of. Permit me to mention two or three particulars' (i. 419). Newton proceeded to describe, in tones reminiscent of Richard Baxter's *Saints' Everlasting Rest*, the possibilities of a contemplative life in which one is weaned from all earthly attachments, and the awareness of one's sin causes one to turn the more readily to Christ. There was always the danger of Calvinist spirituality slipping into quietism. At its worst there was the temptation (to which Newton gave in not a little) to pour exaggerated abuse on oneself as a way of exalting the power of Christ to save. Romaine's rhetoric could be easily construed this way when he wrote, 'Depend upon it, man cannot be laid too low, nor Christ set too high. I would therefore, always aim, as good brother Grimshaw expresses it, to get the old gentleman down, and keep him down: and then Christ reigns like himself, when he is ALL and man is nothing!'[35] While the determination not to wink at sin and the desire to exalt Christ were admirable, the keeping oneself low could easily lead to low expectations of sanctifying grace altogether. Newton sought to temper such excesses in his Calvinist spirituality by gathering insights from Wesley's doctrine of perfection.[36]

Indebted to Wesley for theological method and constructive criticisms of Calvinism, Newton was also influenced by Wesley's evangelical latitudinarianism.[37] Wesley emphasized, despite their differences, the basis which they had in religious

[35] *LyH* i. 330.
[36] For a description of other ways that Calvinists assimilated insights from Arminians during this period, see Walsh, 'Methodism at the End of the Eighteenth Century', 298–9.
[37] See further, Baker, *John Wesley and the Church of England*, 120–36.

experience for shared Christian communion. He wrote that
though they differed on some things, 'notwithstanding this, we
tasted each other's spirits, and often took sweet counsel
together'.[38] Jean Orcibal comments on Wesley's efforts in this
direction: 'Totally opposed to religious indifference, he was
the exponent of a toleration which was mystical rather than
doctrinal, such as he had seen John Byrom champion from the
time of his youth.'[39] Newton sounded remarkably like this
when he wrote to John Ryland about a disagreement in 1772,
making appeal to their common experience of the thing they
described differently. He said, 'If we hold the *head* and love the
Lord, we *agree* in him, and I should think my time ill employed
in disputing the point with you' (ii. 111). Or, again, when
writing to John Campbell, Newton said, 'I congratulate you
and myself on the progress of what some may call latitudinarianism in Scotland. May we not say with the apostle,
"Grace be with all that love the Lord Jesus Christ in
sincerity?" I think that is a latitudinarian prayer—I hope
many agree in loving him, who sadly disagree about trifles.'[40]
Newton and Wesley could both ground latitude on common
religious experience.

When it came to straightforward discursive theology the
situation was more difficult. Initially Newton was able to treat
his differences with Wesley simply as adiaphora. He was
satisfied with Wesley's distinction between opinions and
essential doctrines. But then the problem came, as always
with this formula, when they could no longer agree over which
principles were essential and which were non-essential. As

---

[38] *JWL* iv. 292.

[39] J. Orcibal, 'The Theological Originality of John Wesley and Continental
Spirituality,' trans. R. J. A. Sharp, in *History of the Methodist Church*, i. 110. Cf. Eamon
Duffy, 'Wesley and the Counter-Reformation', in Garnett and Matthew (eds.),
Revival and Religion, 1–19.

[40] *Letters* (Campbell), 107. After quoting this same verse in correspondence to
Hannah More, Newton added, 'I hope I have attained a little of this Catholic spirit,
and that my high regard for you in particular owes nothing to non-essentials,
concerning which *true Christians may differ* . . . but is founded in a union of heart on the
great points in which all those who are taught of God do, and must agree,' *Memoirs of
the Life and Correspondence of Mrs. Hannah More*, ed. William Roberts, 4 vols., 2nd edn.
(1834), iii. 23.

noted above, by 1765 Newton's convictions about predestination had become more firm, and he refused to think of it as only an opinion. Still, he was able to work out a revised formula of concord that would maintain evangelical solidarity, by saying, 'Though a man does not accord with my view of election, yet if he gives me good evidence, that *he* is *effectually called of God*, he is my brother' (vi. 199).[41] Thus, he reverted to the shared experience of grace. He was not, however, able to work out such a formula for perfectionism.

JOHN NEWTON, JOHN RYLAND, JUN., AND HIGH CALVINISM

Newton had several links with Particular (Calvinistic) Baptists during his curacy at Olney (1764–80). Already in Liverpool he had become well-acquainted with the Baptist ministers Oulton and Johnson, and while at Warwick earlier he had gone to hear Beddome despite the disapproval of his own paedobaptist congregation. Within a month of settling at Olney, he 'set the door of acquaintance wide open' with William Walker, the Baptist minister in town, attending his meeting and dining with him. Often he went along to the Baptist meeting, especially when there was a visiting preacher in the pulpit. In May 1776 he attended the large gathering of the Northamptonshire Baptist Association at Olney and heard with pleasure sermons by John Ryland, Robert Hall, and others. He provided accommodation in his home for several who were attending from out of town and had several of the ministers to breakfast; several likewise came to the church to hear him preach. 'We all seemed mutually pleased', he wrote in his diary.[42] Not infrequently, a visiting Baptist minister would also be invited to speak at Newton's weekly religious society; at other times, Newton would cancel the society meeting so members could go to the Baptist meeting to hear the newcomer. Newton was present at the ordination service for the new Baptist minister at Olney, John Sutcliff, in

---

[41] Likewise, Newton wrote to Hannah More about Calvinists on one occasion, and told her: 'I believe you are one yourself, though you are not aware of it,' *Memoirs of Hannah More*, ii. 410.   [42] Diary (1773–1805), 1 June 1776.

1776; Joshua Symonds, the minister of Bunyan's Old Meeting at Bedford, was one of Newton's closest friends with whom he regularly exchanged visits; and for the poor Baptist minister of Arnesby, Robert Hall, Sen., Newton intervened with John Thornton to obtain financial assistance. His links with Calvinistic Baptists were thus many and close.[43]

Early in 1765 he was introduced to John Collett Ryland of Northampton, and in July he visited him and then brought him back to Olney, where he heard him preach at Walker's meeting a 'good and seasonable discourse'. Thus began a series of annual visits to Northampton where Newton would conduct house preaching, particularly for the young scholars at the school for boys kept by Ryland, and that for girls kept by Martha Trinder, a member of Ryland's College Lane congregation. In September 1774 he recorded his reflections after a journey to Northampton,

Indeed the Lord's work seems to flourish there, and Mr. Ryland, amidst the many particularities which give him an Originality of Character beyond most men I ever knew, appears to new and greater advantage every time I see him. The Lord is pleased always to own me to the comfort of the serious young persons in Mrs. Trinders school, of whom I conversed with about 12 this time, who seem very promising.[44]

In 1776 he committed his own orphan niece to Mrs Trinder's care and noted in his diary with thanksgiving that he continued to be used 'to the awakening of many of her scholars'.[45]

John Ryland, Jun., (1753–1825) was one of the scholars in his father's school, and when he was only 15 years of age Newton invited him to visit him at Olney. This was the beginning of an intimate and lasting friendship. They saw each other often while Newton lived at Olney, and even after Newton removed to London, and Ryland to Bristol, they

---

[43] See further, Thomson, 'Newton and His Baptist Friends', 368–71; Nuttall, 'Baptists and Independents in Olney', 26–37.

[44] Diary (1773–1805), 11 Sept. 1774.

[45] For Newton's ministry to Mrs Trinder's scholars, see further, *Life of Mrs. Dawson.*

continued a correspondence which lasted over thirty years.[46]
While their epistolary relationship is a fine specimen of
evangelical friendship—the younger Ryland consulting
Newton about his plans to be married, about his father's
financial problems, about his move to Bristol; the older
Newton counselling Ryland about his preaching, comforting
him after the death of his wife, and so on—it also provides
evidence that Newton played an important role in Ryland's
life, helping him to make a theological shift away from high
Calvinism ('Gillism') to evangelical Calvinism ('Fullerism').

High Calvinism in Northamptonshire and Environs

To understand the significance of this shift, and of Newton's
part in it, it is necessary briefly to consider the history of the
area around Northampton and Olney as a traditional
stronghold of high Calvinism.[47]

A letter written to Isaac Watts by three local ministers
indicated the tenor of Olney Dissent in 1732. It was reported,
'Most of the dissenters in this town have for some time been
extremely fond of lay preachers in the Antinomian strain.'[48]
This tendency can be traced to Richard Davis (1658–1714),
an Independent itinerant minister in Rothwell who combined
vigorous circuit evangelism (planting over a dozen Dissenting
churches far and wide) with views of justification which could
easily be construed as antinomian. At the centre of the
Crispian controversy of the 1690s, which followed on the
republication of the antinomian sermons of Tobias Crisp
(1600–43), Davis acceded late in life to the extreme views of
Joseph Hussey (1660–1726), repenting of the practice of
having 'offered Christ and Grace' freely to the unconverted.[49]

---

[46] Fifty-eight of Newton's original letters to Ryland are preserved in the library of
Bristol Baptist College. These are described in L. G. Champion, 'The Letters of John
Newton to John Ryland', *Baptist Quarterly*, 27 (1977), 157–63.

[47] For what follows, see Nuttall, 'Northamptonshire and *The Modern Question*', 101–
23; Brown, *English Baptists*, 71–95; O. C. Robison, 'The Particular Baptists in
England', unpublished doctoral thesis (Oxford, 1963); Peter Naylor, *Picking up a Pin
for the Lord* (1992); Toon, *Emergence of Hyper-Calvinism*.

[48] Cited in *Calendar of the Correspondence of Philip Doddridge*, ed. G. F. Nuttall (1979),
64. Cf. Scott, *Life of Scott*, 585.

[49] The significant works here were Tobias Crisp, *Christ Alone Exalted; Being the
Compleat Works of Tobias Crisp* (1689–90), and Joseph Hussey, *God's Operations of Grace
but No Offers of Grace* (1707).

This strain of high Calvinism in the Northamptonshire congregational churches was significantly reduced under the influence of Davis's successor Matthias Maurice and, following Maurice, that of Philip Doddridge. Maurice had floated the so-called 'modern question' of duty-faith, asking whether repentance and faith could properly be urged upon all sinful men as a duty, if only the elect have the power to fulfil such an obligation. Maurice affirmed that repentance and faith were indeed obligatory. Still, the 'modern question' remained a matter of heated debate among Calvinistic Dissenters for many years. It remained so particularly among many Baptists, for whom high Calvinism represented theological orthodoxy for a much longer period than for Independents, extending well into the time of Newton at Olney.

Of great moment, therefore, was the shift of a younger generation of Baptist ministers with roots in Northamptonshire away from this heightened version of Calvinism which had held sway in parts of the denomination for fifty years under the powerful influence of John Gill (1697–1771) and John Brine (1703–65).[50] Gill and Brine, who in various ways owed a debt to Hussey, Davis, and Crisp, had given persistent and popular expression to the view that preachers ought not to use moral suasion in presenting the claims of the gospel, because if none but the elect have the power to repent and believe, then none but they have a duty to do so; that is, they answered the 'modern question' in the negative. Gill and Brine were not doctrinal antinomians, but many of their followers were less careful. John Ryland, Jun., later noted how there had been a dangerous tendency to see individuals as below the law before conversion, and above the law after it.[51] Moreover, the constraints that preachers such as Gill and Brine placed upon evangelism perpetuated an introspective and separatistic piety for many years among a number of the Particular Baptist congregations. Chief among the younger generation

[50] Note however that Roger Hayden, 'Evangelical Calvinism Among Eighteenth-Century British Baptists', unpublished doctoral thesis (Keele, 1991), has questioned the extent of the influence of Gill, Brine, and Skepp beyond London, stressing the long-standing evangelical tradition of the Western Association in general, and the Broadmead Baptist church and academy in particular.

[51] Ryland, *Life of Fuller*, 11.

who challenged the hegemony of Gill and Brine in Baptist theology were Andrew Fuller of Kettering, Robert Hall, Jun., of Arnesby, John Sutcliff of Olney, and John Ryland, Jun., of Northampton. Fuller's *Gospel Worthy of all Acceptation* (1785) gave expression to a more evangelical Calvinism that injected new life into the denomination and stimulated a burst of activity in education, associational life, prayer for the unconverted, and foreign missions. This new outlook was key to the foundation of the Particular Baptist Society for Propagating the Gospel among the Heathen (1792) and the missionary career of William Carey, which in turn inspired similar growth in missionary society activity on the part of other denominations at the end of the century. The theology of Fuller was the fulcrum upon which several Calvinistic Baptist congregations turned from tending towards inward-looking, exclusive sects to become part of an expansive and confident denomination.

John Ryland, Jun.

How did John Ryland, Jun., whom Newton knew so well, come to make this shift himself? In his youth Ryland had imbibed the heightened Calvinism of Brine and Gill largely from his father.[52] He recorded his adolescent conversion experience in a contemporary manuscript of twenty-three pages, entitled, 'The Experience of Jo/n R.l..d jun[r] as wrote by himself in a Letter to Tho[s]: R..t dated Feb[y]: 1770', and it is bound up with another manuscript which recounts the spiritual experiences of some of the other 'awakened' boys at his school who had formed themselves into a religious society.[53] In these documents, Ryland related how he was given pause to question his own spiritual condition when, at 13 years of age, he learned that one of his fellow boarders had excused himself from Ryland's company to talk with two other

---

[52] On the elder Ryland, see Hayden, 'Evangelical Calvinism Among Baptists', 125–40.

[53] There was one society among the boys and another among the girls. The second manuscript, also by Ryland, was 'An Account of the Rise and Progress of the Two Society's at Mr. Rylands and at Mrs. Trinder's Boarding School in Northampton'. Both manuscripts are at the Angus Library, Regent's Park College, Oxford.

boys about 'something better'. Ryland discovered this 'something better' was 'Jesus Christ and the salvation of their souls'. These three boarders had been provoked by the death of another boy the previous year into taking religion more seriously, forming themselves into a society which met twice weekly for prayer and to review one another's conduct. Ryland wondered if they were bound for heaven and he was not. This set in motion a long period of 'convictions', lasting until May 1768, during which he sought earnestly for spiritual consolation in the midst of tortured doubts and agonizing introspection. On one occasion he overheard his father talking with John Edwards of Leeds and Robert Hall, Sen., of Arnesby about their own conversion experiences. Edwards confessed to having been 'in the darkness' for four years before being awakened, Hall, for six, and his father, for twelve. This drove the young Ryland almost to despair. A sermon by Bradbury, Whitefield, Hall, or Taylor, heard at Northampton or while out travelling with his father, might give him consolation for a time, but then he would be plunged right back again into self-doubt and anxiety about his spiritual state.

During one of these temporary seasons of consolation he was baptized and joined the church, but it was not until eight months later, after a sermon of his father's, that he found a sense of assurance which remained. Ryland soon took a leading role in the boys' religious society and began to attempt formal prayer and to develop skills in religious discourse with a view to public ministry. On 10 March 1771, at 18 years of age, he was approved by the congregation to preach and to assist his father, and ten years later he was ordained and officially united with his father in the pastoral office. After another five years, when his father had left Northampton, he was given sole charge of the church.

It was sometime during the ten years preceding his ordination that Ryland's theological outlook changed; prior to this he had been a staunch high Calvinist. Not long after Ryland first became 'serious' about religion, he spent a full year reading volumes of divinity from his father's bookcase, and, as he later confessed, he soon fell in with the sentiments of authors such as Hussey, Gill, Brine, and Toplady. A small

versed catechism for the use of young people, written by
Ryland when he was only 16, gives an indication of the
opinions he had formed based on this reading. Question 40 of
the catechism asks, 'Is union a consequence of faith?' and the
answer follows,

> No, this was in election done,
> God put and chose us in his son,
> Cause we're united, faith he gives,
> That in communion we may live.[54]

Though cryptic, this was a version of the high Calvinist
doctrine of eternal justification; namely, that the elect are
already justified in the eternal covenant of redemption rather
than at the time of exercising faith in the gospel promises.
This provides a clue to the kind of piety revealed in Ryland's
conversion narrative, the passive but anxious waiting for God
to reveal his election to him. As a second-generation high
Calvinist, inheriting a grammar of predestination before he
had himself experienced conversion, Ryland was led inevitably
down labyrinthine paths of introspection, searching for
interior graces that might prove his election. He stated in his
catechism that the people of God were 'those whom Jehovah's
firm decree, elected from eternity'. Believing this, it was of
surpassing importance to descry whether he was included in
that number. As narrated above, after two years of darkness,
passively waiting for faith to be revealed to him, he came at
long last to feel that he had indeed been divinely converted.

Still, he remained a high Calvinist, and even after he began
publicly to preach, he was inhibited by his heightened
predestinarian belief from appealing to the consciences of his
hearers. 'For a few years', he recalled, 'I imagined, that these
later divines [i.e. the high Calvinist writers] were more
accurate than their predecessors; and accordingly, when I first
entered on the work of the ministry . . . I was shackled by
adherence to a supposed systematic consistency, and carefully
avoided exhorting sinners to come to Christ for salvation.'[55]

[54] John Ryland, Jun., *Compendious View of the Principal Truths of the Glorious Gospel of Christ* (1769), 16.
[55] John Ryland, Jun., *Serious Remarks on the Different Representations of Evangelical Doctrine* (Bristol, 1817), 8.

But sometime during the next few years, in a process which was paralleled in the lives of Fuller and Hall, Ryland became convinced that he had needlessly deviated from an orthodox and scriptural pattern of practice. Observing the evangelical sentiments of older Puritan divines, reading Samuel Rutherford's *Letters* and especially Jonathan Edwards's *Inquiry into Freedom of Will*, helped to remove the difficulties which had previously troubled his mind. By the time Fuller published his *Gospel Worthy of all Acceptation* in 1785, Ryland's scruples were gone, and he was prepared to join him in the vanguard of the new evangelicalism which transformed the Calvinistic Baptists. With Ryland's move to the academy at Bristol in 1793 he was able to spread his evangelical views to a new generation of Baptist ministers, and to take up a significant leadership role in the denomination.[56]

Newton and Ryland

In after years Ryland described Newton as having been one of his 'wisest and best counsellors'.[57] To what extent then did Newton influence Ryland to moderate the theological views he held as a young man?

(*a*) *Newton's letter of 17 October 1771.* Ryland first visited Newton at Olney in 1768, when his spiritual turmoil was finally coming to an end. Sometime shortly after this they began their long epistolary relationship. The extant correspondence dates from just after the period when Ryland began ministering publicly in 1771. In this same year Ryland published a collection of his adolescent verse entitled, *Serious Essays on the Truths of the Glorious Gospel, and the Various Branches of Vital Experience*. It included a 22-page preface defending his high Calvinist principles and disclaiming that he had had help with, or prior models for, his poems. Wanting to speak with Ryland about the book, but seeing no immediate prospect of meeting with him in person, Newton wrote to him in October. He criticized Ryland sharply for the vanity implicit in his disavowal of any assistance, pointing out several places where

---

[56] See further on Ryland, James Culross, *The Three Rylands* (1897); 'Memoir of the late Rev. John Ryland, D.D.', *Baptist Magazine*, 18 (1826), 1–9; Ryland, *Pastoral Memorials*.   [57] Ryland, *Pastoral Memorials*, 345–53.

his poems might have benefited from criticism and a more careful attention to detail. What was of even greater concern to Newton, however, was the way that Ryland felt he had to thrust upon his readers his views about eternal justification. Wrote Newton, 'For a young man under eighteen, to pronounce ex cathedra upon a point in which the majority of the most learned, spiritual and humble Divines, are of another opinion, was such an offence against decency as grieved me.'[58] Furthermore, Ryland's swaggering declaration in his preface that he aimed explicitly to displease Arminians struck Newton as unnecessarily belligerent. Newton advised him as a young minister rather to aim at 'plain and experimental things', to touch the hearts of his listeners with the evil of sin and the love of Jesus, rather than 'to fill their heads with distinctions'.

Evidently, Ryland took Newton's letter to heart. Not only did he copy the letter out by hand, but in the second edition of his poems in 1775 he made changes which reflected Newton's criticisms. For example, the offending line about Arminians was changed subtly, and the material on eternal justification was removed to a postscript. Moreover, when Newton wrote a second letter to Ryland, three months after the first, he acknowledged that Ryland had shown a teachable spirit and had made satisfactory amends to him.[59]

(*b*) *Newton's letter of 16 January 1772.* In this second letter Newton also went into more detail with Ryland about some points in his high Calvinist theology, though he reiterated that it was chiefly the 'positive manner' in which Ryland expressed his views of justification that had bothered him. Ryland's doctrine of eternal justification had evidently been linked to a position on the order of the decrees, since Newton explained that to his mind the difference between a judicious supralapsarian and a sound sublapsarian was largely verbal. He recommended a scheme in Thomas Halyburton (1674–1712) in which he thought the moderate of both parties might unite.

---

[58] Newton to John Ryland, Jun., 17 Oct. 1771, copy in autograph notebook, 'Omicron to Dr. R.j.', BBC.

[59] This letter is included in Newton's published correspondence with Ryland, covering the period 1772–7. *Works*, ii. 112–32.

The issue of the order of God's decrees was the provenance of high Calvinism. It belonged to that specialized discourse in which predestination was discussed in the context of the doctrine of God and his providence, rather than in the context of the doctrine of salvation and the question of non-response to the gospel. Supralapsarians held the minority view which placed the decree to predestine some creatable beings to life, and to reprobate others to damnation, *before* the decrees to create and to permit the Fall. Sublapsarians (or infra-lapsarians) based predestination on God's prescience of the Fall, thereby placing the decree to predestine and reprobate *after* the decrees to create and permit the Fall. The nature of this dispute was confined principally to those who followed the Swiss Reformed order of salvation. Supralapsarians had a problem of theodicy, for their position could easily be construed as making God the author of sin; sublapsarians had a different problem in seeming to detract from God's absolute government over human history, because of the way their position could be construed as making God in some measure unable to accomplish his designs.

The tract by Halyburton that Newton thought reconciled these positions was entitled, *A Modest Enquiry whether Regeneration or Justification has the Precedency in Order of Nature* (1714). The dilemma addressed was the relationship of predestination in eternity to regeneration and justification in time. How could a person spiritually dead exercise justifying faith without being first regenerated? But, conversely, how could a sinner be given new life in Christ without first being declared righteous in justification? Which came first? Halyburton concluded that regeneration did, at least in the order of nature, ruling out any idea of eternal justification. Effectively, the separate decrees of the *ordo* were contemplated together in the eternal design of God. Halyburton referred only to one divine decree: 'to save elect sinners, to the Praise of Grace, by Jesus Christ'. Despite Newton's suggestion that this might solve an old high Calvinist problem, the concept of God electing to save *sinners* suggests the scheme would, in the end, more easily have satisfied sublapsarians than supralapsarians.

Newton did not tease out Halyburton's argument in detail for Ryland, since the immediate point could be argued from experience. His principal concern with high Calvinist doctrine was the way it so often came across in practice:

> Though I know several in the Supra-lapsarian scheme, at whose feet I am willing to sit and learn, and have found their preaching and conversation savoury and edifying; yet I must say I have met with many who have appeared to be rather wise than warm, rather positive than humble, rather captious than lively, and more disposed to talk of speculations than experience. (ii. 112).

Newton felt that too many high Calvinist writings had hard and paradoxical passages which went beyond experience, puzzling plain people and endangering those weak in faith and judgement. Hussey's writings, for instance, which Ryland esteemed, Newton thought contained 'more bones than meat'. He exhorted Ryland rather to give himself to Scripture and to prayer, making every truth food for his soul. True knowledge, he argued, ought to make sin more hateful and Jesus more precious, and to stir the soul to use the means appointed and to fulfil its duties without reservation. The danger, thought Newton, sprang from using Scripture selectively and separating things which God had joined together.

In 1783 Ryland asked Andrew Fuller about his position on the order of the decrees. Fuller responded that he had formerly considered himself a supralapsarian but without fully understanding what that meant. Though he was not now well-versed in arguments on either side, he felt that the sublapsarian scheme was more useful, allowing him to address men as sinners, not merely as creatures without a case before the Almighty. It was hard to convict someone of sin according to the supralapsarian scheme.[60] This practical, pastoral concern on Fuller's part was similar to that which had motivated Newton throughout his discussions with Ryland.

(c) *A book recommended by Newton.* Ryland's immediate response to Newton's letter in 1772, and the discussions which must have ensued between them, have gone unrecorded. But four years later there was a further episode in Ryland's theological formation which involved Newton. In his *Life of Fuller* (1816), Ryland recalled,

[60] Ryland, *Life of Fuller*, 350.

In 1776, I borrowed of Mr. Newton, of Olney, two sermons on this subject [i.e. the distinction between moral and natural inability], by Mr. Smalley, which Brother Sutcliff afterwards reprinted from the copy which I transcribed. I well remember lending them to Mr. Hall of Arnsby, to whom I remarked, that I was ready to suspect that this distinction, well considered, would lead us to see, that the affirmative side of the Modern Question was fully consistent with the strictest Calvinism.[61]

Hall was at first doubtful but, soon after, was fully satisfied that Ryland was correct. Here Newton's role was small—lending a book to Ryland—but the consequence was significant: Ryland and two of his colleagues were convinced that they could be both consistent Calvinists and fully evangelical preachers.

The book which Newton loaned to Ryland was *The Consistency of the Sinner's Inability to comply with the Gospel; with his inexcusable guilt in not complying with it, illustrated and confirmed in two Discourses, on John VIth, 44th* (1769), written by John Smalley (1734–1820), a Yale College graduate who, as a Congregationalist minister at New Berlin, Connecticut, had distinguished himself as a theologian and preacher.[62] In short compass and in clear terms, Smalley reiterated in these sermons an argument that another more famous New Englander, Jonathan Edwards, had published fifteen years previously in his more formidable *Careful and Strict Inquiry into the Modern Prevailing Notions of the Freedom of Will* (1754).[63] Smalley left the philosophical issues dealt with by Edwards largely to one side and stated plainly the practical problem which Calvinists were facing at the time: 'There is a difficulty, in the minds of many, how to reconcile this total helplessness of sinners, with the sincerity of the gospel offers, or with the justice of men's being condemned or punished for their impenitence and unbelief.'[64] Smalley answered this objection by distinguishing, as Edwards had, between two kinds of

[61] Ibid. 9 n. Ryland also mentioned Smalley in the *Theological Miscellany*, 3 (1786), 604.
[62] W. Allen, *American Biographical and Historical Dictionary*, 2nd edn. (Boston, 1832).
[63] The relevant section in Edward's *Freedom of Will* is pt. 1, s. 4, 'Of the Distinction of Natural and Moral Necessity and Inability'.
[64] Smalley, *Two Discourses*, 4.

helplessness or inability, one natural, the other moral: 'Whatever a man could not do, *if he would*, he is under a natural inability of doing; but when all the reason one *can't* do a thing, is because he has not a *mind* to, the inability is only of a moral nature.'[65]

Smalley provided an example. Some people are so feeble and infirm that they can scarcely do any physical labour, even though they are willing to put forth all their strength in the attempt. Others are strong and healthy enough but their invincible laziness is such that their hands refuse to labour. In like manner sinners labour only under a moral inability to respond to the gospel, and for this they themselves are alone culpable. Moral inability is none the less a real and universal condition: 'as certain and never-failing a connection in this case, as any natural connection whatever'.[66] None are therefore able to comply with the gospel but those who are the subjects of the special and effectual grace of God.

To Ryland the distinction between moral and natural inability meant that sinners could be freely invited to respond to the gospel because they were under no natural inability to comply with its terms. It was precisely this argument that unhinged the high Calvinism of Ryland and his circle. It was an important contribution from New England to the Evangelical Revival in the mother country. The stature of Jonathan Edwards for Newton and his circle is reflected in an incident, recalled by Ryland, in which Newton introduced the intellectually promising Thomas Scott to a group of local Baptists as 'the man who, he hoped, would prove the Jonathan Edwards of Old England'.[67]

There is little record after 1772 of conversations or correspondence between Newton and Ryland about high

<hr/>

[65] Smalley, *Two Discourses*, 10. [66] Ibid. 13.
[67] Ryland, 'Remarks on the *Quarterly Review*', 346. Note, however, that Edwardsean New England divinity was never revered as highly by Newton as by the Fuller–Ryland circle. Newton wrote to Ryland during the American War: 'I long as earnestly as you for an end to the Unhappy war—not so much for the sake of American Divinity. For I think so far as Scheme, System, & Notion are concerned, we have as tolerable stock at home. We have likewise the Bible, & I trust the Holy teaching Spirit has not yet said *migrimus hinc*,' Newton to John Ryland, Jun., 26 July 1779, ALS, LPL.

Calvinism, but it seems probable that Newton continued to be an important influence behind the scenes in the reshaping of Ryland's theology. In any case, it was not long until Ryland met Andrew Fuller and began reading Jonathan Edwards for himself, not long before he made it known that he too now believed that the gospel could be offered unreservedly to sinners. His brother-in-law wrote later that Ryland now agreed on this issue with Calvin himself and all the 'principal Calvinistic Divines', including several of Newton's favourite authors such as Owen, Halyburton, Witsius, Bunyan, and Whitefield. When in 1817 Ryland thought he descried the spectre of a non-evangelical, high Calvinism rearing its head in the Established Church, he wrote to the *Christian Observer* to recount how this was an extreme from which he and the Baptists had recovered forty years previously. Theologically, he wished to continue to keep company with such clergymen as John Newton and Thomas Scott who had established a tradition of lively, evangelical Calvinism.[68]

Summary: High Calvinism and Newton's Evangelical Piety

Newton's correspondence reveals that he was remarkably familiar with the intricacies of high Calvinist discourse. His genial manner, his focus on experience, and his conversational prose style, so different from the discursive scholasticism of the previous century, can easily obscure how well-acquainted he was with the theological issues. His almost throw-away comments to Ryland were all to the point, treating knowledgeably such issues as eternal justification, the order of the decrees, the propriety of exhorting the unconverted, and the use of the law. The frequent and happy interaction between Newton and John Collett Ryland and Robert Hall, Sen., as between George Whitefield and these men, indicates how blurred the lines could be during this period between Old Dissent and New Dissent, between high Calvinists and evangelical Calvinists. The debates were still highly intra-mural and there was a good deal of common ground. While Newton could state quite baldly, 'What is by some called high Calvinism, I dread', he still read the literature and kept up

---

[68] Ryland, 'Serious Remarks', 38.

acquaintance with many of its votaries. For all the evangelical latitudinarian rhetoric noted earlier in his correspondence with Wesley, he still identified himself plainly as an avowed and strict Calvinist:

> If you mean by a rigid Calvinist, one who is fierce, dogmatical, and censorious, and ready to deal out anathema's against all who differ from him, I hope I am not more such a one than I am a rigid Papist. But as to the doctrines which are now stigmatized by the name of Calvinism, I cannot well avoid the epithet rigid, while I believe them. (vi. 245–6).

Newton's Calvinism was stripped down to basics, but it was still in the tradition of confessional orthodoxy.

Secondly, in the Newton–Ryland correspondence it was again issues of piety which came to the fore, for Newton was generally drawn into theological debate only in so far as the issues bore upon vital, religious experience. As a pastor, he thought that it was dangerous to lead people into speculation beyond the scope of their experience. Hence Newton's criticism of high Calvinist manner as captious, positive, and wise-headed to the careless neglect of plain and weak people. As he wrote to Hannah More some time later, 'The talk of some reputed Calvinists is no more musical in my ear, than the mewing of a cat.'[69] He demonstrated his own preferred approach a few years after the Ryland episode when Thomas Scott, then a Socinian, was trying to draw him into a controversy on predestination. Newton refused. When he sent Scott a tract on faith by Thomas Halyburton, ironically, he specifically directed Scott *away* from the very essay bound up with it, which he had earlier recommended to Ryland. Newton worried that speculation upon election might improperly distract Scott from his simple duty to exercise faith in the gospel promises.[70] Evidently, predestination was not a doctrine for beginners. To Newton's eye, Scott was at a

---

[69] *Memoirs of Hannah More*, ii. 410. But note also that Newton owned the label Calvinist and added to More, 'I believe Calvin to have been an eminent servant of God, and his writings, especially his later writings, to be scriptural, judicious, and accurate' (ibid. 411).

[70] Newton's correspondence with Scott took place in 1775. *Works*, i. 521–80.

different spiritual stage from Ryland, whose experience of converting grace appeared more compatible with mature theological self-reflection. What Newton clearly did not do with either man was to make predestination a leading speculative principle from which could be derived an entire religious system. Predestination functioned more to enshrine the experience of grace, to account for the discovery that God had done something for him which he could not do for himself.

Strict in orthodoxy, weighted toward experience, Newton's Calvinism was above all evangelistic. About the same time that he was seeking to soften Ryland's high Calvinism, Newton published a letter in the *Gospel Magazine* in 1772 which drew on the distinction between moral and natural inability to defend the propriety of issuing a general invitation to sinners. The letter was written originally to the Dissenter Robert Jones of Hull. Newton concluded that while sinners were wholly dependent upon grace, they were not for that reason incapable of doing anything. They could, for example, consider their ways, keep from open sin, and attend upon the means of grace (i. 153). In this way, Newton upheld 'duty faith'.[71]

Earlier, this issue had come up with Thomas Jones (*c.*1744–1817), an 18-year-old hairdresser who had given up his business and written to Newton in 1765 about his desire to enter the ministry. Jones studied privately under Newton for an interval before going up to St Edmund Hall, Oxford, where he became one of the Calvinistic students expelled in 1768 for their 'Methodistical tenets'. Notwithstanding this, he was admitted to orders and became curate of Clifton, a village near Olney.[72] Newton's published correspondence with Jones

---

[71] Newton directed Robert Hawker (1754–1830) to this same Omicron letter, when he learned that Hawker was entertaining high Calvinist notions restraining the 'free offer'. Newton appealed to scriptural precedent and to common sense, defending himself, 'We need not fear being reproached as legal preachers, while the charge will equally apply to our Lord and his Apostles!' and, 'Plain common sense, tho' slighted by many who are wise in their own conceit, is worth a thousand refinements and distinctions.' With respect to antinomianism, Newton exhorted Hawker, 'What God has joined together let no man put asunder. He has joined the means and the end— Faith and Holiness.' Newton to Robert Hawker, *c.* Aug. 1800, copy of letter, LPL.

[72] On Jones, see further *LyH* i. 424.

dates from 1765 to 1772 (ii. 44–60). In 1767, when Jones was at Oxford, he wrote to Newton that he had met with some who were objecting to the way Newton exhorted sinners in his printed sermons. In response, Newton appealed to biblical precedent and warned against the 'sour and unsavoury' conversation of those Calvinists who would hamper evangelistic preaching. He claimed that to address the conscience of one's hearers was fully consistent with Calvinism, and he excused himself from proving the point further by referring Jones to Jonathan Edwards, who had 'unanswerably proved' the point in his *Inquiry into Freedom of Will*, and to John Owen's *Practical Exposition on the 130th Psalm* (1669). It has been observed how Edwards was important for the theological shift made by Ryland. To Owen Newton liked also frequently to appeal, since he was a writer esteemed by high Calvinists, from the very centre of seventeenth-century Puritan orthodoxy. The *Practical Exposition* included a section, 'Exhortations unto Believing', which Newton described as 'one of the closest and most moving addresses to sinners I ever met with' (ii. 54). Owen grounded the free offer of the gospel in the definite way of salvation God had provided through Christ. And, as Newton said to his detractors, Owen was no mean Calvinist.

Newton shuddered away from any notion of predestination that might quench evangelical zeal for the conversion of sinners. He sought rather,

to address them as reasonable creatures; to take them by every handle; to speak to their consciences; to tell them of the terrors of the Lord, and of his tender mercies; to argue with them what good they find in sin; whether they do not need a Saviour; to put them in mind of death, judgement, and eternity, etc. (ii. 53).

While Newton felt that this was biblical and consistent with his Calvinistic principles, he was not beneath also adding an argument from success, commenting on another occasion:

Those ministers whom the Lord has honoured with the greatest success in awakening and converting sinners, have generally been led to adopt the more popular way of *exhortation* and *address*. . . . it is not easy to conceive, that the Lord should most signally bear testimony in favour of that mode of preaching which is least consistent with the truth, and with itself. (i. 150).

Thus, however much Newton sought to exalt the sovereignty of God in salvation, he remained equally concerned boldly to address the will of individual men and women.[73] His proselytizing ardour contrasts significantly with the high Calvinist reluctance to preach the gospel indiscriminately to all people. One local Dissenter at Olney considered his zealous preaching and constant visiting from house to house positively 'Jesuistical'. Such aspersions were more usually cast on the Arminian Wesley.

In sum, Newton's relationship with high Calvinists in the Northamptonshire area points up how thoroughly conversant he was with the trade language of high Calvinism but also how determined he was to avoid the extremes of that system which ran counter to his biblical instincts and evangelical experience. Said Newton in 1765, 'I am what they call a Calvinist; yet there are flights, niceties, and hard sayings, to be found among some of that system, which I do not choose to imitate' (ii. 98). Like Wesley's perfectionism, high Calvinism lay outside the dialectic which he sought to maintain between predestination and piety.

John Newton's Evangelical Calvinism

Two selections from Newton's *Works*, one a letter and the other a sermon, may serve to illustrate his own theological position between the extremes mapped out above.

Newton's Ninth Omicron Letter

The ninth letter in Newton's *Omicron* series was entitled, 'On the Doctrines of Election and Final Perseverance'. It had been published previously in the *Gospel Magazine* for June 1772, and the original correspondent was Joseph Milner of Hull, the church historian and pioneer of evangelicalism at Hull.[74] Milner was converted to evangelicalism in 1770 but was not

---

[73] A good example of this is Newton's hymn, 'The Leper', 'Come lepers, seize the present hour, | The Saviour's grace to prove; | He *can* relieve, for he is pow'r, | He *will*, for he is love' (*OH* 1. 82, st. 8).

[74] Bull, *Newton*, 175, 203; cf. *Works*, vi. 279.

finally settled in his views until 1772.[75] It was during this uncertain interval that he wrote to Newton, identifying himself as a candid enquirer and asking Newton to comment on election and perseverance. At the time, Milner found too many difficulties in these doctrines to give them his assent.[76]

Newton prefaced his remarks in this letter by saying that he would not seek to prove these doctrines at large, nor counter objections, nor refer to books on the subject. Rather than aim at the exactness of a disputant, he would offer a few thoughts as they occurred, in a way appropriate to a familiar letter. Besides, he did not think that it was by intellectual and controversial enquiry, but by reverent prayer and study of Scripture, that one came to an experimental knowledge of spiritual truth. He gave several hints for one who would proceed thus experimentally. First, in the reading and study of the Scriptures one ought to employ the 'analogy of faith', realizing that there was a certain comprehensive view of biblical truth which reconciled difficulties with detached texts. Secondly, one ought to consult one's own experience along the way as an authority subordinate to Scripture, noting what sense of a matter was most agreeable to what passed within and without oneself. Thirdly, when led to view Calvinist doctrines favourably, one ought not to be afraid to embrace them on account of some remaining unresolved objections, recognizing there might be greater difficulties on the other side. One could have sufficient knowledge to embrace Calvinistic doctrines before attaining fully to a comprehensive view of things. And fourthly, one ought to compare the tendency of different opinions, observing their consequence in

---

[75] Isaac Milner, *Account of the Life and Character of the Rev. Joseph Milner*, new edn. (1804), pp. xviii, xxi.

[76] Milner's own position appears to have emerged as a hypothetical universalism, i.e. that Christ's redemption was sufficient for all but efficient only for the elect. He himself described his theology as somewhere *between* Newton and Wesley. Thus in 1780 he wrote, 'As to Mr. Newton, I believe him to be an humble, holy man; but he is no more my master than Mr. Wesley is. I have ever thought for myself, I hold universal redemption and preach it constantly: for "I believe in God the Son, who redeemed me and *all mankind*." But when we come to think of the application of this doctrine to particular persons . . . yet I must add with the Catechism, "I believe in God the Holy Ghost, who sanctifieth me and all the *elect* people of God," ' Joseph Milner to Mr. D.H——e, 21 Dec. 1780, printed in *EM*, NS 1 (1823), 232.

practice. Newton then sought to apply these principles to the issues themselves. He argued that Scripture taught election in definite terms and that the experience of evangelical conversion demonstrated how God's initiative always preceded human response. Likewise, the perseverance of the saints was a comfortable doctrine into which one was led gradually as one realized that God infallibly accomplishes what he begins. Newton concluded that both election and perseverance exalted God and abased man more than the alternatives, and both were according to godliness.

Newton's four points of reference in this letter—the analogy of faith, experience, intellectual objections, and practical consequences—were worked out earlier when, in a series of expository lectures on Romans given at Olney, he came to the 'golden chain' passage on predestination in chapter 8, verses 29–30.[77] Lecture 42 was essentially prolegomenon and spelt out the four interpretative 'rules' above, and hatch marks in the manuscript indicate where Newton extracted material that he reproduced verbatim in his letter to Milner. He spent nine lectures on the passage in all, proceeding carefully according to the rules he set out at the beginning. This fourfold hermeneutic was for Newton therefore an explicit and self-conscious theological method.

Despite the 'experimental' nature of Newton's method, his published letter drew at least one antagonistic response. Nicholas Manners (b. 1732) was a Methodist preacher who, after returning from Ireland with Wesley, was appointed as one of four preachers in the Manchester circuit. In 1760–1 he became acquainted with Newton at Liverpool, recalling having even breakfasted with him on one occasion.[78] Manners shared Wesley's views and preached perfection. In a rare tract of fifty-eight pages, *Strictures on Omicron's Ninth Letter* (1778), he disputed Newton's letter line by line in the controversial style of the period. Little of Manners's scriptural exegesis and few of his theological arguments cannot be found in Wesley, or, indeed, do not have seventeenth-century antecedents. His chief objections were common enough criticisms of Calvinism.

[77] 'Lectures on Rom. ch. VIII', MS sermon notebooks 13 and 14, CNM.
[78] *Life and Experience of Nicholas Manners* (York, 1785), 28.

He charged Newton with impugning the character of God by
making God the agent of sin, and he accused Newton of
retarding the progress of believers in holiness by teaching
fatalistic doctrine. Although Newton and Manners shared a
common concern to appeal consciously to Scripture, reason,
and experience, Manners mistook Newton for a confessional
combatant when Newton really understood himself more as a
pastoral theologian. Newton let the dispute die in silence. He
was increasingly convinced that a person became a Calvinist
through personal experience, not by argument.

Newton's Sermon, 'The Lamb of God, The Great Atonement'

'The Lamb of God, The Great Atonement' was a sermon
preached by Newton in 1785 and printed the following year
as part of a topical series based on the libretto of Handel's
Messiah, timed to coincide with the commemoration of Handel
at Westminster Abbey (iv. 184–97). The text, which opens
the second part of the Oratorio, was John 1: 29: 'Behold the
Lamb of God, which taketh away the sin of the world!' Upon
the announcement of such a text, the ears of every evangelical
hearer would have been pricked, for this verse was, like 1 John
2: 2, a test passage for the doctrine of the limited atonement.
And the limited atonement was in turn a test doctrine for
strict confessional orthodoxy. The sermon is therefore a good
site in which to observe Newton's Calvinism at work. It was to
this sermon he pointed the non-Calvinist Hannah More in
1794 for 'a summary of my thoughts' on the subject of
Calvinism.[79] Ever the middleman, he pointed the high
Calvinist Robert Hawker to the very same sermon a number
of years later.[80]

Newton opened the sermon by arguing that the manifold,
great, and marvellous works of God in creation, everywhere
observable, ought to be enough to incite all men to adore their
creator. That they do not is signal proof of their depravity. In
order to soften such obdurate creatures, God appointed an
even greater wonder by offering a suffering saviour in the
person of his own son. As the Lamb of God, Christ superseded

[79] *Memoirs of Hannah Moore*, ii. 410.
[80] Newton to Hawker, *c*. Aug. 1800.

the sacrificial system, dying as the one voluntary substitute for death-deserving sinners. This way of redemption satisfied the rights of God's justice, the demands of his law, and the honour of his government, and provided an atonement which was fully efficacious to deliver a believer from the guilt and penalty of sin. Sin removed, the soul is open to Christ whose grace is richly imparted for a life of continuing obedience.

Newton continued, contending that although the atonement is plainly spoken of in John 1: 29 in a large and indefinite manner as taking away the sin of the world, it is certain from Scripture that all people will not in the end be saved. Moreover, Scripture speaks of those finally redeemed in peculiar language, such as when it says that Christ laid down his life for his own sheep, and so on. They are spoken of not in the language of conjecture or hypothesis but in the definite language of predestination. And is this not the experience all those truly spiritual and enlightened? Not that they first sought God but that he first sought them? Nevertheless, those who would explain away the sermon text by saying that Christ died for the whole world, merely in the sense of having died for some men of all nations, do not follow the scriptural manner of expression. Though there is an election, Scripture speaks typically of Christ having died for sinners. Because all are sinners, there is warrant for all to apply to him for forgiveness. The atonement was not a substitution in the sense of a precise calculation of so much suffering for so many sins. God's way is always more magnanimous than that. The atonement God provided is sufficient for all the world and more. Again, this is warrant for the gospel to be extended to all men. Under the gospel God commands all men everywhere to repent and believe. That some do not is a moral defect on their part, not a natural one, and they are themselves culpable for their rejection of Christ. It is wrong and dangerous to exalt God's grace to the place where one speaks to men and women as though they are unable to comply with his requirements, and therefore not responsible for their own disobedience. The whole may be summed up thus: salvation is wholly of grace, but for those who reject the Lamb of God, offered for the sins of the world, their blood will be upon their own heads.

How did Newton's sermon relate to the conditions of the evangelical world around him and to inherited theological traditions? By beginning with the predicament of human beings as depraved creatures in a glorious creation, he characteristically started at a point upon which all evangelicals and all Calvinists could agree. As he proceeded to discuss God's generous response of providing a saviour, he drew lightly on insights from several traditional theories of the atonement, collating Abelardian (moral incitement), Anselmic (satisfaction), Reformational (penal substitution), and Grotian (governmental) emphases. Although he stressed the penal substitution, he did not use the language of precise imputation or of Christ's passive and active righteousness which, while dear to some high Calvinists, would have alienated followers of Wesley. Rather, he related penal substitution to the simple experience of justification by faith, another point upon which all parties would be able to agree.

When Newton came to deal with the question of the extent of the atonement, he picked his footing along a path between a hypothetical and a commercial view of the atonement. The former was characteristic of Richard Baxter. Under this view Christ's death was seen as an equivalent penalty (not exact) for the sins of all men, satisfying the honour of God's government by displaying his public displeasure against sin, while allowing God to establish a 'new law' of grace whereby only faith and repentance were required for a title to forgiveness. Thus, a 'hypothetical universalism' was advanced which, while still upholding a high view of predestination, sought to get around the offensive notion of a limited atonement. In the loose way that Newton referred to this position, he may also have meant to include the more extreme language of hypothesis in Wesley's Arminianism, in which election was based simply on God's foreknowledge of faith and obedience. In contrast, the commercial view, championed historically by John Owen, was a variation on the concept of penal substitution. In tight Aristotelian logic, Owen contended that the intent, the means, and the end were all one where God is concerned and that God could not have therefore intended Christ's death for all men, since it is plain that all men are not saved. Thus far Newton followed him. The strict logic of Owen's position led him, however, to describe the atonement in terms of a debtor–creditor relationship between man and God, wherein Christ suffered the exact amount necessary to balance the ledger of the sins of the elect, and then cried, 'It is finished'. The concept of imputation naturally figured largely in this view. Characteristically, Newton rehearsed the positions of both Baxter and Owen only to reject them in so far as they were taken to be comprehensive theories of the atonement.[81]

Effectively, Newton subordinated the whole question of the extent of the atonement to evangelical priorities, however much he knew he would be criticized by some Calvinists for a failure of nerve. For him it was enough that Scripture spoke of Christ dying for *sinners*, because this excluded no one from the offer of the gospel. However, this was more to shift the ground of the debate than it was to solve the theological problem. The question could still be asked whether Christ died for *all* sinners or just for *some*. But, acutely aware of partisans to the right and to the left on this issue, Newton sought not so much to resolve the logical tensions inherent in relating divine and human agency, as to live with them as a mystery integral to Scripture itself. It was precisely here that his Calvinism dissolved into his evangelicalism. Following Owen, Newton stressed not that Christ died for everyone, but that a sure and certain way of salvation was open for all, and sufficient for all. Thus he protected the universal offer of the gospel, an evangelical concern, against the high Calvinists without necessarily giving up the belief in a limited atonement *per se*. He likewise defended duty faith by an Edwardsean appeal to the distinction between moral and natural ability. The duty of faith could be urged upon all men, since by nature all have a capacity to respond. If there were a lack of will, due to a disposition to sin reinforced by habit, that was a matter of moral culpability and personal responsibility. That God freely

---

[81] On these views of the atonement, see further, Alan Clifford, *Atonement and Justification: English Evangelical Theology 1640–1790* (Oxford, 1989), 69–166; von Rohr, *Covenant of Grace*, 123–9. Note, however, that Newton was not, as Clifford argues from this sermon, one of the moderate Calvinists who 'shared Wesley's view of the extent of the atonement' (80–1).

elected to remove this disposition in some, such that they could trust in the gospel promises, did not make him responsible for those who continued in unbelief. Thus, Newton upheld the idea of preterition over the more severe notion of double predestination. Again, he used predestination chiefly to explain the mystery of non-response to the gospel, and the distinction between natural and moral ability, to attack the sort of high Calvinist preaching that incited antinomianism.

The sermon reflected the hard-won balance between predestinarian grace and evangelical voluntarism that Newton had struck only after learning from the perfectionism revivals of 1758–62 that Wesley's beliefs lay outside his own theology in one direction, just as surely as the high Calvinism encountered in Northamptonshire in the early 1770s lay outside it in another.

The Moderation of Newton's Calvinism

Newton's sermon on the atonement appeared in 1785, some years after his Calvinism had been tested through disagreements with Wesley and Ryland during the period 1762–72. Chronologically, it may be placed on a curve of increasing moderation in Newton's theology over the years following these disagreements. This later moderation may be illustrated by two further examples.

First, the distributive argument dismissed by Newton in this sermon (i.e. that atonement for all men meant atonement for some men from every nation) had earlier been used by him without reservations. Shortly after arriving at Olney, Newton preached a sermon on John 3: 16. It was organized according to Owen's means–end argument, and one of his first points was, 'The object of [God's] love was the world—that is mankind—not the Jews only . . . but the Gentiles also—not every individual, but some of all nations, people[s] & languages.'[82] Later, he came to see this as too nice a distinction, distorting the plain sense of the text.

Secondly, Newton gradually moved away from the high esteem in which he held such sophisticated Calvinistic

[82] MS Sermon notebook 4, CNM.

theologians as Edwards and Owen. In 1762 Newton claimed Edwards was 'my favourite author'. In 1778 he gave him 'the laurel for divinity in this century'.[83] While Newton realized all along that Edwards's complex argumentation was unfashionable, this did not keep Newton from extolling his works. By 1794, however, he repented altogether of ever having recommended books such as the *Inquiry into Freedom of Will*: 'I was younger then than I am now. I do not now recommend it . . . Mr. E. was an excellent man, but some of his writings are too metaphysical, and particularly that book. If I understand it, I think it rather establishes fatalism and necessity, than Calvinism in the sober sense.' [84] Newton changed his mind likewise about Owen. In 1767 he described Owen as a 'steady, deep-sighted Calvinist'. A little later he could assign him 'one of the first places' as a teacher of theology (ii. 54, 101).[85] But then in 1778 he began to wonder if Owen did not give in to a 'needless display of erudition'. Finally, as an old man he was reported to have said in informal conversation: 'Dr. Owen will be ashamed of his wisdom and clearness, five minutes after he has been in heaven.'[86]

It would be wrong, however, to think that Newton considered himself less a Calvinist as the years went by. His theological moderation was chiefly a matter of eschewing controversy and conforming to contemporary ideals of simplicity and refinement over against discursiveness and minute argument. Newton recognized that scholastic theology was in his own age 'now exploded as uncouth and obsolete' (iv. 523). Cultural norms relating to toleration and taste led him to seek to pare down the gospel to its essentials, rather than to exhaust its implications. He turned increasingly to experience itself as a lowest common denominator between evangelicals who disagreed about details of systematic theology, and he refused to trumpet Calvinistic orthodoxy. His Calvinism remained intact, but it was deliberately sublimated in his preaching and writing in order to reach the widest possible audience. William Jay recalled the old Newton

---

[83] *Private Journals of Byrom*, ii. 638; *Letters* (Barlass), 60; cf. *Works*, ii. 52, 102.
[84] *Letters* (Coffin), 91.   [85] Cf. also *Works*, i. 155; vi. 441.
[86] Cecil, *Newton*, 250.

saying once, 'I am more of a Calvinist than anything else; but I use my Calvinism in my writings and my preaching as I use this sugar.' Newton then took a lump, and putting it into his tea-cup, and stirring it, added, 'I do not give it alone, and whole; but mixed and diluted.'[87]

Thus, while Newton's involvement with Wesley and John Ryland, Jun., during the 1760s and 1770s clearly demonstrates what it meant for Newton, in theological terms, to be 'a middle man', this intermediate position was itself capable of further moderation. As Newton grew old, he became less concerned to give his theological convictions precise or sophisticated definition, wishing simply to accept all those who had experienced the grace of Christ.

[87] *Autobiography of William Jay*, ed. George Redford and John Angell James (1854; repr., Edinburgh, 1974), 272.

5

'There is, without doubt, an awakening and reviving work in and about Olney'
The Olney Curacy, 1764–1780

Would I describe a preacher, such as Paul,
Were he on earth, would hear, approve, and own,
Paul should himself direct me. I would trace
His master-strokes, and draw from his design.
I would express him simple, grave, sincere;
In doctrine uncorrupt; in language plain,
And plain in manner; decent, solemn, chaste,
And natural in gesture; much impress'd
Himself, as conscious of his awful charge,
And anxious mainly that the flock he feeds
May feel it too; affectionate in look,
And tender in address, as well becomes
A messenger of grace to guilty men.
Behold the picture!—Is it like?—Like whom?

William Cowper

NEWTON formed a high conception of the character and duties of an evangelical clergyman as he contemplated entering the ministry and engaged in lay religious activity during the period from 1757 to 1764. Many of these ideals were recorded privately in his diary or expressed in familiar correspondence with friends. He believed that a minister must aim above all to awaken sinners through the preaching of the gospel. He must also be zealous, disciplined, and humble, expert in the Scriptures and widely experienced in spiritual matters, athirst for the glory of God and the salvation of souls. He must pray often and earnestly in private and in public, must preach plainly and affectionately, must speak individually to his hearers of Christ, and must seek to spread the gospel near and far. After finally obtaining orders in 1764, Newton entered immediately upon a vigorous round of pastoral activity, seeking to realize these ideals and to fulfil the spiritual charge he had been given at Olney.

Newton's Olney curacy stands as an important case in eighteenth-century evangelical pastoralia. From his diary, his day-to-day pastoral activity may be recounted in some detail, and local history sources help to set this activity in context. His characteristic practices, and the dilemmas he faced as he sought to provide conscientiously for the cure of souls, illuminate some of the special problems and opportunities encountered by evangelical clergy of his generation, particularly with respect to the relationship between Church and Dissent. Moreover, his ministry at Olney was itself an important episode in the religious history of the surrounding region where the borders of Buckinghamshire, Northamptonshire, and Bedfordshire converge.

OLNEY AND ENVIRONS

In 1712 the ancient parish of Olney in the East Midlands comprised approximately 500 houses and 2,000 inhabitants in an area of over 3,000 acres. The adjacent parishes were for the most part much smaller and less populous.[1] Located at the extreme north-eastern end of Buckinghamshire, the parish measured 4 miles long by 2½ wide, and included the hamlet of Warrington as well as the borough of Olney. A part of the deanery of Newport Pagnell and the archdeaconry of Buckingham, it was then in the southernmost corner of the large divided diocese of Lincoln (though now in the diocese of Oxford). Olney was the largest town in the surrounding area but was only 12 miles from the sizeable towns of Bedford, Northampton, Wellingborough, and Stony Stratford; Newport Pagnell, through which the main road to London passed, was only 5 miles away.[2]

[1] For example, a survey of the region in 1788 reported 417 families at Olney, and fewer than 150 in most of the surrounding parishes. Clifton Reynes, Hardmead, Newton Blossomville, and Weston Underwood had fewer than fifty families. Diocesan Speculum, 1788–92, MS, Lincolnshire Archive Office.

[2] The local history and topography of Olney is recounted in Thomas Wright, *Town of Cowper* (1893); Oliver Ratcliff, *History and Antiquities of the Newport Hundreds* (Olney, 1900); id. and H. Brown, *Olney: Past and Present* (Olney, 1893); George Lipscomb, *History and Antiquities of the County of Buckingham*, iv (1847), 298–310;

The parish was low, open country and lay on the north-west bank of the River Ouse. Only a small fraction of the land was wooded. The largest proportion was laid down in grass and the remaining one-third was arable. Cowper immortalized much of the countryside in pastoral verse, celebrating the Edenic virtues of rural 'retirement', but Newton's first impression was much more bleak: 'The people here are mostly poor—the country low and dirty.'[3] Although the farmland belonged principally to the lord of the manor, Newton's patron the Earl of Dartmouth, the vast majority of houses in town were freehold, so that fewer than twenty families were directly dependent upon Lord Dartmouth as tenants, though many more people from town would have been employed as agricultural day-labourers.[4] An Act of Parliament in 1767 brought about the enclosure of the parish commons, but there is little evidence that this significantly disrupted local patterns of life, since Olney itself was a market town inhabited principally by artisans and tradesmen. Cowper reported to Lady Hesketh in 1786 that the town contained only one other house, besides his own, that was not occupied by a trade.[5] His and Newton's were also the only households with servants. In addition to essential rural craftsmen such as blacksmiths and carpenters, and small retailers such as grocers, bakers, and butchers, Olney had large numbers of cordwainers, watch-makers, straw-workers, tailors, breechesmakers, millers, fell-mongers, innkeepers, and a variety of other trades important to the local economy and the support of nearby villages. A survey of the parish in 1798 found that 337 men were engaged in over fifty occupations.[6] Daniel Defoe noted that

---

William Page, *Victoria History of the Counties of England: Buckinghamshire,* iv (1927), 429–39. See also Browne Willis, 'Parochial History of the Newport Pagnell Hundreds' *c.*1732, with additional notes *c.*1755 and later, MS, Bodl.

[3] *Letters* (Clunie), 43.

[4] Thomas Bainbridge, 'A Survey, Valuation and Plans of the Estates of the Right Honourable The Earl of Dartmouth situate at Olney, Warrington and Bradwell Abbey, in the County of Buckingham', 1796, MS, CNM.

[5] *Letters and Prose Writings of William Cowper,* ed. James King and Charles Ryskamp, 5 vols. (Oxford, 1979–86), ii. 503.

[6] Detailed statistical data for the occupational structure of Olney, with comparative figures for other parishes, may be found in the *Buckinghamshire Posse Comitatus 1798,* ed. F. W. Beckett, Buckinghamshire Record Society, 22 (n.p., 1985).

Olney was famed especially for its 'considerable Manufacture of Bone-lace,' a cottage industry which had been important locally since the late sixteenth and early seventeenth centuries, when many religious refugees from France and the Low Countries settled in the district, bringing the trade with them.[7]

The area was not, however, prosperous. Cowper, who like Newton often interceded with distant benefactors on behalf of the poor at Olney, once remarked, 'Olney is a populous place, inhabited chiefly by the half-starved and the ragged of the Earth.'[8] The lacemakers seem to have been particularly vulnerable to price fluctuations, and were often among the poorest of the town. Those involved as buyers and dealers might do well, but the lacemakers themselves, despite long hours of meticulous labour, frequently became a charge to the parish.[9] It was at Olney that Matthew Maryott, once sexton and clerk of the parish, established and publicized his first workhouse experiment in the 1720s, one of the early initiatives in private enterprise designed to relieve pressure on parish poor rates.[10] In addition to the women and children, who made up most of the numbers of lacemakers, many men who were labourers by day supplemented their income by making lace at home. In 1780 Cowper wrote of 'near 1200 Lace Makers in this Beggarly Town', hundreds of whom he claimed were on the point of starving because of the loss of a domestic market for English lace due to import tariff reductions.[11] If his numbers were not exaggerated, then more than half the parish consisted of such poor people. Local

[7] Daniel Defoe, *A Tour*, 7th edn. 4 vols. (1769), ii. 238. See further, Thomas Wright, *Romance of the Lace Pillow* (Olney, 1919).

[8] *Letters of Cowper*, ii. 91 cf. 316. Cowper's poem, 'The Task', Bk. 4, ll. 374–428, was a conscious portrait of the poor of Olney.

[9] Cf. the comments of Lord Dartmouth's surveyor in 1796: 'The Poor Rates in Olney are very high, owing to the great number of Lace-makers who are employed in the Town, and who frequently become chargeable to the Parish.' The rates in 1795 had been 8s. in the pound, but the average was 6s. in the pound. Bainbridge, 'A Survey of the Estates'.

[10] *Register of the Parish of Olney, Co. Bucks, 1665 to 1812*, transcribed by O. Ratcliff [Olney, 1909], 501–4. See also the 'Olney Workhouse Book Bought 1746' and similar MS records of the disbursements of the Overseers, CNM.

[11] *Letters of Cowper*, i. 363 cf. 358.

crises—a severe winter or a failed harvest, a sudden rise in prices or a loss of property through fire or theft—were often occasions of acute suffering for those who barely managed in good times to live at a subsistence level.

ECCLESIASTICAL HISTORY

The religious history of the surrounding area points up how deeply rooted Nonconformity was in the region for more than a century and a half before Newton came to Olney. It may be useful to recount this history so that Newton's ministry can be seen in proper perspective as one episode in the religious life of the region.

Puritanism and Early Nonconformity

For William Worcester, Vicar of Olney (1624–38) under Charles I, the royal command to read the anti-sabbatarian Book of Sports from the pulpit had rankled. When in 1636 some of his parishioners danced in town after evening prayer, he raised the constables against them armed with bills and halberts. The Dean of the Arches, Sir John Lambe, called on him, admonishing him to read the offensive Book, but Worcester refused and was subsequently suspended. Backed by his patron, Sir Robert Gorges, he continued by various evasions to maintain his influence in the parish until the threat of excommunication and sequestration sent him to his bishop, John Williams (1582–1650). Worcester promised the Bishop he would conform. It was later certified at the archdeaconry court that he duly read the Book to his parishioners. When, however, Lambe congratulated him on his change of heart, Worcester started and replied that he was not at all converted, but only did what he had to do to comply with the Bishop's command. After further argument, Lambe reprimanded him and insisted he declare to his people that he not only read the book but approved of it too. Worcester remained intransigent. He resigned his living and, early in April 1639, set sail for New England to make a new start for himself, as more than a dozen young families from Olney and the surrounding villages had done four years earlier. He settled in Salisbury, Massachusetts, and became the first

173

minister there, continuing until his death on 28 October 1662. He was remembered by Cotton Mather as a 'reverend, learned and holy divine' and headed an impressive dynasty of New England ministers.[12]

As the emigration of many local families to New England testifies, Worcester's Puritanism was shared by numbers of the parish laity. John James was excommunicated and forced to sell his inheritance to cover more than £100 in fines and court fees for going to hear a sermon in the parish church while Worcester was suspended. After making satisfaction to Lambe, James was again excommunicated for being found at his own house with Worcester. He petitioned the House of Lords to declare the proceedings against him unjust.[13] On another occasion Raphael Britten, a lace buyer from Olney, heard someone being reproved in the Archbishop's authority for not reading the Book of Sports, and commented regarding Laud, 'No matter! He is a papist; no good man will read it or cause it to be read.'[14]

Britten's name and trade suggest Huguenot descent, and his case is an example of how native traditions of Protestantism and Puritanism in Olney were augmented by the immigration of religious refugees. Many fled to the area from France and the Low Countries after the St Bartholomew's Day Massacre in 1572, and again after the Revocation of the Edict of Nantes in 1685. Consequently, as Thomas Wright observed, 'Almost every town and village within thirty miles of Olney has persons with Flemish or French names, and practically the whole population must be partially of Flemish or French descent.'[15] Some of the names of those who later took a leading part in Newton's prayer meetings, such as Robython and Raban, can be traced back to these origins.

[12] *Calendar of State Papers, Domestic Series, of the Reign of Charles I* (1635–6), ed. John Bruce (1866), 47, 182–3; J. F. Worcester (ed.), *The Worcester Family: or the Descendants of Rev. William Worcester* (Lynn, Mass., 1856); Cotton Mather, *Magnalia Christi Americana* (1702), iii. 3. I am grateful to Elizabeth Knight, the archivist of the Cowper and Newton Museum at Olney, for lending me her research notes on William Worcester and the Olney families who emigrated to New England.
[13] Quoted in Wright, *Town of Cowper*, 35–6.
[14] *Cal. SP Dom. Chas. I* (1635–6), 37.
[15] Wright, *Romance of the Pillow*, 38.

The area around Olney was well known for the dedication of the populace to Nonconformist ideals. One historian has remarked that the majority of the clergy and local gentry had 'but one idea in coming to church, and that was to hear sermons'. A contemporary letter to William Laud mentioned that the habit of wandering from church to church for the sake of hearing sermons was likewise common, and at a visitation of 1637 it was reported that 'this corner of the diocese [of Lincoln], being most distant, is much suspected of Puritanism'.[16] Not surprisingly, then, when the Civil War began in 1642, Buckinghamshire was found with Bedfordshire and Northamptonshire on the side of the Parliament for the most part. A strong detachment of the Parliamentary army was stationed at Olney during the war, for the bridge over the River Ouse at the end of the town had a strategic importance.[17] Ralph Josselin (1616?–83), curate to the incumbent at Olney who followed Worcester, was himself said to be 'a staunch Parliamentarian, a worshipper of Cromwell'.[18]

During the Commonwealth several beneficed ministers from the area surrounding Olney were 'open communion' Baptists, admitting paedobaptists and baptists alike to membership and the Lord's Supper. They and their members often acted co-operatively and maintained a loose association of churches. After the Restoration, the labours of a few strong leaders who came from these congregations established Dissent as a permanent feature in the region. John Bunyan (1628–88) was a major influence in and around Bedford. His near-contemporary John Gibbs (1627–99) of Newport Pagnell was equally active and played an important part in the history of Olney. Gibbs had been placed by Parliament in the living at Newport Pagnell to replace an incumbent thrust out by Cromwell's party in 1648. He was himself ejected after the Restoration (but before the Act of Uniformity brought about the wider 'Great Ejection'), ostensibly for refusing the

---

[16] *VCH Buckinghamshire*, i. 321–2.

[17] A skirmish took place in and about Olney between Royalists and Parliamentarians, the former commanded by Prince Rupert, in Nov. 1643. Ratcliff, *Newport Hundreds*, 59–60.

[18] Thomas Wright, 'Olney Men, 7', *Olney Advertiser* (13 Nov. 1909).

sacrament to an influential parishioner. His political activities
as an informant to Parliament during an insurrection in 1659
had also told against him. During the 1660s, when Nonconformists were legally proscribed and persecuted, Gibbs
maintained a congregation at Newport Pagnell and gathered
others nearby at Olney, Newton Blossomville, Astwood,
Cranfield, and Roade.[19] The Conventicle and Five Mile Acts
were responsible for some of this itinerancy, and many of his
people travelled far to be with him at these meetings. The
Olney and Newport Pagnell churches were especially closely
linked and seem for a time to have been regarded as one
congregation. In response to Archbishop Sheldon's 1669
survey of conventicles, local clergy noted Gibbs's activity at
Newport Pagnell, and mention was made also of Olney:
'Olney; two meetings; one, Anabaptist, at the house of Widow
Tears; number, about 200, but decrease; mean people; led by
Mr. Gibbs, one Breedon, and James Rogers, lace buyers, and
one Fenne, a hatter.' Another meeting of fifty or sixty was
recorded at Newton Blossomville.[20] The 'Dissenting Interest'
at Olney and in the surrounding area originated chiefly in
these labours by Gibbs.

Under the Declaration of Indulgence in 1672, twenty-seven
licences to preach and to hold religious meetings were granted
in Buckinghamshire, and licences were likewise numerous in
Bedfordshire and Northamptonshire. Bunyan submitted an
application for several licences for places nearby Bedford
including one on behalf of William Henseman for 'the house
or barn of Joseph Kent, Olney'.[21] When licences were recalled
in 1675 and the persecution resumed, the names of Nonconformists from Olney began to appear regularly in the
Buckinghamshire Quarter Session records. Then, after Joseph
Kent's barn was raided in 1684, and forty people were
arraigned and fined for attending an unlawful assembly at

[19] See Fig. 1 for many of these places and others referred to in this section.
[20] Maurice F. Hewett, 'John Gibbs, 1627–1699', *Baptist Quarterly*, 3 (1926–7),
315–22; Nuttall, 'Baptists and Independents'; Wright, *Town of Cowper*, 129–35. The
full parish responses to Sheldon's survey for Olney and the surrounding towns and
villages are given in John Broad (ed.), *Buckinghamshire Dissent and Parish Life, 1669–
1712* (Aylesbury, 1993), 1–72. The other meeting at Olney was Quaker, and
attended by about forty.   [21] *Cal. SP Dom. Chas. II* (1672), 62, 119.

Olney, the Dissenters would frequently meet three miles away at Northey: 'The meeting place was only a few yards from "Three Counties' Point", where Northamptonshire, Bedfordshire and Buckinghamshire adjoin. Here Bunyan and Gibbs preached; and here, when they were persecuted in one County, they could flee into the next.'[22] This may also explain why many other licences were taken out at places likewise close to the borders of these counties.

Comparatively little is known of the character of the parish church itself at Olney from the turbulent years after the beginning of the Civil War until well into the Hanoverian period. Such records as do exist, however, suggest that incumbents were aware of, and regretted, the strength of Dissent in the town. The advowson and rectorial tithes were held from 1642 by the Johnson family who built and resided for many years at the Great House where Newton would later hold his parish prayer meetings. They appointed a succession of six vicars. Henry Elliot, Vicar of Olney during the first two decades of the eighteenth century, reported that 40 per cent of his parish was comprised of Dissenters, and he confided to his visitation return in 1715 that he was exasperated by his 'divided and untractable parish', adding with St Paul, πρὸς ταῦτα τίς ἱκανός; ['Who is sufficient for these things?'][23] In 1735, Wolsey Johnson became the incumbent and soon afterwards inherited the impropriation as well.[24] Whatever the predilections of his forebears, Johnson himself opposed local evangelical and dissenting activity vigorously.

In the late seventeenth and early eighteenth centuries, the old Puritan impulse was sustained in the region chiefly through the efforts of Dissenters such as Gibbs and Bunyan and their followers. Still, while Dissent was well on its way to becoming an established part of local life in and around Olney, its patterns were fluid, and its organization and distribution changed significantly within short periods. The Old Meeting founded by Gibbs was open communion and

[22] Hewett, 'Gibbs', 320.
[23] 'Parochial Returns to Bishop Wake's Questionnaires of 1706, 1709, and 1712', Wake MSS 275–6, Christ Church, Oxford.
[24] See further, Lipscomb, *History and Antiquities*, 305–7.

survived the difficult days of the Clarendon Code to be given more permanence with the erection of a meeting-house a few years after the Act of Toleration. However, a little earlier, a number of Olney Dissenters were received into the membership of a paedobaptist church at Rothwell in Northamptonshire. The minister at Rothwell was Richard Davis, the popular high Calvinist evangelist mentioned in Chapter 4, who maintained a kind of connexion of congregations across Northamptonshire, Huntingdonshire, and Cambridgeshire. Most of the Olney members of Davis's Rothwell congregation went on almost immediately to help establish a new church at Wellingborough, whose pastor was a shoemaker named Robert Bettson. In later years the Congregationalist church at Olney would identify Davis as its founder, and Bettson as its second minister, but already at this time the group at Olney had an identity distinct from the baptists. In the visitation return for 1706, the Vicar of Olney indicated the presence of a 'Davisite' meeting under the local leadership of an apothecary named Thomas Bere, who had earlier been an associate of Gibbs and leading member of the Old Meeting.[25]

To this Gibbs–Davis factionalism in Olney was added in the following years a growing tension over terms of communion. In about 1712 Matthias Maurice (1684–1738) came from Wales to pastor the Old Meeting, but some members had already discarded Gibbs's open-communion ideals and become strict baptists, maintaining that only those baptized as adult believers should be allowed full membership in the church and admission to the Lord's Supper. Within very short order, Maurice led a paedobaptist secession to establish the Lower or Independent Meeting at Olney, augmenting the Davisite group meeting in the High Street. Then, in 1718, the

[25] For this and the following two paragraphs, see Nuttall, 'Baptists and Independents'; Hewett, 'Gibbs', 320–1; *History of the Congregational Church at Olney* (Olney, 1929); Wright, *Town of Cowper*, 129–38; Josiah Thompson, 'History of Dissenting Churches of the Congregationalist, Presbyterian and Antipaedobaptist Denominations in England and Wales' [1774], Meen MS, DWL; Broad (ed)., *Buckinghamshire Dissent*; 'Parochial Returns to Bishop Wake's Questionnaires', Wake MSS. Note that the dates given in the visitation records for Maurice's ministry, and for Davisite and Independent meetings in Olney, appears to conflict with some of the other sources. I have given what seems to me the most plausible reconstruction above.

members of this congregation were formally dismissed from the church at Wellingborough to stand on their own as a self-governing Independent church. From this time forward there were two principal Dissenters' meetings in the town.

By the 1730s the fortunes of both congregations had declined. The Baptists disbanded; the Independents decreased considerably in numbers. The latter were slowly resuscitated by the attentions of Philip Doddridge (1702–51), who had begun his famous pastorate at Northampton in 1730, and John Drake (d. 1775), the minister at Yardley Hastings just across the county border from Olney. Doddridge, Drake, and others took turns preaching a lecture once a month in the town, even though most of the Olney Dissenters had 'for some time been extremely fond of lay preachers in the Antinomian strain'.[26] Nearly 500 people turned out to hear them, including a great number of Churchmen. From 1738 Drake began to preach once a Sunday at Olney, and from 1759 until his death in 1775 he resided there permanently.

The Baptist cause too depended on other churches in the surrounding area to regain its strength in Olney.[27] When the members were dispersed in the 1730s, several joined the strict communion church at Walgrave in Northamptonshire. This congregation, together with another at Northampton recently 'enchurched on a strict bottom', served the Olney Baptists until thirteen members finally reconstituted themselves as a distinct church again in 1738. They had difficulty sustaining their own minister until William Walker (d. 1793) finally settled among them in 1753 and remained at Olney for the following twenty years. John Drake was thus the Independent minister, and William Walker the Baptist minister, when John Newton came to Olney in 1764. In 1775 John Whitford succeeded Drake as minister of the Independent Meeting, and John Sutcliff replaced Walker at the Baptist Meeting.

Summary: The Puritan Constituency

From this brief sketch of the religious history of Olney and environs, prior to the beginning of the Evangelical Revival, it

[26] *Correspondence of Doddridge*, ed. Nuttall, 64.
[27] See further, Michael A. G. Haykin, *One Heart and One Soul: John Sutcliff of Olney, His Friends and His Times* (Darlington, 1994), 100–6.

is clear that Nonconformity was especially strong in the region. Michael Watts's analysis of the Evans List of 1718 corroborates this assertion.[28] The density of the Dissenters in Bedfordshire was strongest, at over 10 per cent; but Northamptonshire was still 8.5 per cent, and Buckinghamshire close to 7 per cent—all above the national average of just over 6 per cent. Diocesan records paint a picture of Dissent as even stronger in Olney and the Newport deanery to which it belonged.[29] In 1712, for example, when parishes in Buckinghamshire were rarely reporting that Dissenters formed more than 10 per cent of the local population, they formed nearly 25 per cent at Olney. Moreover, the numbers of Independents and Particular Baptists, among whom Calvinistic beliefs were strongest in the early eighteenth century, were disproportionately high in nearby Bedfordshire, and Northamptonshire. The extreme north-east corner of Buckinghamshire, in which Olney and Newport Pagnell were located, protruded into these two counties, and it shared with them many common geographic, social, and religious characteristics. The history of the Olney area demonstrates how widely Dissenters in the region co-operated: they shared in each other's services; large congregations assisted smaller ones; and ministers conferred with one another and exercised wide pastoral oversight. Olney was at the centre of this region, where Calvinistic Dissent had attained some of the highest proportions of the English population that it had gained anywhere.

Several factors account for the vitality of Nonconformity in the region at the time of the Evans List. First, it is evident from the history of the region that the Puritan tradition continued strong throughout the seventeenth century. The

---

[28] Watts, *Dissenters*, 267–9, 509.

[29] Broad (ed.), *Buckinghamshire Dissent*, pp. xvii–xlv, and the parochial returns beginning on p. 73. The figures for Dissent in the period after Newton's curacy were generated slightly differently, but Dissenting congregations continued to prosper significantly in comparison to other parishes. The most remarkable increase was in nearby Lavendon, where Newton had participated in a local prayer meeting. Olney was reported to have 417 families, of whom 715 persons were Dissenters; Lavendon-cum-Brayfield, 130 families, of whom 200 persons were Dissenters. Diocesan Speculum, 1788–92, MS, Lincolnshire Archive Office.

progress of Puritanism from a protest movement within the Church, through a period of ascendancy within the Establishment, to a dissenting movement outside the Church may be seen in microcosm at Olney. Worcester was a Nonconformist within the Church under Charles I; Gibbs was a beneficed Baptist under the Commonwealth; and then, ejected at the Restoration, he became a Dissenter outside the Establishment under Charles II. This is one instance of several similar cases from the surrounding area. Michael Watts suggests, moreover, that large numbers of Independents, and the Particular Baptists who sprang from them, were present in those counties which were during the Civil War well behind the Parliamentary lines, since it was here that Puritanism was sufficiently secure to afford the luxury of internal dispute.[30] This would further account for the prominence of more radical Puritan ideals in the East Midlands counties.

It is also clear that the region around Olney saw a number of strong and gifted Nonconformist leaders. The influence of 'Pope Bunyan' was enormous in Bedfordshire, and his extensive itinerancy is itself enough to account for the strength of Calvinistic Baptists in that county. The labours of Gibbs in Buckinghamshire and Davis in Northamptonshire were likewise prodigious. Doddridge was yet another remarkable leader a few years later. The individual genius and dedication of these men and others did much to create a loyal following for Dissent.

Recent studies have demonstrated that Dissent also tended to prosper most in areas where parochial organization was ineffective, and deference to traditional authority was weak.[31] Olney and the surrounding parishes were not unwieldy in size as were many of the parishes in, for example, Yorkshire. Nor did Olney see significant demographic shifts or an unusual rise in population, such as occurred in pre-industrial areas such as the North-West; on the contrary, the local economy and population remained static throughout most of the eighteenth century. But Olney was a market town inhabited by artisans and merchants, and repeatedly the names of tradesmen occur in the records of Nonconformity in the

---

[30] Watts, *Dissenters*, 281–2.   [31] See e.g. Gilbert, *Religion and Society*.

region. This was the occupational group most often associated with Dissent and with later evangelicalism. Reliance upon trade for a living allowed individuals a measure of independence from local social control associated with conservative landed interests, the so-called traditional alliance of squire and parson which favoured the Church. Moreover, those involved in a commercial economy were much more mobile, and the history of Olney in particular demonstrates how far many Dissenters were willing to travel—sometimes more than twenty miles—to worship according to conscience.

In the immediate vicinity of Olney it does not appear that the local gentry and clergy had much influence in restraining Nonconformist activity, especially once the penalties of the Clarendon Code were moderated. It may be significant also that two of the most ancient seats in the area belonged to recusants, the Throckmortons of Weston Underwood and the Digbys of Gayhurst. Without legal status themselves, these aristocratic families were not in a position to exercise religious coercion on the immediate population. Contemporaries also noted the problems there were in maintaining ecclesiastical discipline in the archdeaconry of Buckinghamshire, the farthest corner of the largest diocese in the kingdom. The religious monopoly of the Established Church had been broken in law by the religious provisions of the Revolutionary settlement; it was further weakened in and around Olney through the relative independence of the local population from traditional forms of rural paternalism and church discipline.

The Evans List statistics were mostly collected in 1718. In the decades which followed, Olney participated in the general decline in the numbers and morale of Dissenters as a whole which prompted several self-searching tracts lamenting the 'Decay of the Dissenting Interest'. Internal debates over Socinianism, Calvinism, and terms of communion fragmented a movement whose principal bond of union—opposition to the State–Ecclesiastical—was already weakened in the environment of religious toleration of the early eighteenth century. Doddridge wrote in 1730 of the danger that a Dissenting minister might soon find himself 'entertained with the echo' of his own voice. In Olney, however, the problem was more that

Dissenting lay people were in danger of being entertained only by their own voices, for in the generation which followed that of the Ejection, they were often without local pastoral oversight. Yet when Doddridge and Drake lectured there in the 1730s, some 500 turned out, nearly one quarter of the local population. Clearly, Puritanism had left a large constituency at Olney which could be exploited by effective evangelical leadership.

Early Evangelicalism: Whitefield and Browne at Olney (1739–64)

This was the situation when in May 1739 George Whitefield, having long promised to come, first visited Olney. Denied the pulpit, he preached in a nearby field to an estimated 2,000 people. He travelled on the same day to Northampton where he visited Doddridge, preached to large audiences, and remarked upon the 'many righteous souls' that lived in the area. He was encouraged that people of all denominations prayed for him. Then, on his way back to Bedford, Whitefield stopped again at Olney since the people were begging to see him once more:

Great numbers were assembled together; but on account of it being a rainy day, it was judged inconvenient to preach in the fields. I therefore stood upon an eminence in the street, and preached from thence with such power as I have not for some time experienced. Though it rained all the time, yet the people stood very attentive and patient. All, I really believe, *felt*, as well as *heard*, the Word, and one was so pricked to the heart, and convinced of sin, that I scarce saw the like instance.[32]

Newton's history of evangelical religion at Olney began with this event. He wrote in 1765, 'The Gospel seed was first sown in Olney by Mr Whitfield and his brethren, about the year '39. We have several precious souls of so long standing in the kingdom of God. Soon after a little place was built, a society formed, and Mr Whitfield's preachers came frequently.'[33]

The influence of Whitefield and his preachers at Olney

[32] *George Whitefield's Journals* (Edinburgh, 1960), 272–4; Tyreman, *Life of Whitefield*, i. 231. [33] *Letters* (Jones), 66–7.

began precisely when organized Dissent in the town was weakest, when neither the Baptists nor the Independents had a settled minister. But for Newton to date the origins of 'the Gospel' at Olney from Whitefield's first visit obscures the over-whelming continuity of Calvinistic Methodism in the 1730s with local religious tradition.

The incumbent who refused Whitefield his pulpit was Wolsey Johnson (d. 1755), a man of property and some social standing, since, as noted above, he possessed the advowson and impropriated tithes for Olney along with the vicarage. Two years before his death Johnson appointed Moses Browne (1704–87) to the living, intending himself to move with his family to an estate in Lincolnshire. At one time a pen-cutter, Browne had distinguished himself as a man of letters while still young, writing poetry for the *Gentleman's Magazine* and publishing his own dramatic compositions. Under the influence of evangelical preaching, he was later converted and sought to enter the ministry. Like Newton he did not have a university education, but because of the patronage of James Hervey and the influence of Lady Huntingdon he was at length able to obtain orders.[34] After serving as curate to Hervey at Weston Favell for a time, he was appointed to the vicarage of Olney. Several local history sources refer vaguely to 'great disputes and squabbles' that ensued between Browne and Johnson's widow. Describing Browne's ministry on one occasion, Newton filled in the details:

By him the Gospel was preached in the church; and then the Methodist preachers withdrew, and went where they were more wanted. The gentleman [Johnson] who gave Mr Browne the living resided in the parish, and soon became his open enemy. With such head, the spirit of opposition and enmity exerted itself with great courage. Mr Browne went through a great deal—was often abused to his face—put in the spiritual court . . .[35]

The advowson was not by this time any longer in Johnson's hands, however, having passed sometime earlier to the trustees of Frances Nicoll in whom also the moieties of the Olney manor were recently united. When in 1755 she married

---

[34] *LyH* i. 164–8.   [35] *Letters* (Jones), 67.

Lord Dartmouth, the estate and advowson became vested in him by right of marriage. It was soon after this that Lord Dartmouth met Lady Huntingdon and through her influence, and that of several leading evangelical preachers, embraced evangelical principles himself. Newton commented, 'By the favour of such a patron, Mr B. was held up; and at last the Lord gave him the victory, and put his enemies to shame.'[36] Compared to the wealth of evidence for Newton's Olney curacy, next to nothing is known of the fourteen-year ministry of Whitefield and his lay preachers, or the twelve-year ministry of Browne at Olney. But Newton acknowledged that these men had not only prepared the way for him, but had also taken the brunt of local opposition.

John Drake, the Independent minister at Yardley Hastings who used to preach once a week at Olney, and then came and resided there in 1759, provided information on Dissent in Olney for the editor of a manuscript account of Dissenting churches in England and Wales in 1774. Regarding Olney, the editor recorded, '[Drake] says when he first came there both the meetings were considerable but both are now greatly reduced. This was first owing to the preaching of Mr. Brown the Vicar which drew many from the Meetings.'[37] Here then is a clear link between the Evangelical Revival and Old Dissent. Early evangelicalism at Olney drew on the constituency which had been created in large measure by a long history of Nonconformity in the area. But because Browne had a large family and a small income, he eventually accepted the chaplaincy of Morden College at Blackheath in Kent and, later, the rectory of Sutton in Lincolnshire. It was originally agreed that he would resign the living at Olney, upon which resignation, Lord Dartmouth would offer it to Newton. In the event, Browne did not resign the vicarage, and Newton remained curate throughout his period at Olney. During this time, Newton drew on the same catchment as Browne, with the result that Drake complained that he, even more than Browne, gave 'a mortal wound to the Dissenting Interest in this place'.[38]

[36] Ibid.   [37] Thompson, 'History of Dissenting Churches'.
[38] Ibid.

It would be hard to imagine an individual better suited to take advantage of the Puritan–Nonconformist constituency at Olney than Newton. An evangelical Calvinist with the highest regard for Whitefield, Newton had deep roots in the Dissenting tradition and his churchmanship was of the lowest sort and unlikely to cause offence. As demonstrated below, Newton co-operated widely with Dissenters and integrated many of their practices in his own ministry. His initial popularity at Olney had much to do with the fact that he was able to offer his adherents everything that could be had at the local Meeting, along with additional perquisites which accrued to member-ship in the Church. It was as though the parish had been specially groomed for him. He saw this in providential terms: '[God] has a people in this country, that were in danger of being scattered as sheep without a shepherd: they did not seek me, nor I them; but the Lord has brought us together.' And shortly after he arrived at Olney he identified his situation with that described in John 4: 38: 'I sent you to reap that whereon ye bestowed no labour: other men laboured, and ye are entered into their labours.'[39]

NEWTON'S CURACY

Initial Reception

At first Newton's congregation was not as large as he had been given to expect from reports in London. But after only a few months, he described it in enthusiastic terms as not much smaller than that which met in London at the fashionable Lock Chapel patronized by Lord Dartmouth. Week by week he learned of more 'experienced' people from the country around Olney. By the end of 1764 he could write that there was unquestionably 'an awakening and reviving work in and about Olney', though it was not attended with 'noisy, or very remarkable appearances'.[40] People travelled from five or six miles around to hear him, and within a year a gallery was added along the north side of the nave. Newton claimed in 1765 that with this addition the church could hold almost

---

[39] *Letters* (Clunie), 32, 40.   [40] Ibid. 62.

2,000 people, and that it was still well filled. Even if this estimate was overly optimistic, his congregation would still have represented an exceptionally high proportion of the surrounding population. Olney itself possessed not many more than 2,000 inhabitants, while the surrounding parishes contained far fewer potential hearers still.

When Newton's *Authentic Narrative* was published toward the end of his first year at Olney, he hoped it would give some additional weight to his ministry. 'The people stare at me since reading [it],' he wrote to Alexander Clunie.[41] At the centre of Newton's religious self-consciousness was the belief that he had been remarkably converted through a decisive experience of God's grace. When he described Olney as 'reviving' and 'awakening', he understood numbers of his parishioners to be themselves experiencing this same converting grace. From several casual phrases in his correspondence, it is evident that, in his own mind, he naturally divided those who came to church into three categories: hearers, professors, and believers. For Newton, the general awakening at Olney involved many mere hearers or nominal professors becoming experienced, serious believers through the preaching of the gospel. The careless were being awakened and those distressed in conscience comforted. While he saw this to be a gracious work of the Holy Spirit, he did not flag in his own efforts to see his parishioners thus quickened spiritually. It was the chief end of his pastoral labours. At intervals he reported to his friends small numbers of persons whom he felt had been truly converted under his ministry. In January 1765 he wrote that he had 'a score or two believers' to show Clunie, one or two of whom were not yet born when Clunie was last at Olney. A month later he announced that he had admitted two individuals to the sacrament who could now 'give a solid reason of the hope that is in them,' and that six others had been awakened in the past few weeks. In May 1766 he related that 'a young lamb or two' had lately been added to his fold; in January 1767 that he also had good hopes of two unlikely persons—a disturbed woman and a 70-year-old man, both poor. On another occasion Newton wrote, '[Jesus] was

41 Ibid.

pleased to bless what he enabled me to say, to the deliverance of one poor soul who has been some time in great distress. She came to me this morning, rejoicing as a bird that has just escaped out of the snare of the fowler.'[42] By 1775 he could report to Lord Dartmouth that some 100 souls had been awakened in this way under his ministry (i. 468).

He saw his role of preaching and counselling as an instrumental one, like a midwife attending the labour and delivery of spiritual children. Through the preaching of the gospel he sought to awaken sinners; then, through pastoral visiting he aimed to observe, and through counselling to hasten, the work of grace in particular cases, testing its genuineness before finally announcing his hope that this or that person had been truly converted. This understanding of ministry was expressed in his hymn on Galatians 4: 19, 'Travailing in Birth for Souls'. Mixing metaphors of birth and harvest, Newton described the task of evangelical ministers:

> If some small hope appear,
> They still are not content;
> But, with a jealous fear,
> They watch for the event:
> Too oft they find their hopes deceiv'd,
> Then, how their inmost souls are griev'd!
>
> But when their pains succeed,
> And from the tender blade
> The rip'ning ears proceed,
> Their toils are overpaid:
> No harvest-joy can equal theirs,
> To find the fruit of all their cares.
> (*OH* 2. 26, st. 4–5)

Public preaching and private counselling were thus directed to the end of individual conversion. This was for Newton the essence of a gospel ministry.

Pastoral Activity

It remains to survey how Newton carried out this ministry at Olney by examining the required services he performed, the

---

[42] *Letters* (Clunie), 100.

additional weekly meetings he conducted, the round of pastoral calls he typically made, and the wider activities he engaged in outside the parish.

(a) *Stated and prescribed services.* Two services a Sunday were regarded in contemporary pastoral handbooks and episcopal visitation charges as a 'relatively uncontroversial minimum', and at only one of these services did bishops typically require a sermon. Yet, despite some regional variation, there were still many parishes that did not measure up to even this unambitious eighteenth-century ideal.[43] Newton certainly met these basic obligations, since he had two 'stated services' on Sundays, at both of which he preached a one-hour sermon. 'I cannot wind up my ends to my own satisfaction in a much shorter time,' wrote Newton, 'nor am I pleased with myself if I greatly exceed it' (ii. 163). These services were supplemented by many other meetings, so that he often preached five or six sermons a week. On one single Sunday in 1765 he preached for a total of six hours at church and at home, commenting afterwards, 'if there was occasion I could readily go and preach again'.[44] He kept close to the liturgical rubrics in his Sunday services, and read the prescribed forms of the Prayer Book without variation or omission, but he used extempore prayer before and after the sermon. Many of his parishioners attended only one of the services on Sunday.

Although not always his pattern, Newton generally preached 'experimentally and to believers' in the morning and 'more to sinners' in the afternoon.[45] For these latter services he preached, for example, a series of sermons in 1773 against sins particular to the town, such as whoredom, adultery, drunkenness, and profane swearing.[46] Often his Sunday discourses drew on Old Testament typology. This was the case in 1766 when he preached on Joshua 4: 10, 11 and 1 Kings 17: 7, collating references to the drying up of the river Jordan in order to apply these to Christ and to death: 'O how

---

[43] F. C. Mather, 'Georgian Churchmanship Reconsidered: Some Variations in Anglican Public Worship 1714–1830', *Journal of Ecclesiastical History*, 36 (1985), 265–6; cf. Walsh and Taylor, 'The Church and Anglicanism', 11–12.

[44] *Letters* (Clunie), 85.   [45] Diary (1773–1805), 30 Jan. 1774.

[46] Ibid., 17 Jan. 1773.

valuable is an interest in Him, who is an abiding spring when every stream fails, and who can . . . make a safe and pleasant passage through the swellings of the black river—Death!'[47] His 'interesting manner of preaching' was noted by contemporaries, and many enjoyed his emblematic imagination, his knack of pithy proverbial expression, his ear for local colour and anecdote, and his willingness to display his emotions from the pulpit.[48] Richard Cecil recalled the effect of Newton's preaching on his hearers: 'He frequently interspersed the most brilliant allusions, and brought forward such happy illustrations of his subject, and those with so much unction on his own heart, as melted and enlarged theirs.'[49]

Some of this directness is retained in more than two dozen, hand-sewn sermon notebooks that survive from this period. For example, in a sermon on the love of God in Christ, during his first year at Olney, Newton turned to his hearers:

Now are there any hearts so hard, so much like stones, so much like tigers, as to pay no regard to this love? It has been found that sinners who have stood it out against the terrors & judgments of God denounced in his word, have been captivated & melted down by love. Are there any here, that have added sin to sin, thro despair of mercy, thinking all help was past—O say not so, see how God has loved the world—there is indeed then forgiveness with him. Nothing can ruin you but impatience & unbelief. . . . The Lord in the Gospel proclaims a free pardon, to all who believe in his son, & will you despise the gospel & spirit of grace & make your own damnation sure, by refusing to hear his voice? O Lord God prevent it, & rend the heavens & come down, [and] touch the stoney heart, that it may stand out no longer. . . . You that feel the weight of sin. See what encouragement . . . Believers, Let this subject, engage you to trust the Lord with Soul & body, what can you fear after such an earnest of his love. . . . Let us chide our cold unfeeling hearts—& pray for a coal of fire from the heavenly altar to send us home in a flame of love to him who has thus loved us.[50]

Like many of his contemporary evangelicals, Newton preached earnestly for a response from his listeners. Besides its obvious emotional immediacy, this passage illustrates some of the

---

[47] *Letters* (Clunie), 129; Diary (1767), 4 Jan.   [48] *Letters* (Palmer), 30.
[49] Cecil, *Newton*, 227.   [50] MS Sermon notebook, 4 [1764–5?], CNM.

classes (sinners, seekers, believers) to which Newton typically appealed.

Early in Newton's ministry he carefully wrote out detailed outlines for almost all his spoken sermons, but in after years he took such pains much less often. Even during his Olney curacy there were occasions when he would write in his diary of producing sermons 'hand-to-mouth,' or of only 'catching at a text . . . upon the Pulpit stairs'. If he was not 'straightened', but found 'liberty' and 'enlargement' in the pulpit, he took this as a sign of God's blessing upon his extempore habit. His open acknowledgement later in life of his usual lack of any sort of sermon preparation drew sharp criticism from his nineteenth-century biographers.

Like many conscientious clergy of the period, Newton usually administered the sacrament twelve times a year, on the first Sunday of each month. When one of the major festivals of Christmas, Easter, or Whitsuntide fell in a given month, he would exchange the nearest first Sunday for the feast day.[51] On rare occasions he would take the controversial step of refusing a parishioner the Lord's Supper if he felt there was enough evidence to warrant such discipline, but more often he sought to 'fence off' the communion table by preaching rather than by examination. When he moved to St Mary Woolnoth in London, he used to preach a preparation sermon on the Friday morning before each sacrament Sunday, but there is no evidence that he adopted this practice at Olney. Still, he surmised, 'Perhaps there are not many assemblies in the kingdom where there are fewer come to that ordinance, whom the minister would wish absent, than at Olney.'[52] He sometimes recorded in his diary with satisfaction the names of repentant sinners who came forward for the sacrament. Although his eucharistic theology was 'low' and he regarded Holy Communion chiefly as a commemorative ordinance, he understood the Lord's Supper as a special opportunity of covenant renewal where one might expect a heart-felt experience of the divine presence.

The practice of catechizing the young people of a parish in

---

[51] Cf. Mather, 'Georgian Churchmanship', 269–74.
[52] *Letters* (Barlass), 52, 129.

preparation for confirmation, although a canonical require-
ment and a rubric of the Prayer Book, varied a great deal in
different regions during the eighteenth century, but very few
ministers, including high churchmen, catechized regularly
throughout the year.[53] Yet, soon after Newton arrived at
Olney, he began catechizing the children of the parish every
Thursday morning. His way of proceeding is discussed below,
but here it is important just to note that the practice was, for
him, virtually unrelated to the rite of confirmation; his
motives in this activity arose much more from his evangelical
preoccupation with conversion.

Norman Sykes has exhibited in detail how, even for
conscientious bishops, the practice of confirmation was beset
with practical difficulties in this period.[54] In the large diocese
of Lincoln there was often only very short notice given of an
intended confirmation. Although not supported by any
sacramental impulse, Newton did preach a preparatory
sermon for an upcoming confirmation in May 1773. Since he
received parishioners at home on the Wednesday and Friday
beforehand to give out tickets for the confirmation, he
presumably also spent some time carefully examining individual candidates.[55] He brought fifty-five parishioners to the
bishop for the rite, 'some of them, I hope, already devoted to
the Lord, but others, I fear, too little sensible of the
engagement they were to make, though I endeavour to keep
such away'.[56] Bishop Burnet had considered confirmation,
rightly managed, as 'the most effectual means possible for
reviving Christianity'.[57] While Newton used the opportunity
which confirmation offered, he was more concerned on a day-
by-day basis with other means for effectually reviving
Christianity among his parishioners.

The ordinances of the Prayer Book and the rhythms of the
church calendar with its liturgical seasons provided only the
barest outline for the annual cycle of Newton's parish
ministry. One of the frequent nineteenth-century criticisms of

---

[53] Mather, 'Georgian Churchmanship', 279–81.
[54] *Church and State*, 115–37.
[55] Diary (1773–1805), 2 and 7 May 1773.
[56] Bull, *Newton*, 194.   [57] Quoted in Sykes, *Church and State*, 117.

the *Olney Hymns* (1779) was how little its contents related to the Christian year. At Olney, Christmas, Easter, and Whitsuntide had their counterpoint in the rhythms of secular and commercial town life. Associated with gift-giving and revelry in the eighteenth century, New Year's Day had by this time become a secular holiday. Locally, however, it was also the occasion of what was perhaps the most significant communal religious event of the year, initiated by Newton, when on three successive nights the ministers of the three churches would preach to the young people of the town in the presence of the adults. This was a time when expectations ran especially high that revival and awakening would attend the preaching. Newton usually wrote a new hymn for the occasion and remarked in 1773 about the approaching New Year's Day sermon, that it lay upon his heart 'with more weight than any other opportunity in the course of the year'.[58] The solemn theme on these occasions was the passing of time and relentless approach of death. Newton's hymn, 'Uncertainty of Life', was typical:

> See! another year is gone!
> Quickly have the seasons pass'd!
> This we enter now upon
> May to many prove their last:
> Mercy hitherto has spar'd,
> But have mercies been improv'd?
> Let us ask, Am I prepar'd,
> Should I be this year remov'd?
> (*OH* 2. 3, st. 1)

The other significant annual occasions at which he preached a sermon were the Fair days: Easter Monday and 29 June. People came from long distances to join the townspeople of Olney on these ancient days of local trade and festivities. Cattle chiefly were traded, but there was a good deal of carousing as well. Newton recorded on one Fair day that a drunken curate from the nearby parish of Harrold in Bedfordshire, in a fit of excitement, had enlisted himself as a soldier and was now exposed to much embarrassment and inconvenience.[59] On the evening of these Fairs Newton was

---

[58] Bull, *Newton*, 183–4.   [59] Diary (1773–1805), 20 Apr. 1778.

often able to draw larger than normal crowds to hear him preach, including many people from out of town. He described his preaching on these occasions in the metaphors of trade:

On the evening of our fair-days I usually preach, which I call opening my booth. Sometimes I invite them to buy the truth or to come and see; sometimes I depreciate the wares and objects of the fair, and endeavour to convince them that all is vanity and vexation of spirit in comparison to what is set forth to view and to sale, without money or price, in the ordinances of the Gospel; but alas, I have the fewest spectators and the fewest buyers. A mountebank or a dancing dog can gather a crowd, but there are only here or there, one who have [*sic*] leisure or desire to attend the things which belong to their peace. But a few there are, usually amongst them some strangers whom the novelty of preaching at such a time, induces to come and hear . . . For the sake of such . . . I began this custom upon my first coming to Olney.[60]

Newton's conceit here of taking the gospel as a commodity into the consumer marketplace was a way of talking about evangelism that had scriptural precedent and had been common enough among the Puritans. Yet, it was also an innovative local adaptation to an increasingly commercial society.

Another different sort of occasional service, which Newton took with the utmost seriousness, were the national fast days. During the War of American Independence, Newton took great pains to prepare for the declared fast days. In terms which recalled the Puritan sense of the 'godly nation', he preached three times each day and held local prayer meetings, believing that a national repentance could avert providential judgement through defeat in war. On 27 February 1778, he felt the response of his congregation at Olney to the fast was sincere, and he prayed, 'Surely Thou hast seen many of thy children sighing and mourning before thee, under a sense of sin, & from a prospect of judgements being at the door.'[61]

He performed many baptisms, churchings, and marriages, but rarely were these the occasion for any written reflections. Funerals, however, he used as solemn opportunities to put his

---

[60] *Letters* (Dartmouth), 209–10.   [61] Diary (1773–1805), 27 Feb. 1778.

hearers in mind of the precariousness of life and the awfulness of eternity. 'As I know funerals bring those to hear who will not often come, & rather quicken the attention of the auditory,' wrote Newton, 'I am glad to embrace the opportunity when it fairly offers.'[62] If there was a corpse in the church on the day of his midweek lecture, he would likewise give his discourse a 'funeral turn'. When the deceased had lived a pious life, he sought to stir up the affections of his people to follow this example. Thus, in the autumn of 1778 he preached a funeral sermon for one Sarah Crawbyd, setting her before his congregation as a poor and aged woman who had been an 'honourable disciple', and urging his listeners to follow in her steps. When the deceased had been an open sinner, his task was more difficult. A week after Sarah Crawbyd's funeral sermon, he had the much more disagreeable task of speaking to those who came to the graveside of one Samuel Robython, a man who died at 25 years of age through drink, after having been often warned and convicted. Newton did not know what to say. He did not want to add to the grief of the parents, especially because they had another son set on the same course, who did not come to the burial, but spent the funeral Sunday at the alehouse.[63] In these cases, Newton confessed he would usually 'omit a clause in one of the prayers', doubtless the phrase, offensive to evangelicals, that all those buried had a 'sure and certain hope of the Resurrection'.[64]

(*b*) *Additional meetings.* One of the first ways in which Newton augmented these customary and prescribed services was to set up a weekly lecture. When he came to Olney in May 1764, he was, however, in deacon's orders only. Because of how uncertain his path to ordination had been, he chose not to risk any controversy and waited until after he was priested in the middle of June to establish this lecture. Thereafter, Newton regularly gave a sermon in the church on Thursday evenings, which was attended by many Dissenters besides his own church members. Usually, he preached a series of expository sermons, working his way, for example, through the Psalms, Acts, or Hebrews; but he departed from this plan

[62] Ibid., 5 Sept. 1779.   [63] Ibid., 18 and 24–7 Oct. 1778.
[64] Bull, *Newton*, 130–1.

from time to time to treat topical subjects. Thus, when in the winter of 1773 Cowper entered his third period of serious depression, Newton spoke from 1 Corinthians 10: 13 about God's sufficiency in times of temptation. After performing the wedding of Susanna Unwin and Matthew Powley in 1774, he turned the lecture into 'a sort of wedding sermon'. When in 1779 a poor young woman from out of town was taken in by Mrs Unwin, after having been nearly killed in the street, Newton abandoned the intended subject of his lecture and preached instead on Jesus's words of dying forgiveness in Luke 23: 34, so that the woman could hear the gospel explained in a way suitable to her case.[65]

At the beginning of 1765 Newton proposed setting up three meetings: 'one for the children, another for young and enquiring persons, and a third to be a meeting with the more experienced and judicious, for prayer and conference'.[66] The first of these he established immediately on Thursday afternoons (although also held sometimes in the mornings) at the nearby Great House, the uninhabited mansion of the former lay rectors which was now owned by Lord Dartmouth. Newton recorded the names of eighty-nine children who turned up for the initial meeting.[67] He explained to Clunie that his plan was not so much to catechize them formally, though he would attend to that too, as to 'talk, preach, and reason with them, and explain the scriptures to them in their own little way'.[68] The following week he had another forty-four children and had to move for a time to the chancel to accommodate them all. The popularity of these meetings can be accounted for by the 'little donatives' Newton used as an incentive for the children to attend and learn the catechism. At the first meeting he gave most of them a copy of a catechism, written by a Dissenter. At the second he proposed they learn the Lord's Prayer and the first six catechetical questions by heart, adding that he would next time call one girl and one boy by lot; if they could repeat the memorized

---

[65] Diary (1773–1805), 6 Jan. 1773, 5 May 1774, and 2 Feb. 1779.
[66] Bull, *Newton,* 137.
[67] 'A List of the Children', 1765, MS Notebook, CNM.
[68] *Letters* (Clunie), 67.

passages well, they would each receive sixpence. By the end of the month he had given out several more catechisms and thirty or forty Prayer Books. In February, when none of the children did very well repeating the set passages, he weakened and gave everyone a printed sermon.[69] By April Newton had a steady attendance of over 200 children. To control the behaviour of such numbers, Newton told them he would at Whitsuntide give a Bible and five shillings to the best behaved boy and girl under 10 years of age, the same for the best two above that age, and smaller rewards to other children who still did well. With such 'premiums', he was even able to get three-quarters of the children to return and sit still for the evening lecture.[70] 'About a hundred of them', he reported to Lord Dartmouth, 'come constantly to Church and sit in a body before the pulpit.'[71]

It was principally Nonconformist literature Newton used with the children. After his second meeting he wrote in his notebook, 'I have a considerable number of Dissenter's Children, & it is partly to avoid discouraging them, that I begin with Mason's Catechisms.'[72] Newton was probably referring here to a book by the Dissenting divine and author John Mason (1706–63), grandson of the millenarian John Mason of Water Stratford. Newton also used books such as *A Token for Children, Being an Exact Account of the Conversion . . . of Several Young Children* by the seventeenth-century Non-conformist James Janeway, and *Sermons to Young Persons* by Philip Doddridge, and he furnished all the children with a small hymnbook by Isaac Watts.[73] Newton procured these books with the help of his friend Clunie in London, who belonged to the Society for Promoting Religious Knowledge Among the Poor, or, as it was popularly known, the Book Society. This society, which Newton himself joined in 1768, in many ways anticipated the ideals of the interdenominational Religious Tract Society, and the subscribers list included prominent evangelicals of several denominations, though Dissenters tended to predominate.[74] At Olney, however, even

---

[69] Probably the sermon by John Mason, *Serious Advice to Youth* (Macclesfield, 1762?).   [70] *Letters* (Clunie), 67.   [71] *Letters* (Dartmouth), 175.
[72] 'List of Children', CNM.   [73] *Letters* (Clunie), 66, 72.
[74] *An Account of the Society for Promoting Religious Knowledge Among the Poor* (1769).

among the children, Newton found his desire for harmony between denominations tested. At the end of January several of his young people were displeased because two of the rewards fell to the children of Dissenters. Newton used this occasion to point out 'the nature & evil of a party spirit', taking them through the parable of the Good Samaritan at the next meeting and explaining it with reference to 'their little prejudices about Church & meeting'.[75]

Newton's pattern varied at the children's meetings. At different times he set them hymns to learn by heart, talked to them of the death of a pious young person, preached a series of sermons on Luke, or illustrated the story of the prodigal from his own life. While speaking to the children, he would also sometimes address bystanders indirectly in the hopes that such a 'random-shot' might hit the mark. He was pleased to see several of the young people awakened through his efforts. The effect of the rewards in maintaining high attendance was, however, of limited duration. After various disruptions in the spring and summer, he resolved to resume the meetings in the autumn on a different plan and with a smaller group, recognizing that 'too many came, not with a view to instruction but for the sake of money & books'.[76] The attendance seems to have come down in the autumn to an average of about forty. When he was able later to recruit Samuel Teedon to come from Bedford to set up as schoolmaster in Olney, he found the numbers of children attending his meeting pick up again to fifty, sixty, or seventy, and he recorded once more the 'liberty' and 'enlargement' he felt in speaking to them.

Newton soon set up other meetings which fulfilled his desire to have something for enquirers and serious believers. Early in 1765 he began a regular prayer meeting on Tuesday evenings. At first there were about forty persons. Although Newton wanted none but were 'downright in earnest,' the numbers steadily increased.[77] The meeting was held in the first instance at the vicarage, but early in 1768 the assembly had to be moved to a room of the Great House that could

---

[75] 'List of Children', CNM.   [76] Ibid.
[77] *Letters* (Clunie), 72.

accommodate 130 people.[78] At these meetings one or two men would pray extempore, there would be time for 'spiritual converse' and the singing of a hymn, and Newton would provide an informal discourse. Beginning in June 1767 Newton began a popular series of expositions at these meetings based on *Pilgrim's Progress*, which he continued for two and a half years; he repeated the series again in 1772.[79] Newton selected those who would pray at these meetings and kept a record of their names; he was delighted when another 'mouth was opened' to pray extempore, enlarging the ranks of the 'praying men'.[80] The members of Newton's society were conscious of others in London and Yorkshire, meeting on the same night, with whom they felt spiritually united as they met. Not infrequently, a visiting Dissenting minister—friends of Newton's such as William Bull from Newport Pagnell, Samuel Brewer from London, or Joshua Symonds from Bedford—would be present with them and would give a sermon or pray. After a good meeting, Newton might write simply: 'good time, affections stirring and earnest prayer'.[81]

A third regular weekly meeting begun in Newton's first year at Olney was held on Sunday evenings after tea at the vicarage, for 'an hour or more in prayer and singing'. Here too Newton would often use a hymn as the basis of an informal lecture. Frequently the subject of concern and prayer on these occasions was the need for personal and corporate revival. Very similar to the Tuesday meeting, this meeting seems to have been intended to open Newton's intimate family worship to a select circle of his most promising parishioners, but it soon grew well beyond these bounds. By the autumn of 1765 he resorted to the expedient of issuing tickets to those he hoped were truly serious in order to exclude the merely curious; still, even with this measure, he reckoned there were

---

[78] *Letters* (Dartmouth), 185.

[79] Newton later described these expositions to Hannah More, and added, 'in those lectures I came nearer the apprehensions of the poor lace-makers, and engaged their attention more, than when I spoke from the pulpit'. *Memoirs of Hannah More*, iii. 7. Cf. Newton's preface to his published notes on *Pilgrim's Progress*, 3rd edn. (1798).

[80] Records were kept in the final few pages of his Diary (1773–1805).

[81] Diary (1767), 19 May.

about seventy persons of both sexes attending regularly. Upon
the completion of a new vicarage, which Lord Dartmouth
built for Newton in 1767, the meeting was held in Newton's
best parlour, but the following year this meeting too had to be
moved to the Great House. With the increased space, Newton
opened the meeting in 1769 more widely to members of the
congregation. In February 1779, the weather being warm, he
decided to replace the meeting for an interval with a third
Sunday service at the church in hopes of getting a large
congregation.

From his animated diary entries, it seems that this prayer
meeting, at the close of a busy sabbath, was over the course of
his curacy the one with which he was most personally
satisfied. Society meetings like this and the one on Tuesdays
had meant so much to Newton when he was introduced to
evangelical religion in 1754. At Olney, they became the
nerve-centre of his ministry. He commented on the prayer
meetings in 1766, 'I think nothing has been more visibly
useful to strengthen my heart, and to unite the people closely
together in the bonds of love.'[82] Again, he wrote in 1778 to a
Scottish Secessionist to explain his position as an evangelical
in the Church of England, saying, 'At Olney, (and it is much
the same in all the parishes where the Lord has placed
awakened ministers) we are Ecclesia intra Ecclesium [*sic*]. I
preach to many, but those whose hearts the Lord touches are
the people of my peculiar charge.'[83] Here then at Olney was
the *ecclesiola* of Pietism which had become so characteristic of
Evangelical Revival in England.

The Thursday evening lecture, the children's Thursday
catechetical instruction, and the prayer meetings on Tuesday
and Sunday evenings were a permanent fixture of Newton's
ministry throughout his time at Olney. There were other
occasional meetings as well, and some which seem to have
been maintained only for short periods before they were
dropped again.[84] In September 1765 there is one passing

[82] *Letters* (Jones), 74–5. [83] *Letters* (Barlass), 52.
[84] G. R. Balleine, *History of the Evangelical Party in the Church of England*, new edn.
(1951), 83, gives a schedule of Newton's regular meetings, which is inaccurate and
misleads by including several of these *ad hoc* meetings. He is followed by Demaray,
Innovation of Newton, 126–7.

reference to a Monday evening vicarage meeting for 'the few men who belong to our little society'.[85] This may have anticipated his experiment during the summer of 1767 with class meetings, an idea borrowed from the Moravians and Methodists. As he explained to Clunie, he divided his 'sheep and lambs' into 'small flocks' of anywhere from eight to a dozen individuals of the same sex, and he intended to meet with each small group every six weeks.[86] His diary for 1767 records a cycle of these meetings on Fridays, with entries such as, 'a pleasant meeting in the evening with Class A', and so on. After 1767 there are for several years very few documents in which to follow Newton's activities; then, from 1773, when it is again possible to follow his activities in his diary, he mentions no more of these class meetings.

Some of the 'younger, and more lively sort', began in the spring of 1765 to meet at six o'clock on Sunday mornings to pray for Newton and the services of the day.[87] It was at one of these morning prayer meetings in 1767 that Cowper famously found his heart overcome with feelings of sweetness as one line from a hymn the poor folks were singing seized his attention all in a moment.[88] Cowper later recalled that these meetings lasted until about 1772 and were attended chiefly by the lacemakers; there would always be forty or fifty poor folks present.

Other lay-initiated prayer meetings began in 1772. There was a group of young people who had been awakened and formed their own society at the cottage of Molly Mole (or 'Mohl'); Newton called their prayer meeting 'Mole Hill' and took pleasure in joining them several times. The following spring Newton wrote in his diary, 'There seems something of a revival. Prayer meetings set up from house to house by the young people. I was at one of them last night and spoke.'[89] In Scotland and New England it had been prayer cells like this, often among young people, that formed the nucleus of wider

[85] Bull, *Newton*, 141.   [86] *Letters* (Clunie), 129–30.
[87] Ibid. 77. Cf. *Letters* (Jones), 69–70; *Letters* (Dartmouth), 185, entry for 1768. Newton also recorded a Sunday morning prayer meeting, Diary (1773–1805), 4 July 1773.   [88] *Letters of Cowper*, i. 180.
[89] Diary (1773–1805), 7 May 1774.

revival movements. Such impromptu meetings were very different, however, from the others laid on by Newton, with far more potential for lay fervency to burst the banks of propriety and threaten clerical authority. In the autumn of 1774 Newton joined—he does not at first say that he initiated—an early morning prayer meeting on Tuesdays 'chiefly on account of the present appearances of the times'.[90] The immediate crisis was due to a poor harvest, but there was concern too over instability in the country, perhaps because of the dissolution of Parliament and the upcoming election, or on account of the rebellion fomenting in the American colonies, or perhaps for other reasons. This meeting must soon have lapsed, though, for in June of the following year it was begun afresh, this time focusing definitely on the 'present troubles in America', since news of the first shots of the War of American Independence had just broken that week. Newton reported to John Thornton and Lord Dartmouth that between 150 and 200 people turned out at five o'clock in the morning. They met for an hour; for the first ten minutes Newton spoke about the state of the nation, and then the balance was spent in hymn singing and prayer.[91] By the autumn the attendance had dropped to about forty, but the meeting was still spirited enough to draw the notice of some who accused Newton and his people of siding improperly with the Americans. On 1 October Newton preached a patriotic sermon in his defence, but the following February the accusation still had enough currency that he was forced to write to Lord Dartmouth to explain that he was not meddling in politics or complaining against the government. (Lord Dartmouth, in addition to being Newton's patron, had been Secretary of State for the American Colonies at the onset of the crisis.) Earlier, John Collett Ryland of Northampton had been censured for making political statements from the pulpit. Newton always protested his own loyalty to the government, but Olney and the

[90] Diary (1773–1805), 4 Oct. 1774.
[91] Newton to John Thornton, 13 June 1775, ALS, CUL.; cf. *Letters* (Dartmouth), 216. One of the Olney Hymns, 'On the Commencement of Hostilities in America', was written for this occasion (*OH* 3. 64).

surrounding area had a history of religious and political radicalism of which others were only too aware.

(c) *Pastoral visits and counselling.* When not otherwise occupied, Newton would use his mornings for reading and writing, and spend his afternoons visiting about the town and countryside. In 1765 he told Lord Dartmouth, 'My afternoons are generally spent in visiting the people, 3 or 4 families a day, and so, in course.'[92] He later remembered these pastoral visits with fondness: 'The most of [God's] people there were poor, afflicted, ignorant and illiterate, but they were taught of God *before I saw them.* I was their official teacher from the pulpit; but I taught them chiefly by what I first learned from them in the course of the week, by visiting and conversing with them from house to house.'[93] In 1767, recalling Richard Baxter's practice earlier at Kidderminster, Newton resolved to 'converse singly' with each of his people in turn for an hour at a time.[94] Week by week he recorded the names of the parishioners he visited. Sometimes individuals would come to him, often from great distances, and he would meet with them in his study. Other times he would take parishioners with him on his rounds, or encourage spiritually mature lay people to visit the ill and afflicted. Richard Stamford (1745–79), one of the first converts from his ministry, had been particularly useful and acceptable in visiting the sick.[95] Cowper was likewise active for many years calling on the poor and needy of the parish; so much so that Richard Cecil said Newton considered him a sort of unpaid curate.[96] When Betty Abraham died in 1774, Newton remarked similarly that she had been a 'Mother in our Israel . . . exceedingly useful, especially to the lambs of the flock', and he lamented having few left so qualified to help enquirers forward.[97]

Many times Newton's visits were pastoral calls on persons in particular need. So, for example, in 1773/4 he breakfasted with Mr R. at Warrington who was distressed by the unhappy

[92] *Letters* (Dartmouth), 175. [93] *Letters* (Coffin), 134.
[94] Diary (1767), 3 June 1767.
[95] Diary (1773–1805), 26 Aug. 1779; cf. *Register of the Parish of Olney*, ii. 347.
[96] Cecil, *Newton*, 150.
[97] Newton to John Ryland, Jun., 14 Feb. 1774, ALS, BBC.

conduct and elopement of his daughter; he called day after
day on the dying Mr Bayes at Weston Underwood to establish
him in the hope of eternal life; and he spent time with Mr and
Mrs Cooke at Warrington, seeking to comfort them after their
13-year-old son John was killed in an overturned cart.[98] As
parish minister, he was often called on as physician of both the
bodies and the souls of his people. He had an 'electric
machine' with which he treated the rheumatic disorder of a
woman from nearby Sherrington who came to him and was,
on the same occasion, converted under his preaching.[99] He
studied the merits and demerits of the smallpox inoculation,
convinced of the need for faith whether or not one took the
inoculation (ii. 129–31).[100] In 1776 he explained to Foster
Barham, a Moravian friend from Bedford, that a certain pious
young woman from his congregation was in spiritual agony as
her death approached but that this was, he was certain, the
result of a shattered constitution, not the result of any moral
failing on her part (i. 589–91). Many parishioners suffered
various degrees of derangement.[101] There were suicides and
attempted suicides, and poverty and alcoholism were widespread. And all the while there were sin-sick souls to be
comforted and unfeeling profligates to be upbraided. All of
this required that he be a skilled casuist. Indeed, Newton
confessed that his favourite branch of spiritual medicine was
'anatomy', studying the intricate workings of the human heart
(i. 442). It was in routine visits and emergency pastoral calls
that he sought to enforce and to apply his public teaching to
the particular cases of individuals in the parish.

In one further respect Newton was able to be of help to
those he visited, since through the largess of the wealthy
evangelical merchant John Thornton (1720–90) he was
permitted to draw £200 a year—and more if occasion
demanded—for hospitality and to help the poor and needy.[102]
This accounts for the weekly entries in the ledger section of
Newton's pocket-book diary for 1767, recording expenditures
of a few shillings a week for the poor; it also explains how he

[98] Diary (1773–1805), 17 Feb. 1773, 10 Mar. 1773 and *passim*, and 21–4 Apr.
1774; cf. *Register of the Parish of Olney*, ii. 374.   [99] Bull, *Newton*, 135.
[100] See also, Newton to John Ryland, Jun. [1777], ALS, BBC; *Letters* (Dartmouth),
192.   [101] *Letters* (Taylor), 102.   [102] Cecil, *Newton*, 142.

could afford to distribute bread to the poor in the winter and make frequent gifts of Bibles and other books to his parishioners. It also accounts for the pique in the comments of the Independent Minister John Drake that Newton's 'indefatigable visiting and many little artifices among the poor and the young people' carried all before him.[103] When Thomas Scott took possession of the vicarage in 1781, a year after Newton's move to London, he found himself embarrassed that he could not match Newton's liberality in the parish.[104]

(d) *Extra-parochial activity*. 'Passing through Emberton', Newton wrote to his wife not long after arriving in Olney, 'an old woman came after me, and invited me to her cottage. I went. Five or six women soon joined us. We talked, sang a hymn, and prayed, and I thought it a good bait by the way.'[105] Emberton was a village just a mile and a half south of Olney on the road to Newport Pagnell. It was also a discrete ecclesiastical parish. Here is an example of the simple cottage meetings which Newton held at one time or another in nearly all the parishes adjacent to Olney. In several instances the cottage meetings were held *ad hoc*, as this one was with the women from Emberton. In other cases, the meeting was regularly established, well attended, and included a sermon from Newton. After visiting the nearby village of Ravenstone in January 1766, Newton wrote in his diary, 'Walked to Ravenstone. Endeavoured to put the few people who know the Lord there (as I did at Denton) upon forming themselves into a little society to meet for prayer. I have seen some good effects, I trust, from these prayer-meetings at Olney, and would therefore recommend the practice to others.'[106] At Lavendon to the north-east of Olney, Newton began another prayer meeting in May 1767. Later, at the nearby Lavendon Mill he would also often visit the miller Mr Perry for tea, and then preach afterwards in his barn to as many as 150 people.[107] A more rare opportunity offered when he was asked in 1766 by the widow of the minister at Bozeat, five miles

[103] Thompson, 'History of Dissenting Churches'.
[104] Scott, *Life of Scott*, 161.   [105] Bull, *Newton*, 131.
[106] Ibid. 144.
[107] Diary (1767), 31 May 1767; Diary (1773–1805), 21 Apr. and 10 June 1775; 30 Mar., 31 July, and 2 Nov. 1776; Bull, *Bull*, 69; Wright, *Town of Cowper*, 82.

from Olney, to supply the church services. Newton took it as a providential call. For two or three Sundays he preached to a crowded church, several standing along the walls outside, unable to get in. Newton estimated the numbers of hearers at 800, three-quarters of whom he was convinced had never heard the gospel in their lives.[108] The neighbouring clergy, so he surmised, soon intervened to have him shut out of the services, but still he expected another pulpit to be open to him soon at a place eight miles off. Realizing these opportunities would not last, he maintained his services at Olney unabated despite Clunie's fear that he would strain himself.

Newton understood himself to be a strictly regular minister despite the visiting, cottage meetings, and preaching he did in other men's parishes. Although he did not engage in field preaching, he still quickly established a reputation as a local Methodist. The first sign of opposition came soon after he arrived at Olney, when several ministers from the area denied him testimonials for his priesting. The opinion of the diarist William Cole, from the same archdeaconry as Newton, confirms what was his local reputation. Upon seeing Newton at a visitation in 1765, he described him as 'a little odd-looking man of the Methodistical order, and without any clerical habit'.[109] A year later Newton announced to Lord Dartmouth his chagrin that he had been unable to gain the co-operation of the justices of the peace to suppress Sunday trading at Olney, since the justices would not countenance proposals from 'a reputed Methodist'.[110] This may be what Cowper was referring to later when he wrote of seven or eight ministers from the neighbourhood of Olney who were in league to prevent the closure of public houses on Sundays.[111] The resentment of neighbouring clergy may be illustrated also from an incident in 1769 when Newton's friend Mr Perry asked the minister at Lavendon, probably a curate named Dixie, if Newton might preach the funeral sermon for a member of his family. When the minister not only refused, but

---

[108] *Letters* (Clunie), 112–17; cf. Bull, *Newton*, 148–9.
[109] Quoted in Thomas Wright, *Life of William Cowper*, 2nd edn. (1921), 68.
[110] *Letters* (Dartmouth), 183; cf. *Works*, vi. 553.
[111] *Letters of Cowper*, i. 482.

took the occasion to preach himself against 'enthusiasm', Newton took the same sermon text the following Sunday at Olney and sought to overturn the hostile interpretation. Newton then preached a funeral sermon on behalf of the Perrys at his next Thursday lecture. When in 1773 the Bishop of Lincoln talked to him about his prayer meetings, he had reason therefore, given his reputation, to worry that he might be disciplined for intruding into adjacent parishes, but afterwards he was able to remark simply, 'through the Lord's goodness all ended well'.[112]

Figure 1 below shows many of the places where Newton at various times preached, made pastoral calls, or set up cottage meetings; Figure 2 shows the parish boundaries which applied to the same area. It is apparent that even a self-consciously regular evangelical like Newton could exercise wide influence within the neighbourhood of his own parish. The area of Newton's most intensive activity was generally within a triangle defined by Northampton, Bedford, and Newport Pagnell, towns that were also home to some of his closest friends. Because these friends were Dissenters, Newton's ministry at these places usually took the form of 'parlour preaching', the other end of the social scale from cottage preaching. Here he would often stay for several days at a time, preaching at the home of John Ryland, Sen., or at Mrs Trinder's school, when in Northampton; or at the home of the Moravian Foster Barham when in Bedford. Newport Pagnell was nearer, and here Newton often repaired for spiritual conversation with William Bull and simply returned home the same day. The villages within the triangular area defined by these points, if not quite constituting a circuit in the Methodist sense of the word, were still frequently visited by Newton as pastor and preacher. It was walking, or at least easy riding, distance to most of the places, and he could carry on this regional ministry without unduly disrupting his scheduled services in his own parish. To many, he must have seemed like an evangelical rural dean. Shortly after Newton arrived at Olney, he set up a monthly meeting of 'six or seven clergymen who preach the Gospel in this and the adjoining

[112] Bull, *Bull*, 194; cf. *LyH* ii. 139.

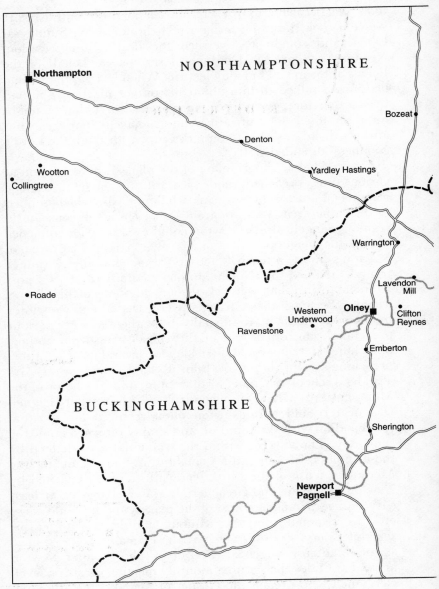

FIG. 1 Olney and Surrounding Settlements

Based on original Ordnance Survey maps of Northamptonshire, Bedfordshire, and
Buckinghamshire

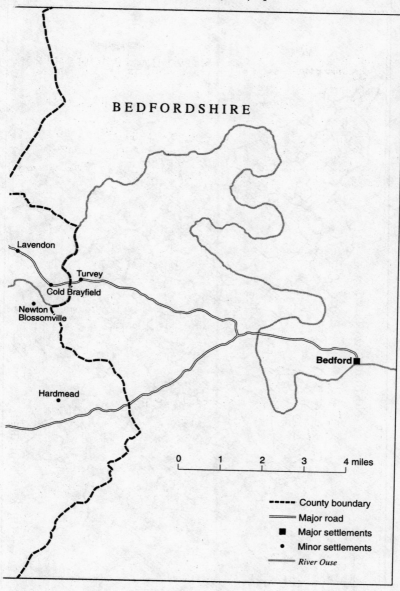

BEDFORDSHIRE

Lavendon

Turvey

Cold Brayfield

Newton
Blossomville

Bedford

Hardmead

0   1   2   3   4 miles

- - - - County boundary
——— Major road
■   Major settlements
●   Minor settlements
~~~~~ *River Ouse*

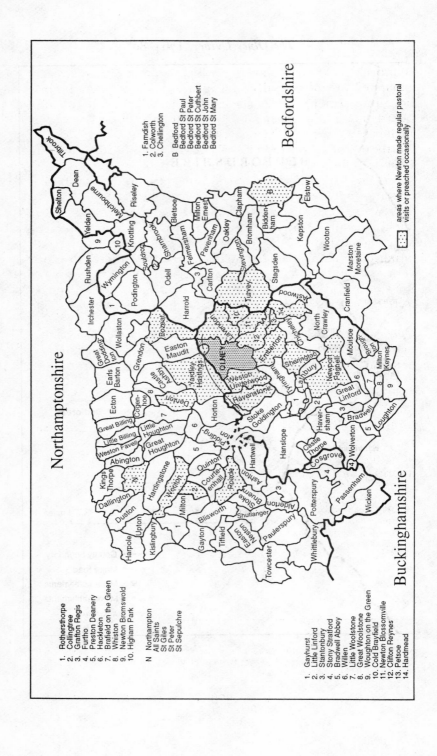

Northamptonshire

Bedfordshire

Buckinghamshire

1. Famdish
2. Colworth
3. Chellington

B   Bedford St Paul
    Bedford St Peter
    Bedford St Cuthbert
    Bedford St John
    Bedford St Mary

1. Rothersthorpe
2. Collingtree
3. Grafton Regis
4. Furtho
5. Preston Deanery
6. Hackleton
7. Brafield on the Green
8. Whiston
9. Newton Bromswold
10. Higham Park

N   Northampton
    All Saints
    St Giles
    St Peter
    St Sepulchre

1. Gayhurst
2. Little Linford
3. Stantonbury
4. Stony Stratford
5. Bradwell Abbey
6. Willen
7. Little Woolstone
8. Great Woolstone
9. Woughton on the Green
10. Cold Brayfield
11. Newton Blossomville
12. Clifton Reynes
13. Petsoe
14. Hardmead

▨ areas where Newton made regular pastoral
   visits or preached occasionally

counties'.[113] Clearly, however, his religious circle quickly expanded to embrace all evangelicals of whatever denomination. In a region which had previously seen a strong ideal of interdenominational concord in the ministries of Bunyan at Bedford, Gibbs at Newport Pagnell, and Doddridge at Northampton, and would later be the scene of the Bedfordshire Union of Christians, an experiment in evangelical ecumenism, it was not surprising to see such ministerial dialogue and co-operation in evangelism.

Newton's extra-parochial activities took him even further afield than this, however, for he was linked to a large number of evangelical ministers from around the country in a network of mutually supportive friendships. He did not have to travel very far to exchange visits or church services with, for example, Abraham Maddock at Kettering, Henry Venn at Yelling, or John Berridge at Everton. With many Dissenters too there was an exchange of hospitality and, at an informal level, of pastoral labours. The visits with these friends, and between Newton and ministers from points more distant yet, brought a steady stream of preachers through Olney who invigorated and reinforced his local ministry. As his reputation grew through his correspondence and publications, and as during the last half of his curacy he began to take would-be ordinands under his roof and act the part of their mentor, his parishioners shared the stimulation provided by the many newcomers who took part in services and in formal and informal meetings.

[113] *Letters* (Clunie), 35. This was probably the group which met every Easter at Creaton in Northamptonshire, where the minister was Abraham Maddock, and later Thomas Jones. Out of this developed an important regular clerical meeting in the nineteenth century. J. Owen, *Memoirs of Thomas Jones* (1851), 189-92.

FIG. 2 Olney and Surrounding Parishes

Adapted from C. R. Humphery-Smith (ed.), *The Phillimore Atlas and Index of Parish Registers* (Chichester, 1984). By kind permission of the trustees of the Institute of Heraldic and Genealogical Studies.

TENSIONS IN EVANGELICAL PASTORAL PRACTICE

From the foregoing sketch of the character of Olney and of Newton's pastoral labours there, three principal points of tension in his evangelical ministry may be observed.

Lay Initiative and Pastoral Control

Clearly, Newton involved the laity of the parish extensively in the work of the ministry, and he encouraged them to be active in praying and speaking at his society meetings, just as he had been earlier in London and Liverpool. He sought freely to win the affections of his people. Yet he also desired to maintain his clerical authority in the parish, and increasingly this was challenged by the very forces of lay voluntarism which he unleashed. As Cowper put it, 'Instrumentality is generally taken up with some Reluctance, and laid down with a great deal more.'[114]

At various times Newton had to intervene to maintain control of the prayer meetings. He also referred on occasion to the work being at a stand, or to isolated cases of opposition. Already in 1776, he felt he needed to preach a sermon on Romans 11: 13, 'I magnify my office.'[115] But the principal challenge to his authority came after a fire in October 1777 that consumed twelve houses in town. When his first Thursday evening lecture in November fell on Guy Fawkes Day, Newton tried through appropriate remarks to restrain the reckless behaviour which could be expected on that night, realizing the danger of fire, but he was met with unusual defiance. In particular, the Baptists 'in a body' set themselves against Newton's authority.[116] He wrote with sadness in his diary that 'the Sons of Belial' terrorized the town, and that his own house was threatened by the mob. In the end, it had been necessary to give them money to keep them from laying violent hands on the vicarage. What grieved him most was that the mob was encouraged by the conduct of those whom he thought would rather have suppressed immorality for the

---

[114] *Letters of Cowper,* i. 439.
[115] MS Sermon notebook, 35 (1776), CNM.
[116] Newton to John Thornton, 18 Nov. 1777, ALS, CUL.

Lord's sake.[117] This was a turning point for Newton. He confessed in later years to Richard Cecil that he should never have thought of leaving Olney were it not for the incorrigible spirit which prevailed in a place he had so long laboured to reform.[118]

Newton felt keenly the death of each of his long-standing believers and worried that new converts were simply not coming forward to take their place, as they had in the first period of his ministry. Before the fire he confessed to John Ryland that because of the general deadness of the towns-people, 'the bulk of whom seem sermon-proof', he had thoughts of leaving.[119] At the annual service to give thanks for 'Gospel privileges'—the anniversary of the day ten years previously when Newton was prevented from moving to Cottingham near Hull—he noted that not one person prayed for his continuance at Olney.[120] Many opportunities to leave had offered before, but Newton had been unwilling to consider them. Now the people were complaining of a lack of power in his preaching, and he wondered if his time in the town was drawing to a close. Were it not that an important letter from John Thornton miscarried, Newton might well have moved to Hull that very year.[121] When in 1779 Thornton offered him the living of St Mary Woolnoth in London, he accepted it with mixed feelings of regret and relief.

The main challenge to clerical prerogative at Olney came after Newton left. Thomas Scott's son and biographer, John Scott, wrote about the offensive temper of the people at Olney, a 'much divided place', and he laid the blame for this at Newton's door: 'the exquisite candour and tenderness of Mr. N.'s temper had failed of adequately counteracting the existing tendency of things. Many indeed were nursed up to a morbid delicacy of feeling, which could not bear the faithful application of scriptural admonitions, even by his gentle hand, without expostulation and complaint.'[122] The way that ministerial authority was thus undercut by Newton's

---

[117] Diary (1773–1805), 5 Nov. 1777.   [118] Cecil, *Newton,* 166.
[119] Newton to John Ryland, Jun., 15 Feb. 1777, ALS, and 14 Feb. 1774, ALS.
[120] Diary (1773–1805), 1 Feb. 1777.
[121] *Memoirs of Hannah More,* ii. 260.   [122] Scott, *Life of Scott,* 180–1.

encouragement of lay activism at Olney may be illustrated by the case of Thomas Raban (d. 1784).

Raban was a carpenter who acted for many years as Newton's churchwarden and was his most loyal disciple. Newton's immediate successor at Olney was not Thomas Scott, whom the people did not at first want, but Benjamin Page, an appointment Newton left to Moses Browne. Page was very unlike Newton, and Raban led the local opposition against him when Page and Maurice Smith, the vicar's warden, ordered a new pew for the Warrington parishioners and expected the vestry to pay for it. Raban, who as church carpenter had done the work, was left unpaid by either vestry or curate. Page countered Raban's opposition by withholding from Raban the employment he should have gained from coffins for sixteen smallpox victims. Cowper kept Newton abreast of the whole episode of the Warrington pew as it developed. On one occasion he rendered his opinion of the affair in verse:

> The Curate and the Church warden,
> And eke the Exciseman too,
> Have treated poor Tom Raban,
> As if he was a Jew.
>
> For they have sent him packing
> No more in Church to work,
> Whatever may be lacking,
> As if he was a Turk.
>
> Thus carry they the Farce on,
> Which is great Cause of Grief,
> Until that *Page* the Parson,
> Turn over a *New Leaf*.[123]

The affair wound up in the hands of the Archdeacon before it was finally concluded.

Page was soon replaced by Scott, but Raban was not much happier with his appointment, since he had been accustomed to speaking in the meetings and Scott retained this prerogative to himself. Scott asked Raban to desist. Raban wished to be set up formally as the assistant to the meetings at the Great

---

[123] *Letters of Cowper*, i. 384–5.

House and to speak on Sunday evenings. Part of the problem arose because Scott was finding it difficult to maintain the number of services which Newton had begun, since he still had parochial obligations at Weston Underwood. Even so, he conceded to Raban that he would himself be willing to give the people a third sermon on Sundays. Raban responded that this would not do: 'It is not what the people wish, they want variety.'[124] Although Raban eventually acquiesced outwardly to Scott's authority, the wound he felt from this episode continued to fester. The year before Raban died in 1784, his name occurs as the newly ordained minister of the Independent Meeting at nearby Yardley Hastings.[125] This kind of story was not unique to Olney, recurring in other evangelical parishes in which lay participation in ministry was encouraged.[126]

Regular and Irregular Ministry

Charles Smyth has shown the various responses of eighteenth-century evangelicals within the Established Church to the demands of church order and canonical obedience.[127] Some, like John Berridge of Everton, made wide 'Gospel rambles' into other men's parishes, never hesitating to preach in a barn or an open field, since it was a matter of conscience to preach the gospel to dying sinners wherever they were to be found. Others, like Samuel Walker of Truro, refused to countenance any such breaches in church discipline and parochial order. Newton's case stands somewhere midway between these two positions.

He was conscious before his ordination that to enter orders, already an evangelical, was to subscribe to the canons and

---

[124] Ibid. 530.

[125] Bull, *Bull,* 122; cf. *History of Congregational Church at Olney.* The whole case of Thomas Raban may be followed in Cowper's correspondence with Newton after the latter removed to London in 1780 until Raban's death in 1784, q.v. *Letters of Cowper,* vols. i–ii. See also, Ella, *William Cowper,* 344–7.

[126] At Creaton, for example, where Abraham Maddock was minister for thirteen years, his evangelical ministry similarly fostered independence among the laity: 'Several Dissenting congregations were formed, in the neighbourhood, out of his congregation at Creaton; and they rebelled against him as disobedient children.' Thomas Jones, upon arrival at Creaton in 1785, quoted in Owen, *Memoir of Jones,* 78.

[127] Smyth, *Simeon and Church Order.*

make vows of submission to his diocesan 'with his eyes wide open'; he would not be able, after the fact, to claim that his conscience required him to set aside church order to preach itinerantly. Newton excused those of an earlier generation like John Berridge who had been converted in the ministry. But to the lay itinerant Captain James Scott (d. 1807), who had sought Newton's advice about obtaining orders, Newton wrote,

Things are so well understood now on both sides, that for a man to apply for ordination with a design to act contrary to the general rule of a parochial cure, carries the appearance of disingenuity; and if the canons are silent, I believe the laws of the land give every minister such a right in his own parish, as not to allow any other person to preach in it without his consent, unless he claims as a Dissenter the benefit of the Act of Toleration (vi. 117).

Although Newton allowed that the canons did not expressly forbid indiscriminate preaching, and he suggested that there might still be rare cases where it was necessary, he thought itinerancy was generally for those of lesser ability, who were only good for about a dozen sermons; more skill was required to be a 'burning, shining, steady light' in one parish year after year (ii. 164–7).

By what casuistry then did Newton defend his own meetings, sometimes of more than 100 individuals, in parishes such as Lavendon, where almost certainly he proceeded without permission, to judge from the hostility of the local vicar? Newton did not explain. Perhaps he would have argued that unless he was expressly forbidden, he had an implicit right to proceed. He did not, in any case, feel any heat from his ecclesiastical superiors. He recounted to William Barlass the cycle of archidiaconal and episcopal visitations, and explained, 'At those times I wait on them, answer my name, dine with them, and then return home. And this is all the weight of church power that I feel. Except for about four days in three years, I know no more of a superior, than if I was an archbishop myself.'[128] When the Dissenter Samuel Palmer asked Newton about exchanging pulpits, Newton replied that he could not do so, not from any high theological principle,

[128] *Letters* (Barlass), 53.

but rather for the sake of expediency and consistency. For the present, he could not justify preaching in a Nonconformist chapel or in the fields. This evidently was where he drew the line. Thomas Scott at first followed Newton's pattern by expounding to private gatherings in the neighbourhood, but he later repented of such 'irregular engagements', and a few years after moving to London dropped them altogether. As Charles Smyth has demonstrated, this was increasingly the situation as the century wore on, and evangelicals in the Established Church were forced to grapple with the problem of retaining the laity in the Church following the death or removal of an evangelical incumbent.[129]

Dissenting Sympathies and Establishmentarian Prerogatives

'The Dissenters here, most of them at least who are serious, forget that our Meeting House has a Steeple to it, and we that theirs has none.'[130] So wrote Cowper of Olney's cheerful spirit of interdenominational co-operation after living in the town for a little more than a year. It was indeed remarkable the degree to which co-operation was sustained during Newton's curacy between the parish church, the Independent Meeting, and the Baptist Meeting. Newton established cordial relations with Samuel Drake and William Walker soon after he arrived at Olney, and this cordiality was maintained as they frequently met for tea or gathered with visiting ministers from out of town. Several Dissenters thanked Newton for bringing his old friend Samuel Brewer, the popular Independent preacher from London, to visit the town around the end of 1765. Brewer preached on Tuesday for Newton, on Wednesday for Drake, and on Thursday for Walker. The four dined together at the vicarage on the Thursday, and then on Friday Newton called a special prayer meeting for Brewer to take leave of the people.[131] Given the confraternity of the ministers, it is hard to imagine that there would have been much to restrain parishioners from circulating between venues to hear Brewer as often as they liked.

Newton would often cancel or curtail one of his society

---

[129] Smyth, *Simeon and Church Order*, 246.
[130] *Letters of Cowper*, i. 197–8.   [131] Bull, *Newton*, 142–3.

meetings so that his people could go to hear a visiting preacher at one of the Dissenting chapels. At the New Year's Day services for the young people, when the three churches each held services in turn, Newton sat contentedly under the preaching of his fellow ministers and often recorded his desires for their good success. He identified himself with them in common cause as on one occasion he prayed, 'Help us to travail in birth for souls, and give us to labour in a spirit of love and peace.'[132] After Samuel Drake's death in 1775, the Independent congregation called Newton's erstwhile Liverpool acquaintance, John Whitford, as their minister. When Whitford and his family were permanently settled, Newton prayed, 'Help me to be serviceable to them, and to pray for their comfort and prosperity . . . perserve me from narrowness of spirit, enable me to see thy hand in every event, and to pray for a blessing upon every instrument.'[133] William Bull testified of Newton's relations with local Dissenters in the same vein, 'Not infrequently was [Newton] found a hearer at the Dissenting meeting-house; he was habitually present at the gatherings of the Baptist Association in Olney, at ordination services, and generally living on most friendly terms with his Dissenting brethren.'[134] This co-operation was based on a deep conviction on Newton's part that the true church transcended the distinction between Churchman and Dissenter, since it was called into existence by the gospel, and its members could recognize one another easily enough by the sole criterion of loyalty to that gospel.

Despite these catholic aspirations and the mutual goodwill between denominations, the ministers harboured some serious reservations about one another. After a conversation with Drake in 1773, Newton recorded alongside his desire to be kept from a 'party spirit', his concern to prevent the young people from being 'staggered and puzzled by fine words and artful speech'.[135] Drake reciprocated the suspicion when, around the same time, he wrote that although Newton's preaching marked a true disciple of Jesus, 'his carriage to the Dissenters always reminds me of Iscobar Tomburin or some

[132] Diary (1773–1805), 3 Jan. 1776.   [133] Ibid., 15 Mar. 1776.
[134] Bull, *Bull*, 51.   [135] Diary (1773–1805), 18 Dec. 1773.

other Disciple of Ignatius Loyola'.[136] Each worried that the other was guilty of strategic manipulation, seeking to gain an untoward influence over his own people. In the interregnum between the departure of the Baptist minister William Walker in 1773 and the arrival of John Sutcliff in 1775, Newton complained that the Baptists were intentionally drawing people away from his meetings by setting up parallel services on the same nights. No doubt they would have argued that their action was defensive. One woman, after fourteen years among Newton's people, defected to the Baptists in 1778. The scores were made even, however, when a few weeks later a long-standing member of the Baptist church, named Mary Brittain, having been dismissed by the church, came over to Newton's people and chose (in his words) 'to walk with us entirely'.[137] Thus while the threshold between Church and Chapel at Olney was, and remained, very low throughout Newton's curacy, this cross-denominational traffic could sometimes stir up mistrust and suspicion, instead of a spirit of co-operation and goodwill.

In Chapter 2, Newton's debt to Puritanism and Old Dissent was described; in this chapter, it has been demonstrated that the Olney area owed just as deep a debt to the same traditions, which prepared the way for Newton's popular ministry in the town. Newton's day-to-day activities as a 'Gospel minister' have been described, and his methods clearly borrowed much from Dissenting and Methodist practice. He co-operated with local Dissenters in the task of promoting a corporate spiritual awakening in the town, but by the mid-1770s his own authority had begun to weaken. When, after the fire of 1777, he had cause to try to exert his authority over the parish as a whole, it was too late. Already he had fostered a popular religious culture with a life of its own; he had demonstrated a low regard for ecclesiastical authority and parochial order; and he had established an *ecclesiola* within the parish church which implicitly acknowledged the legitimacy of dissent. These were principles at odds with that mutual relationship of deference and paternalism

[136] Thompson, 'History of Dissenting Churches'.
[137] Diary (1773–1805), 10 Nov. and 6 Dec. 1778.

which might have been expected between people and parson. The local tradition of Calvinistic nonconformity and the lay activism of the independent artisan population, to which Newton's own sentiments had seemed so well suited at first, led in the end to his undoing. This experience at Olney forms part of the background to the statement of his ecclesiological principles Newton would offer in London in 1784.

6

'O for the lively exercise of grace
in my own soul'
Newton and the Spiritual Life

> He was the St. Francis de Sales of the Evangelical
> movement, the great spiritual director of souls through
> the post.
>
> G. R. Balleine

I T is evident from Newton's ministry at Olney that he was an
active parish evangelist, immersed in a round of formal and
informal services, conscientiously visiting the homes of his
parishioners to promote their spiritual well-being. His lasting
reputation would, however, be built less on his parish ministry
than on his spiritual influence within a wider circle of
individuals through familiar correspondence, domestic hospitality, and periodic tours to preach and visit in various parts of
the country. This chapter therefore examines Newton's
evangelical spirituality by describing his private devotional
practices from his diary, tracing his emergence as a public
spiritual adviser, and analysing some of his most important
teachings on the interior life of the Christian.

NEWTON'S PRIVATE DEVOTIONAL PRACTICES

The man revealed in nearly 1,000 pages of manuscript from
Newton's private diary is a man at his prayers. Newton began
and maintained a diary principally as an aid to devotion, and
much of it was written in the form of first person prayers to
God, especially after 1775 when he made this formal pattern a
conscious practice. But even so, the diary does not give a
balanced picture of the whole of Newton's interior life, since
he used it for a specific purpose and it formed only part of his

221

typical spiritual regimen. Fasting, mental prayer, contemplative walks in the countryside, meditation, and devotional reading routinely took up more of Newton's time than writing in the diary itself. In the larger pattern of his devotion, the diary was used chiefly as a means of disciplined self-examination and a way of focusing his religious affections. Its picture is therefore not only of a man at his prayers, but also, more often than not, of a man in the confessional.[1] This perspective is important to establish at the outset, for while Newton's diary is the primary source for understanding his spirituality, it does not necessarily give a rounded picture of his spiritual life. In particular, its sometimes self-recriminatory tone ought to be seen in part as a distortion created by the medium itself.

The Rhythm of Newton's Devotional Life

Newton began his diary in 1751 while still at sea: after his conversion experience in 1748 and his marriage in 1750, but before his introduction to evangelicalism in 1754 or the consolidation of his Calvinistic beliefs about 1756. Some themes and practices in his devotional life remained constant throughout the half-century covered in the diary; others modulated or were replaced by new emphases. But the times that he set aside as special devotional occasions continued very much the same from the beginning.

(a) *Daily exercises.* On a day-to-day basis, he usually set aside time in the morning and evening for the reading of Scripture and for prayer, which he considered the two 'prime ordinances' and the most indispensable of the believer's 'secret exercises' (i. 236). About such Bible reading and prayer, he wrote, 'The one is the fountain of living water, and the other the bucket with which we are to draw' (i. 117). He confessed that his mind wandered unless he used various forms of artifice with himself in his Scripture reading: 'Thus sometimes I turn them into a prayer form, sometimes I suppose myself in imaginary conversation, sometimes that I am call'd upon to speak to a point.'[2] His private prayers,

[1] Cf. William Haller on the Puritan diary, *Rise of Puritanism* (New York, 1938), 38.
[2] Diary (1751–6), 29 Apr. 1755.

while reverential, did not follow a strict form of words but tended to be fairly natural and extempore conversations with God, expressed often in biblical phrases and responding to an awareness of God's presence and grace. His prayers were sometimes vocal, sometimes written, sometimes mental, but he never sought to transcend or to do without words and images. Newton offered his prayers from the heart, with an intense awareness of his present feelings. 'I often find', he observed during a week in which he was able to sustain spiritual feeling, 'that prayer is an index of my present state. It is indeed the gate of heaven.'[3] To his lections and prayers he added meditation and self-examination. By meditation he did not mean ruminating upon a text of Scripture, or focusing the imagination upon episodes in the life and passion of Christ (although he did meditate in these ways on different occasions); rather, he described meditation in very eighteenth-century terms as 'the observations we are able to make upon what passes within us and without us, which is what we call *experience*' (i. 287). On another occasion he further described this meditation upon inward and outward experience as taking 'what we see, hear, and feel, and [applying] all for the illustration and confirmation of the written word to us' (i. 117). This then was the rationale for the time he took frequently, though not strictly every day, to record in his diary the state of his soul and his private prayers, as well as reports of sermons, religious conversations, or other spiritually significant events in his life.

His diary was more introspective during the first few years, while he was at sea, than it was after he returned permanently to England in 1754. After this, sermons and conversations began to play a relatively larger role in his reflections. This shift corresponded to Newton's movement during the winter of 1754/5 from relative religious isolation and patterns of piety owing much to his upbringing in Old Dissent, to an enlarged circle of religious associates and patterns of piety owing more to Methodism. There were other changes in Newton's diary after he entered orders in 1764. As a devotional discipline, Newton had read and commented upon

---

[3] Bull, *Newton*, 118.

writers on the spiritual life on a fairly regular basis before his ordination. This was less often the pattern when he took up the itinerary of a busy parish minister. As a layman he had been able at various times to devote entire days, or several hours on certain days, to prayer. Often while on duty at the Watch House at Liverpool, he had the leisure and privacy to spend two or more hours in religious exercises. Once a minister, these extended opportunities came less frequently, though he would still note the occasions for leisurely prayer which he enjoyed while walking in solitude to local villages to make routine pastoral calls or visit friends. His diary inevitably took on something of the character of a clergyman's journal once he was in ministry, registering sermon texts, parishioners visited, letters received and sent, and other matters of professional concern. But the journal element never entirely took over from the original purpose of self-examination, and ministerial concerns were always contained within the perspective of what was still essentially a confessional diary recording his own spiritual aspirations and exercises.

(*b*) *Weekly exercises.* Throughout the period covered in his diary, Saturday evenings were devoted from about six o'clock to a review of the past week's mercies and sins in preparation for the following sabbath. 'My weekly confession and acknowledgement', he called it. He recorded his 'balancing and summing up the week' with more than usual brevity one Saturday in 1755, writing simply—'great mercies and blessings on God's part, great sins and mistakes on mine'.[4] These were consistently the two foci of his recollections. While on board ship he would conduct his review, whenever possible, walking on deck, inspired by the open sky and the vast ocean (untroubled, it seems, by the miseries of his human cargo below deck).[5] Later, at Chatham, Liverpool, and Olney he

---

[4] Diary (1751–6), 8 Feb. 1755. Cf. st. 2 of his hymn, 'Saturday Evening' (*OH* 2. 40): 'Mercies, multiply'd each hour, | Thro' the week our praise demand; | Guarded by almighty pow'r, | Fed and guided by his hand: | Tho' ungrateful we have been, | Only made returns of sin.'

[5] It is this, more than any other episode, that has brought the charge of hypocrisy on Newton. However, it should be noted that Newton himself came to recognize the moral contradiction of this scene. He wrote to a correspondent in 1788: 'I had a

would venture out into the fields whenever the weather permitted. His heart was simply gladdened by the beauty of creation, and the vastness of sea and sky corresponded to his desire to find his heart 'enlarged' in prayer. Sometimes these walks also afforded subjects for emblematic meditations when he returned to write in his diary. A decayed Great House near Chatham was, for example, a picture of the postlapsarian state of natural man, majestic though in ruins.[6] But meditations of this sort were secondary to the serious work of spiritual stock-taking and sabbath preparation. To this end, a Saturday evening 'serious walk' or 'retired hour' remained an important fixture of his spirituality throughout his adult life.

(*c*) *Monthly exercises*. The Saturday evening before the sacrament was to be administered became an occasion for particular spiritual seriousness, though, viewing the Lord's Supper as a commemorative ordinance, Newton did not worry himself over questions of sacramental efficacy or the nature of the divine presence in the sacrament. As early as 1751 he expressed himself satisfied with his doctrinal knowledge of the Lord's Supper but still felt keenly the need to prepare his soul for the communion. While at sea he had felt it the greatest inconvenience of his vocation that he was unable regularly to communicate. In October 1752 he had made a detailed personal covenant, pledging himself to high standards of religious duty and discipline, and he then sealed, and subsequently renewed, this covenant by taking the sacrament. Equally important as this subjective self-dedication was the objective contemplation of the atoning Passion of Christ at the Lord's Supper. In this way the sacrament offered a particular opportunity for focused prayer involving the imagination. In classic Puritan terms the Lord's Supper was for him the sign and seal of the covenant in both its human and divine dimensions. During the 1750s the sacrament was often attended for Newton with intense spiritual emotions of

certain fervour of spirit in communion with God upon the vast ocean, at a distance from the public means, without the help of Christian friends (yea, though I was engaged ignorantly in the wretched slave-trade) . . .' *Life of Mrs. Dawson*, 108; cf. *Works*, i. 88.

[6] Diary (1751–6), 2 June 1755.

contrition, gratitude, and self-surrender. The disciplines of preparation which he learned from Dissenters' handbooks such as Matthew Henry's *Communicant's Companion*, and the seriousness of preparation sermons he heard at London and Liverpool, all contributed to raise his expectations of heightened religious affections at the Lord's Supper. Rarely, however, in Newton's later diary entries were his expectations fulfilled, and he most often recorded his lament that he was 'cold and wandering' or 'dull and stupid' at the sacrament. On the first Sunday of March 1776 he remarked on his languid frame at the sacrament, making only the concession, 'Yet perhaps herein consists the strength of that faith Thou hast been pleased to give me that I am capable of maintaining hope, under a succession of such frames, and such proofs of vileness.'[7] Only occasionally did he find again the sweet and comfortable sense of God's presence which he had in his early years. The tone latterly was more one of disappointed longing.

On Easter in 1773, in the midst of a long season of inward spiritual dissatisfaction, Newton recorded that he had been 'stupid' as usual at the sacrament, adding,

Then I am always nearly alike—my judgment is satisfied and my Wish, Choice, and Desire on the Lord's side, but my sensible affections are so little exercised, that I can hardly give attention to what is passing. Nor is it thus now and then, the only season I can remember it to have been much otherwise is now near twenty years ago.[8]

Although he tried at various times stoically to steel himself against this loss of 'sensible affections', and to face courageously a devotional and sacramental life without the old warmth of spiritual emotion, he could not keep up the effort. The sense that something was missing in his spiritual life overwhelmed him again in January 1775: 'Seasons of melting in my own soul are sadly infrequent. I have formerly too little valued them and spoken of them lightly. O that the Lord would again give my heart to feel and my eyes to flow.'[9] His continual self-reproach month after month for not feeling

---

[7] Diary (1773–1805), 3 Mar. 1776. [8] Ibid., 11 Apr. 1773.
[9] Ibid., 29 Jan. 1775.

more, even while 'holding the memorials of Christ's dying love in my hands', bore repeated witness to the way that a deeply felt awareness of God's presence remained the great desideratum of his sacramental devotion. Although he did not want to live upon his feelings, he never stopped hoping he would find his affections deeply stirred through prayer and devotional discipline.

(*d*) *Annual exercises.* To the daily, weekly, and monthly cycle of Newton's private religious exercises may be added a number of annual occasions he set aside for serious devotional reflection. The timing of these bore little relation to the ecclesiastical calendar, for the 'memorial days' which he observed commemorated significant events, not from the history of the Church, but from his own salvation history. Even the great Christian festivals usually passed with very little mention in his diary. The first entry in his diary, six pages in length, was a solemn meditation written in preparation for the approaching Christmas season in 1751. He reminded himself at the outset, however, that he was not conducting this meditation because Christmas was a red-letter day of some numerical significance, but because there would be an administration of the Lord's Supper. Hence the subject of the ensuing pages was not the incarnation of Christ but rather, following the pattern of his sacramental preparation, his own past experience—the moral collapses and personal folly on his part, the general and specific mercies on God's. This was the usual form of his meditations. Meditations on his annual memorial days tended to survey the sweep of his past life, rather than to confine themselves to the past week or month, but the twin focus on mercies and sins remained. Almost fifty years after he began his diary, he noted how important these days had been, and prayed that each remaining anniversary would 'deepen the impression in my heart of thy goodness and my own vileness'.[10] After moving to London in 1780, he ceased keeping a daily diary, and the pattern of recording his religious experience at weekly and monthly intervals was telescoped into these more periodic

[10] Diary (1793–1805), 2 Feb. 1796.

entries, which therefore assumed an ever greater symbolic weight as he advanced towards old age.

The occasions which he chose to commemorate were chiefly New Year's Day, his and his wife's birthdays (4 August and 2 February), their wedding anniversary (12 February), and the North Atlantic storm (21 March) which signalled his return to God.[11] Because he made his solemn surrender to God for the work of the ministry on his birthday in 1758, this was remembered alongside his birthday reflections after he entered orders. After his wife's death on 15 December 1790, he added this too to his calendar of memorial occasions. Other events were commemorated from time to time, if not every year, such as the epileptic fit which took him out of the Atlantic slave trade, or his move from Olney to St Mary Woolnoth in London. As observed in the discussion of Newton's auto-biography, these memorial days were the anvil on which his self-understanding was hammered into shape as he relentlessly studied his own biography to discern the meaning of his inward and outward experience, to see the ways in which 'grace and providence concur'. From his natural birth, through his declension into immorality and apostasy, to the dawning of grace in his soul on the occasion of near-shipwreck; from his initial passion for Mary which made him heedless of authority, through the scenes of untold misery which resulted, to his ultimate determination to make good in the world for her sake; from his gracious entry into the ministry, through his unfaithful returns to God, to his temporal and spiritual well-being in old age—each of these patterns was rehearsed time and again in his annual cycle of anniversary recollections. Perhaps the most poignant reflections of this kind are contained in an interleaved copy of his *Letters to a Wife* (1793), where Newton traced the lines of his grief following Mary's death in meditations placed side-by-side with letters he wrote to her some forty or fifty years earlier. In many of these meditations he was remembering past events through two filters, recalling, for example, at 79 years of age the recollection at 28, of an experience of God's

---

[11] As here, from the beginning of his diary he used New Style dates for these anniversaries.

mercy at 23. The same lines were painted over again and
again.

The Design of Newton's Devotional Practice

(*a*) *Communion with God.* What were for Newton the final
goals of the life lived under grace? On New Year's day in
1753, he described his ultimate desire: 'to make it the end and
aim of my life (as it is the privilege and perfection of my
nature) to obtain fellowship and communion with God the
Father and with his son Jesus Christ'. Then he restated this
purpose again, in words recalling Richard Baxter's *Saints'
Everlasting Rest*: 'to have my heart and conversation in Heaven
and Heavenly things, walking with an eye of faith as seeing
Him who is invisible'.[12] A few months later he recorded his
fervent prayer to 'grow in grace, and advance though by slow
degrees towards perfection'.[13] Newton's private religious
exercises were thus a means to the ends of perfecting his
nature and maintaining an unbroken experience of communion
with God. He understood that these two ends were mutually
dependent: 'I must lead a mortified life if I really propose to
find life and enlargement in spiritual duties; but then it is in a
way of prayer that I must expect assistance for practising that
self-denial: thus I am in a circle.'[14] At various times (as on this
occasion) this seemed a vicious circle, which could become
unbalanced and carry him in a downward spiral; at others
(and this was the ideal) it seemed to him more of an upward
spiral which could move him dialectically towards his
spiritual goals. When he first expressed these sorts of desires
he was within the orbit of Calvinistic ideas but did not yet
have an abiding assurance of his salvation. By 1756, however,
he was looking less anxiously into his soul for evidence of
saving grace, remarking that his final hope of acceptance
before God was based objectively on the atonement. Still, he
acknowledged that his inward sense of peace with God would
vary in daily life, according to God's gracious dispensation
and his own faithfulness in attending to the normal means of

[12] Diary (1751–6), 1 Jan. 1753. The biblical allusions were to 1 John 1: 3 and
Hebrews 11: 27.   [13] Ibid., 25 May 1753.
[14] Ibid., 4 Apr. 1756

grace. It was this communion with God in the daily routines
of life that he sought after throughout the remainder of his life.
All his devotional exercises were but means directed to the
goal of achieving communion with God as an abiding inward
experience.

'Communion presupposes union,' wrote Newton. The
theological framework for his devotional practice was the
Calvinistic teaching that the bond which indissolubly united
the believer to Christ was, subjectively, faith, and objectively,
the Holy Spirit. Out of this union, which signalled the
initiation rather than the culmination of the spiritual life,
flowed the twin benefits of justification and sanctification. It
was faith which, by the agency of the Holy Spirit, realized
here and now what God has done for the believer in Christ.[15]
Significantly, Newton understood there to be degrees of faith,
and that one's experience of communion with God largely
depended on the strength of its exercise. 'It is plain from
Scripture and experience', he wrote, 'that all our abatements,
declensions, and langours, arise from a defect of faith'
(i. 285). Not inconsistently (because faith was a gift of God),
he wrote also that the believer's sensible perception of his
communion with Christ varied because it 'depends upon the
communications we receive from the Lord, the Spirit', which
were dispensed according to the present needs of the believer
(i. 279). Crucial to Newton's spirituality, however, was the
belief that faith could ordinarily be expected to grow through
the diligent use of 'appointed means' of grace. And among
these means he included chiefly the sorts of private religious
exercises exhibited in his diary.

(*b*) *The lively exercise of faith.* How precisely did Newton's
devotional routines function to keep faith in lively exercise? It
appears that the typical form in which his meditations were
cast was designed to this end. Almost invariably there
recurred a threefold pattern following a curve through past,

[15] The classic text here is Calvin's *Institutes*, bk. 3, especially chaps 1 and 2. Note,
however, that John Gill, *The Doctrines of God's Everlasting Love* (1732), discounten-
anced the idea that faith, by the agency of the Holy Spirit, was the believer's bond to
Christ, arguing rather that an 'everlasting love-union' between the elect and the Holy
Trinity was anterior to the believer's temporal experience of faith.

present, and future in exercises of recollection, penitence, and resolution. Each of these three phases of his meditative prayer can be described further in binary terms, because Newton would usually first recollect sins and mercies, then express contrition and thanksgiving, before finally offering up self-dedication and resignation. That this was a conscious mould into which Newton directed his thoughts and prayers was especially apparent on days when, whether on account of fatigue or because of constraints on time, his entries were cryptic; one day in 1755, for example, he simply noted exercises of 'contrition, praise, and self-dedication', after he went for a long walk to review the events of his near-shipwreck. At other times, as on 2 February 1796, the actual paragraph structure of his diary entries followed these three stages of meditation. While numerous changes were rung on this pattern of prayer, the basic form remained constant over the years. The desired effect of these 'exercises of praise and humiliation' seems to have been to recreate and maintain the emotional landscape of conversion. Newton brought himself back again and again in his mind to the point of helplessness at which an entire dependence on Christ was his only hope of acceptance before God. In this way, his faith was rekindled.

The emotions of conversion were the key interior link between justification and sanctification. In a period when the relationship between religion and ethics, grace and obedience, was so disputed—when it was only with difficulty that evangelicals could escape the charge either of antinomianism or legalism—it was crucial to Newton to keep his feelings of gratitude for sins forgiven at a high pitch. This, he felt, was the all-important impulse that could sustain authentic Christian ethical endeavour, since it was the motive of gratitude which made one's obedience 'evangelical' rather than 'legal'. In 1753 he noted that one of the principal benefits he derived from his memorial day exercises was the motivation to persevere in Christian obedience. Specifically, he recalled the relapse which followed his first attempt at serious religious observance, and exhorted himself, 'I ought to use the utmost caution in examining and watching my own heart, because I have reason to remember that within 6 months after making a covenant with my Lord, I again returned for a season like a dog to my vomit'.[16] Newton realized that a collapse of ethical motivation was fearfully possible, despite having experienced overwhelming grace. 'Examining and watching' were therefore necessary to keep from falling from the path of obedience into heedless lawlessness, as well as to avoid the opposite danger of slipping into self-sufficient moralism.

The threefold pattern of Newton's typical exercise of meditative prayer illustrates these concerns. The first stage—rehearsing his past life—was usually the most lengthy, and his division of these recollections into 'blessings enjoyed and deliverances vouchsafed' and 'offences committed notwith-standing' specifically heightened his sense of unworthiness. The second stage of his exercises turned upon his consideration of the atonement, as he recalled the present benefits of sins forgiven which he now enjoyed because of Christ's Passion. This turning point is evident, for example, in Newton's meditations on 18 September 1779, when, after lamenting an indolent and wasted day, he recovered in a crescendo of inwardly directed exhortations, saying, 'But now I may, I must, I do mention the Atonement. I have sinned, But Christ has died.' The spiritual emotions piqued by this exercise were of both contrition and gratitude, humiliation and praise. As just observed, this pattern of tension and resolution was intended to produce, as Newton put it, 'a motive to stir my heart up and to awaken my drowsy powers to a quicker persuit [sic] after Holiness. The exceeding goodness of the Lord and my own unfaithfulness are topics which mutually heighten each other.'[17]

It was in this 'mutual heightening' that the emotions of conversion were reawakened. In Lutheran terms this was to emphasize the state of the Christian as 'at one and the same time righteous and a sinner [*simul iustus et peccator*]'. There were times when the pattern was not thus dialectical or climactic, as when on one occasion the contemplation of his temporal well-being led him in prayer to describe God's gifts as 'so many steps to rise to thee'. But the usual tendency of his

---

[16] Diary (1751–6), 21 Mar. 1753.   [17] Ibid., 22 Mar. 1756.

meditations was in the first instance to look intently upon his own wretchedness and moral incapacity, and then to praise God for undeserved mercy in Christ.[18]

This led to the final stage in his devotional exercises in which he resolved for the future to offer a better obedience to God in return for all the benefits he enjoyed. During the 1750s this was expressed rigorously in terms of a written covenant of duties to which he dedicated himself; later in life, particularly during his wife's declining health and after her death, this was expressed more passively in terms of resignation to the will of God, even if this meant suffering. A few months before her death in 1790, when it was clear that she would not live long, Newton's birthday meditation ended with the simple prayer: 'What thou wilt, when thou wilt, how thou wilt.' Throughout his life Newton's practice of prayer and meditation typically ended on a note of intense moral seriousness.

(c) *Memory and affections*. Newton's devotion might be described further as a kind of 'Ebenezer spirituality', since not infrequently he referred to his spiritual inventories as 'monuments', 'memorials', or 'Ebenezers' (cf. 1 Samuel 7: 12). As he wrote to one correspondent, 'Let us sit down and draw up our inventory, if we can, of the benefits and comforts temporal, spiritual, personal and relative, by which he has distinguished us from thousands: that gratitude may be excited.'[19] He signposted the most significant events of his spiritual biography, and returned again and again in memory to the emotions and lessons which these experiences offered. He quite literally erected such a monument in the study of the vicarage at Olney, one of the finest houses in the vicinity, built for him by Lord Dartmouth in 1767. Finding his status enhanced in so many ways since entering orders, he placed a plaque above his desk on which were juxtaposed two texts of Scripture, which would always remind him of stark contrast between his present and former positions in life:

---

[18] Cf. Donald Davie, *The Eighteenth-Century Hymn in England* (Cambridge, 1993), 125–7, where he discusses Newton's hymns and their sometimes conflicting states of emotion, such as grief crossed with pleasure, or mournfulness with joy.

[19] *Life of Mrs. Dawson*, 87–8.

Since thou wast precious in my sight,
thou has been honourable,
  Isaiah XLII. 4th

BUT

Thou shalt remember that thou wast
a bond-man in the land of Egypt,
and the Lord thy God redeemed thee:
  Deu.[my] *XV. 15*[th]

The key word on this monument was the word 'remember' in
the first line of the second verse. This plaque illustrates what
recurred in his diary, how Newton's biography took on a kind
of sacramental quality, as outward and visible events were
contemplated at regular intervals as signs of inward and
spiritual grace. It is one of the distinguishing marks of his
devotional practice that the usual subject of his meditation
was not, for example, the *lectio divina* (St Benedict), the love of
God (St Bernard of Clairvaux), the passion of Christ (St
Ignatius Loyola), the eternal rest of believers (Richard Baxter),
the transcendent excellence of divine things in themselves
(Jonathan Edwards), or any other external object of spiritual
attention, but was rather his own personal experience of
providence and grace.

Newton's devotional practice may also be understood as the
attempt, by preaching to himself, to compose his heart to feel
what he outwardly professed. He did not analyse this in terms
of faculty psychology, as Puritan writers on the spiritual life
did at great length, such as when Richard Baxter wrote, 'The
understanding must take in truths, and prepare them for the
will, and it must receive them and commend them to the
affections.'[20] Newton would have agreed none the less with
Baxter's basic definition of the great task of meditation as 'to
get these truths from thy head to thy heart'; that the sermons
one heard and the notions one entertained should not 'flit
around in the top of the brain', but 'be turned into the blood
and spirits of affection'.[21] When Newton wrote about
communion with God, it was in the language of the heart and
of sense experience. 'Fresh communications of grace' did not

---

[20] *Saints' Everlasting Rest* (1650; modern repr., 1960), 142.
[21] Ibid. 143.

234

mean that messages or visions were imparted directly into the mind. Indeed, Newton was suspicious of those who claimed such inspired revelations. A minister who visited him in 1778 was 'wrong in being so much guided by impressions', and Newton noted likewise with disapproval the famous case of Whitefield, who had publicly announced a revelation of his son's future greatness, only to be proved wrong when the son grew sick and died soon afterwards.[22] It was this kind of activity which, for Newton, justified the charge of 'enthusiasm'. What he sought in prayer was not revelation, but rather a 'spiritual and abstracted love', the 'warming of my heart into a thankful frame', 'a sensible advance in spirituality', 'liberty of communion', 'spiritual breathings' and a 'personal revival'. What he detested were 'formal dead prayers', 'barren uncomfortable sabbaths', and 'confused and veiled sacraments'. It was the religion of the heart which mattered most.

Newton's preoccupation with his own spiritual biography, his relentless concern with the weight of indwelling sin, and his focus upon his feelings, were at times indulgent, and his prayers were sometimes lost in a kind of solipsism. Although there was usually a counterpoint between his quest for self-knowledge and the knowledge of God, the predominant tone of the diaries was one of lamentation and disappointed desire, sometimes even of self-condemnation. In a short entry on 1 May 1756 he called himself simply, 'a lump of sin'. Increasingly, however, he realized the danger of dwelling too much upon self-examination and noted the importance of losing all thoughts, even of his own vileness, in thoughts of God's person, work, and love. It may be that the decreasing frequency of his diary entries after 1780 reflected a concern to move on to a more disinterested pattern of prayer. In old age, his meditations certainly became more self-forgetting as he sought to contemplate Christ and to anticipate his heavenly rest. In 1793, William Bull returned from seeing Newton and wrote, 'He looks very old, and has got exceedingly fat since I saw him last, but he is full of piety, holiness, and heavenly-mindedness.'[23] Wilberforce too noticed that Newton was

---

[22] Diary (1773–1805), 7 Feb. 1778; Cecil, *Newton*, 252.
[23] Bull, *Bull*, 220.

preoccupied with thoughts of God and heaven, comparing his appearance to Moses coming forth with shining face from the presence of God.[24] In one of Newton's last diary entries, he recorded his simple desire to be able in the approach of death to retire graciously as a thankful guest from a full table.[25]

The Historical Context of Newton's Private Devotional Practice

Through his contact with evangelicals of many denominations and through his reading, Newton was in touch with contemporary and historic traditions of Christian devotion, all of which influenced the way he understood the spiritual life. Ernest Stoeffler argues in *The Rise of Evangelical Pietism* (1971) that all experiential Protestantism during the post-Reformation period, *c.*1590–1690, can be treated as an essential unity characterized by four dominant traits: stress upon the personally meaningful relationship of the individual to God, religious idealism, biblicism, and opposition to prevailing norms of faith and life. These four characteristics seem on first impression to represent a lowest common denominator which would allow almost anyone in the seventeenth century to be described as a pietist, blurring theological distinctions which were regarded at the time as essential to defining the experience of God's grace. Looking back from a later perspective, however, particularly in the wake of advances in religious toleration in England and on the Continent, it was often possible to discern such commonalities between individuals who had fiercely disagreed with one another in earlier historical context. This was certainly the case for Newton, who, like Joseph Milner in his *History of the Church of Christ* (1794–7), was always looking for the vein of 'experimental godliness' in the eclectic assortment of spiritual writers he read.

The pattern of piety which recurred in Newton's diary betrays a particular debt to his upbringing in orthodox Dissent and his reading of the Puritans, noted in Chapter 2. For not only was the theological context of his devotion drawn from English Calvinism, but many of the characteristics of his

[24] William Wilberforce to Newton, 8 June 1804, ALS, Bodl.
[25] Diary (1773–1805), 21 Mar. 1804.

piety were found in this tradition too. To these roots can be traced, for example, his biblicism, his intense moral serious-ness and preoccupation with indwelling sin, his tendency to stress words over symbols as instruments of devotion; and his emphases upon introspection, discursive meditation, and the importance of the affections.[26]

Methodism and Moravianism, on the other hand, provided precedent for a devotional life which centred in the feelings in a more direct way than the scholastic or rationalistic context of Puritan nonconformity allowed. Jonathan Edwards's pain-staking scrutiny of the inner structure of religious feeling in his *Treatise on the Religious Affections* (1746) was a bridge between the concern to retain a rigorous intellectual context for the emotions aroused by religion, characteristic of Puritanism and Dissent, and the willingness to indulge pious emotion more widely, characteristic of the Evangelical Revival (apparent, for example, in popular preaching, corporate revivalism, missionary zeal, intimate society meetings, and hymn-singing). The sense of having come into a new world of this latter sort appeared in Newton's diary after he had ended his religious isolation by visiting London in 1754/5. And the Christ-centred focus of his devotion, the joyous sense of sins forgiven, the close fellowship with other believers, and above all, the simple dependence upon God for which he strove, drew on his exposure to Methodists and 'awakened' clergy up and down England from 1754 onwards. The Moravians did not impress Newton in the same way at first, but after a few years at Olney his opinion of them changed dramatically. Soon he found some of his most endeared friends were Moravians, and he recorded his admiration for them as 'excellent, spiritual, evangelical' people.[27] In 1794, Newton declared that August Spangenberg's statement of Moravian doctrine, published in English in 1784 as *An Exposition of Doctrine*, accorded with his own sentiments more than any other system of divinity he knew (vi. 439). The simplicity of Newton's devotion borrowed much from the Moravians.

---

[26] See further Gordon Wakefield, *Puritan Devotion* (1957); Watkins, *Puritan Experience*; Nuttall, 'Methodism and the Older Dissent'.
[27] *Letters* (Barlass), 131.

The Moravians were an important conduit through which Continental traditions of spirituality passed into English evangelicalism, and Newton's friend William Bull was particularly indebted to them for his introduction to a number of foreign spiritual writers.[28] Bull became a devotee of the mystical tradition, and in the 1770s, largely through his influence, Newton himself began dipping into works such as Jakob Boehme's *Way to Christ* and the autobiography of Mme Guyon. It was Bull who introduced William Cowper to Mme Guyon and persuaded him to translate some of her verse in 1782. At some point Newton also went on to read Mme Guyon's most famous follower, François de Fénelon, and studied some of the writings of the opponents of Quietism, such as Jacques Bossuet (chiefly his *Universal History*) and the Port Royalists Pierre Nicole, Blaise Pascal, and Pasquier Quesnel. As Jean Orcibal has written of Wesley and other evangelicals, Newton read these writers chiefly for their spirituality—the inward religion of the heart which they taught and exemplified—and largely ignored the polemics which divided them sharply from each other.[29] Newton wrote, for example,

If such persons as De Fenelon, Paschall, Quenell, and Nicole (to mention no more), were not true Christians, where shall we find any who deserve the name? In the writings of these great men, notwithstanding incidental errors, I meet with such strains of experimental Godliness, such deep knowledge of the workings of the Spirit of God and the heart of man, and such masterly explications of many important passages of Scripture, as might do honour to the most enlightened Protestant. (v. 29)

Newton extolled in similar terms elsewhere the spirituality of Boehme and Guyon, excusing their unavoidable mistakes in doctrine.[30] Effectively, he gave these writers the status of honorary experimental Protestants. As he read them on the spiritual life, he simply edited out their 'Popish errors'. Yet, on balance, Newton's reading of Continental spiritual writers was of limited range and had little influence on him in

---

[28] Bull, *Bull*, 106.   [29] Orcibal, 'Theological Originality', 103.
[30] Bull, *Bull*, 52; Diary (1773–1805), 4 Oct. 1778.

comparison with the native English traditions of spirituality so important to his early theological formation. At least part of the motive for reading foreign writers was curiosity. There was also a social appeal to be found reading what was still considered polite (French), if pious, literature. In the end it was left to Wesley, among Newton's contemporaries, to attempt more seriously to integrate various strands of Catholic spirituality into his own evangelical theology.

Newton's devotional pattern had been established earlier, before he had begun much of this reading, when he was immersed in Calvinistic writings on the spiritual life. Although he had read William Law while at Liverpool, and was impressed with much that he found in him, Law's mystical piety was not destined to have much lasting influence on him.[31] In about 1764 Newton wrote to Thomas Haweis, enclosing a copy of a poem by the famous shorthand diarist and follower of Law's 'inward religion', John Byrom. Newton commented to Haweis, 'Perhaps you may think this second [poem] has rather a Mystic air. For my own part I like the Evangelic strain best, but I believe that every expression is capable of a good sense.'[32] To the Principal of St Edmund Hall at Oxford, Dr Dixon, with whom Newton debated the merits of William Law's writings in a correspondence from 1768 to 1779, he likewise conceded the value of mystical writers only grudgingly, allowing that occasional statements could be construed in a 'Gospel sense' (vi. 207). Newton remained wary of mysticism and quietism, for he suspected that such modes of devotion might obliterate the distinction between nature and grace, failing to observe the radicality of sin and the necessity of coming always to God through Christ. He consistently translated mysticism into his own evangelical grammar. It was evangelical theology which, above all else, shaped his devotional practice and teaching. Newton identified his spiritual pedigree as descending from the indigenous protest against the medieval Church, through English Calvinism, to Moravianism and Methodism, when he explained to his parishioners in London that those who

---

[31] Cf. *Journals of Byrom*, ii. 637; Overton, *William Law* (1881), 395–8.
[32] Newton to Thomas Haweis [?1764], ALS, FLP.

maintained an evangelical strain of doctrine were now called Methodists, but earlier had been described as Lollard and Gospeller, or Puritan and Pietist (vi. 571).

NEWTON'S EMERGENCE AS A PUBLIC SPIRITUAL ADVISER

Although Newton stressed the importance of private devotional disciplines as the hidden secret of the life of godliness, his spirituality was not formed or expressed in isolation. In addition to the means of grace to be employed by the believer in solitude were other religious exercises involving corporate Christian activity. Principally, Newton explained, these were 'an attendance on the preached Gospel, and free converse (as proper opportunities are afforded) with [God's] believing people' (ii. 380). These social exercises were important in Newton's own spiritual formation, and he made them central to his ministry at Olney. Exchanging preaching and 'free converse' with other clergy and influential laymen beyond the parish connected him to a large fellowship, in which he gradually emerged as an exemplar and teacher of evangelical spirituality. Years later, in a funeral sermon for Newton, Richard Cecil could look out over his congregation and identify many ('among whom I stand as witness') who had been thus enlarged and confirmed by Newton 'as by a father in Christ'.[33] Newton's status as a kind of evangelical patriarch for nineteenth-century evangelicals owed much to his emergence among his peers as a 'nursing father' in Christ during his Olney pastorate.

The Evangelical Clerical Network

Before examining what Newton taught about the spiritual life through his printed publications, it may be useful to trace specifically how the private piety of his diary passed over into public teaching, noting the communication patterns within evangelicalism involved in his rise to a position of prominence in the movement.

At the outset it is important to emphasize that Newton's

[33] Cecil, *Works*, 85.

spirituality, in the third quarter of the eighteenth century, was incubating within a culture of religious friendship, dominated chiefly by clergy (though including some laymen as well) with evangelical views and experience. This culture was expressed in informal interaction through the exchange of pulpits by ministers, and the exchange of household hospitality and familiar correspondence by ministers and laymen alike. It was a world which partly overlapped with the connexional world of Methodism and the localized life of Moravianism in its settlements, and which partly, though never wholly, obscured the differences between Churchmen and Dissenters. Propriety was generally at a premium; 'singularity' at a discount. It was also a world in which Calvinistic views of one sort or another predominated, but the bases of co-operation can almost without exception be traced to two concerns: to promote individual spirituality and to further local evangelism.

The network of relationships sustained by this culture can be observed in Newton's principal friendships, which stretched out in concentric rings from Olney as he cultivated religious acquaintances on a local, regional, and national basis. John Edwards of Leeds cast a wistful look towards Olney when, on a journey to London, he passed within twenty miles but was unable to stop at the town he described (in words more usually associated with the Virgin) as 'highly favoured Olney'.[34] During the 1760s and 1770s the Olney vicarage hosted what must have seemed one continual religious conversation, as students, laymen, and clergy of various denominations came from around the country to stay as houseguests for a night or, in some cases, several weeks. Just as often, Newton was to be found elsewhere on annual preaching assignments or as the pulpit supply for another Gospel clergyman. There were also more prolonged trips for preaching and the renewal of acquaintances. In May and June of 1765 he preached at least fourteen times in London. The following spring, while the new vicarage was being built, he took a three-month circular tour of 650 miles, visiting and preaching for old friends in Yorkshire, the North-West, and the West Midlands. Journeys like these refreshed Newton. 'I

[34] Bull, *Newton*, 176.

came down, as you know,' Newton wrote to Clunie from Helmsley, 'to collect honey this spring, to carry home for a sort of winter's stock.'[35] Although this was probably his most extensive tour, Newton usually made a tour of some duration at least once annually throughout his ministry. He was keenly aware, however, especially at the beginning of his ministry, that he could not leave his parish unless he had himself a 'Gospel Preacher' for a replacement. After 1772, when Thomas Jones became curate of nearby Clifton, he and Newton were able in many cases to cover for one another's absences; Thomas Scott became a third in this preaching pool after his conversion in 1776. Earlier, Newton had to draw in support from further afield. But the impulse to visit neighbouring and distant clergy, once set going, created its own momentum as every visit created a vacancy which could be filled only by displacing another evangelical clergyman, and so on. John Berridge wrote to Newton in 1773, 'I entreat you not to pass by Everton without warming a bed, and a pulpit. If the Lord gives me strength, I will pay off all my debts; but if I am forced to be insolvent, do you act like a generous Christian, and continue your loans.'[36] And Newton did. This mutual exchange of domestic hospitality and preaching was the framework for the expression of evangelical solidarity beyond the boundary of a minister's own parish or local congregation.

With Dissenters the exchange functioned a little differently. They might come and speak or pray at Newton's weekday meetings in his home or at the Great House; he might go and preach in their house; or they might each attend Church or Meeting to hear the other preach. Newton explained to Samuel Palmer in 1797 how he understood his relationship with Dissenters in this respect:

We may love and pray for each other in our own respective pulpits and parlours, though we cannot make an exchange of public services. Were it not for the sake of expediency and consistency, I would very gladly preach in your meeting-house or under your pear-tree, if you asked me; for I believe whenever two or three meet

[35] *Letters* (Clunie), 160.   [36] *Works of Berridge*, 386.

together in the Saviour's name . . . the spot whereon they stand is, for the time, *Holy Ground*.[37]

Thus, for Newton, prudential restraint prevented the full exchange of public preaching. But there was still evidently plenty of opportunity for Churchmen and Dissenters to participate together in a wide, interlocking network of supportive evangelical friendships.

The Evangelical Familiar Letter

The culture just described, which thrived on religious conversation and mutual assistance in the work of local evangelism, was naturally expressed in a network of familiar correspondence, or, as Newton sometimes called it, 'paper converse'.[38] In the first instance, it was necessary to correspond simply to arrange household visits and to schedule preaching assignments. But the impulse to correspond went much deeper than this. Many times the focus of letters was on personal spirituality, seeking to get and inspire 'more warmth and light' in one's devotional life, or simply to express spiritual solidarity in times of joy or sorrow. Thus, Newton began a letter to a London correspondent suffering under severe illness, 'I have been thinking of you and yours upon my knees' (vi. 76). At other times the focus with such friends was upon evangelism, exchanging narrative accounts of the progress or decline of local revival, or discussing the opportunities and problems of the Gospel ministry. Points of doctrine might be raised, or practical advice and exhortation given regarding the work of the ministry.

Such letters were naturally exchanged between ministers and laymen who could consider one another, in essence, social equals. Within Newton's correspondence were other letters whose tone suggested a degree of stratification up and down the social scale. His tone was deferential when writing to superiors such as Lord Dartmouth or (to a lesser extent) John

---

[37] *Letters* (Palmer), 105.
[38] Ward, *Protestant Evangelical Awakening*, 2, has described this kind of networking and exchange of letters as a general phenomenon across the 18th-c. Protestant world. Whereas the 16th c. produced public confessions of faith, the 18th c. produced archives.

Thornton. While evangelical conviction went far to overcome social distinctions, it could not obliterate them; these were client–patron relationships in which Newton functioned as a faithful epistolary chaplain. In other letters it seems that Newton was writing from a position notionally above that of his correspondent. These might be described as director–enquirer relationships in which he responded, for example, to cases of spiritual concern addressed to him by needy individuals, or to requests for advice from young men entering the ministry. Newton wrote other kinds of letters, including a number which were evangelistic, written to those outside the Gospel milieu such as his brother-in-law Jack Catlett or Thomas Scott prior to his conversion. But it was chiefly through his correspondence within the evangelical network that he was recognized as possessing a particular genius for spiritual letter-writing. One of Newton's clerical correspondents from Scotland, who used to keep a volume of Newton's published letters by him constantly, wrote in 1774, ''Tis pity Mr. Newton should do anything but write letters.'[39]

(a) *Considerations of genre.* Howard Anderson and Irvin Ehrenpreis have described how a steady increase in the efficiency of the Post Office, the influence of French and Latin specimens, and the trend to more natural prose after the Glorious Revolution helped make the eighteenth century 'the great age of the personal letter'. The aesthetic question which dominated the century was how art combined both personal expression and objectivity, nature within and without. The familiar letter in many ways exemplified these concerns, since in the best letters a writer's own character was revealed through candid accounts of other subjects. The goal was a spontaneous veracity in which art was subordinated to nature, the composed to the unplanned; the great failure was for a letter to appear studied and artificial.[40] Herbert Davis has described letter-writing among the cultured élite as 'an art which they naturally looked upon as a continuation of the art of conversation; which for a generation that liked to imagine itself as Augustan was the very mark of polite society, possible

---

[39] *Letters* (Barlass), 10.
[40] Anderson and Ehrenpreis, 'Familiar Letter', 269–82.

only among civilized men and women—an art which at its best should be the triumph of wit and humour and imagination'.[41] These ideals describe well the studied naturalness in the correspondence of such poets as Pope and Cowper. Similar aspirations also motivated evangelicals such as Newton who could not pretend to such high levels of sophistication. John Overton's comments, prefacing his discussion of William Law's epistolary style (which he compared with Newton's), provide a delightful Victorian panegyric on these same ideals among eighteenth-century letter-writers generally:

In the eighteenth century the art of letter-writing reached its perfection . . . In an earlier age the English style was not sufficiently easy and flexible to admit excellence in an art which, above all things, requires ease and flexibility. In a later, the penny post, the electric telegraph, and the general rush and hurry of life, have, among them, well-nigh improved letter-writing off the face of the land. Men make known their wants, express their sentiments, and so forth, to their friends in writing, but they no longer write letters. In these degenerate days an average letter hardly contains as many lines as in the last century it contained pages. *Then* almost every able man left behind him many more or less good specimens of this delightful branch of literature.[42]

And Overton certainly felt that Newton was much more than just an 'able man' in this respect.

The familiar letter was a particularly fitting genre for spiritual direction. The very demands of the genre, requiring both spontaneity and discipline, substance and personality, created a courteous context for discussing the spiritual life. Needless abstraction and controversy were ruled out by making them marks of bad taste, while at the same time the writer felt bound to say something worthy of the recipient, or at least worthy of the cost of the postage (normally paid by the recipient). Because the letter was still a form of literary culture, and the writer was generally aware (as noted with respect to Newton's autobiography) that his letter might be read aloud, reread or passed around to others, it was

[41] Davis, 'Correspondence of the Augustans', 13.
[42] Overton, *William Law*, 335.

incumbent upon him to make sure his letter included matter of more than ephemeral value. For the cultured élite, this might mean the letter could be returned to time and again for entertainment; for evangelicals, it meant the letter would provide lasting edification.

(*b*) *Newton's epistolary style*. Newton wrote to his orphan niece encouraging her to writer better letters. 'The whole art', he explained, 'is to write with freedom and ease. . . . Tell me something about the fowls in the yard, or the trees in the garden, or what you please; only write freely' (vi. 304). To another correspondent he offered the excuse, when he had reached the end of his paper before he intended, 'I love to give up my heart and pen, without study, when I am writing' (vi. 42). At other times, when the subject of the letter was paramount, he was forced to be more disciplined than either of these examples would suggest. And so, writing on the nature of communion with God in 1772, he explained to his correspondent at the start of the letter that he would have to come straight to the point, for he intended to limit himself to a single sheet of paper.

This was also an aesthetic point. When in the 1750s Newton wished to write beautiful letters to his wife while away at sea, he worried he wrote too digressively, remarking, 'The great beauty of an epistolary style is conciseness' (v. 355). Over the years he sought to develop a style which would nicely balance compression of meaning with ease of manner. When John Thornton sent John Berridge a copy of twenty-six letters by Newton published under the pen-name Omicron, Berridge praised the letters for their Christian simplicity which contrasted with a merely human eloquence, and he spotted the author immediately by both the matter and style of the volume: 'Omicron is Mr. Newton. He wears a mask, but cannot hide his face. Pithiness and candour will betray the Curate of Olney.'[43] Berridge then, at least, felt that Newton achieved his ideal of saying something substantial and memorable in correspondence, without violating the spirit of familiarity germane to a personal letter. The creative tension of letter-writing lay precisely in this balance between ease and

---

[43] *Works of Berridge*, 395.

concision, freedom and control, within the narrow limits of the medium.

There is a parallel here to the tension which existed in Newton's spirituality between the desire to have his devotion arise spontaneously from the heart, out of an overwhelming experience of grace, and the recognition that he needed to attend patiently to the means of grace to keep faith in exercise. Fittingly then, Newton wrote in his diary in October 1775:

I am thinking of a new plan for my diary. The Lord has given me many friends with whom I correspond. He is my best friend. He knows my all. A thought came into my mind yesterday, that it might be [to] his blessing [and] affecting [to] my own heart, and lead me to a more exact notice of what passes, if I address myself to him, something in the Epistolary form, laying my cares, desires, wants and connections before him as they arise.[44]

From that time forward, therefore, the tension between freedom and discipline became a matter of both form and content in Newton's private devotion.

Newton's Emergence as an Author on the Spiritual Life

The gap between manuscript and print culture in the eighteenth century was not wide. This was observed in connection with the progress of Newton's autobiography from personal letters to a published book, and it is apparent again in the case of Newton's religious letters. He emerged gradually from the situation of a Christian whose private piety was known to a small circle of friends, to become an author on the spiritual life widely read by evangelicals.

In the correspondence between Newton and Thomas Haweis before Newton's ordination in 1764 they had discussed at great length the possibility of launching a new Christian magazine. Newton had urged Haweis to set the project afoot, but Haweis had challenged Newton himself to take the initiative. In the end, the project appears to have died. The idea was soon taken up by others, however, for in 1766 the first issue of the *Gospel Magazine, or Spiritual Library, Designed to*

[44] Diary (1773–1805), 15 Oct. 1775.

promote Religion, Devotion, and Piety, from Evangelical Principles
was launched. If any magazine symbolized Newton's circle of
friendships, this did. Although Calvinistic in theology, its
stated aims were practical and evangelical, and it embraced
both Dissenters and Churchmen. Most magazines in the
eighteenth century, particularly new ones like the *Gospel
Magazine*, depended heavily for copy on correspondents from
around the country who would send in regular contributions.
In the spring of 1771 Newton contributed in this way,
sending in a copy of a personal letter he had written originally
to Mr Symonds (presumably his friend Joshua Symonds
(1739–88), Baptist minister of the Old Meeting at
Bedford).[45] It was published in the May issue, at the back of
the magazine in the section set aside for miscellaneous
contributions from correspondents, and was signed Omicron.
The June and July issues saw another two of Newton's
personal letters recycled in this same way. These first three
letters had each originally been written in response to specific
enquiries of a practical or casuistical nature, such as whether
one is obliged after marrying to contribute to the poor in the
same amount as before one married, or whether one need
worry that the specific sins of believers would be publicly
declared on the Day of Judgement. Then, in the July issue,
there was a note from the editor at the end, saying, 'The
queries proposed to the consideration of our very valuable
correspondent Omicron have been transmitted to that gentleman.' Thus, on the strength of three contributions, Newton
had been seen as a potential spiritual adviser by one of the
readers. The enquirer, who used the *nom de plume* Thereon,
had asked about how to begin conducting family worship. In
the August issue Newton's response appeared as a letter, 'To
Thereon, on Family Worship,' signed, 'Your friend and
servant in the gospel, Omicron.' In the September issue
Thereon's public gratitude to Omicron was recorded, and a
further contribution from Newton was given pride of place as
the first item in the issue.

Newton's contributions to the *Gospel Magazine* were of a

---

[45] Cf. Bull, *Newton*, 203 n.

practical nature and not in the least controversial, but they sat side by side in the magazine with articles reporting on the Minutes Controversy which erupted after the Methodist conference of 1770. From the beginning, the *Gospel Magazine* was not a friend to Wesley, but throughout 1771 the tone of its articles grew increasingly antagonistic toward the Arminian evangelist. Wesley called the magazine, 'that Monthly Medley of truth and error, sound Words and Blasphemy, trumped up as a vehicle to convey Calvinism and slander the nation'.[46] It is interesting, therefore, that just as the mutual acrimony was reaching boiling point, Newton's first original contribution to the *Gospel Magazine*, not based on a prior personal letter, should appear (again in first position) as a letter 'On Controversy'. The context of the Minutes Controversy made Newton's comments in this letter extremely topical. Readers of the *Gospel Magazine* would have seen the import immediately of Newton's statement, for example: 'Of all people who engage in controversy, we, who are called Calvinists, are most expressly bound by our own principles to the exercise of gentleness and moderation' (i. 242).

Newton continued to contribute regularly to the *Gospel Magazine*, off and on, for several years, sometimes publishing what was previously a personal letter, sometimes using the epistolary form more artificially for a new topical essay, sometimes even answering a personal letter through the press. By 1774 he had made twenty-six contributions, in addition to several hymns, which he then collected and republished as a single volume of letters on religious subjects by Omicron.[47] Six years later he published *Cardiphonia, or the Utterance of the Heart; in the Course of a Real Correspondence* (1780), comprising collections of Newton's familiar letters to twenty-four different recipients. With the publication of this volume, Newton's place as the gentle casuist of the Revival, spiritual director of souls through the post, was secure. As his reputation grew, and as he himself became older, he found it increasingly

---

[46] Quoted in *GM* 6 (1771), 360.

[47] This volume was republished in 1793 with some additional letters which had been contributed by Newton to the *Gospel Magazine* after 1774 under the pen-name Vigil.

difficult to keep up with his personal correspondence. Although still devoting a great deal of time to letter-writing, he was always working in the 1790s from a stack of fifty or sixty unanswered letters. Besides several minor pieces cast in epistolary form, the only significant collection of private letters which he published after *Cardiphonia* was an edited version of his correspondence with his wife in 1793. Posthumously, a sequel to *Cardiphonia* was included in Newton's collected works, and throughout the nineteenth century many more collections of his letters to single recipients were published by their descendants.

NEWTON'S PUBLIC TEACHING ON THE SPIRITUAL LIFE

In all, over 500 letters, written by Newton to correspondents stretching from Bodmin Moor in Cornwall to Tayside in Scotland, were published during his lifetime or shortly afterwards. It is difficult, however, to extract a unified core of teaching on the spiritual life from this body of literature, for most of Newton's letters were by definition *ad hoc* compositions reflecting the particular concerns of the correspondents, an occasion within Newton's personal milieu, or a theme of immediate topical relevance. None the less, there was a short series of letters published in the *Gospel Magazine* in the summer of 1772, and then reprinted in the Omicron volume in 1774, which provided a simple outline of the spiritual life. Republished many times as a stand-alone tract in the nineteenth century (even translated into Russian), these letters offer one of the finest specimens of what he taught more widely in his correspondence (i. 171–91).

Newton on the Spiritual Life: Three Omicron Letters (1772)

These letters were first prompted by a query from John Thornton about how Newton thought the work of divine grace typically progressed in a believer. Newton responded in three personal letters with thoughts based loosely upon the text from Mark 4: 28*b*, '—first the blade, then the ear, after that the full corn in the ear'. Sometime near the beginning of 1772 Newton asked Thornton to return copies of the letters he had

written, so that he could publish them.[48] In these letters
Newton explained that he would deal, not with what was
uniquely personal or occasional in the experience of believers,
but only with what he observed was common to all. He set out
to trace three stages of spiritual development, corresponding
to the growth of corn described in his text, which he
denominated simply A, B, and C; stages which he compared
also to those of a child, a young man, and a father (1 John 2:
12–14). The process of spiritual formation described by
Newton may be summarized as follows.

By nature all men are incapable of receiving or approving
divine truths, being dead in sin. A is a person, however, who is
under the drawings of God that will bring him infallibly to
Christ for salvation. The beginning of this work is instantaneous, effected by 'a certain kind of light communicated to the
soul, to which before it was an utter stranger' (i. 172). This
light is at first weak and indistinct, but once begun it increases
steadily. Conviction, though often thought of as the first work
of God in the soul, is an immediate effect of this prior
illumination by the Holy Spirit, a reflex of the spiritual
apprehension of God's perfections revealed by God's own
Spirit. This light is always mediated through the Scriptures
and leads to the perception of its principal truths. There may
be some temporary efforts by A to gain God's approval
through religious exercises and moral earnestness, but these
efforts are quickly proved ineffectual, and he is brought to see
the necessity and sufficiency of the salvation outlined in the
gospel. Though a believer, he is longing to enjoy 'a sure and
abiding sense of his acceptance in the beloved' (i. 176). He
believes in the power of Christ to save, but through ignorance
and legality, and the remembrance of past sins and present
corruptions, he questions his own willingness and fears that
Christ may spurn him. God gives him encouragement,
however, to keep him from being swallowed by sorrow, and
enlarges his heart at various times in religious exercises. His
problem is that he rests in these feelings, rather than taking
his comforts as encouragement to press on. When comforts are
withdrawn, he finds it much more difficult to pray, or to read

---

[48] John Thornton to Newton, 4 Jan. 1772, ALS, CUL.

and hear God's word, and his temptations seem to increase. His spiritual hopes are easily dashed in this condition, and he longs to feel again something to assure him personally of Christ's promises. His views of grace are still narrow, but by these fluctuations between comfort and fear he is brought slowly forward, and with a tender conscience he fights against sin. Although his chief hindrances are weak faith and a legal spirit, his appetite for spiritual things is keen and his zeal lively. The state of A is remarkable for the strong exercise of his affections more than for mature views of Christ. It is towards such views that God's grace advances him, for though he is a believer, he seldom thinks himself one.

Newton went on in his next letter to describe the second stage of Christian experience. It commences, and the alternating hopes and fears of the young convert are resolved, when he is enabled by 'appropriating faith' to rest in Christ, spiritually apprehending Christ's entire suitableness and sufficiency for all who trust in him. B then knows that he belongs to Christ, and Christ to him. However, 'There are various degrees of this persuasion; it is of a growing nature, and is capable of increase so long as we remain in the world. I call it assurance, when it arises from a simple view of the grace and glory of the Saviour, independent of our sensible frames and feelings' (i. 178). Now that faith is stronger, though, it has more to grapple with. If the state of A could be described as one of *desire*, the state of B is one of *conflict*. The Lord appoints specific trials to humble B and show him all that remains in his heart, for though he may be free from the guilt and dominion of sin, he is not free from its indwelling presence. Although he desires sanctification, he does not really understand the deceitfulness of his own heart: it is beyond what he would have believed had he been told beforehand. The sinfulness of sin is made manifest to him, above all, through his capacity to violate the light and love God has tenderly shown him. Through God's testing of his heart, and by the agency of the Holy Spirit, he is trained up in a growing knowledge of himself and of God, and is gradually led thereby to cease completely from boasting, complaining, and censuring others.

The third stage, C, Newton describes in his last letter as one chiefly of *contemplation*. Here the believer does not necessarily

have stronger affections than the young convert, nor does he
have an assurance that B does not also have, since he is in the
same state of absolute dependency as he was in the beginning.
He has no special inherent grace, but as a mature Christian
his assurance is more stable and simple. His greatest strength
is his constant sense of his own weakness. Weaned from
trusting to himself, he has learned through long experience to
turn to the Lord at once and has therefore clearer and deeper
views of Christ. God has blessed his use of the means of
prayer, reading and hearing God's word, and meditating on
his experience to give him likewise a more comprehensive
knowledge of spiritual things. Although his feelings are not as
warm as A, his judgement is more solid, and his thoughts are
more steadily fixed on Christ. Contemplating the glory of
Christ is the great business of his life, and by so doing he is
morally transformed day by day and grows in humility,
heavenly-mindedness, resignation to God's will, and tenderness to others. Finally his heart is united to the glory and will
of God alone, in so far as this is possible, given the remnants of
a fallen nature. Although he loves God because of all that he
has received from him, yet he has now a more simple and
direct love in which self is forgotten in consideration of the
glory and perfection of God as he is in himself. This
experience of the believer is compatible with happiness or
suffering, riches or poverty, learning or illiteracy, lively or low
spirits; and it may be had by minister and layman alike. There
is nothing on earth to be found so beautiful, wrote Newton, as
a believer continuously contemplating Christ in this state of
the spiritual life.

An Evangelical Formative Spirituality
Believing that Scripture taught a Calvinistic understanding of
justification and sanctification, Newton simply sought in these
letters to unite this understanding with what he had carefully
observed over many years of his own and others' religious
experience. Newton believed that if one looked hard enough,
one ought to be able to discern a consistent pattern beneath
the variety of Christian experience, for it was the same Spirit
at work in all: 'These exercises which form what may be called
the *outline* of a Christian's experience, are, like the features in

253

the human face, as to the grand and leading points, universally the same in all, but so modified and diversified . . . that each one may be considered an original.'[49]

With this working assumption, Newton's letters on growth in grace became an essay in interpreting his empirical observations by his theology, and vice versa. This was consistent with the theological method he displayed elsewhere, which sought to co-ordinate Scripture, reason, and experience. In one sense Newton's theory of spiritual development was not very sophisticated, for once the possibility of development was allowed, then at least three stages— beginning, middle, and end—were bound to emerge.[50] Yet its genius was its simplicity. And by his use of biblical typology (exodus–wilderness–Canaan) and imagery (child–young man–father) he gave these stages symbolic associations which would help his reader to see the soul's progress as part of a larger pattern of redemption as well.[51]

Newton wanted to be careful not to universalize his own experience in these letters, but the spirituality reflected in his diary and in his private devotional practice nevertheless surfaces at many points. Some of the insights which he had discovered and expressed in private, he was able to spell out much more clearly in these letters. Outside the confessional isolation of the diary, with a specific correspondent or general readership in mind, he was required to write with discipline to communicate effectively to others. For example, the dialectic between self-knowledge and knowledge of God which recurred

---

[49] Newton, *Memoirs of Grimshaw*, 82.

[50] William Romaine's concept of the spiritual life was similar to Newton's, as the 19th-c. title of his trilogy on the Christian life suggests: *The Life, Walk, and Triumph of Faith* (collected edn., 1824). Romaine's method and approach was, however, miles apart from Newton's. It was a treatise, not a series of letters; it correlated principally systematic theology with the Scriptures, rather than experience with the Scriptures; and its style was scholastic and digressive (if substantial), rather than familiar and epigrammatic. Henry Venn's evangelical spiritual classic, *The Complete Duty of Man* (1761), on the other hand, was principally a practical handbook, almost casuistical in nature, and it did not reflect a developed concept of formative spirituality, reflecting very little on the temporal nature of growth in grace.

[51] The simple threefold pattern of formative spirituality in Newton's writings is in some ways parallel to Catholic ascetical theology, with its ancient division of the spiritual life into the stages of 'beginner', 'proficient', and 'perfect'. Cf. Pierre Pourrat, Preface to *Christian Spirituality*, 3 vols. (Tunbridge Wells, 1922–7).

in the diary was given in the letters an almost visual clarity as
he described such knowledge expanding in both depth and
height in the course of Christian experience. Likewise, the
concept of the spiritual life progressing from an anthropo-
centric to a theocentric focus, from attending to one's own
feelings to contemplating the perfections of Christ himself, is
an insight latent in the diary, which was more fully developed
in the letters. Still, at the time when he wrote the letters, he
identified most clearly with the character of B in the middle
stage of *conflict*. In writing about the case of B, Newton
tellingly shifted from third-person pronouns to first-person
pronouns more often than he did in either of the other cases.
When a friend hinted a few years later that to write about C he
must have arrived at that level of experience, he demurred,
though he insisted the state was still attainable (ii. 37).

The evangelical spirituality that Newton described exhibited
signs not only of his personal experience, but also of his
contemporary religious context, for like his theology it steered
a middle course between positions which he regarded as
compromising the Gospel. The first volume of the *Gospel
Magazine* for 1771—the year Newton began contributing—
included a note to the reader: 'Here the Reader's mind is in no
danger of being corrupted by the proud, pharisaical tenets, of
the *Arminian*; nor poisoned with the licentious tenets of the
Antinomian.'[52] While Newton was anxious to avoid controversy (and he described freedom from contention as a final
mark of the character of C), he would have identified entirely
with this editorial ideal. Against antinomianism he stressed
the use of appointed means of grace and the morally
transforming nature of contemplation. His whole concept of
development in the spiritual life was in contrast to the high
Calvinist ethos, where the focus upon God's eternal purposes
in salvation often obscured the temporal dimensions of the
believer's experience. Against Arminianism, which he conceived of as a form of moralism, Newton emphasized the
passive reception of God's grace. Most of his verbs were, in
fact, in the passive, and the soul's progress at every stage was
accounted for in terms of divine agency. Moreover, although

[52] Preface to *GM* 6 (Jan. 1771).

Newton identified lofty possibilities for the spiritual life, his teaching differed from Wesley on both assurance and perfection. Newton did not base assurance on inward feeling, but on 'judicious views' of Christ's sufficiency; and he taught explicitly that assurance belonged, not to the essence of faith, but to its establishment (i. 178–9). And for Newton sanctification was never, as it was for Wesley, either entire or instantaneous. There were always the 'inseparable remnants of a fallen nature' to contend with, even in one's highest attainments. The whole thrust of Newton's teaching emphasized the progressive, lifelong nature of the believer's growth in holiness.

These three letters on growth in grace represent only a specimen of Newton's religious correspondence. And in one sense they are atypical in treating the theory rather more than the practice of the spiritual life. Most of Newton's letters were much more occasional. But in all of his correspondence—even in his letters of almost wholly disinterested friendship—he treated the subject at hand within the context of this basic evangelical understanding of formative spirituality.[53]

---

[53] For a specimen of Newton's actual practice of spiritual direction, see his letters to James Coffin and his wife, a couple from Cornwall who had been awakened by reading his works, and then wrote to him for advice. *Letters* (Coffin); cf. Sidney Kolpas, 'The Quest for James Coffin', *Book Collector*, 39 (1990), 220–34.

7

'For my own part I like the evangelic strain best'
The Hymnody of John Newton

Oh God, the Olney Hymns abound with words of grace
John Betjeman

THE hymn was an apt literary form for the expression of Newton's spiritual ideals, since like the familiar letter it allowed him to treat a substantial theological subject without the loss of personal, or even autobiographical, immediacy. While serving an evangelical end in its possible modes as an instrument of hortatory, didactic, pastoral, evangelistic, or devotional concern, the hymn also justified Newton's participation in a pleasurable form of literary art. This participation and this pleasure was shared with William Cowper, and Newton stressed in his preface to the *Olney Hymns* (1779) that publication was originally planned in part simply as a celebration of their Christian friendship—as a kind of mutual *Festschrift*. As a shared pleasure, hymn composition and singing accorded well with the importance Newton placed upon Christian friendship, hospitality, and correspondence. Likewise, hymns—often compared with ballads and folksongs—had a semi-anonymous nature which made them suited to the extra-ecclesiastical and transdenominational solidarity which Newton believed was formed through adherence to a simple gospel. Raised in Old Dissent under the hymns of Watts, acquainted with the hymns of later Non-conformists through his renewed contact with Dissent after his conversion, Newton was also familiar with the powerful effusion of sacred song which accompanied the ministry of Whitefield and the Wesleys, the Moravians, and other preachers of the Evangelical Revival. It was the pastoral occasion of his work at Olney and his friendship with Cowper in the late 1760s that provided the impulse for Newton to contribute himself to this growing stock of congregational religious verse.

THE OCCASION AND CONTEXT OF NEWTON'S OLNEY HYMNS

A part of the Christian intimacy which Newton discovered after leaving the slave trade included the singing and reciting of hymns. One Sunday in the summer of 1755, when he was at Chatham, he rose before dawn for private prayer and then set out with a friend at half past five for a Meeting. After the friends prayed together, Newton records how they passed the rest of their walk 'in singing & repeating hymns of praise, & in spiritual conversation'.[1] They did the same when they returned that evening. Later, at Liverpool, Newton spent a solitary walk in the country one Saturday in devotional exercises and noted in his diary: '—enlarged in intercession till I came near the town, which was about an hour, concluded with a hymn'.[2] In both private and 'social' piety, hymns had meant much to Newton as a layman. The earliest record of hymns actually written by Newton himself comes also from the period at Liverpool, just before his ordination, for in 1763 he included two of his hymns (later published in the *Olney Hymns*) in correspondence with Thomas Haweis.[3]

Once settled as Curate of Olney, Newton immediately made hymns a vital part of his ministry. He noted in his diary at the beginning of 1765, 'We have now a fixed little company who come to my house on sabbath evening after tea. We spend an hour or more in prayer and singing, and part between six and seven.'[4] A month later he was giving out

[1] Diary (1751–6), 6 July 1755.
[2] Ibid., 20 Sept. 1755.
[3] This precedes by four years the earliest date yet assigned to any of Newton's contributions to the *Olney Hymns*. The hymns are preserved as what appears to be a fragment of a cover letter Newton sent to Haweis in 1763 with a bundle of manuscripts (John Newton Collection, FLP). They are, ''Tis past—the dreadful stormy night' (*OH* 3. 21), and, 'When my Saviour, my Shepherd is near' (*OH* 3.30). There are some minor emendations in the published versions.
[4] Entry for Sunday, 27 Jan. 1765, cited in Bull, *John Newton*, 138. Robin Leaver mistakenly places this meeting earlier at Liverpool in 'Olney Hymns 1779: 1. The Book and its Origins', *Churchman*, 93/4 (1979), 237.

hymnbooks to the children at his Thursday catechetical
meetings and employing one Mr Hull to teach them to sing.
Expounding and singing hymns continued as a regular part of
the children's meetings, and Newton saw in this the biblical
promise fulfilled that praise should come out of the mouths of
babes. He only prayed that it would be from their hearts. This
seemed to be the case for one boy in February, John Stamford,
who Newton noticed had become 'serious & retired' and wept
often.[5] A part of the value of hymns in this didactic context
was also mnemonic, since Newton had the children learn the
hymns by heart, effectively, catechizing them in verse.[6]

Whether Newton wrote his own hymns for these occasions
early in his ministry is not known, but with the arrival of
Cowper in Olney in 1767 the most creative period of hymn
composition certainly began. The hymns 'O Lord, our
languid souls inspire' by Newton, and 'Jesus, where'er thy
people meet' by Cowper, were written when the sabbath after-
tea prayer meeting was moved into the large room of Lord
Dartmouth's vacant Great House in the spring of 1769. Both
the occasion and the collaboration nicely symbolize the piety
of the *ecclesiola* which Newton fostered at Olney and which was
expressed in these hymns.[7] Newton's hymn is a prayer, and
each phrase in the first five stanzas invites God to act on
behalf of the gathered people: to inspire their souls, send
heavenly fire, hear prayer, display his presence, raise hopes,
pour out blessings, and so on. The suppliant posture
acknowledges revival as a matter of divine initiative, and the
aspirations point to Newton's most ardent pastoral ideals:

> 4. Within these walls let holy peace,
>   And love, and concord dwell;
>   Here give the troubled conscience ease,
>   The wounded spirit heal.

---

[5] 'List of Children', CNM.   [6] Diary (1767), 1–7 June.
[7] The close connection between the hymns and the non-liturgical setting of
Newton's small groups meeting for prayer and fellowship is suggested further by the
fact that Newton wrote very few hymns after he moved to London, since the
congregation at St Mary Woolnoth was largely from outside the parish and Newton's
ministry there was chiefly a matter of preaching. The prayer-meetings were no more.

> 5. The feeling heart, the melting eye,
>   The humble mind bestow;
>   And shine upon us from on high,
>   To make our graces grow!

Christian *koinonia*, release from guilt, stirring affectionate piety, modesty, and growth in virtue comprised the ideal evangelical fellowship, to which Newton added in the last stanza the wider hope of numerical increase through conversion:

> 6. And may the gospel's joyful sound
>   Enforc'd by mighty grace,
>   Awaken many sinners round,
>   To come and fill the place.   (*OH* 2. 43)

During the 1770s Newton regularly wrote a hymn for these meetings and, as noted in Chapter 5 above, often used the hymn as a basis for his discourse.[8] As with the children's meetings, so with the adults' prayer meetings, the hymns themselves were sometimes enough to elicit a spiritual response from those present. At the end of May 1778, Newton noted that his speaking on a hymn, written in response to an incident in the parish that week, 'revived the spirit of T. Old'.[9] Sometimes, Newton would speak from a hymn of Cowper's, or from extant hymnbooks such as Richard Conyers' *Collection of Psalms and Hymns* (1767) or William Hammond's *Psalms, Hymns, and Spiritual Songs* (1745).[10] In the preface to the *Olney Hymns*, Newton related that he and Cowper conceived at a very early date that they might themselves publish a volume of their collected hymns one day.[11] With the onset of Cowper's

---

[8] Ella, *William Cowper*, 193, states that neither Newton nor Cowper intended their hymns to be sung and that Newton wrote his hymns for 'exposition only'. This goes well beyond the evidence. While hymns were probably sung in formal worship only before and after divine service, and while Newton may sometimes have expounded a hymn without having his people sing it, there is good evidence that many of the hymns were in fact sung in meetings and that this was the original intention. See e.g. Newton to John Thornton, 3 Aug. 1775, ALS, CUL, and Cowper to Mrs Madan, 26 Sept. 1767, *Letters of Cowper*, i. 180.

[9] Diary (1773–1805), 31 May 1778.

[10] See e.g. ibid., 4 Feb. 1776, 26 Oct. 1777, and 10 Jan. 1779.

[11] King, *William Cowper*, 82, dates the beginning of the formal collaboration between Newton and Cowper early in 1771.

third period of serious depression in 1773, however, the whole project was cast into doubt, for from that point on Cowper wrote very few more hymns. For his part, Newton continued to write hymns regularly, and even published a number in 1774 as an appendix to his *Omicron* volume of letters. Over the course of his ministry at Olney in the 1770s he eventually amassed a large corpus of his own compositions, which he appears to have kept in a separate notebook and numbered consecutively. In the end, he decided to publish, even without a commensurate number of hymns from Cowper.[12]

While there remains much work to be done on the textual background and occasion of the hymns written by Cowper and Newton, it is evident that the composition and dissemination of the hymns before publication in 1779 took place within a milieu wider than that of 'the Curate of Olney & his poor people'.[13] In their *English Congregational Hymns in the Eighteenth Century* (1982), the critics Madeleine Ford Marshall and Janet Todd do not adequately distinguish the occasion of Newton's hymnody in the pastoral task at Olney from the intended audience for his hymns. The hymn-writing task was indeed for Newton first and foremost a response to the spiritual needs of his people, and many hymns arose from very specific situations in the parish. For example, the death of parishioner Betty Abraham in February 1774 prompted Newton to write a funeral hymn.[14] However, although the occasion might be

---

[12] John Baird and Charles Ryskamp, Introduction to *The Poems of William Cowper*, i. *1748–1782* (Oxford, 1980), pp. xiv–xix, rehearse the view of Lady Hesketh that hymn composition was a burdensome task imposed on Cowper by Newton and ill-suited to his delicate sensibilities. Contrast J. R. Watson, 'Cowper's Olney Hymns', *Essays and Studies*, NS 38 (1985), 45–65, who argues that this is a false portrait and that hymn-writing was for Cowper 'anything but a bleak task: that it was rather a matter of joy'. On Cowper's contributions to the *Olney Hymns* see further, Madeleine Forell Marshall and Janet Todd, *English Congregational Hymns in the Eighteenth Century* (Lexington, Ken., 1982), 119–46; Davie, *Eighteenth-Century Hymn*, 137–53. On the textual history of Cowper's hymns, see Norma Russell, *A Bibliography of William Cowper to 1837* (Oxford, 1963), 15–20.

[13] Phrase from Newton's letter to Thornton, 3 Aug. 1775. The best historical reconstruction of the writing of the Olney hymns is Leaver, 'Olney Hymns 1779: 1'; 'Olney Hymns 1779: 2. Hymns and their Use', *Churchman*, 94/1 (1980), 58–66; 'Olney Hymns: A Documentary Footnote', *Churchman*, 97/3 (1983), 244–5. See also Demaray, *Innovation of John Newton*, 226–59.

[14] Diary (1773–1805), 20 Feb. 1774.

local and the first audience his own parishioners, he certainly wrote with an awareness of a much wider audience from the beginning. Just as Newton's letters were often written both for the recipient and, so to speak, over the recipient's head for the press, so his hymns were written with an eye to eventual publication. Newton and Cowper had publication in mind from as early as 1771; both writers published hymns themselves in the *Gospel Magazine* that same year; and throughout the following years dozens of hymns were 'published' in the sense that they were disseminated through letters and personal exchanges within the informal network of ministers and prominent laymen in which Newton played so key a role. John Thornton was particularly interested in Newton's hymns, and Newton regularly sent him hymns as a part of his 'epistolary chaplaincy'.[15] In consequence of such exchanges several hymns were picked up and published, sometimes anonymously or altered or wrongly attributed, in various sources such as the *Gospel Magazine* or later editions of Conyers' *Collection*. All of this was well before the formal publication of the *Olney Hymns* in 1779. As discussed below, this ability to write at the same time for the particular and the general situation was characteristic of Newton, and it was grounded in principles both doctrinal and cultural.

EVANGELICAL HYMNODY IN THE 1760S AND 1770S

The English congregational hymn, as distinct from the devotional lyric, metrical psalm, and office hymn, was barely sixty years old when Newton began writing hymns himself. Although there were earlier hymnbooks, it was really with Isaac Watts's *Hymns and Spiritual Songs* (1707) that the English hymn came of age. Watts aimed to liberate Christian worship from the hegemony of metrical psalmody, and as a result he

---

[15] See e.g. Newton to Thornton, 25 Jan. 1775, ALS, CUL. In Thornton to Newton, 16 July 1774, ALS, CUL, Thornton suggests an emendation to the last verse of 'The Barren Fig Tree' (*OH* 1. 103), and though Newton did not finally print the version as Thornton suggested, he did change the lines from the original version. Newton submitted his work ('I have called it mine, but I consider it as yours') to Thornton's judgement as his patron, and he privately dedicated the volume to him (Newton to Thornton, 13 Feb. 1779, ALS, CUL).

grounded his hymnody at every stage in self-conscious theory. He retained the metres and tunes of the old psalmody but he shifted the hermeneutical horizon. Instead of worshippers accommodating themselves to the horizon of Davidic Judaism, Watts would have the psalms and other scriptural texts and Christian doctrines accommodated to the contemporary horizon of the assembled worshippers. Famously, he said he wished to see 'David converted into a Christian'.[16] The battle of hymn-singing versus psalm-singing raged throughout the eighteenth century and was by no means dead by the time Newton was writing, but hymnbooks proliferated in the decades between Watts and Newton.[17] As William Romaine put it in 1775, there was 'a vast variety, collection upon collection, and in use too, new hymns starting up daily—appendix added to appendix—sung in many congregations, yea admired by very high professors'.[18] Hymns won their way first among Dissenters (though not among all) before becoming one of the distinctive marks of Methodism, borrowing much along the way from immigrant Moravians. Associated thus with irregularity (Dissent), enthusiasm (Methodism), and non-Englishness (Moravians), hymns were tolerated only slowly within the Established Church and not given official recognition until a consistory court at York settled a controversy over the use of hymns which arose in a Sheffield church early in the nineteenth century.[19]

The most conservative contemporary of Newton with respect to hymnody was Romaine, whose *Essay on Psalmody* appeared in 1775 along with his own liturgical psalter. Romaine wished to see psalmody done well, rather than to see it supplanted by human compositions. In a concession to contemporary aesthetics, he defended the psalms, saying, 'the

[16] Watts, *Hymns and Spiritual Songs*, 17th edn. (1751), p. x.

[17] Before Newton's time, Olney itself had seen a bitter controversy over the singing of hymns among the Baptists, and the minister William Walker left the congregation in 1752 in part because of the resistance of many to singing in church. Naylor, *Picking up a Pin*, 56 (quoting a MS at the Olney Baptist Church); cf. Haykin, *One Heart and One Soul*, 105.

[18] William Romaine, *An Essay on Psalmody* (1775), 104–5.

[19] This history is reviewed, together with specimen hymns, in Richard Arnold (ed), *English Hymns of the Eighteenth Century: An Anthology* (New York, 1991).

sentiments are sublime'.[20] More particularly, he saw Watts's enterprise as a failure of biblical theology attendant upon the more secular culture introduced since the Restoration. Human compositions crept in because the general Christological meaning of the psalms had been lost 'when vital religion began to decay among us, more than a century ago'.[21] Romaine referred to 'Dr. Watts' flights of fancy', and quarried terms of derision from past debates when he wrote of 'Watts' jingle', and 'Watts' whyms' instead of Watts's hymns. His central argument for psalm-singing he stated thus: 'And this should silence every objection—*It is the word of God.*'[22]

Newton did not feel he needed to enter the psalms-versus-hymns debate when he penned the preface to the *Olney Hymns*, but he confided to John Thornton what he thought of Romaine's *Essay*:

I have received (I suppose from the Author) a book Mr. Romaine has lately published on the subject of Psalmody. I wish he had treated it in a different manner . . . I am afraid it will hurt some weak well meaning people . . . to be told, that whatever comfort they may think they have received from singing hymns in public worship was only imaginary. . . . He seems to ascribe all the deadness that is complained of in many places when the gospel is preached (I suppose He chiefly means the London Dissenters) to their not singing Sternhold & Hopkins. Strange that a Wise Man can advance such Paradoxes. This judgment involves not only the Dissenters, & the Lock, but the Tabernacle, Tottenham Court, Everton, Helmsley, & many other places where I should think He must allow the Lord has attended his blessing. The Curate of Olney & his poor people may be content to be ranked amongst so much good company. . . . Some of us here, know that the Lord has comforted us by Hymns, which express Scriptural truths, tho not confined to the words of David's Psalms. And we know by the effects we are not mistaken. I believe Dr. Watts' Hymns have been a singular blessing to the Churches, notwithstanding Mr. Romaine does not like them.[23]

Newton's argument is here an argument from success, rather than a theological argument, but it is significant that he links

---

[20] Romaine, *Essay*, 10.   [21] Ibid. 104.   [22] Ibid. 136.
[23] Newton to Thornton, 3 Aug. 1775.

revival with hymnody, and that he aligns himself with the hymnody of Martin Madan and Thomas Haweis at the Lock Chapel, the followers of Whitefield at the Tabernacle and Tottenham Court, John Berridge at Everton, and Richard Conyers at Helmsley. This was the *Gospel Magazine* circle once again. (It may be significant that Newton did *not* include the Foundery or Fetter Lane among the centres of hymnody with which he identified.)

By the 1760s and 1770s, Newton had inherited a tradition of hymnody which had expanded well beyond Watts's programme. Methodism in particular made Watts's revolution look tame, introducing a new freedom and variety in metre, setting hymns to popular Handelic tunes, and expressing a new energy of piety in naturalistically broken speech, including sighs, groans, interjections, and exclamations.[24] By the time Newton was writing there was clearly a restrained tradition of hymnody represented by Watts and followers such as Philip Doddridge, and a more rhapsodic tradition represented by Charles Wesley and contemporary Methodists and Moravians such as John Cennick. Robin Leaver, in a bicentenary article on the Olney Hymns in which he speculates about what tunes might have been used in Olney, suggests that Newton and Cowper may best be positioned between these two poles, at least with regard to music. Leaver states first, 'Most [Anglican] evangelicals were more than willing to use hymns and sing them to tunes which were warmer than the traditional psalm tune but not as extravagant as those used by the Methodists and the Madan circle, while at the same time being careful not to overstate the importance of the music.'[25] Then, based upon Cowper's criticism of Martin Madan's 'sabbatical concerts' and the known antipathy of both Cowper and Newton to sacred oratorios, such as the Messiah, performed in churches, Leaver continues:

[24] On Charles Wesley, see Marshall and Todd, *English Congregational Hymns*, 60–88. Frank Baker, in his introduction to *Representative Verse of Charles Wesley* (1962), emphasizes more the classicism of Wesley in his careful diction and skilled use of rhetorical devices, as does Donald Davie, 'The Classicism of Charles Wesley', in *Purity of Diction in English Verse* (1952), 70–81. See also Bernard L. Manning, *The Hymns of Wesley and Watts: Five Informal Papers* (1942), and Henry Bett, *The Hymns of Methodism*, 3rd edn. (1945). [25] Leaver, 'Olney Hymns 1779: 2', 61.

If Newton applied the same criteria to the melodies for the *Olney Hymns* [as he did to the poetry] then they would have been of a type mid-way between the traditional psalm tune (which, no doubt, also continued to be sung in Olney) and those of the Madan circle: that is, simple, direct, with moderate use of repetitions and avoidance of dance forms and over-decorated melodic lines. This was certainly the type of tune used by Newton's friends.[26]

For these friends, Leaver cites the examples of William Cadogan of Reading and Charles Simeon of Cambridge. The few examples we have of tunes probably used at Olney, while not sufficient to make any final judgement, help to support Leaver's reconstruction, and point to the moderate tone of the *Olney Hymns* within the contemporary context of hymnody.[27]

CRITICAL PRINCIPLES OF NEWTON'S HYMNODY

The origins of the congregational hymn in the early eighteenth century suggest several continuities with contemporary literary ideals. Clarity, simplicity, and didacticism were as much valued in satire, serious drama, the novel, and the essay as they were fundamental to the hymn. Moreover, the hymn reflected the general conviction that literature could and ought to appeal to common, public sentiment, and that the duty to instruct and to delight were not antithetical.[28] Beyond this, most of the attempts of modern critics to define the hymn

[26] Leaver, 'Olney Hymns 1779: 2', 62.

[27] In addition to the example cited by Leaver, see 'O for a Closer Walk—a Note on its Original Tune', *Hymn Society of Great Britain and Ireland: Bulletin*, 8/5 (Winter, 1974), 87, and, from a later period, the tune Ebenezer, by Thomas Bowman of Martham, Norfolk, interleaved in the pamphlet of Newton's anniversary poems following the death of his wife in 1790, CNM. Despite Cowper's suspicion of Madan's excessive fascination with music, he did sing hymns from Madan's tunebook with the Unwin family (*Letters of Cowper*, i. 153). This would have been Madan's *Collection of Psalm and Hymn Tunes Never Published before* (1769). Note also below the discussion about music held by the Eclectic Society in London in 1787.

[28] Cf. Marshall and Todd, *English Congregational Hymns*, 149: 'The congregational hymn, in all its manifestations, incorporates the common poetic values of its day, most particularly the sought-after balance between specific expression and general experience and the careful alliance of poetic delight and instruction. . . . The positive accomplishments of congregational hymns as poetry may in fact be seen as the result of the interplay between just such a traditional understanding of poetic purpose, of general truth and the instructive duty of literature, and the evangelical challenge to make religion matter.'

as a genre reduce to the same principle: the hymn must be written for the gathered, worshipping congregation, contributing to its purposes and respecting its limitations. Its sentiments cannot therefore be private or idiosyncratic, and its language must be lucid so that meaning will be conveyed instantly.[29]

It was Watts, again, who first gave classical definition to the critical principles of hymnody. In the preface to his *Hymns and Spiritual Songs* he explained that he would restrict his choice of metre to allow the hymns to be sung to common tunes, and he would refrain from enjambment and mid-line caesuras to allow the hymns to be lined out. Then, famously, Watts continued, 'The Metaphors are generally sunk to the Level of vulgar Capacities, I have aim'd at Ease of Numbers and Smoothness of Sound, and endeavoured to make the Sense plain and obvious.'[30] It was this that Pope ridiculed as 'the art of sinking'. Nevertheless, if it was to be congregational hymnody, then the desire to edify the whole people required something like Watts's stated aim 'to promote the pious Entertainment of Souls truly serious, even of the meanest Capacity' without, as he hoped, at the same time disgusting persons of richer sense and education.[31]

Newton openly acknowledged his indebtedness to Watts and his use of Watts's hymns as a pattern. Of his own principles Newton wrote,

There is a stile and manner suited to the composition of hymns, which may be more successfully, or at least more easily attained by a versifier, than by a poet. They should be *Hymns*, not *Odes*, if designed for public worship, and for the use of plain people. Perspicuity, simplicity and ease, should be chiefly attended to; and the imagery and coloring of poetry, if admitted at all, should be indulged very sparingly and with great judgment.   (iii. 302)

This is little more than a restatement of Watts and a shrewd summary of the restrictions of the genre: public not private,

---

[29] On definitions of the hymn genre, see e.g. M. Pauline Parker, 'The Hymn as a Literary Form', *Eighteenth-Century Studies*, 8 (1975), 392–419; Marshall and Todd, *English Congregational Hymns*, 1–3, 147–65; Erik Routley, *Christian Hymns Observed* (Princeton, 1982), 1–5.   [30] Watts, *Hymns and Spiritual Songs*, p. viii.
[31] Ibid. ix.

lucid language, and restrained metaphor. Further light is shed on these principles in a letter to John Ryland, Jun., examined earlier for its bearing on high Calvinism. Newton chided his young friend for being too self-aggrandizing in the preface of his volume of poems, *Serious Essays on the Truths of the Glorious Gospel* (1771), and too careless in the poems themselves. Newton was bothered by Ryland's vanity in disclaiming any assistance and wished Ryland had spent more time in careful revisions with a 'severer Eye of Criticism'. He thought Ryland would not easily qualify for Waller's commendation, 'Poets lose half the praise they should have got | Could it be known what they discreetly blot.' Following up some of Ryland's printed comments, Newton argued that he need not write disagreeable verse like that of Ralph Erskine's *Gospel-Sonnets* in order to be understood by plain and pious people:

Watts's Hymns are as intelligible as Erskine's Sonnets. If you will you can make your lines smooth and your rhymes true, and avoid improper expressions which you have sometimes used, merely for the number or the sound of the Syllables . . . I observed several expressions that were false English . . . I was sorry to see them as coming from a house where literature was professedly study'd.[32]

Here then are the technical elements of good taste in the traditions of Watts. The rhythm must be smooth and the rhymes true; the diction must be proper and the syntax correct.

In the preface to his hymns Newton noted that Watts might have had the right to say it was hard work condescending to the capacities of common readers—'But it would not become me to make such a declaration. It behooved me to do my best' (iii. 302). Newton saw himself as a journeyman in the trade, not a master; a skilled versifier, not a sophisticated poet. Watts had written with a clear distinction between élite and popular in mind, and was manifestly a member of the former class, seeking to condescend to plain persons of mean capacities without offending his peers. Newton, on the other hand, places himself squarely *between* élite and popular readers. He wrote,

[32] Newton to John Ryland, Jun., 17 Oct. 1771.

But though I would not offend readers of taste by a wilful coarseness, and negligence, I do not write professedly for them. If the Lord whom I serve, has been pleased to favor me with that mediocrity of talent, which may qualify me for usefulness to the weak and poor of his flock, without quite disgusting persons of superior discernment, I have reason to be satisfied. (iii. 302).

His 'mediocrity of talent' would both permit him to be useful to the simple parishioners beneath his status and education and, he hoped, keep him from appearing repugnant to those above.

Newton's middling cultural status is recognized by Lionel Adey in his recent study, *Class and Idol in the English Hymn* (1988), in which he traces the two traditions of Learned (university) and Popular (back-street chapel) hymnody through the modern period. He further refines the latter category, distinguishing between hymns which were 'popular by origin', such as Negro Spirituals, and those which were 'popular by destination', such as the hymns of the Wesleys. When Adey comes to Newton, however, his categories are defeated:

The Wesleyan and Olney hymns were 'popular by destination,' yet in their richness of scriptural and poetic allusion the former and those of Cowper also belong to the Learned tradition. In regard to those of the half-educated Newton, the distinction breaks down, for in their unevenness and restriction to biblical sources his hymns approach the category of 'popular by origin' although as an Anglican priest he belonged in principle to the Learned tradition.[33]

Newton himself pointed to his failure to measure up to the standards of the cultural élite when in playful mock-humility he acknowledged to Cowper in 1780, 'how destitute I am of taste or vertù' (vi. 162).

Beyond the issues of status and the techniques of 'sunk poetry', however, the single most important critical principle for Newton was a religious one. As he outlined in his letters on growth in grace, so in his preface again he stated his belief in the fundamental solidarity of Christian experience: 'As the workings of the heart of man, and of the Spirit of God, are in

[33] Lionel Adey, *Class and Idol in the English Hymn* (Vancouver, 1988), 33.

general the same, in all who are the subjects of grace, I hope most of these hymns, being the fruit and expression of my own experience, will coincide with the views of real christians of all denominations' (iii. 302–3). Here then was the doctrinal basis for Newton's 'transparency' and for his capacity to write as the representative or universal 'I' in his hymns. Here too is that characteristically eighteenth-century concern with the specific expression of general and universally applicable truths.

DISTINCTIVENESS OF NEWTON AS A HYMN-WRITER

The arrangement of a hymnbook gives some clue to the distinctiveness of its themes and of its conception of hymnody. Watts divided his into three books, in large part in response to the polemical context in which he was writing. The first book presented hymns closely tied to scriptural texts and in canonical order, since this would suit the Scripture-only faction. The second book presented hymns of 'human composure' on devotional themes, and the third offered a number of sacramental hymns. This arrangement underlay several subsequently produced hymnbooks, but none more so than the *Olney Hymns*, which was also in three books, the first of which was canonically arranged, and the second of which was on 'occasional subjects'. The third book, however, was a departure from Watts in treating 'the Rise, Progress, Changes, and Comforts of the Spiritual Life'. This was a new development. Most evangelical hymnbooks after Watts, such as Martin Madan's popular *Collection of Psalms and Hymns* (1760), had no apparent arrangement, except that hymns with similar themes or metres were sometimes clustered together. Joseph Hart's popular *Hymns, &c., Composed on Various Subjects* (1759) anticipated the Olney arrangement in part, since Hart's hymns were set out to follow the chronological pattern of the author's own spiritual autobiography through all its ups and downs, but even here this is not rationalized into generally applicable headings and subheadings. The *Olney Hymns* appears to have been the first to be patterned, at least in book 3, on an evangelical conception of normative spiritual formation. The more famous volume of hymns to do so was published a year later by Wesley as *A Collection of Hymns, for the Use of the People Called Methodists* (1780) and quickly became the Methodist standard.[34] The two tables of contents reveal something of the differences between the Wesleys' and Newton's concept of the spiritual life. The Wesleys' hymnbook is divided into 5 parts and 24 subheadings and includes 49 hymns on 'Groaning for Full Redemption', which expressed the perfectionism which had become a sore point between Wesley and Calvinists like Newton.[35] Newton's arrangement is less elaborate and follows the basic pattern of his letters on growth in grace: the sinner is first awakened to contrition and spiritual desire (1. Solemn Addresses to Sinners; 2. Seeking, Pleading, Hoping) before experiencing testing (3. Conflict) which, intermingled with divine assistance (4. Comfort), leads to a more perfect obedience and resignation to God (5. Dedication and Surrender; 6. Cautions), leading in time to a more contemplative frame of mind, focused upon Christ (7. Praise).[36] In its arrangement, the correlation of the Olney hymnbook to Watts on the one hand, and Wesley on the other, is another indication that it was itself between the hymn traditions of Dissent and Methodism.[37]

In the last chapter, it was observed that Newton's private devotional exercises aimed to recreate the emotional landscape of conversion as way of keeping gratitude to God at a high pitch, since gratitude was, from the human point of view, the inward motor of growth in Christian virtue. Many of Newton's hymns function in much the same way. 'The rebel's

---

[34] See further, the editors' introduction to John Wesley (ed.), *A Collection of Hymns for the use of the People called Methodists*, ed. F. Hildebrandt and O. A. Beckerlegge, with J. Dale, vol. vii of The Oxford Edition of the Works of John Wesley (Oxford, 1983), 1–69.   [35] Cf. Manning, *Hymns of Wesley and Watts*, 11.

[36] A few short hymns follow under heading 8; these are for before and after the sermon, and the Gloria Patri. They were added during the final compilation of the hymnbook, to make it more serviceable to those who would use such short hymns in public worship. See Diary (1773–1805), 28 Jan. 1779.

[37] Several later Dissenters' hymnbooks were arranged topically in traditional theological categories. See e.g. Benjamin Beddome, *Hymns Adapted to Public Worship, or, Family Devotion* (1818), and John Rippon, *A Selection of Hymns From the Best Authors* (1827).

surrender to grace', for example, redraws the crisis of conversion in a hymn based on St Paul's experience on the Damascus road. Although Acts 9: 6 is in the subtitle of the hymn, Paul is nowhere mentioned in the hymn text, so that the 'I' who speaks quickly becomes the voice not just of Paul, but of Newton and of each of the singers. In the biblical passage Paul responds to the voice from heaven after the bright light, saying, 'Lord, what wilt thou have me to do?' This becomes the kind of response Newton puts into his own and his singers' mouths:

> . . .
> But mercy has my heart subdu'd,
> A bleeding Saviour I have view'd,
>   And now, I hate my sin.
> 5. Now, LORD, I would be thine alone,
> Come take possession of thine own,
>   For thou hast set me free;
> Released from Satan's hard command,
> See all my powers waiting stand,
>   To be employ'd by thee.
>
>   (*OH* 1. 121, st. 4–5)

Newton's choice of metre works with his theme of rebellion and surrender, for the movement from a couplet of eight syllables to a shorter line of six syllables has a restraining, yielding effect throughout the hymn which parallels the theme. The metre is not typical of Newton, but this affective response of self-surrender to the atonement, fortifying the will for present obedience, recurs often. Newton's image of a 'bleeding Saviour' is also handled in a characteristic way. It is a common enough representation for Newton, but, as here, he does not often dwell especially long on the physical suffering of Christ in the kind of graphic blood-and-wounds imagery— what Marshall and Todd call the 'pietist baroque'—of the Moravians, which became a particular fascination during their 'sifting time' in the 1740s.[38] Again, the metaphor of

---

[38] The word 'blood' occurs about sixty times in the *Olney Hymns*, and Cowper's use of the word is generally more graphic than Newton's. For Newton 'blood' is used most often as synecdochal shorthand for the substitutionary atonement ('without shedding of blood is no remission', Hebrews 9: 22); the focus is more often upon this signification than upon a particularly gory tableau. The contrast in this respect is

surrender in battle is understated, present only in 'subdu'd', 'take possession', 'Satan's hard command', and 'my powers waiting stand'—common, prosaic words when taken individually. It is a chaste and restrained metaphor when compared with Donne's 'Batter my heart, three-person'd God', or Herbert's two-layered plea, 'Captivate strong holds to thee'.[39] While Newton's hymn may not have the passion of these Caroline lyrics, its very modesty helps to communicate something of the chastened, quiet submission which follows the conquest achieved by divine love, rather than by power.[40]

Another hymn which illustrates Newton's ability to match metre to theme treats a 'Sinners in the hands of an angry God' theme which runs counter to most modern sensibilities. 'Expostulation' is the first hymn of book 3:

> No words can declare,
> No fancy can paint,
> What rage and despair,
> What hopeless complaint,
> Fill Satan's dark dwelling,
> That prison beneath;
> What weeping and yelling,
> And gnashing of teeth!

The recurrent pounding of the two-stress lines hauntingly reinforces the theme of impending damnation, just as the starkness of the negated 'words . . . declare' and 'fancy . . . paint' is as literal and either/or as the prospect Newton is announcing. As one of the four traditional last things of Christian theology, hell was not an untypical theme of eighteenth-century hymnody. It must perhaps be added, however, that Newton took no delight in tormenting his

striking between Newton's contributions to the *Olney Hymns* and the Moravian collection edited by John Gambold, *A Collection of Hymns of the Children of God in all Ages* (1754).

[39] John Donne, 'Holy Sonnets, XIV' (1633); George Herbert, 'Nature', *The Temple* (1633).

[40] Cf. Donald Davie's description of modest poetic diction as having the effect of 'a taunting gravity and sobriety which chastens the reader as it pleases him'. *Purity of Diction*, 35.

singers and that his vivid conception of such eternal verities was part of what informed his evangelical earnestness. He could only close such a theme with, 'It is not too late | To Jesus to flee,' and a bold invitation to sinners to accept the free offer of the gospel.

More usually Newton worked in the neutral metres of hymnody of four-stress lines, in the typically rising rhythms of iambic common and long metre or the stronger trochaic rhythms of various combinations of 'sevens'. Often Newton expounded his scriptural passage or theme with unadorned didacticism. In 'Jacob's ladder' Newton simply talks to his readers and explains the relevance of Genesis 28: 12 for the Christian now:

> Well does Jacob's ladder suit
> To the gospel throne of grace;
> We are at the ladder's foot,
> Ev'ry hour, in ev'ry place:
> By assuming flesh and blood,
> Jesus heav'n and earth unites;
> We by faith ascend to God,
> God to dwell with us delights.
>
> (*OH* 1. 9, st. 4)

The ladder was a symbol which much exercised the thought of Christian devotional writers from John Climacus in the seventh century to the late medieval mystics. But Newton accommodates the story of Jacob and the symbolism of the ladder to a more typically Protestant biblical theology, matching the literal ladder to the spiritual throne in Hebrews 4: 16 and developing the mediatorial role of Christ which is unbounded by time and space. Faith, rather than mystic love or contemplation, raises the believer to God, and corresponds to the divine initiative in creating fellowship between God and man. It is a typological habit of mind which was always uniting the Old Testament to the New in terms of promise and fulfilment, and, in the process, reiterating and sometimes invigorating the biblical symbols (ladder, throne) which were the Christian inheritance. But in this hymn the figuration is less enjoyed than it is simply expounded.

One further characteristic of Newton's hymnody (and of

Cowper's) helps to distinguish it from that of the Wesleys. The Calvinism of Newton and Cowper, perhaps even their temperaments, lent to their verse a plaintive or resigned tone much more often than for the Wesleys. This is particularly the case when the hymns for believers in Wesley's *Collection* are compared with the hymns in the middle section of book 3 of the Olney hymns. Against Wesley's 'Finish then thy new creation, | Pure and spotless let us be,' must be set Newton's 'My best is stain'd and dy'd with sin, | My all is nothing worth.' It is of course possible to find contrary strains in both hymn-writers, but on the whole the *Olney Hymns* assume a more reticent spiritual posture and have less immediate expectations that sin will be purged by divine grace in the life of the believer. The emotional tone of the poetry is correspondingly more moderate.

Personal Directness and Salvific Vision

In their study of eighteenth-century hymnody, Marshall and Todd helpfully compare and contrast Newton's hymnody with that of his predecessors. They see Watts's hymns, such as 'When I survey the wondrous cross' as consisting typically of 'fine tableaux', painting scenes to which his congregation of London burghers could be trusted to respond with appropriate emotions, cultivating a refined interiority and abstraction from the world. Charles Wesley's hymns, such as 'O for a thousand tongues to sing', on the other hand, they distinguish as ecstatic, charismatic verse, designed to inculcate exemplary sensibility in the context of the dramatic flurry of the revival. Newton's distinctiveness lay, for Marshall and Todd, in his entire sense of identity with one particular congregation and his comprehensive, transhistorical vision, which led him to write in transparently simple language as the representative 'I'. He was therefore able to express paradigmatic sentiments of and for his people, and to set their lives on a large eschatological canvass. Thus, conclude Marshall and Todd, 'Newton's most remarkable hymns are fired by a vision of Christian experience that begins with Newton's conviction of God's providential intervention in his own life and proceeds to sweep across history.' Or again, 'Newton's best hymns proceed from his total identification of himself with his people, for whom he then stands and whom he can then instruct in the basics of the faith, placing them in a world full of providential signs.'[41]

This analysis reflects the stated conviction of Newton of the fundamental solidarity of all truly evangelical experience. A hymn that well illustrates Newton's use of simple first-person language to represent experience shared by poet and singers alike, interpreting this experience in a large salvific frame, is 'Faith's review and expectation', or, as it is better known, 'Amazing Grace'. The first three stanzas reflect on a climactic evangelical conversion in the past:

1. Amazing grace! (how sweet the sound)
    That sav'd a wretch like me!
    I once was lost, but now am found,
    Was blind, but now I see.

2. 'Twas grace that taught my heart to fear,
    And grace my fears reliev'd;
    How precious did that grace appear,
    The hour I first believ'd!

3. Thro' many dangers, toils and snares,
    I have already come;
    'Tis grace has brought me safe thus far,
    And grace will lead me home.

The initial exclamation of 'Amazing grace!' accomplishes what Pauline Parker claims a good hymn must; that is, it invites immediate congregational consent and release of emotional energy.[42] The following parenthetical response ('how sweet the sound') simply enacts the amazement just proclaimed, and focuses the whole line back upon the word 'grace'. Then the balance of the stanza lays out the stark contrasts that evoked the initial cry of wonder. The last two lines perfectly match cadences with the contrasting images, and the simple antitheses (lost/found, blind/see) are expressed in equally simple monosyllables. The second stanza, ringing changes on the thrice repeated 'grace', harks

---

[41] Marshall and Todd, *English Congregational Hymns*, 88–9, 92, 102, 148. Note also, in this context, Newton's use of 'for me my friends and you' in *OH* 1. 19 and 109. Cf. on Christopher Smart, Guest, *Form of Sound Words*, 247–53.

[42] Parker, 'Hymn as Literary Form', 401–2.

back to the first exclamation while developing the paradox in evangelical theology that the preaching of the law, and the remorse which it provokes, is itself a part of the very grace which brings powerful psychological release from the guilt of sin and the fear of damnation. The precision of 'the hour I first believed' pinpoints the experience of grace as climactic in the same way the earlier dialectical images did. And by the end of the second stanza the singers have been led to express the exemplary sentiments of the amazement, sweetness, and preciousness of divine grace. Of the danger and toil of stanza 3, both Newton and his poor parishioners had had much, but the last half of the stanza becomes a pivot upon which the whole hymn turns, gathering the past up once more into the word 'grace' and then turning with faith to face the future.

The last three stanzas trace the path of the believer through, respectively, the balance of this life, death, and the final dissolution of the elements of this world.

> 4. The Lord has promis'd good to me,
>   His word my hope secures;
>   He will my shield and portion be,
>   As long as life endures.
>
> 5. Yes, when this flesh and heart shall fail,
>   And mortal life shall cease;
>   I shall possess, within the vail,
>   A life of joy and peace.
>
> 6. The earth shall soon dissolve like snow,
>   The sun forbear to shine;
>   But God, who call'd me here below,
>   Will be for ever mine.

> (*OH* 1. 41)

It is a strong final quatrain which can draw the circle from 'the earth' in its final eschatological consumption, to the simple reassurance of the final small word 'mine'.

Critics and compilers of anecdotes for hymn handbooks have been quick to point out the autobiographical significance of this hymn as a metaphorical description of Newton's sensational conversion. But it is important to note that the hymn was based on the scriptural passage 1 Chronicles 17: 16, 17, in which David responds in amazement to the prophet

Nathan's announcement of the Davidic covenant: God's promise to maintain David's line and his kingdom forever. David went before God and said, 'Who am I, O LORD God, and what is mine house, that thou hast brought me hitherto?' The passage is one of the high points in biblical theology and the weight of accumulated Christian covenantal and typo-logical interpretation meant that Newton would certainly have seen in this text the anticipation of Christ as that greater son of David; the one presented as the fulfilment of the divine promise to David in the genealogies of the Gospels. The typology had only to be extended to see in God's grace to David an anticipation of God's grace to Newton in his experience, as much as to the poor of Olney in theirs. The title of the hymn and the turning from past to future in stanza 3, suggest the kind of amazed backwards and forwards looking, along the line of salvation-history, which David was doing in 1 Chronicles, which Newton did persistently in his own devotional life, and which Newton presented for his people as an exemplary pattern for their own piety. The force of this is even greater when it is remembered that Newton probably expounded this hymn as a part of his regular hymn discourses on Sunday evenings, making all these implicit typological connections explicit for his people. 'Amazing Grace' was thus grounded not only in Newton's spiritual autobiography and his devotional discipline, but also in his biblical theology.

That this hymn has become so nearly a folksong in many countries, suggests that Newton's capacity to universalize his own experience was indeed one of his distinctive traits as a hymn-writer. In Newton one can also observe how the hymn genre, with its requirements of simplicity and commonality, creates a situation in which the line between archetype and cliché was very fine. To write in simple words which retain an 'extra poetic dimension'[43] because of scriptural resonances and the evocation of the common human condition, without simply falling into stock epithets and dead metaphors, defines a particularly demanding poetic task. Certainly, only a few of Newton's 281 hymns achieve this 'high simplicity' un-ambiguously.

---

[43] Davie's phrase, *Purity of Diction*, 73.

Naïve Expression or Self-Conscious Artistry

One of the most interesting questions about Newton's hymnody stems from this very simplicity and seemingly transparent language: Was Newton's plain style the product of unaffected *naïveté*, or was it the result of self-conscious artistry? Between 1977 and 1993 Donald Davie's judgement about Newton shifted with respect to this question. In 1974 and 1977 he identified Newton as the one outstanding hymn-writer of the eighteenth century who presented 'a different language from the purged but still educated and elegant English of the eighteenth-century gentleman'. Newton was 'a remarkably simple, even obtuse man' and represented a much less sophisticated level of society than such contemporaries as his friend Cowper. Davie argued that whereas the simplicity of Watts was the result of studied artistic discipline, the simplicity of Newton was a natural habit of mind, grounded in his natural *naïveté* and the literalness of the language of common people. The result was an 'absence of conscious intention and strategy' in Newton's hymns, which, as poems, did not rise to the level of Herbert, Watts, and Cowper, but had real, if minimal, poetic virtues just the same.[44]

By 1993 Davie changed his mind. He had earlier spoken of Newton's 'wide-eyed concern to get the point home': 'Now, after fifteen years, the word I'm not sure about is "wide-eyed"; for I've come to suspect that Newton is a more artful writer than I had supposed, and never more so than when he seems most artless.'[45] Davie goes on to retract his earlier evaluation of the minimal poetic virtues of Newton's hymns. In the same essay, he marks the phrase from Newton,

> But, when I see Thee as Thou art,
> I'll praise Thee as I ought,

as anything but quaint. 'The tautness of such an expression', confesses Davie, 'does not come by inspired accident to a man

---

[44] Donald Davie, 'The Language of the Eighteenth-Century Hymn', address delivered at the William Andrews Clark Memorial Library, Los Angeles, 1977, repr. in *Dissentient Voice* (Notre Dame, Ind., 1982), 77–80.

[45] Davie, *Eighteenth-Century Hymn*, 135.

too naïve to ask himself if he is sincere.' The self-portrait of Newton as a 'bluff and forthright sailorman' Davie now takes as at least partly a persona. Still, however, Davie, like Lionel Adey, is not quite sure what to make of Newton: 'Newton's simplicity and artlessness are partly authentic, partly assumed; and only sometimes can we afford to take them at face value.'[46]

There is good evidence, however, that Newton laboured over his hymns and sought to achieve the very best craftsmanship he could according to his principles, which his letter to John Ryland indicated were simple but strict. It was not the case that any doggerel would do. Indeed, his diary confirms that he did not simply dash off verse on the run. In December 1773 he remarked, 'Making hymns now & then, which is with me generally a work of time', and again in July 1774, 'I usually make a hymn weekly & sometimes it cost[s] me so much thought & study that I hardly do anything else.'[47] Time, thought, and study do not equate with sophistication or ingenuity, but Newton's investment in the task of hymn-writing should at least argue that the simplicity of his verse was not the result of inattention or carelessness.

NEWTON AND EVANGELICAL AESTHETICS

Suspicion of Polite Culture

The source of Davie's critical uncertainty may be traced in part to Newton's middling rank between the learned and the uneducated, but also it can be traced to Newton's own ambiguous attitude towards polite culture. Newton *himself* was not sure how far he could indulge in artistic creation before he would be guilty of distracting himself and his readers from the simplicity of the gospel. The desire to edify and the desire to please were often felt by Newton as a tension. For Watts, writing at the height of the Augustan period when didacticism and delight were most easily harmonized, this

---

[46] Davie, *Eighteenth-Century Hymn*, 125.
[47] Diary (1773–1805), 7 July 1774.

tension was felt almost wholly as a gap between élite and popular; that is, how might he edify plain people while still pleasing the polite. Watts recognized the problem and resolved it in his 'art of sinking'. In other hymn-writers the tension was less easy to resolve, as was sometimes implied by the special pleading of a final disclaimer, often in the form of a prayer-wish, stating that the writer was prepared to face the censure of the critics for the sake of advancing the cause of true devotion.[48] Only with John Wesley did this become an outright challenge to the critics to see whether his brother's hymns were not strong English, excellent verse, and even in some cases, true poetry, while yet being 'the handmaid of piety'.[49]

'Handmaid of piety' suggests that the relationship between religion and culture (edification and pleasure) was not always felt by evangelicals as a tension between the church and the world. Why, in fact, write verse, or sing, at all? Clearly there was enclosed within evangelicalism something which can only be called an aesthetic culture. There were 'solid joys and lasting treasures' which 'none but Zion's children know'. The central doctrine of the new birth, and the insistence that the experience of regeneration gave the believer a new 'taste' (the word itself is significant) for spiritual things, meant that this aesthetic was to some extent self-referential. You had to be one to know one. The analogy might be that one who has experienced romantic love has a different capacity to appreciate an Elizabethan love sonnet than one who has not. Regardless of what their critics might think, there were evangelicals who found the imagery of 'a fountain fill'd with blood | Drawn from Emmanuel's veins' not merely acceptable, but beautiful. And this corresponded to a spiritual experience of regeneration which they acknowledged one had to have, to understand.

Newton's attitude towards religion and culture may be further gauged from his notes of the discussions of the Eclectic

---

[48] See e.g. Benjamin Wallin, Preface to *Evangelical Hymns and Songs* (1750); and Thomas Haweis, Preface to *Carmina Christo; Hymns to the Saviour* (Bath, 1792).
[49] John Wesley, Preface to *A Collection of Hymns*, 74–5.

Society in London some nine years after the Olney hymnbook was published. On 9 June 1788 the society discussed, 'How far Music may be subservient to true devotion'. Newton's minutes record,

Scientific Music not subservient but hurtful, & therefore not expedient. It too much occupies the Mind in performance or in hearing. The effects Mechanical. Tends to give a Ceremonial, Judaizing Cast to worship, & to hurt the simplicity of the Gospel. It substitutes a dead Carcase for the Living power of religion.

In private, it is ensnaring without great Care, & may insensibly steal away the heart & consume much procrastination.[50]

The last sentence could have been applied as equally to literary art as to music. The *OED* gives, as one historical definition of 'scientific', an adjective which may be applied to an art, practice, or operation based upon or regulated by science, or, 'also, more loosely: systematic, methodical'.[51] Evidently, then, Newton and his fellow Eclectics were resolving upon an ideal of music which corresponded to the ideal of plain style in the language of hymns. Above all, one must not contemplate the music or the poetry for its own sake. Art is not to be a matter of contemplation and enjoyment, so much as it is to be simply an instrument of devotion. And it is a potentially dangerous ('ensnaring') instrument.[52] The ground has shifted subtly from Watts's linguistic concern to achieve intelligibility for the uneducated to a more religious concern to resist the seductive temptations of the world. What is the relationship, then, between religion and culture for

---

[50] Newton, 'Minutes of the Eclectic Society [1787–9]', MS notebook, FLP; cf. Newton's attitude toward the *Messiah* and the Handel commemoration at Westminster Abbey in 1784, *Works*, iv. 1–15. See further, Robert Manson Myers, 'Fifty Sermons on Handel's Messiah', *Harvard Theological Review*, 39/4 (Oct. 1946), 217–41.

[51] Note especially the historical example from Jane Austen, 1817, in the supplement, vol. iii, to the *OED*.

[52] Cf. Doreen Rosman, *Evangelicals and Culture* (1984), who argues that this was typical of evangelical attitudes around the turn of the 19th c., even if evangelicals did reflect contemporary taste more than is often recognized. Says Rosman, 'The concept of a God who delighted in creativity and beauty for their own sake was alien to evangelical thinking, and even to the most cultured and intellectual of evangelicals' (p. 47).

Newton? If the gospel is simple, so must be the music and the language of devotion.[53]

For Cowper the layman, literature became a vocation and he was able in poetry itself to protest against the artifice of cosmopolitan life and to extol the virtues of nature and the comforts of the domestic life as some of the greatest goods given to men and women in a postlapsarian world. For Newton the minister, evangelical earnestness would not permit anything more than a brief excursion into poetry, just as his sense of urgency had made it much easier for him to write letters than to labour over the production of lengthy treatises. There would be hymns perhaps, but whether he had the ability or no, there would be no epic poems. It was pastoral utility alone that justified even slight forays into literary art.

The tension between art as the servant of religion versus art as a distraction from religion helps to illuminate Newton's statement about hymns being better written, or at least more easily written, by a versifier than a poet. The implication was that it was more possible for the poet to fail in the religious aims of hymn-writing than the versifier, since the poet was the more likely to distract his readers with fancy. And indeed, it was fancy and imagination ('the imagery and coloring of poetry') which posed the greatest threat of distraction. This explains why Newton could still have a high view of the versifier's task. Smooth rhythm, true rhymes, strong sense, and taut syntactical construction were still to be worked at with discipline; it was flights of fancy that were to be eschewed.

Here, however, another cultural attitude intrudes which can best be labelled 'prudence'. The persistent awareness of 'superior taste' and the desire not to appear vulgar or offensive suggests that Newton felt it useful not only to have enough culture to do the work of the ministry (art as an instrument of devotion, edification, etc.), but also that it was prudent to

---

[53] Cf. Newton's 'Minutes of the Eclectic Society [1787–9]' for 1 Oct. 1787, when the society's discussion was of the question, 'What is the most useful style & manner of public and private address?' Again, the consensus was that style must be 'simple' and 'perspicuous'.

have enough culture to take into account prevailing standards of taste and, wherever possible, accommodate them (art as a measure of social standing).[54] Prudence is not perhaps a very heroic basis upon which to establish a religious aesthetic, and the result is correspondingly ambiguous. As Doreen Rosman has written of evangelicals and culture at the turn of the nineteenth century, 'evangelicals shared in the tastes and interests of the more cultured of their contemporaries to a far greater extent than is always recognized, but were unable to justify their enjoyment within the terms of their world-denying theology'.[55]

Shifts in Contemporary Taste

Despite his ambiguous attitude towards polite culture (suspicious but prudent), and despite the self-enclosed nature of the evangelical aesthetic represented by Newton, it may still be asked how his particular integration of religion and literature, in theory and in practice, relates to the shift in cultural taste from Augustan to Romantic ideals in mid- to late eighteenth-century England. The transitional period, during which Newton was active, is sometimes called Sentimental, or the 'Age of Sensibility'.[56]

Taking into view the fields of religion, philosophy, and literature, John Hoyles in his study, *The Waning of the Renaissance* (1971), has identified Isaac Watts as one of the best representatives of the Augustan or classical aesthetic, characteristic of contemporary taste during the early eighteenth century.[57] The Augustan ideal emerged as the English Enlightenment eroded Renaissance ideals and was comprised

---

[54] As late as 24 Feb. 1794, Newton recorded the Eclectic society's discussion of the question, 'What concession may Ministers make to the customs of Polite Life?' He noted the conclusion: 'No concessions to the Spirit of the World. But Civility and Respect to superior stations.' 'Minutes of the Eclectic Society [1789–95]', MS notebook, CNM.

[55] Rosman, *Evangelicals and Culture*, 43. On evangelicals' attitude of prudence toward the social order, see also Willmer, 'Evangelicalism, 1785–1835'.

[56] The phrase comes from Northrop Frye's seminal article, 'Towards Defining an Age of Sensibility', *Journal of English Literary History* (1956), 144–52.

[57] But note that Marshall and Todd dissent, arguing for the coexistence in Watts's writings of both Augustan ideals and the older tradition of metaphysical wit and pietist baroque imagery. *English Congregational Hymns*, 3.

above all in the word 'refinement', which meant 'rubbing off the rough edges left over from a gothic and scholastic past'.[58] In the field of thought, this meant that minute philosophy which relied on elaborate deductive arguments was eschewed, and the axiom was preferred over the syllogism.[59] As Bolingbroke wrote, 'The improvement of real knowledge must be made by contraction, and not by amplification.'[60] In literature, this meant something like Samuel Johnson's description of the English style in Addison: 'familiar but not coarse, elegant but not ostentatious'.[61] The insistence of the Royal Society at the turn of the century upon a clear and plain style of English compatible with scientific exposition and the call for clarity and distinctness in Cartesian ideology ran parallel with Watts's classicism, particularly the self-conscious theoretical confidence by which he defined the generic limits of the hymn as 'sunk poetry', and the careful attention which he paid to a literary ideal of restrained sensual pleasure. Donald Davie has noted how the Calvinistic values of simplicity, sobriety, and measure also helped to inform this ideal.[62]

Newton imbibed precisely these sorts of aesthetic ideals in his formative years. Raised in Old Dissent and learning the hymns of Watts from childhood, Newton's programme of reading as a young man also included authors such as Shaftesbury, and Addison and Steele. Seeking to write polite letters, striving after an epigrammatic wit, and most of all, embarking on a massive course of self-study in the classics— all of this pointed to Newton's desire to achieve an ideal of refinement. Particularly, he wished not to offend what he perceived as the superior elegance of Mary Catlett. While his evangelical conversion introduced a new influence which would in time significantly alter these values, Newton's call for 'perspicuity, simplicity and ease' in hymnody is one of many examples of the persistence of the Augustan aesthetics of Watts, just as William Cowper's negative evaluation of

[58] John Hoyles, *The Waning of the Renaissance, 1640–1740* (The Hague, 1971), 80.
[59] Ibid. 115. [60] Ibid. 156.
[61] Quoted in Parker, 'Hymn as Literary Form', 393.
[62] Donald Davie, *A Gathered Church* (1978), 24–8.

George Herbert's poems as 'gothic and uncouth', if admirably pious, is another.[63]

Despite this persistence of Augustan propriety, however, Newton's case illustrates how such ideals gradually waned as intellect and doctrine were increasingly, if never wholly, dissolved into feeling and piety. Married for seven years, associated with Methodism for three, Newton wrote a letter to his wife on her birthday in 1757, beginning with the disclaimer, 'You will not expect me to address you in the strain of modern politeness, but I am persuaded that you will favourably accept why I may write, because you approve of my motive and sincerity' (v. 515). Refinement was not now needed to woo his lover but was seen as an artifice which distracted from the spontaneous expression of what his heart felt (his 'motive and sincerity'). Sincerity now precluded premeditation or fastidiousness about diction. In the autumn of 1779, concluding a good-natured epistolary controversy with Dr Dixon at Oxford about William Law's mysticism, Newton wrote,

Methinks my late publication comes in good time to terminate our friendly debate. As you approve of the Hymns, which, taken altogether, contain a full declaration of my religious sentiments, it should seem we are nearly of a mind. If we agree in rhime, our apparent differences in prose must, I think, be merely verbal, and cannot be very important. (vi. 246)

The turning towards the heart in this case was emphatically a solvent of doctrine, and precision in religious language was valued not at all. It was seen in fact as a barrier to catholicism. The gap is wide between the phrase, 'merely verbal', and such characteristic terms of Augustan critical approbation as 'strength' or 'niceness' of expression.

What has been observed here with respect to Newton, Hoyles argues in a later study, *The Edges of Augustanism* (1972), was in fact a general phenomenon: 'By the 1740s, classicism

---

[63] William Cowper, from his conversion narrative, 'Adelphi', in *Letters of Cowper*, i. 9. Though Herbert was a favourite poet of Newton's (Cecil, *Newton*, 318), Newton shared Cowper's evaluation of the literary style of the 17th c. as 'uncouth and obsolete'.

and the Enlightenment were being seriously undermined by the forces of preromanticism and evangelicalism.'[64] Hoyles links the quietism of John Byrom and William Law—who 'elevated the thing over its name, moving the debate from external evidences to the inward religious consciousness'—to the evangelicalism of the Wesleys, but 'the Wesleys, unlike the Quietists, would not stay still'.[65] Not only would they not stay still, but they, like Newton, would never entirely reject the Augustan values of public truth, didacticism, and external evidences. Hoyles appropriately takes Law and Byrom, with their high conception of the imagination and its creative symbolic potential, as the anticipation of Romanticism rather than the early evangelicals, like Newton, who remained more truly between the times.

In the end, Newton's poetics represent a transitional phase in the integration of religion and culture, between Augustan and Romantic conceptions of beauty and taste. Thus, commenting on Newton's lines, 'With pleasing grief, and mournful joy, | My spirit now is filled' (*OH* 2. 57), Davie observes that the emotional state described appears 'enervated, even luxurious', and that it reveals the hymn to be very much of the Age of Sensibility, a period more usually associated with Henry Mackenzie's *Man of Feeling* (1771) than with evangelicalism. As Davie notes, however, in Newton the occasion of the oxymoronic state of sentiment, the crucifixion, is clear and momentous, so that one cannot quite say that the emotional compound is indulged in for its own sake. Still, Davie suspects that Newton was in step with secular literary taste and made prudent overtures towards Sentiment, just as Watts had earlier toward Augustanism.[66]

Several critics have probed the relationship between evangelicalism and the origins of Romanticism, and Newton himself has variously been seen as anticipating Blake's prophetic vision, or as a source for Coleridge's 'Ancient Mariner' or for episodes in Wordsworth's 'Prelude'. Others have seen the evangelical focus upon experience and the

---

[64] John Hoyles, *The Edges of Augustanism* (The Hague, 1972), 83.
[65] Ibid. 114.   [66] Davie, *Eighteenth-Century Hymn*, 126–8.

insistence on 'plain language for plain people' as an anticipation of the famous preface to Coleridge and Wordsworth's *Lyrical Ballads* (1798), with its rejection of poetic diction.[67] For all this, however, Newton remains chiefly a poet of religious sentiment. Newton's concept of the imagination remained restrained, and his habit of mind was one of signification rather than of symbol. It would be a very different generation that would return to a concept of the direct sensuous apprehension of the spiritual world, and affirm the spiritual significance of the least material phenomenon.[68] For Newton the material and the spiritual remained largely isomorphic categories, and the imagination was more often the source of distracting fancies than it was an organ of perception and creativity. The universal 'I' of his hymns remains chastened by exemplary pedagogical intention and the evangelical conviction that sin has tainted all. Newton's 'I' does not become the Romantic 'self'. Newton would never cry with Coleridge, '—O I have had a new world opened to me, in the infinity of my own Spirit!'[69]

[67] See e.g. Janet Todd, 'The Preacher as Prophet: John Newton's Evangelical Hymns', *The Hymn* (1980), 150–4, 158; Martin, *John Newton*, 358–62; Brantley, *Locke, Wesley, and Romanticism*; id. *Wordsworth's 'Natural Methodism'* (New Haven, 1975); Frederick Gill, *The Romantic Movement and Methodism* (1937).

[68] See further Robert J. Barth, *The Symbolic Imagination* (Princeton, 1977); and James Engell, *The Creative Imagination: Enlightenment to Romanticism* (Cambridge, Mass., 1981).

[69] S. T. Coleridge, Letter to Mrs. J. J. Morgan, quoted in the editor's Introduction to *Biographia Literaria*, vol. i. of *The Collected Works of Samuel Taylor Coleridge*, no. 7, Bolligen Series, 75 (1983), p. xiv.

8

'My connections have enlarged—my little name is spread' Newton in London, 1780–c.1790

Oh thou resort and mart of all the earth . . .!
William Cowper, apostrophizing London

NEWTON was 54 years of age when he moved from Olney to London where he would serve as Rector of St Mary Woolnoth, in the heart of the city, until his death in 1807. Earlier, at 29 years of age, he had spent most of one winter in London as a new convert eager to increase his faith by living 'at the fountain-head, as it were, for spiritual advantages', and the time he divided there between Church and Chapel, formal society meetings and informal conversation, left a lasting impression on him. Now, twenty-five years later, he returned to the metropolis less to be moulded by, than to exert, religious influence; less to learn than to teach. Through conversation and correspondence, through pulpit and press, Newton had steadily emerged as a prominent figure among his evangelical contemporaries. Just as Lord Dartmouth had previously exerted the necessary influence to secure Newton's ordination and raise him to his first title in 1764, John Thornton now used his patronage to enlarge Newton's sphere of ministry by presenting him to an important city living. Newton disliked the frantic pace of urban life but saw this new opportunity as both an honour and a calling, at a time when there were so few evangelical incumbents in the nation's capital. Active to the end, he developed in London the stature of a patriarch within the evangelical movement by the time he died.[1] He grew old contentedly, even as he watched a younger

---

[1] Already in 1798, Newton noted that he had a dozen books in duodecimo and that his writings had spread to Ireland, Scotland, and America, and had been

generation of evangelicals rise up to take his place under changing religious and political conditions. This chapter describes Newton's ministry in its evangelical context in London up to *c.*1790, and then singles out his ecclesiology for more detailed examination in the light of contemporary concerns about church order among evangelicals. Newton's defence of his own ecclesiological principles provides the basis for assessing how he reconciled his loyalty to the gospel, and therefore to all those converted by it of whatever denomination, with his loyalty to the Established Church in which he ministered.

EVANGELICALISM IN LONDON, *c.*1780

What was the state of evangelicalism when Newton arrived in the city in 1780? It was over forty years since Whitefield first stood up in Moorfields and Kennington Common to broadcast his simple gospel message to the thousands that thronged to hear the sensational 'boy preacher'; nearly as many years since Wesley's organizational genius appeared in the 'General Rules of the United Societies' (1743) which would give discipline and direction to his growing number of recruits. Evangelicalism had advanced in the capital on several fronts during these years. By the 1780s the 'Gospel world' was complex, made up of several disparate groups and popular preachers who yet formed a recognizable religious bloc in London. Shortly after arriving in the city, Newton wrote to a Scottish correspondent and outlined the state of evangelicalism in the Established Church, among Methodists and Moravians, and among Dissenters.[2] His anecdotal evidence, together with other contemporary testimony, provides a basis for reconstructing the context of his London ministry in the 1780s.

translated into German and the Low Dutch languages. *Memoirs of Hannah More,* iii. 48.

[2] Newton's correspondent was William Barlass (1758?–1817), minister of an Antiburgher Secession church near Aberdeen, and the letter is Newton to Barlass, 23 Feb. 1781. *Letters* (Barlass), 117–39.

Within the Established Church

William Romaine (1714–95) at St Andrew-by-the-Wardrobe was the only beneficed evangelical north of the Thames before Newton arrived in London, but evangelicalism had spread more extensively and found a larger constituency within the Established Church than might appear from how poorly it was represented among city incumbents.[3] Evangelicalism had been steadily advancing within the Church by alternative means, especially through proprietary chapels and lectureships. Newton explained that though only two gospel ministers (he and Romaine) had churches, 'we have about ten clergymen, who, either as morning preachers or lecturers, preach either on the Lord's day, or at different times of the week, in perhaps fifteen or sixteen churches'.[4] This was only to say that evangelicalism in London was thriving within the same ecclesiastical underworld as had Puritanism 200 years earlier, when the first lectureships appeared and 'godly ministers' depended widely upon private patronage. Patrick Collinson has commented regarding Elizabethan Puritans,

The London preachers whose strategically central position made them natural leaders of this movement would not be incumbents . . . When the puritans spoke of 'the church in London' they meant, in effect, a group of unbeneficed stipendiary curates and preachers, some of them lecturers in parish churches or the inns of the court, others lacking even that measure of settled responsibility.[5]

In many cases Newton's evangelical contemporaries were able to exploit the network of endowed lectureships left behind by

---

[3] There were a few other evangelical incumbents in the environs of London. Roger Bentley, another Thornton nominee, had the living of St Giles, Camberwell (1769–95); and Richard Conyers, the brother-in-law of Thornton and likewise his nominee, had St Paul's, Deptford (1767–86). William Bromley Cadogan, who converted to evangelicalism in 1780, held St Luke's, Chelsea (1775–97), but did so in plurality with St Giles, Reading (1774–97), the primary scene of his labours. By Thornton's will, John Venn was later presented to the valuable living of Clapham (1792–1813); Henry Foster became Vicar of St James', Clerkenwell in 1804; and William Jervase Abdy was first Curate-in-charge (1782–1805) and then Rector of St John's, Horsleydown (1805–23). See further Eliott-Binns, *Early Evangelicals* (1953), 234–47, 270, 311; Balleine, *Evangelical Party*, 41–51; Michael Hennell, *John Venn and the Clapham Sect* (1958), 79–80.   [4] *Letters* (Barlass), 129.

[5] *Elizabethan Puritan Movement*, 1st paperback. edn. (Oxford, 1990), 84–5.

their Puritan forefathers to much the same ends, capturing from below a grass-roots constituency within the Established Church. For example, the oldest lectureship in the city was established at St Antholin's in the reign of Edward VI and became for years a citadel of Puritan preaching. But in the 1780s it was the evangelical Henry Foster (1745–1844) who occupied the post there as popular Friday evening lecturer, and Newton often went and assisted him, St Antholin's being the next parish but one to St Mary Woolnoth. Foster, like other evangelical lecturers, strung together a number of such stipendiary preaching assignments. When Newton exchanged duties with him in 1779, just before moving to London permanently, he had to preach a full eleven sermons in a fortnight.[6] Foster could attract large numbers too. Newton went to hear him open a new lecture at Christ Church, Spitalfields, in 1783, and remarked that, large as the church was, it could not hold all those who wanted to attend; many went away, unable even to get near the door.[7] Other well known lecturers in this period included Romaine himself at St Dunstan's-in-the-West; George Pattrick at St Leonard's, Shoreditch, and St Bride's, Fleet St.; Watts Wilkinson at St Mary, Aldermary, and St Bartholomew, Exchange; George Dyer at St George-the-Martyr; and William Goode at St Lawrence, Jewry.[8]

Normally elected by the vestry, these lecturers possessed an authority independent of the incumbent of the church, with whom they sometimes were in conflict. But once licensed, they seldom came under the scrutiny of their ordinary. Hostile testimony to the way evangelicals exploited these lectureships to gather large popular audiences may be observed in a slightly earlier period from a printed notice preserved at the British Library entitled, 'To the Beneficed Clergy of the Diocese of London, The Humble Address of their (as yet

[6] *Letters* (Bull), 60.
[7] Newton to John Thornton, 8 Sept. 1783, ALS, CUL.
[8] There were also evangelical lecturers at St Alban's, Wood St.; St Swithin's, London Stone; St Mary Somerset; St Margaret's, Lothbury; Bow Church; All Hallows; St Peter's, Cornhill; and St Bartholomew-the-Great. See further, Eliott-Binns, *Early Evangelicals*, 241–7; Balleine, *Evangelical Party*, 48–51. On lectureships in London, in general, see Barrie-Curien, 'Clergy in the Diocese of London', 96–7.

uninfected) Parishioners' (1759).[9] The purpose of the notice was to urge incumbents to refuse evangelical lecturers—'irregular Teachers', 'utter Enemies to Decency and Order', 'Idols of the Populace', and so on—access to their pulpits by more strictly adhering to the Canons respecting the licensing of preachers. The wish in the closing paragraph that 'the Reverend Gentlemen in Possession may never be ousted their Churches by a Fanatical Faction' testified to contemporary fears that evangelical lecturers represented the revival of Puritan radicalism. The opposition of the parochial (and propertied) interest in the city to the mass appeal of evangelical lecturers continued, as Newton would discover, in the 1780s.

Chaplaincies, like the lectureships, also allowed numbers of unbeneficed evangelical clergy direct access to large congregations. District and private chapels were allowed as an important expedient for extending the ministry of the Church, at a time when parochial reform and church building inadequately kept pace with changes and growth in population. It was for this reason that the first district chapel in London was established when Richard Baxter, upon the encouragement of Tillotson, entrusted his chapel in Oxenden St. to the new incumbent of St Martin-in-the-Fields in 1676. Proprietary chapels were, however, like lectureships, outside the parochial system. These chapels were generally built by subscription and maintained by private individuals who controlled the appointment of the minister. Although a proprietary chapel might be supported in several ways, it often depended as a commercial enterprise upon a popular preacher who could attract some well-to-do hearers willing to pay high pew rents for the best seats. The Lock Hospital, for example, languished until Martin Madan's preaching attracted large numbers and led to the building of a new chapel in 1762. It quickly became the most important evangelical pulpit in the growing and fashionable West End. Thomas Haweis, Charles De Coetlogon, and Thomas Scott were at various times the stated preachers and Lord Dartmouth a regular hearer. In the year Newton began his

[9] See Fig. 3 below.

TO THE

Beneficed CLERGY of the Diocese of *London*,

The Humble Address of their (as yet uninfected) Parishioners.

REVEREND SIRS,

T is well known, that since the Introduction of Lectureships, there have crept into our Pulpits a Set of very irregular Teachers; utter Enemies to Decency and Order, and Propagators of moſt abſurd Doctrines; whereby they unſettle the Minds of the Laity, and allure them to forſake their lawful Paſtors: Men, who deſpiſe all Rule and Authority, and openly declare they know no Superior in the Church; who are puffed up with ſpiritual Pride, and proclaim themſelves the only True-Goſpel-Preachers: By which Device, with the Help of myſterious Nonſenſe, plentifully diſcharged among their Admirers, they are become the Idols of the Populace, and the Vulgar Herd from all Quarters of the Town, dance after their Summons, weekly publiſhed in *The Advertiſer*, &c.

By theſe diſorderly Crowds of their Followers, We your helpleſs Pariſhioners are driven out of our Churches, and deprived of the Benefit of Public Worſhip; this, Gentlemen, is our deplorable Situation, and it is only in your Power to relieve us therein.

Our Canons enjoin, That " neither the Miniſter, Churchwardens, nor " any other Officers of the Church, ſhall ſuffer any Man to preach within " their Churches or Chapels, but ſuch as by ſhewing their Licence to " preach, ſhall appear unto them to be ſufficiently authorized thereunto." See the 50th and 52d Canons.

Now, we humbly conceive, the putting this Injunction in Force may greatly tend to remedy the Evil; for it is not likely that One in Five of theſe new Guides can produce any Licence at all *.

A Trial whereof hath been lately made by a worthy Gentleman, who has the Cure of a ſmall Pariſh, and thinks it incumbent on him to guard his little Flock againſt Error and Enthuſiaſm; and if his Example ſhould prevail in this Metropolis, we may again hope to ſee our Worſhip reſtored, in the Bond of Peace and Unity of Spirit.

That the Enormities complained of may be ſpeedily cured, and that the Reverend Gentlemen in Poſſeſſion may never be ouſted their Churches by a Fanatical Faction, but that we may long enjoy the Benefit of their orthodox Miniſtry, is the hearty Prayer of

Their moſt Affectionate Pariſhioners,

1 January, 1759.

A, B, C, D, E, F, &c. &c. &c.

---

* *N. B.* No Licence to any Lecturer whatever can authoriſe him to Preach in any other Church than that whereto he is appointed, without or againſt the Conſent of the Rector or Vicar of ſuch Church; nor can any Lecturer depute another Perſon to Preach in his Stead.

ministry at St Mary Woolnoth, Richard Cecil, on the strength
of a bond from the evangelical aunt of William Wilberforce,
assumed personally the lease at St John's Chapel, Bedford
Row, and commenced his long and successful ministry there.
Henry Foster in the same year began preaching at Long Acre
Chapel; and Cecil and Foster together supplied for many
years the congregation which Augustus Toplady had built up
at the Orange Street Chapel. While Newton was in London,
Basil Woodd too commenced his lengthy ministry at Bentinck
Chapel, Edgware Road. Proprietary chapels were in some
cases notoriously exploited by West End developers for
commercial ends, but evangelicals in this period used them,
like the lectureships, as another vehicle for extending their
gospel message in the capital.[10]

During the 1780s there was thus a strong company of
evangelical preachers in London, united in purpose and
linked in friendship, who, without livings of their own, drew
large numbers to chapels and lectures to hear their preaching.
By this means an evangelical constituency within the Church
was gradually built up. One of the characteristics of the
growth of evangelicalism along these lines, outside the
traditional patronage and organization of the Church, was its
direct dependence upon popular appeal. As Thomas Scott put
it, 'In London . . . almost all are either *hugged* or *kicked* to
death, according as they are popular or unpopular.'[11] From
the perspective of the 1820s, Charles Jerram reflected
similarly on his earlier ministry at St John's Chapel, Bedford
Row:

[The congregation] was not altogether of the character I liked. It
was not parochial, and such as I could consider as peculiarly my

---

[10] *DNB*, s.v. Martin Madan (1726–90); Josiah Pratt, *The Life, Character, and
Remains of The Rev. Richard Cecil*, 5th edn. (1816), 9–23; Scott, *Life of Scott*, 218–38,
364–72; Elliott-Binns, *Early Evangelicals*, 241–7; Balleine, *Evangelical Party*, 48–9.
[11] Scott, *Life of Scott*, 394.

Fig. 3 'To the Beneficed Clergy of the Diocese of London' (1759)
British Library 816m.22/118.

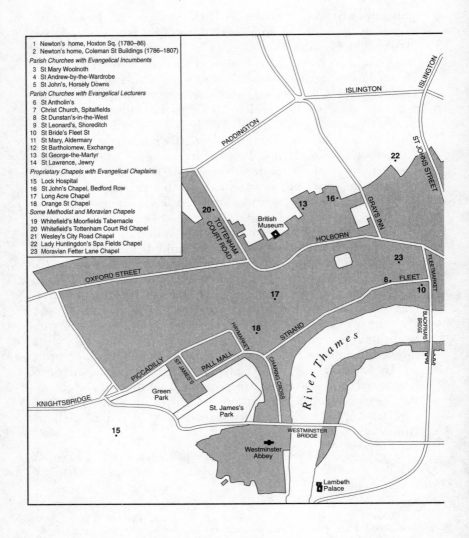

1 Newton's home, Hoxton Sq. (1780–86)
2 Newton's home, Coleman St Buildings (1786–1807)
Parish Churches with Evangelical Incumbents
3 St Mary Woolnoth
4 St Andrew-by-the-Wardrobe
5 St John's, Horsely Downs
Parish Churches with Evangelical Lecturers
6 St Antholin's
7 Christ Church, Spitalfields
8 St Dunstan's-in-the-West
9 St Leonard's, Shoreditch
10 St Bride's Fleet St
11 St Mary, Aldermary
12 St Bartholomew, Exchange
13 St George-the-Martyr
14 St Lawrence, Jewry
Proprietary Chapels with Evangelical Chaplains
15 Lock Hospital
16 St John's Chapel, Bedford Row
17 Long Acre Chapel
18 Orange St Chapel
Some Methodist and Moravian Chapels
19 Whitefield's Moorfields Tabernacle
20 Whitefield's Tottenham Court Rd Chapel
21 Wesley's City Road Chapel
22 Lady Huntingdon's Spa Fields Chapel
23 Moravian Fetter Lane Chapel

FIG. 4 Newton's London, *c.*1784
Based on a map in the Guildhall Library, London.

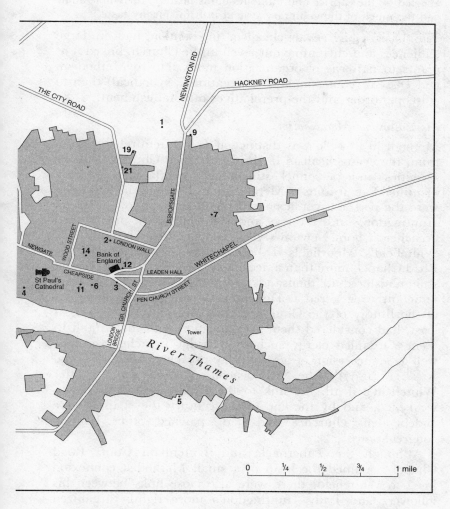

own; but collected from various parts of the metropolis, the larger portion of which were entire strangers to me, and for whom I could not, therefore, feel the sympathies which unite the pastor and his flock in an appropriated parish. As, moreover, a congregation of this description is usually of a more fluctuating character than a parochial charge, and the comfort of the minister, and that independence which he ought to feel, are liable to be more or less

297

affected by the caprice and humours of his hearers, the whole affair had too much of the voluntary system in it to suit my taste.[12]

The basis which evangelicalism in London had in large audiences and current favour, even in the Church, linked it at points to patterns of organization more akin to Methodism and Dissent (connexional, congregational, synodical) than to episcopal order and the prerogatives of Establishment.

Methodism and Moravianism

Methodism in 1780 was distinct, if not yet entirely separate from, the evangelicalism in the Established Church, and the activities and personnel still largely overlapped. Newton identified four strands of Methodism in London: the first three were the personal connexions of Whitefield, the Countess of Huntingdon, and Wesley; and the fourth, the unattached preachers whom Newton styled 'Independent Methodists'.[13] Whitefield's Moorfields Tabernacle and Tottenham Court Road Chapel, more than a decade after the evangelist's death, still ministered to thousands. Although these chapels were reluctantly registered as Dissenting Meetings, they made use of the liturgy of the Church of England and Whitefield, at least, had considered them in connection with the Establishment. Ordained clergy such as Berridge preached there as well as a succession of powerful lay preachers such as Torial Joss (1731–97), 'the Archdeacon of Tottenham'. After Whitefield's death the link to the Established Church was weakened, and by the end of the century the chapels were Independent churches and had spawned other London congregations.[14]

Although the Tabernacle and Tottenham Court Road Chapel remained the head of a small Methodist connexion loyal to Whitefield, there were also close links between his followers and Lady Huntingdon's more tightly organized

---

[12] James Jerram, *Memoirs and a Selection from the letters of . . . Charles Jerram* (1855), 305. [13] *Letters* (Barlass), 129–30.
[14] Albert Belden, *George Whitefield: The Awakener*, 2nd edn. (1953), 192–206; Edwin Welch (ed.), *Two Calvinistic Chapels, 1743–1811* (1975), p. xv; Tyerman, *Life of Whitefield*, ii. 372–6.

connexion. Lady Huntingdon (1707–91) had long used the drawing-room of her residences in London as a venue for her chaplains to address the aristocratic guests who gathered there at her personal invitation. But since 1770 she had also sought to reach a wider public in London through chapels acquired or built for such a purpose. She obtained control of her most important chapel in Spa Fields less than a year before Newton arrived in London. Newton remarked that it could hold 2,000, and her Westminster Chapel, where Dr Henry Peckwell was chaplain, was nearly as large. The Countess also had a large chapel at Mulberry Gardens, Wapping; and by 1790 she could add to her 'Plan of Association' Sion Chapel and Holywell Chapel. Initially her chapels had much the same status within the Church of England as the proprietary chapels mentioned above. But upon losing a well-publicized legal battle over the status of Spa Fields Chapel, she was forced after 1783 to register all her chapels as Dissenting Meetings. In 1780 her chapels were, however, still within the purview of the Establishment, and among those who wore her chaplain's scarf were yet strict churchmen such as Romaine, as well as those who (as time would show) scrupled little about church order.[15]

Wesley's City Road Chapel, said to hold almost as many as Whitefield's Tabernacle, was 2 years old when Newton arrived in London. Wesley had likewise many preaching rooms and several smaller chapels around the city including Snowfield's, Southwark (1743), Spitalfields (1750), and Wapping (1764). A plan for the London circuit in 1792 included some thirty-two preaching places. Because of the Calvinistic controversy, there was a theological divide between Wesleyan Methodism and the rest of the evangelical world which, except perhaps for the cleavage between Church and Dissent, was sharper than that between any other partisans of the Revival. These theological differences were only aggravated by the commencement in 1778 of Wesley's periodical bearing the provocative title, *The Arminian Magazine.* Still, Newton conceded of Wesley's London followers, 'Though

---

[15] *LyH*, ii. 294–311; Welch, *Two Calvinistic Chapels*, pp. xvi–xix, 93.

they are Arminians, as we say, there are many excellent
Christians, and some good preachers among them.'[16]

To the personal connexions of Whitefield, the Countess,
and Wesley, Newton added 'several preachers, whom I may
call Independent Methodists, of the Methodist stock, and
something in the dissenting form, but who stand singly, not
being connected with any of the dissenting boards'.[17] In this
category he would likely have included men such as Rowland
Hill who preached indiscriminately in chapels, streets, and
fields around London until his followers built Surrey chapel
for him in Southwark in 1782. Hill was himself in deacon's
orders, but the pulpit at Surrey chapel was open to Churchmen
and Dissenters alike. Newton's friend William Bull of Newport
Pagnell preached there frequently from its opening until
shortly before his death in 1814.

For Newton, at the beginning of his London career in 1780,
these several branches of Methodism could all still be viewed
as broadly within the outline of the Church, however irregular
they might appear. While he did not like the label 'Methodist',
he would, if pushed, accept the appellation for himself and,
regular though he was, throw in his lot with these others
(v. 507 cf. vi. 271).[18] He estimated that the churches and
chapels open on the Lord's Day for those 'whom the world
calls Methodists' (including himself), as distinct from
Dissenters, had a combined attendance of about 30,000.[19]

There was also an important Moravian work in London.
The chapel was in Fetter Lane and its origins were tied up
with those of Methodism. In 1738/9 the Fetter Lane religious
society, which figured so prominently in Wesley's early
journals cradled together what would later emerge as two

---

[16] Luke Tyerman, *Life and Times of the Rev. John Wesley*, 3rd edn., 3 vols. (1876),
iii. 223; *Letters* (Barlass), 130. [17] Ibid.

[18] The seventh Article of Enquiry for Bishop Porteus's Visitation in 1790 asked,
'Are there in your Parish any Methodists or any Dissenters from the Church of
England . . .?' Newton's return is badly mutilated but it is clear that he confessed to
being called a Methodist himself, though disapproving of the term as 'vague and
indeterminate' and refusing for this reason to give a direct answer on behalf of the
parish. Returns to Articles of Enquiry, Fulham Papers, LPL.

[19] *Letters* (Barlass), 131.

distinct movements in the form of Methodism and Moravianism. From it Wesley seceded in 1740 to form his own Methodist society at the Foundery, but from it also came seventy-two members who in 1742 formed the first London congregation of the Moravian Church. Moravianism had by 1780 expanded from this base in London to make great strides in Yorkshire, Wiltshire, and Ireland. (There was also a strong community of Moravians at Bedford which included the Barham family whose friendship Newton valued during his Olney curacy.) The Fetter Lane chapel remained for many years the headquarters of the work and from 1768 was given strong leadership by Benjamin La Trobe (1728–86). Through his preaching and writing and his relationships with other evangelical leaders, La Trobe did much to reverse the hostile opinion which had formed in England, following reports of the sentimental extravagances of certain Moravians in Germany around the middle of the century. When Newton was in London in 1779 waiting to be instituted and inducted into his living at St Mary Woolnoth, he went on Sunday morning to the Moravian Chapel to hear La Trobe preach. To his Scottish correspondent he wrote that though he used to share the strong and widespread prejudices against the Moravians, he now found some of his most dearly loved friends among them, adding, 'I do not know more excellent, spiritual, evangelical people in the land.'[20] By 1786 the Moravian Congregation comprised 166 members. Though their membership was not large in London, they exerted an influence within evangelicalism out of all proportion to their numbers, through their example of simple piety and their zeal for foreign missions.[21]

Dissent

When Newton arrived in London the pace of growth among evangelical Dissenters was quickening. Alan Gilbert has demonstrated how a pattern of 'New Dissent', representing

---

[20] Ibid. 132.
[21] Colin Podmore (ed.), *Fetter Lane Moravian Congregation, London, 1742–1992* (1992); J. E. Hutton, *History of the Moravian Church* (1909), 301–2, 438–42; Wilson, *History and Antiquities*, iii. 420–6.

those sections of Dissent transformed by the Methodist Revival, emerged during the last half of the eighteenth century, reversing the earlier serious decline in Dissenting fortunes. 'Within the dissenting tradition', writes Gilbert, 'the New Dissent was a phenomenon analogous to that of Methodism within the Anglican tradition.' While the Old Dissent cherished seventeenth-century and early eighteenth-century traditions and tended to remain exclusive and élitist, the New Dissent was inclusive and evangelistic. Towards the close of the century Quakers, General Baptists, Presbyterians, and the Unitarian movement which gradually displaced the latter, were in a state of stagnation, or actual decline. Yet at the same time Congregationalists, Particular Baptists, and New Connexion General Baptists, inspired with proselytizing zeal, showed a rapid growth rate akin to Methodism. Fresh initiatives in village preaching, Sunday schools, foreign missions, associational life, education, and inter-denominational co-operation witnessed to the vitality of this new evangelical strain of Dissent.[22]

The nature of the evidence makes it impossible to calculate precisely the density and distribution of Dissent in London during this period or to determine the relative strength of evangelical ideals. But it is none the less clear that the general pattern described by Gilbert, with a few exceptions, holds for the capital. A decade after Newton arrived in London, the first issue of the *Baptist Annual Register* (1790–3) recorded fifteen Particular Baptist congregations in London and another eight in Southwark, as well as one congregation belonging to the New Connexion General Baptists. (Although Dan Taylor, leader of the New Connexion, was in London from at least 1786, the strength of the New Connexion was still in the Midlands and the North.) The concurrent decline and growth in different sectors of the Baptist denomination is apparent from the estimation of one historian that, while eight Baptist congregations ceased in London during the last half of the century, twice as many were newly established near the city's centre and in the suburbs. But above all, the strength of evangelicalism among Baptists may be gauged by the

[22] Gilbert, *Religion and Society*, 36–41.

presence in the capital of outstanding leaders such as John Rippon (1751–1836) and Abraham Booth (1734–1806). Committed to Andrew Fuller's evangelical Calvinism, both of these men were at the centre of the most important Particular Baptist ventures during the period.[23]

Baptists were themselves divided for much of the century over whether believer's baptism ought to be a strict term of communion; inevitably, then, baptism was a potential obstacle to close co-operation with evangelicals of other denominations. Although Newton did not apparently keep up close links with many Baptists in London, he had Baptist friends elsewhere, thought highly of the writings of Fuller, and applauded their many evangelistic activities. Nevertheless, when describing to a correspondent the character of the Particular Baptists in London as sound and numerous, he added the complaint that they were too zealous about baptism and grew more by gaining proselytes from other denominations than through conversions under their own preachers. Newton once teased a Baptist minister that there was a text which he could preach on, but the Baptist minister could not, namely, 'Christ sent me not to baptize, but to preach the Gospel'.[24]

Newton's links with Independency were much closer. It was noted in Chapter 2 that Samuel Brewer, whose influence upon Newton in 1754–5 had been formative, was a particularly good example of the effect Whitefield had upon many young Independent ministers. But Whitefield and the preachers of his and Lady Huntingdon's connexions did not merely kindle evangelical fire among the Independents like Brewer from a distance; they also augmented the growth of evangelical congregational churches directly through the secession of preachers and entire congregations from Methodism. When connexional loyalties weakened, congregational patterns of church government most naturally took their place. This was

---

[23] John Rippon, *Baptist Annual Register* (1790–3), 8–9, 172–5; William Page (ed.), *Victoria History of London*, i (1909), 391. For Rippon and Booth, see Brown, *English Baptists*, 118–19, 123, 126–7. For Baptist statistics for London, see further the *Protestant Dissenters Magazine*, 3 (1796), 433–5; W. T. Whitley, *Baptists of London, 1612–1928*, [1928], 56–7.   [24] *Autobiography of Jay*, 272–3.

true too, though to a lesser extent, of some of Wesley's societies. Although the initial licensing of Calvinistic Methodist chapels as Independent meetings was in many cases reluctant, the drift into outright Dissent after the deaths of Whitefield and the Countess was almost inescapable. With the considerable accession to evangelical Independency of numbers of these Methodists, the situation for Independent chapels in London was similar to that of the Baptists. During the last half of the century four of their Meetings closed, two of which had previously become Unitarian, but at the same time, many new autonomous churches were being established.[25]

The case of John Clayton (1754–1843) illustrates well the impact of Methodism on Old Dissent. Awakened under the preaching of Romaine, Clayton trained for the ministry at the Countess of Huntingdon's College at Trevecka, served at various chapels (including Moorfields, Tottenham Court Road, and Spa Fields) as a Methodist lay preacher, and then sought episcopal ordination. He was refused orders. In 1778 he was instead ordained pastor of King's Weigh House, one of the oldest Presbyterian churches in the city. In 1784 he took it out of the Presbyterian Fund and into the Congregational denomination because of the Unitarian beliefs prevalent among Presbyterians. A lecturer at Pinners' Hall and head of a small dynasty of Congregational ministers, Clayton came to have considerable influence upon the denomination. Though a Congregationalist, he was invited by Newton in 1783 to join the Eclectic Society and remained on the friendliest terms with evangelicals in the Established Church. On matters of ecclesiastical polity his position was by no means the highest—one of his church members called him something of an 'Independent Presbyterian Methodist'. To some later Nonconformists his political and social conservatism was notorious. But his career was testimony to the way in which Methodism captured, or at least infused an entirely new spirit into, the citadels of Old Dissent among Independents in London. This process was only beginning in 1780, however,

[25] Jones, *Congregationalism*, 152–61; Watts, *Dissenters*, 445–50. See further, Waddington, *Congregational History*, 597–8, 675–6.

and Newton still associated Independency with the piety of Old Dissent in which he was raised. Thus, upon his arrival in London, he observed that though contemporary Independents retained for the most part a 'form of sound words', they compared but poorly to the former glory of their denomination.[26]

Presbyterians, Newton regretted, no longer preached the cross and had few attending their polite and elegant churches in London. The one exception to this pattern was the new churches established by immigrant Scots, especially those in communion with the Secession church.[27] In 1796 the *Protestant Dissenters Magazine* listed seven Scottish Presbyterian and three Seceder congregations in the metropolis.[28] Indebted to the indigenous revival in Scotland associated with Ebenezer Erskine (1680–1754), the Secession church and other subsequent breakaway groups were strongly evangelical. Newton had to have his correspondents north of the Tweed explain to him the bewildering series of splits in the Scottish church. But his writings were very popular among the Seceders, and he soon had contacts with several in the city. To John Campbell in Edinburgh he wrote, 'Burghers, Antiburghers, Kirk-men, and Relief-men, all are fish that come to my net; and especially those whom you send.'[29]

The full impact of the rise of evangelical Nonconformity would not be felt until the 1790s and afterwards, when Newton was growing old. It would consequently be a new generation of Anglican evangelicals who would have to respond more seriously both to the threat to Establishment prerogative and the opportunity for interdenominational collaboration posed by the growth of Dissent. But the growing *esprit de corps* of Dissenters brought issues of cross-denominational bickering and co-operation to the fore already in the 1780s. Although Newton would on many occasions observe happily the growth in evangelicalism among Nonconformists, he was also provoked by them to defend publicly

---

[26] Thomas W. Aveling, *Memorials of the Clayton Family* (1867); Jones, *Congregationalism,* 159; *Letters* (Barlass), 131–2.   [27] Ibid.
[28] *Protestant Dissenters Magazine,* 3 (1796), 433–5.
[29] *Letters* (Campbell), 63.

how he reconciled his ecclesiology to his evangelicalism. Not all his brethren were satisfied by his attempted self-vindication, but he gave his opinion on an issue which would often occupy his nineteenth-century successors.

St Mary Woolnoth

As John Thornton passed St Mary Woolnoth on his way to and from his city counting-house in the 1770s, he had no doubt often thought how happy he would be to see a Gospel Minister in its pulpit. The Rector from 1752 until 1779 was a non-resident pluralist, Charles Plumtre, DD, and during his incumbency, though he provided a curate, 'scarcely ever above two or three assembled together in the place, even on a Sunday'.[30] Ever eager to advance the evangelical cause through shrewd patronage, Thornton purchased the right of next presentation not long before Plumtre died in 1779, and immediately thereafter he offered the living to Newton.

One of ninety-seven parishes within the city walls, St Mary Woolnoth was annexed after the Great Fire to the adjacent St Mary Woolchurch Haw, and together the parishes comprised about 500 square yards on the south side of Cornhill and Poultry Streets, opposite the Bank of England and the Royal Exchange. The united parishes, though compact, included the Mansion House of the Lord Mayor. An annual levee for the Lord Mayor, including a sermon, was held at the church. Newton calculated that his cure contained a total of 142 houses, including 'many opulent persons, Bankers & Traders', and that he had from 150 to 200 regular communicants.[31] The smallest of the ten new churches actually built under the Act of 1711, St Mary Woolnoth was completed in 1727 by the famous English architect Nicholas Hawksmoor, and its peculiar baroque style, though rare in ecclesiastical architecture, would have been generally pleasing to eighteenth-century taste (see Fig. 5 below). The living was worth just over £260 per annum and, unlike Newton's income at Olney,

[30] *New Spiritual Magazine,* 3 [1785], 1198.
[31] Returns to Articles of Enquiry for St Mary Woolnoth, Porteus 1790, Fulham Papers, LPL.

it was secure for his lifetime. When Thornton's offer first
came in 1779, Newton confided to his diary that at his time of
life such a 'settlement' might indeed seem desirable.[32] In all,
it was among the most prestigious and comfortable benefices
in the country to be held by an evangelical.

Newton's ministry was not, however, principally to his
parishioners, many of whom retreated on weekends to
suburban villas or abandoned the city altogether for the
summer, while others stayed away explicitly because of
Newton's reputation as a Methodist. To the small number of
parishioners who did attend his ministry on Sunday mornings,
he preached a shorter, more cautious sermon than at other
times, realizing that two or three of his bankers might be
present.[33] The church was generally full for each of Newton's
three weekly services because of the large numbers he drew,
not from within, but from outside the parish. As 'the
shopwindow for the whole country', London could attract
religious consumers as much as it could commercial traders.[34]
'Many of my Evening hearers', Newton wrote, 'come from far,
from most of the Villages around the Metropolis: some from
Chelsea, from Camberwell, Newington and Stoke Newington,
and eastward from Limehouse and Bow—etc.'[35] Some parishioners objected to this intrusion, complaining that their seats
were too often occupied by strangers, or that they could not
get to them because of the crowd in the aisle.[36] But, as noted
in the case of lectureships, this was a frequent grievance by
parishioners where an evangelical was preacher.

The geographically diverse composition of Newton's regular
congregations was matched, moreover, by the denominational
and theological diversity of the hearers he attracted, especially

[32] Diary (1773–1805), 19 Sept. 1779; cf. Bull, *Newton*, 237.
[33] Cecil, *Newton*, 176, 178–9. St Mary Woolnoth had an established Sunday
afternoon lecture. The lecturer, chosen by the parishioners, was Dr David Horne
from the time of Newton's induction until the 1786 visitation; Joseph Griffiths, from
the 1790 visitation until that of 1803; and Josiah Pratt, from sometime before
Newton's death until at least 1810. The name of Pratt (member of the Eclectic
Society and later secretary of the Church Missionary Society) suggests that by the
time of Newton's death evangelicals controlled the vestry.
[34] See Stout, *Divine Dramatist*, 34.
[35] Newton to William Wilberforce, 23 Mar. 1801, ALS, Bodl. See further, *EM*
16 (1808), 106.   [36] Bull, *Newton*, 246.

FIG. 5 Interior of St Mary Woolnoth. The triplet of giant fluted Corinthian pillars and the curved, richly decorated pulpit are original, illustrating the fashionable elegance of Newton's city church. The tapered monument on the north wall, parallel with the pulpit, commemorates Newton.

RCHME Crown copyright.

to his Sunday and Wednesday evening lectures.[37] Although there were only two Roman Catholic families and about a dozen Dissenters residing in the parish itself, he reported to a correspondent after less than a year, 'Churchmen and Dissenters, Calvinists and Arminians, Methodists and Moravians, now and then I believe, Papists and Quakers, sit quietly to hear me' (vi. 198). Unlike Olney, then, St Mary Woolnoth looked out on a highly mobile, cosmopolitan population with little sense of parochial identity. Newton explained to a friend in the country, 'it is but little that ministers in London can know of their congregations, further than by their outward appearance.'[38]

To fulfil his parochial cure in a such a setting, Newton came up with the expedient of printing and distributing to all his parishioners periodic sermons; on one occasion he also sent them an open letter entitled, 'A Token of Affection and Respect to the Parishioners of St Mary Woolnoth . . . from their Minister' (vi. 563–81). By this means, he could be sure that all had the opportunity at least to read what he would have said to them, had they come to hear him preach. Although he was still much occupied by his 'bounden attention to the Sick & the Sorrowful', the former daily round of calls on parishioners, the cottage prayer meetings, the children's meeting, the Great House meetings—all that constituted the parish *ecclesiola* at Olney—these were no more.[39] St Mary Woolnoth was for Newton principally a pulpit. Even the routine surplice duties of the parish were, at least after 1788, supplied by a curate. Newton continued, as at Olney, to care for the needs of the poor as he was able, and he often brought particularly needy cases to the attention of his wealthy friends and acted as a conduit for their philanthropy. On occasion he could be found taking the needy under his own roof, or visiting prisoners at Newgate, or giving small gifts to poor children. Yet, the poverty and distress he encountered, like the spiritual concerns he addressed, could not be confined within the boundaries of his parish.

---

[37] *Letters* (Barlass), 127; *EM* 16 (1808), 105.
[38] *Letters* (Taylor), 46.
[39] Newton to William Wilberforce, 1 Nov. 1797, ALS, Bodl.

NEWTON AS EVANGELICAL PATRIARCH

Besides his pulpit ministry, Newton's principal contribution as a metropolitan religious leader was to the evangelical corps as a whole, in London and around the country, through a range of extraparochial friendships and activities.

In this, his location in London was pivotal. If there was anything that struck him about the contrast between Olney and London, it was the turbulence of the latter—'the throng and hurry of the busy world, and noise and party contentions of the religious world'.[40] The exchanged hospitality, the correspondence, and the round of preaching that had connected Newton to evangelicals outside Olney had been extensive, but the evangelical network in London hummed with a much greater volume of activity and, sometimes, of strife. Upon returning to the city after visiting and preaching in the country, his first letter would typically bemoan the 'throng of engagements' and incessant activity, albeit religious activity, in which he was again caught up. Newton commented whimsically, 'Whatever else be dear in London, the gospel is good, cheap, and in great plenty.'[41] Although no longer able to enjoy moments of rural quiet and solitude in day-to-day life, Newton in London was able to exert a significant influence upon ministers and laymen of all denominations from around the nation as they passed through his church and came to his door. In London, he was bound to know of, and often to contribute to, the most important religious developments and controversies of his day.

As Newton grew old in London he increased in stature. Two regular gatherings in which he participated during the 1780s and 1790s, one informal and one formal, illustrate the ways in which his 'connections were enlarged' and his 'little name was spread' among his fellow evangelicals. The first gathering was at his home, where he routinely received visitors twice a week; the second was at the Castle and Falcon in Aldersgate Street, where he participated in the fortnightly discussions of the Eclectic Society.

---

[40] *Letters* (Bull), 58 cf. 60.   [41] Ibid. 206.

Table Talk

With filial devotion Richard Cecil recalled of Newton after his death, 'His house was open to Christians of all ranks and denominations. Here, like a father among his children, he used to entertain, encourage, and instruct his friends, especially younger ministers, or candidates for the ministry.'[42] On one occasion, when Newton was having trouble arranging a free day to see William Wilberforce, he explained his schedule: 'I have been long in the habit of seeing my friends, *at home* on Tuesdays & Saturdays ... On a Tuesday I frequently have more than Forty in the course of the day, & as some come from a distance, it would grieve me to disappoint them.'[43] This was written in 1797. Earlier too, in 1785, when Wilberforce first sought Newton's spiritual counsel but was shy of his religious seriousness becoming public, Newton warned him that if he came on a Saturday he might well be seen, for there was usually a succession of visitors from morning to night and the house was seldom clear before eight in the evening. The Nonconformist William Jay (1769–1853) of Bath went along to a 'kind of open breakfast' at Newton's whenever he was in town. Typically, Jay recalled, the guests would join in the family worship, led by Newton, after breakfast. Then Newton would withdraw to his study with his friends, 'and there, with his pipe ... he would converse in a manner the most easy, and free, and varied, and delightful, and edifying'.[44]

Newton's table talk on these occasions, like Luther's earlier, was recorded by younger men eager to learn from him and preserve his wisdom for posterity. Richard Cecil followed him around, Boswell-like, and recorded what fell 'at different times, both in company and in private, from his lips'.[45] After becoming minister of Kingsland Chapel in London, John Campbell (1766–1840) likewise recorded his conversations

[42] Cecil, *Newton*, 175. See also the memoir of Henry Foster in *The Bible Preacher; or Closet Companion*, ed. S. Piggot (1824), pp. vii–viii; Josiah Bateman, *Life of the Right Rev. Daniel Wilson*, 2 vols. (1860), i. 13–19; Jerram, *Memoirs of Charles Jerram*, 201–22.
[43] Newton to Wilberforce, 1 Nov. 1797.
[44] *Autobiography of Jay*, 269–70.
[45] Cecil, *Newton*, 240; cf. 'Table-talk', ibid. 241–71.

with Newton. A few examples of the words—sometimes picturesque or whimsical, sometimes aphoristic or pro-verbial—which these men recollected from their visits, may illustrate the way Newton had come to be regarded as one of the aged, wise men of evangelicalism. Jay recalled Newton's droll humour: 'He one day told of a countryman who said to his minister, "You often speak of our FORE-fathers; now, I know only of three—Abraham, Isaac, and Jacob. Pray, sir, who is the *fourth?*" '[46] More seriously, but still memorably, Cecil recounted an illustration Newton used about the need for patience in the Christian life. Newton remarked, 'For an old Christian to say to a young one, "Stand in my evidence," is like a man who has with difficulty climbed by a ladder or scaffolding to the top of the house, and cries to one at the bottom, "This is the place for a prospect,—come up at a step." '[47] Campbell recorded the aphorism, spoken after one man told of narrowly escaping death at sea: 'We are immortal till our time comes.'[48] After the year 1800 Newton's sight and hearing decayed such that it became more and more difficult for him to participate in conversation, but still people came, until he was at last but an unseeing and unhearing oracle. That Newton's words were so lovingly preserved, that his homely conversation was remembered so affectionately by friends of all denominations, demonstrates how he came to be regarded in old age as something of an evangelical patriarch.

The Eclectic Society

Through household hospitality Newton was in effect the convenor, in his own home, of a regular, informal synod of evangelical ministers and leading laymen. In January 1783 this became only slightly more formal when he met with Cecil, Foster, and the layman Eli Bates, to establish what would become known by the end of the year, appropriately, as the Eclectic Society.[49] At first Newton could identify these meetings only by circumlocution. Inviting John Clayton to

---

[46] *Autobiography of Jay,* 271.   [47] Cecil, *Newton,* 247–8.
[48] *Letters* (Campbell), 178.
[49] On the Eclectic society, see further, Michael Hennell, *John Venn and the Clapham Sect* (1958), 200.

become a member, Newton wrote: 'The Society, that bears no name, and espouses no party, meets at the Castle and Falcon, Aldersgate Street.'[50] The group increased to eight by October and included the Moravian La Trobe. Typically, they began with tea at four, and then a short prayer introduced about three hours of discussion on an arranged subject. At least twenty years the senior of most other members, Newton was regarded with respect, and his words must have carried especial authority at these meetings. It was the perfect institutional embodiment of his ideals—a non-partisan group of evangelical believers, gathered in a spirit of friendship for 'improving' spiritual conversation. The composition likewise reflected his sense of ecclesiastical propriety, for it comprised predominantly ministers of the Church of England, but included by design two or three laymen and Dissenters as well. He wrote sometime later to John Campbell, when the Eclectic had swelled by a few more members,

I am not fond either of assemblies, consistories, synods, councils, benches, or boards. . . . [Ministers'] associations, in my judgment, should always be voluntary and free. Thus there are ten or a dozen of us in London, who frequently meet; we deliberate, ask, and give advice as occasions arise; but the sentiment of one, or even of the whole body, is not binding on any.[51]

The contrast here between the Eclectic and formal systems of church government is telling. For, indeed, the Eclectic was, from its inception, an important focus for extra-ecclesiastical evangelical leadership, and in time it would become famous as the matrix of the Church Missionary Society and the *Christian Observer* magazine.[52] It anticipated the great age of the

[50] Aveling, *Clayton Family*, 82.   [51] *Letters* (Campbell), 64–5.

[52] The Eclectic society is best known from the 'Notes of the Discussion of the Eclectic Society, London, During the Years 1798–1814', published in 1856 by John Pratt from his father's notebooks, and reprinted as *The Thought of the Evangelical Leaders* (Edinburgh, 1978). About the earlier period of the society, virtually nothing has been written, and for this period Newton's own manuscript notebooks are a valuable source of information. They were unknown to Charles Hole, *Early History of the Church Missionary Society* (1896), and shed much light on the formative period of the Evangelical party in the Church of England. There are two notebooks: the first covers 1787–9 (FLP); the second, 1789–95 (CNM).

organized religious society, even as it looked back to the
spiritual ideals of religious friendship and intimate *koinonia* in
which the Revival began.

Evangelicalism was emerging in the 1780s as a coalition of
several interlocking denominations, personal connexions, and
ecclesiastical parties. It was united in opposition to unbelief
and to merely notional expressions of Christian faith; united
too in an affective spirituality of conversion—the thing itself
about which 'justification by faith' was only a description. In
the 1790s this would be given enduring institutional expression
through co-operative ventures in publishing and mission
agency. But the very success of evangelicalism made its own
internal fault lines more apparent, and the potential for
friction between coalition members was heightened by the
sheer volume of religious commerce in the city.

This underlying tension was reflected in the evangelical
periodical press in the 1780s. Wesley's *Arminian Magazine*
began in 1778, in direct opposition to the *Gospel Magazine*.
Then, early in 1784, after publishing for some eighteen years,
the *Gospel Magazine* folded. Two magazines, the *New Spiritual
Magazine* (1783–5?) and the *Theological Miscellany* (1784–9),
competed to capture the interdenominational Calvinistic
constituency of the *Gospel Magazine*, but both folded before the
end of the decade. It was not until the *Evangelical Magazine*
(1793–1805) appeared that the *Gospel Magazine* had an
enduring, if less narrowly Calvinistic, successor. Newton
himself was partially implicated in an especially bitter
controversy related to the *New Spiritual Magazine*, which led
eventually to its termination.[53] Though he sought to avoid
controversy in his own contributions to the evangelical press,
he was ridiculed by the editors of the *New Spiritual Magazine*
and labelled 'John Weathercock'.[54] The 1780s were a difficult
decade in which to remain an eclectic 'middleman'.

In the 1780s Newton was involved in another controversy

---

[53] See further, *A Familiar Letter of Reproof and Humiliation to the Rev. Thomas Towle*
[1785], and *A Miscellaneous Collection of Satirical Pieces . . . Respecting 'Master Tommy
Dishclout, B.D., and Some of his Learned Friends* [1785?].
[54] *Collection of Satirical Pieces*, 25. On Newton and controversy in the periodical
press, see further, Newton to John Ryland, Jun., 16 Dec. 1786, ALS, BBC.

that highlighted again the forces which tugged evangelicals apart, even as many sought to draw closer together. It related to Newton's *Apologia* (1784), the public statement of his reasons for joining and remaining in the ministry of the Church of England. From the arguments advanced by Newton in the *Apologia* may be inferred several of the most important characteristics of his evangelical consciousness— what it meant to him to be 'of the Gospel', and how this transcended his own particular ministry in the Church of England. Newton's position as a senior evangelical leader gives his statement a special importance for defining the evangelical moment of the 1780s.

The *Apologia* (1784)

Occasion and Context

Although Newton's *Apologia* was published in 1784, he had written a preliminary draft seven years earlier, which he had laid aside after taking the opinion of Samuel Lucas, Independent pastor at Shrewsbury (1779–97). The full title of Newton's work, when published, was *Apologia: Four Letters to a Minister of an Independent Church, by a Minister of the Church of England*. The anonymous Independent minister to whom Newton chiefly addressed himself was Samuel Palmer of Hackney (1741–1813), author of *The Protestant-Dissenter's Catechism* (1773). Palmer's catechism was designed to instil the principles of Nonconformity in a new generation of Dissenters who, because of a long interval of peace and liberty, had grown indifferent to their heritage and were consequently easily tempted to conform to the Established Church, especially when there could be found a parish with 'an ingenious, popular, or evangelical ministry'. The outline of Newton's tract followed Palmer closely, except that Newton sought to overturn each of his principal arguments for Dissent, and make them arguments instead for conformity. Newton decided better of it after writing his first draft, however, and set his manuscript aside, choosing not to appear publicly as a controversial writer.

But with his growing prominence as an evangelical and his

preferment to a city benefice, Newton found more and more Dissenters murmuring that his motives for being in the Church of England were suspect. Thus he explained the occasion of the *Apologia*:

My habits of friendship and intimacy with many Dissenters, and the readiness and pleasure with which I embraced opportunities of hearing their ministers, caused many not only to take it for granted, but positively to affirm, that I was a Dissenter at heart, and that I remained in the establishment against the light and conviction of my conscience; which could only be for the sake of convenience and emolument.[55]

Given these rumours, Newton felt he had to respond: 'I am willing to be thought mistaken, but I wish to be found honest.'[56]

Chiefly, Newton had in mind about twenty Dissenting ministers in London ('whose persons I love, whose characters I respect'), and it was their reaction he looked for after publication. He gave a copy of the *Apologia* to Clayton and to each of the lecturers at Pinners' Hall—Brewer, Gibbons, Fisher, Davies, Barker, and Winter. To John Ryland, Jun., Newton wrote a few weeks later, 'I am not afraid of making you angry, but I am told that some Dissenters are not pleased, & that I may expect an answer.'[57] He did not have to wait long. His *Apologia* came off the press in March and by June a line-by-line rebuttal was published by Dr Henry Mayo (1733–93), pastor of the Independent congregation in Nightingale Lane, under the title, *An Apology and a Shield for Protestant Dissenters, In These Times of Instability and Misrepresentation* (1784).[58] Palmer himself, who it was rumoured might respond to Newton, felt Mayo had been too mean-spirited.[59] Palmer wrote to Newton to tell him that he would not respond in print. From this beginning, Palmer and Newton carried on a friendly correspondence which lasted until Newton's death.

[55] *Letters* (Palmer), 45–7; cf. *Letters* (Campbell), 91.
[56] *Letters* (Palmer), 43.
[57] Newton to John Ryland, Jun., ALS, 22 Apr. 1784, BBC.
[58] The *Apologia* was also reviewed in the *New Spiritual Magazine*, 3 [1785], 1199; *Theological Miscellany*, 1 (1784), 387–9; *Monthly Review* 71 (1784), 426–9.
[59] *Letters* (Palmer), 41–9.

Mayo, on the other hand, was a seasoned controversialist, having entered the lists against John Gill over baptism in 1763, and against Martin Madan a few years later over the alleged simony involved in placing Thomas Haweis at Aldwinkle. John Berridge wrote to John Thornton in the autumn, 'Mr. Newton has fallen into the hands of a slaughter-man, I hear, Dr. Mayhew, who will certainly cleave him down the chine if he can. He set Mr. Madan on his head about Aldwinkle, and almost made him crazy. I hope my dear brother will bear the Doctor's operation with Christian patience, and make no reply.'[60] Newton did not reply, but still this did not stop another pamphlet from appearing the following year in the form of an anonymous satirical poem, *Apologia Secunda or, a Supplementary Apology for Conformity: Two Epistles, humbly addressed to the Awakened Clergy by a Layman* (1785). It included lines such as,

> Go,—cringe to a patron, or flatter his wife,
> And the bus'ness is done; you've an income for life.

and, in mock defence of Newton's failure to respond to Mayo,

> Thus these graceless schismatics revile our good church,
> As if by her son she was left in the lurch;
> Because to himself he was so much a friend,
> As to keep in the dark what he could not defend.[61]

Although some Dissenters—such as William Bull and Samuel Palmer himself—appreciated Newton's candour, Nonconformist opinion was clearly divided over Newton's tract.

Newton's Dissenting friends could be excused if they were a little vexed by his seeming to come out as an advocate for the Church. Because of the tortuous path he had travelled to ordination, he appeared to some now as simply equivocal. He had vacillated so long between Church and Dissent—even saying at one point that he was through with the Established Church and offering himself up to be a Dissenting minister—that it must have seemed that his ecclesiastical principles were

[60] *Works of Berridge,* 423–4.
[61] *Apologia Secunda,* 10. (The copy in Dr Williams's Library, London, is inscribed 'to the Rev. Mr. [James?] Bennet from the author'.)

not quite solid. Even in 1768 Newton had been prepared to argue, in his first draft of his *Review of Ecclesiastical History*, that primitive church order was at odds with the Church of England. Only the united efforts of Haweis, Madan, and Lord Dartmouth persuaded him to excise these passages, seeing as this was the church within which he presently ministered.[62] Did Newton's position change over the years? He wrote later, 'A dear Dissenting brother of mine who was hurt by the publication of Apologia, said to me, I am sorry you are so much more of a Churchman than you were formerly. I answered, I do not think myself more of a Churchman, but I am indeed less of a Dissenter.'[63] As Newton observed ministers of gathered churches, such as Joshua Symonds of Bedford, imposed upon by their congregations, he began to think of himself as the true 'independent' minister of the gospel. He would never take a strong position on church order, but he grew ever more satisfied as the years went by that his arguments in the *Apologia* were sound.

Argument

The *Apologia* (v. 3–58) is an important document for defining Newton's evangelical consciousness. For in it he provided his theological rationale not only for his conformity, but also for his sense of belonging to an evangelical movement transcending the limits of denomination and party. Newton's line of argument may be summarized as follows.

He claimed that with the demise of the old persecuting high church principles in the Establishment, nothing remained to inhibit reciprocal goodwill between parties, for the gospel was, or ought to be, a much stronger bond between Christians than church order. Although a national religious establishment was not of express divine appointment, it remained expedient none the less, serving to preserve at least minimal Christian influence in many regions which would otherwise be entirely

---

[62] Newton wrote to Lord Dartmouth on this occasion that he had, as he put it, 'corrected what I had wrote upon the government of the primitive church, with a pair of scissors, not a bit here and there, but I cut out every line of it'. *Letters* (Dartmouth), 189. Even with the excision, Mayo did not miss the opportunity to quote Newton's *Ecclesiastical History* against him. See Mayo, *An Apology and a Shield*, 21.

[63] Newton to John Ryland, Jun., ALS, 31 July 1789, BBC.

spiritually destitute. His personal reason for conformity, he added provocatively, was the regard he owed to Christ alone as the head of the church. This was a principle he saw widely acknowledged, but wrongly construed, by many people of God, resulting in countless unhappy divisions. Because the visible church comprised all professing Christians, it was necessarily a *mixed* body of both regenerate persons and nominal Christians. As Christ was not, however, governor of merely nominal Christians ('for his kingdom is a spiritual kingdom, which none can understand . . . until born from above' [v. 24]), he must be understood as head of the church only in its more limited and proper sense as his mystical body, composed of all those who by faith are united to him. There were hidden ones who belonged to him amongst every body of professing Christians—even amongst the Roman and Greek churches. Sadly, men equally eminent in piety and learning—whether from the Church of England, the Church of Scotland, the Independent churches, or the Baptists—disagreed widely over which system of church order was of divine right. Because in the essentials of the gospel he agreed with them all, he would in the disputed matters of church order honour the headship of Christ over his entire mystical body by refusing to call any party or subdivision of God's people the true church to the exclusion of the others. He would maintain friendly relations with all, but allow none to be master of his conscience. When he joined the Church his conscience concurred happily with the articles, liturgy, and rubric of the Establishment, and he saw the probability of greater useful-ness there. Because he had also been led specifically by providence to a suitable situation on that side, he was satisfied that he had done well to seek episcopal ordination. In conclusion, he claimed not to have regretted the decision since.

Analysis: Evangelicals and Ecclesiology

What are the implications of the ecclesiological compromise here worked out by Newton? To begin with, it is remarkable to what extent his experience of religious pluralism marked his exposition. Indeed, his acceptance of a range of religious diversity was probably one of the most basic assumptions underlying his writings. That he rejected the ideal of a confessional state and a monopolistic national church—the two sides of the traditional Anglican Church–State constitution—was at the same time both a simple recognition of the contemporary reality and an act of theological commitment. For, by basing his defence of religious establishments upon their instrumental value, he was acknowledging the *de facto* status of the Church of England as a voluntary, if privileged, society which people would choose to join, or not, as a matter of private judgement. But he also knew that his primary theological concern with true belief over nominal profession would not in any case be advanced by State-coerced, religious uniformity.[64] He thought it simply made good sense, as a matter of expediency, for the State to make wide provision for religious services. This baldly utilitarian approach to Church establishment was criticized by some of his Nonconformist detractors. It was also a markedly different position from the magisterial reformers, who assumed the ideal of a confessional State, or, again, of the non-separatist Puritans, who fought for their particular version of it.

Newton's position reflected the attitudes of a very different generation which, as Palmer noted, had grown up after the Hanoverian succession was secure and had entrenched the Revolutionary settlement of 1689.[65] The constitutional status of the Church had been significantly lowered by the official recognition given to all Trinitarian Protestant denominations, and the passage of time lent this pluralism an added sense of

---

[64] Cf. Newton to Thornton, 17 Mar. 1779, ALS, CUL, 'I shall not be sorry if the Dissenters bill succeeds, for I wish every person the same liberty in Religious matters, which I desire for myself. And I think Human Authority has not much right to interfere with pains and penalties, to force the consciences of those who are peaceable subjects. The Truth is strong, and as able to maintain itself now, as in the early days of Christianity, when it had no protection from Civil Government, but was oppressed with violence in every place. Constraint can only make Hypocrites . . . I wish they would proceed to repeal the Corporation and Test acts, so far as they require, by decree, a profanation of the Lord's supper. I think if I were a Member of Parliament, I would make a motion to this purpose, before I had been a week in the House.'

[65] Ward, *Protestant Evangelical Awakening*, 51 cf. 354, argues that pluralism was one of the most critical conditions shaping the Protestant world in the 18th c. The dominant mood he describes as 'the longing to go behind the present confessional division of Europe into a larger religious unity'.

legitimacy. Newton grew up with some measure of pluralism as part of the world-as-given, and if pluralism, then also voluntarism, for diversity implied the freedom to choose (even if this was still officially understood in the establishmentarian sense of freedom to dissent).[66] From the beginning, therefore, Newton's understanding of evangelicalism was rooted in a religious landscape of acceptable diversity. The force of this assumption can be seen in the central irony that in Newton's *Apologia*, not only did a minister of the Established Church feel he had to justify himself for having dissented from Dissent, but also that he used the classic separatist apologetics, rehearsed by Palmer, to do so. Newton turned the argument that Christ, not the King, is the only true head of the church, and that Christ alone is the Lord of men's consciences, into a peculiar defence for remaining *in* the Establishment—out-dissenting the Dissenters. No wonder that some Dissenters complained bitterly at this treatment, since Newton could be seen to be cutting out from under them their whole *raison d'être*.

The pluralism underlying Newton's evangelical conscious-ness relates to a second point implicit in his text; namely, the inevitable tension that acceptable diversity created between inclusive and exclusive types of evangelicalism. This can be seen even more clearly in the case of Whitefield, whose wide travels across two continents exposed him to more of the varieties of Protestantism within the dominions of Great Britain than probably any of his contemporaries. Whitefield uniquely experienced an 'advanced pluralism' as time and again he crossed the threshold of religious communities whose loyalties had much to do with a local, or even national, history which he himself largely transcended simply by virtue of his extensive itinerancy. As a consequence, very early in White-field's career he encountered, as Newton did later, the problem of separatism. In 1741 in Scotland the Associate Presbytery of the Erskine brothers asked him to preach only for them as it was they who were truly the Lord's people. Famously, Whitefield rejected separatism in favour of trans-denominationalism, saying, 'If the Pope himself would lend

---

[66] See further, Watts, *Dissenters*, 263–393; Gilbert, *Religion and Society*, 1–48.

me his pulpit, I would gladly proclaim the righteousness of Jesus Christ therein.'[67]

Newton resolved the problem of evangelical diversity in a similar way, recognizing that evangelicalism could be trans-denominational only in so far as it subordinated distinctive denominational positions on matters of Church–State consti-tutionality, church order, and sacramental discipline to the overriding concern for the simple gospel. Thus he wrote in 1778 to an Antiburgher Secessionist in Scotland who, unlike those whom Whitefield had earlier met, was disposed to recognize other varieties of evangelicalism: 'My heart is . . . more especially with those who, like you, can look over the pales of an enclosure, and rejoice in the Lord's work where he is pleased to carry it on, under some difference of forms.'[68] But by abandoning the Puritan–Reformed question, 'What constitutes a true church?' for the Evangelical–Pietist question, 'What constitutes a true Christian?' Newton effect-ively committed himself to a low church ecclesiology.[69] This was the price that an inclusive evangelical was willing to pay to maintain maximum evangelical solidarity. And this was the route which Whitefield had taken earlier when he wrote to a Presbyterian minister: 'My one sole question is, *Are you a Christian?* . . . If so, you are my brother, my sister, and mother.'[70] Or as Joseph Milner put it in the preface to his church history, 'Genuine piety is the only thing, which I intend to celebrate.'[71] Among those who held a higher position on church order were many who still recognized a spiritual bond with other evangelicals. But the implication that one's fellow evangelical was schismatic, belonging only to a religious organization, not to the true church, could only act to restrain a fully transdenominational evangelical conscious-ness. Newton realized from the beginning that his *Apologia*

---

[67] *Works of the Revd. George Whitefield*, ed. John Gillies (1771), i. 308.
[68] *Letters* (Barlass), 49.
[69] Likewise, in 1788 and again in 1798 the members of the Eclectic Society agreed in affirming that there is no express form of church order binding upon the consciences of all. Newton, 'Minutes of the Eclectic Society [1787–9]'; *Thought of the Evangelical Leaders*, 3–6. Cf. Ward's description of 'the separation of religious from ecclesiastical life' in the 18th c. (*Protestant Evangelical Awakening*, 46).
[70] *Works of Whitefield*, i. 126.   [71] *History of the Church of Christ*, i. p. iv.

would receive a rough welcome from this quarter. To William Bull—an Independent, but one so broad-minded Newton could call him an Erastian—he wrote, 'I cannot expect that the high church folks, either on my own side or on yours, will be highly pleased.'[72] While inclusive evangelicals inhabited the ecclesiastical valleys, exclusive evangelicals dwelt further up the mountain of their own high churchmanship and were therefore at a further remove from their spiritual fellows on the slopes or peaks of other ecclesiologies. The inference is that, at least for Newton, evangelical consciousness, while not incompatible with either a developed ecclesiology or denominational aloofness, was of itself essentially *not* ecclesiological.

Newton's *Apologia* suggests that the evangelical disregard for ecclesiology was, at least in his case, based on a deeper assumption in evangelical consciousness that the spirit was opposed to the flesh. His discussion of the church as visible and invisible was drawn almost verbatim from Calvin (*Institutes*, 4. 1. 7), but he used it to very different effect. Whereas Calvin was concerned in page after page of the *Institutes* strongly to uphold the divinely ordered authority of the visible church, Newton's concern was principally with the church under its invisible, eschatological aspect; stressing that Christ's kingdom was not of this world and did not consist in 'meats and drinks' or 'forms and parties' (v. 41).[73] In his familiar correspondence he would often, in discussing the differences which separated devout Christians in his own day, conclude his case for mutual forbearance with a pietistic appeal to that future day when all divisions would be at an end. For Newton, the distinction between the church under its visible and mystical aspects gave way to what seemed a much more important distinction *within* the visible church, howsoever constituted, between nominal and true Christians. Here was the focus of evangelical, proselytizing ardour. The dialectic between visible and invisible was subtly exchanged for one between nature and grace. And whereas nominal profession of faith was linked with the merely physical aspects

---

[72] *Letters* (Bull), 194.
[73] Cf. Haweis' similar definition of the 'spiritual Church' in his *Impartial and Succinct History*, quoted in Wood, *Thomas Haweis*, 222.

of church life and discipline, true belief was equated with the wholly spiritual experience of regeneration. That the Christian life was an affair of the spirit was an underlying emphasis in Reformed theology which Newton elevated in his own under-standing of the church. In this he was abetted by the Enlightenment prejudices of his own age which perpetuated the so-called 'dissociated sensibility' found in the philosophical dualism of Descartes and the mechanistic worldview of Isaac Newton, in both of which the spiritual and material spheres appeared divided and detached.[74] Newton's use of the word 'spirituality' itself was always in this sense of something spiritual in contrast with something corporeal. Evangelicalism was to Newton essentially a form of this kind of spirituality.

In the picture Newton drew of evangelicalism, it appeared then as a highly amorphous movement, diverse and little concerned with ecclesiastical tradition or sensuous worship, but universally preoccupied with real belief over nominal profession. Not surprisingly therefore, the locus of evangel-icalism as a movement transcending denomination and party distinctions was largely outside authorized parochial or denominational structures. It was found instead in settings such as the gatherings of friends at Newton's house, or the meetings of the Eclectic Society at the Castle and Falcon, or the attempts to set up a non-partisan periodical. Although evangelicalism would remain an uneasy coalition, it would in the 1790s, under the impetus of its own growth, see this extra-ecclesiastical impulse expand with astonishing alacrity.

[74] On this element in the Reformed tradition, see Brooks Holifield, *The Covenant Sealed* (New Haven, 1974), 1–2. On Enlightenment dualism, see Hoyles, *Waning of the Renaissance*; id., *Edges of Augustanism.*

CONCLUSION

The men who ushered in new ways of christianizing their
world, Spener and Francke, Baxter and Watts, Doddridge
and Wesley all appeared as middle men of one kind or
another. Someone needed to mediate between the world
of ecclesiastical precision, and the world of spiritual
nutriment.

W. R. Ward

But I am a sort of middle man, and consequently no
great stress is laid upon me where the strengthening of a
party, or the fighting for a sentiment, is the point in view.

John Newton

During the last years of Newton's life, as his health deteriorated in old age, his world became increasingly confined to his
study at No. 6 Coleman Street Buildings and his pulpit at St
Mary Woolnoth, a few hundred yards away. After his wife's
death in 1790, he felt that the last cord which bound him to
this world had been severed, and only his potential usefulness
as a Christian minister could distract him from his desire for
heaven. His reputation continued to spread, and many came
to him or wrote to him for advice; but his counsel was spiritual
counsel, and his preoccupation was with the life of interior
piety. Consequently, he was, for the most part, only a passive
observer of many of the significant religious and political
changes which were taking place around him.

A number of factors point to a sea change in evangelicalism
in the early 1790s.[1] William Wilberforce (1759–1833) had
been converted in 1785, and in the 1790s his Parliamentary
career and leadership of the Abolition movement were
involving evangelicals as never before in a high level of public
and political discourse. No longer could public affairs be

---

[1] The periodization followed here is standard in many studies. See e.g. Elliott-
Binns, *Early Evangelicals*, 446–57; Ford K. Brown, *Fathers of the Victorians* (Cambridge,
1961), 1–4; Watts, *Dissenters*, 394–490; Rupp, *Religion in England*, 553–5.

viewed only as remote matters subject to Providence, about which evangelicals could do nothing. Newton's kind of acquiescent piety was increasingly out of step with the new possibilities open to evangelicals in the public sphere. Charles Simeon (1759–1836) was ordained Vicar of Holy Trinity at Cambridge in 1783, and his career, in a way parallel to that of Wilberforce, brought evangelicalism into a whole new level of political sophistication within the Church of England. His influence in raising up a generation of evangelical ordinands at Cambridge ('Simeonites'), his policy of purchasing advowsons to provide them places of ministry and ensure an evangelical succession, his influence upon the choice of chaplains for the East India Company—all of this reflected a shrewdness and level of partisan organization within the Church of England very different from what existed among evangelicals when Newton sought ordination.

To the careers of Wilberforce and Simeon may be added other developments marking the 1790s as a turning point within evangelicalism. In 1791 both John Wesley and the Countess of Huntingdon died, and Methodism was consequently forced into a new phase, in which the pattern of personal loyalty to a connexional leader was increasingly replaced by denominational modes of organization. As noted in the last chapter, evangelical Dissenters were, with Methodism, showing signs of the quickening rate of growth that would carry on well into the nineteenth century. Moreover, the French Revolution created a new point of tension between evangelicals within and without the Establishment, since it became easy to equate political and religious radicalism with Dissent once the Hanoverian Church–State constitution appeared to be threatened. There are signs that Newton himself shared these fears in the 1790s.[2]

But as far as evangelicalism was concerned, the most significant change noticeable in the 1790s was the increased size and visibility of the movement as a whole. The sense of evangelicalism having reached a new phase was captured by Newton in 1795:

[2] Bull, *Memorials of Bull*, 221.

Conclusion

The times are dark; but perhaps they were darker in *England* sixty
years ago, when, though we had peace and plenty, the bulk of the
kingdom lay under the judgment of an unregenerate ministry, and
the people were perishing for lack of knowledge. In this respect, the
times are better than they were. The gospel is preached in many
parts; we have it plentifully in London; and many of our great
towns, which were once sitting in darkness, have now the true light.
Some of those places were as a wilderness in my remembrance, and
now they are as gardens of the Lord. And every year the gospel is
planted in new places—ministers are still raising up—the work is
still spreading. I am not sure that in the year 1740, there was a
single parochial minister, who was publicly known as a gospel
preacher, in the whole kingdom: now we have, I know not how
many, but I think not fewer than four hundred.[3]

Newton noted elsewhere the same pattern of growth among
evangelical Dissenters.[4] He had the distinct sense in the 1790s
that he had lived to see a remarkable revival of religion. It had
begun in the 1740s and was now quickening pace, even as he
was himself preparing to die and pass on the torch to a new
generation of evangelicals.

It was during the half century between the 1740s and
1790s that Newton was converted, came to maturity, and
exercised his ministry in the Church of England. Newton's
genius was not as an original theologian like Jonathan
Edwards, a spectacular preacher like George Whitefield, or a
theological synthesizer and organizational leader like John
Wesley. His achievement was rather as a broker of consensus,
whose spirituality and manner of theological formulation
represented an ideal of evangelical catholicity. From a review
of Newton's life, work, and religious thought, it is evident that
he was a moderate on most matters of theological debate
among evangelicals during the last half of the eighteenth
century. He was pre-eminently a practical theologian whose
concerns were those of the conscientious pastor, parish
evangelist, and spiritual counsellor. In the midst of their
disagreements, John Wesley wrote to Newton, 'You appear to
be designed by Divine Providence for an healer of breaches, a

---

[3] *Letters* (Campbell), 75–6, cf. 141, 146; cf. *Letters* (Taylor), 117.
[4] *Letters* (Campbell), 38–9, 89, 102, 106–7, 141, 142.

reconciler of honest but prejudiced men, and an uniter (happy work!) of the children of God that are needlessly divided from each other.'[5] It is this reconciling breadth in Newton's evangelicalism that makes him so valuable for the religious historian. Newton circulated widely between Church and Dissent, among evangelicals whose beliefs ranged from the high Calvinist doctrine of eternal justification to the Wesleyan doctrine of Christian perfection. Developing his theology in this context, without merely equivocating between factions, he registered in his writings some of the most important, common features of evangelicalism. Moreover, because he disliked controversy and sought to find consensus whenever possible, the few points at which he felt bound to disagree with his contemporaries delimited a particularly broad conception of 'the Gospel world'. It should thus be possible to infer from Newton's experience his consciousness of the centre and the periphery of the evangelical movement in which he participated.

James Stephen declared of Newton: 'He became an absolute latitudinarian on all points of ecclesiastical polity.'[6] This is the first area in which Newton helps to define his contemporary evangelical milieu. Plainly, evangelicals did not have an agreed ecclesiology. 'High church folks' among Churchmen and Dissenters drew away from the principles which bound evangelicals to each other. This point was noted in the last chapter as a clear implication of Newton's *Apologia*. Whatever evangelicalism was, it was not something which could be spelled out into the details of ecclesiastical polity, or the relations of the Church to the State, or the administration and efficacy of the sacraments. However, the pluralism of the evangelical world did not trouble Newton; on the contrary, he celebrated the combined richness of insight it afforded into the gospel. Newton wrote whimsically of his own eclecticism, 'It is impossible I should be all of a colour, when I have been debtor to all sorts, and, like the jay in the fable, have been beholden to most of the birds in the air for a feather or two.

---

[5] *JWL* iv. 293.
[6] 'The Evangelical Succession', *Essays in Ecclesiastical Biography*, new edn. (1875), 405.

Church and Meeting, Methodist and Moravian, may all perceive something in my coat taken from them.'[7] To Newton, church order and ministry were in every sense matters of expediency, subordinate to evangelism and the spiritual nurture of individual believers.[8]

Nevertheless, Newton's famous hymn, 'Zion, or the City of God', expressed his unwavering confidence in the eschatological church of all ages:

> Glorious things of thee are spoken,
> Zion, city of our God!
> He, whose word cannot be broken,
> Form'd thee for his own abode:
> On the rock of ages founded,
> What can shake thy sure repose?
> With salvation's walls surrounded,
> Thou mayst smile at all thy foes.
>
> (*OH* 1. 60, st. 1)

The smiling security of the church was due to the walls of salvation which encompassed it. To change the metaphor, the church was less the ark of salvation, than salvation was the ark of the church. The citizens of Zion, though divided into different communions, were subjects together of the same 'Grace, which like the Lord, the giver | Never fails from age to age'. If the details of church order were on the margins of evangelical self-understanding, the conviction that believers shared in an invisible, transhistorical church was at the centre.

The nature of evangelical theology is a second area illuminated by Newton's biography. Newton's theology endeavoured to steer a middle course between Arminianism and high Calvinism. These positions represented two sides of a

---

[7] *Letters* (Bull), 25.

[8] Note, however, that at the end of Newton's life he regarded church order more highly than he had previously, even if this was still a matter of expediency. See e.g. the discussion of his opposition to the lay catechist scheme of the CMS in Hole, *Early History of the Church Missionary Society*, 65; and Eugene Stock, *History of the Church Missionary Society*, 3 vols. (1899), i. 72. In the mid-19th c., this meant that Newton could be seen, ironically, both as the embodiment of 'the true evangelical alliance principle' (Thomas Palmer Bull) and as the 'founder of the Evangelical Party' in the Church of England (James Stephen).

debate that was carried on within evangelicalism. What was clearly beyond the pale of evangelical conviction was the explicit avowal of outright legalism or antinomianism. Moreover, this study has sought to demonstrate the marked continuity of Newton's theology with a long tradition of Reformation and Puritan theology. While this tradition had been driven underground in the Church of England during the decades before the Evangelical Revival, it was preserved among Dissenters; and Newton's theological formation illustrated some of the ways in which this theological inheritance was transmitted to the new evangelical leaders.

In the eighteenth century, concern continued to focus upon the order of salvation, but Newton and his contemporaries, imbued with Enlightenment ideals, focused upon experience and indulged less rigorously in speculative theology than did their forebears. Newton appropriated the principle that religious experience itself is a more profound bond between Christians than the form of words in which it is expressed. It was thus that he was able to give Arminians such as Wesley the credit of being elect even though they did not maintain his particular doctrine of election. Contemporary aesthetic preferences for simplicity over discursiveness also encouraged the gospel message to be pared down to its most basic form, rather than festooned to its most elaborate, with reason understood to function more along Lockean (or Edwardsean) than Aristotelian or Ramist lines. But above all, Newton's concern was to edify; to offer, like Wesley, plain truth for plain people. At no point did Newton make predestination the leading speculative principle from which he derived an entire religious system; instead, his Calvinism was expressed in subdued tones in biographies, sermons, letters, hymnody—he did not bother to write treatises or polemical tracts, much less a body of divinity.

From Newton's experience, it would seem to follow that evangelical theology was generated in the desire to understand the pattern of divine initiative and human response in each stage of the process of salvation. This was central. Moreover, for the broad evangelical consciousness that Newton represented, this understanding had to be expressed without prolixity, for latitude implied a reduced creed of essential beliefs. 'Nice distinctions' only led away from the essentials on which evangelical solidarity was based. Newton neatly summarized these essentials for one of his enquirers in 1795:

I repeat my advice . . . to read the scriptures with prayer, to keep close to the important points, of human depravity, regeneration, the atonement, and the necessity of divine teaching. If a man is born again, hates sin, and depends upon the Saviour for life and grace, I care not whether he be an arminian or a calvinist. If he be not born again, he is nothing, let him be called by what name he will.[9]

These were fundamental convictions held in common with virtually all of his evangelical contemporaries.

The final aspect of the evangelical movement, which the study of Newton's life serves to elucidate, is its spirituality: the piety about which theology is only a description. The theme Newton celebrated above all others was the converting grace of God. From the *Authentic Narrative* it is plain that the experience of conversion was central to his evangelical conviction. Furthermore, the exposition of Newton's formative spirituality and his hymnody demonstrates that he understood conversion not only as the inauguration of the spiritual life, but also as the progressive, lifelong transformation of the believer. Union and communion with Christ, by the gracious agency of the Holy Spirit, through the lively exercise of faith, was the affective centre of Newton's evangelical spirituality. This was the goal towards which conversion was directed, both as an experience of initiation and as a process of incremental growth toward its full realization. All the benefits of salvation derived from, and were consummated in, union with Christ. It was thus that Newton's pastoral labours were directed towards the spiritual awakening of sinners and the spiritual maturation of believers. Through his conversion narrative, his letters of spiritual direction, and his hymns, Newton's life became a potent symbol of the whole evangelical experience.

[9] *Letters* (Coffin), 94.

APPENDIX

John Newton's Recorded Reading, 1725–1756

Annotated handlist of select authors and titles classified by period during which read

c.1729–32

Isaac Watts (1674–1748), *Catechisms: or, instructions in the principles of the Christian religion, and the history of Scripture, composed for children and youth* (1730), *Divine songs attempted in easy language for the use of children* (2nd edn., 1716), and [?*Prayers composed for the use and imitation of children, suited to their different ages and their various occasions* (1728)]; learned by heart as a child. (The first includes the Westminster *Shorter Catechism* of 1647.)

c.1732–41

Benjamin Bennet (1674–1726), *The Christian oratory: or, the devotion of the closet display'd* (3rd edn., 1732); basis of adolescent devotional practice.

Daniel Defoe (1661?–1731), *The family instructor*, i. (11th edn., 1734) and ii. (2nd edn., 1720), and [?*A new family instructor; containing, a brief and clear defence of the Christian religion in general, against the errors of the atheists, Jews, deists & sceptics: and . . . the Church of Rome* (1732)]; effected a 'transient reformation' in adolescence.

c.1742

Third Earl of Shaftesbury (1671–1713), *Characteristicks of men, manners, opinions, times*, ii. (6th edn., 1738); could nearly repeat the 'Rhapsody' verbatim, 'operated like a slow poison, and prepared the way for all that followed'.

1748

Thomas à Kempis (1380–1471), *The Christian's pattern: or . . . the imitation of Jesus Christ*, trans. George Stanhope [1660–1728] (13th edn., 1746); carelessly took it up 'as I had often done before' but now it occasioned pangs of conscience.

William Beveridge (1637–1708) [?*Sermons concerning the death, resurrection, and ascension of Christ* . . . (1709)]; the sermon on Christ's passion 'affected me much'.

1751–3 (at sea)

Gilbert Burnet (1643–1715), *The life and death of Sir Matthew Hale* (3rd edn., 1721); uses as model for detailed devotional scheme at sea.

Henry Scougal (1650–78), *The life of God in the soul of man* [pref. G. Burnet, R. Leighton's 'Rules' appended] (8th edn., 1749); 10-page extract in diary, had 'particular regard' for it. (An abridgment was published by John Wesley in 1744 and 1748.)

Philip Doddridge (1702–51), *Some remarkable passages in the life of Colonel James Gardiner* (1747); affected by it 'more frequently and sensibly than all the books I ever read'.

James Hervey (1714–58), *Meditations and contemplations*, 2 vols. (2nd edn., 1748); along with Scougal and Doddridge, 'gave me a farther view of Christian doctrine and experience'.

Robert Boyle (1627–91), Isaac Watts (1674–1748), Matthew Hale (1609–76), William Beveridge (1637–1708), John Howe (1630–1705); titles unidentified, but these authors 'and many others by whom God has been pleased to bless this nation' he proposed in July 1752 to read constantly in turn, recording their 'advices and examples' and striving to adopt them into practice. The 'great and good Mr. Boyle' appears again in August as an example of how to reverence the name of God.

1754–5 (at London)

John Owen (1616–83), *Christologia: or a declaration of the glorious mystery of the person of Christ, God and man* . . . (new edn., 1721); led him to pray for more knowledge of the mystery of godliness in Christ, 'a rich book, but the style something obscure'.

Theodosia Alleine, *The life and death of Mr. Joseph Alleine* [by his wife] (1672); prompted tears and expressions of desire to be spiritually useful. (Joseph Alleine, 1634–68.)

Thomas Halyburton (1674–1712), *An extract of the life and death of Mr. Thomas Halyburton*, [pref. by I. Watts] (2nd edn., 1718); of 'particular use' to him. (An abridgment was published by John Wesley in 1739, 1741, and 1747.)

Matthew Henry (1662–1714), *The Communicant's companion: or, instructions and helps for the right receiving of the Lord's Supper* (14th edn., 1752); followed closely in his own sacramental preparation.

James Hervey (1714–58), *Theron and Aspasio: or, a series of dialogues and letters, upon the most important and interesting subjects*, 3 vols. (1755); read and reread often, especially 9th dialogue, noting and approving the emphasis upon the 'glorious and comfortable doctrine of [God's] freely imputed, and only justifying righteousness', hoped the book would be widely useful.

Gilbert Burnet (1643–1715), [*The abridgment of the history of the reformation of the Church of England*, 2 vols. and suppl. (6th edn., 1728)]; reminded of how valuable his privileges are.

Voltaire (1694–1778), *The history of Charles XII, King of Sweden*, trans. from the French (8th edn., 1755); *The age of Lewis [sic] XIV*, trans. from the French (new edn., 1753); drew from these the lesson of the vanity of the world.

[?Edward Fisher (fl. 1627–55)] *The marrow of modern divinity ... touching both the covenant of works, and the covenant of grace* (Glasgow, 14th edn., 1752); 'with which I am much pleas'd, and hope to be benefitted'.

John Calvin (1509–64), *Institutes of the Christian religion* (1536); noted without comment.

John Wesley (1703–91), [?*An extract of the Reverend Mr. John Wesley's journal, from November 25, 1746, to July 20, 1750 [sic, 1749]* (1754)]; [?*Free-grace. A sermon preach'd at Bristol* (4th edn., 1754)]; pleased with the spirit but lamented some errors. (Newton noted in January 1755 having read the 'journal' and 'defence' of Wesley. The journal extract above was Wesley's seventh and most recent; however, there were several tracts related to the Calvinist controversy published in 1754/5 which could be the 'defence' referred to by Newton.)

George Whitefield (1714–70), [?*A letter to the Reverend Mr. John Wesley: in answer to his sermon entitled, Free-grace* (repr., 1752)]; [?*Nine sermons upon the following subjects; viz. I. The Lord our righteousness ...* (5th edn., 1750)]; noted with admiration and respect. (Newton noted in January 1755 having read some 'letters' and other 'pieces' of Whitefield, along with the sermon which stands first in the volume cited above.)

Daniel Defoe (1661?–1731), *Religious courtship: being historical* discourses on the necessity of marrying religious husbands and wives only (7th edn., 1750); 'engrossed my attention a good deal'.

Ralph Erskine (1685–1752), *Gospel-sonnets; or, spiritual songs* (6th edn., 1755); applied to himself the several marks and evidences of the truth of grace.

Henry Rimius (d. 1759?), *A candid narrative of the rise and progress of the Herrnhuters, commonly call'd Moravians or Unitas Fratrum, with a short account of their doctrines, drawn from their own writings* (1753); drew several lessons from the errors of the Moravians and determined never to leave the doctrines in which he had been established.

1755–6 (at Liverpool)

Richard Burnham (1711–52), *Pious memorials; or, the power of religion upon the mind in sickness and at death* [with preface by James Hervey] (1753); 'a choice collection of God's faithfulness'.

Ebenezer Erskine (1680–1754) and Ralph Erskine (1685–1752), *A collection of sermons on several subjects*, 3 vols. (1738–50); read with pleasure, warmed and enlarged his heart, one upon the rent veil of the temple 'a most excellent discourse'.

Thomas Cooper (*c.*1520–94), [?*Brief exposition* (1573)]; read several of Cooper's sermons as part of sabbath preparations.

Blaise Pascal (1623–62) [title unidentified]; noted without comment.

Isaac Watts (1674–1748), [?*Discourses of the love of God, and the use and abuse of the passions in religion* (1729)] or [?*The doctrine of the passions explain'd and improved* (4th edn., 1751)]; felt his own experience testified to the influence of divine love upon the passions.

Philip Doddridge (1702–51), *The rise and progress of religion in the soul: illustrated in a course of serious and practical addresses, suited to persons of every character and circumstances* (6th edn., 1753); aspired to the ideal scheme of managing a day, reviewed the chapter on a Christian temper, looking for evidence of it in himself; also *The family expositor: or, a paraphrase and version of the New Testament: with critical notes*, 2 vols. (3rd edn., 1756); extracted a harmonized life of Christ from it, and began conducting family worship shortly afterwards.

Robert Leighton (1611–84), *A practical commentary, upon the first epistle general of St. Peter*, 2 vols. (1701); 'several excellent things'; and [?*The expository works and other remains of Archbishop Leighton* (1748)]; read sermons and meditated on Leighton's rules to promote holy living.

Samuel Walker (1714–61), *The Christian. Being a course of practical sermons* (1755); read fourth sermon on John 6: 37 with much comfort.

Anthony Horneck (1641–97), *The happy ascetick; or, the best exercise, together with prayers suitable to each exercise* (6th edn., 1724); chose some rules to review every morning as a method of focusing his intention for the day.

Tobias Crisp (1600–43), *Christ alone exalted: being the compleat works of Tobias Crisp*, 2 vols. [ed. John Gill] (new edn., 1755); 'this author is branded an antinomian by many, but I know not why unless for exalting the power and grace of Christ'.

John Flavel (1630?–91), *Husbandry spiritualized: or the heavenly use of spiritual things* (9th edn., 1724); prompted expressions of longing for more spirituality.

Alexander Pope (1688–1744) [title unidentified]; read some of his satires.

Voltaire (1694–1778) [?*Micromegas: a comic romance . . . together with a detailed history of the crusades*, trans. from the French (1753)] and [*The history of the war of seventeen hundred and forty one*, English trans. (1756)]; found in these evidence of man's sin and God's providence.

William Romaine (1714–95), *A practical comment upon the 107th Psalm* (1755); this, with a sermon of Robert Leighton, prompted him to pray for such a faith and temper in the light of the impending war with France.

William Beveridge (1637–1708) [?*Sermons on faith and repentance* (1710)]; read sermon on the believer's call and election.

Elizabeth Singer Rowe (1674–1737), *The miscellaneous works, in prose and verse, of Mrs. Elizabeth Rowe*, 2 vols. (4th edn., 1756) [her popular *Devout exercises of the heart* was published by Isaac Watts]; prayed for a portion of her spirit.

John Shower (1657–1715), *Serious reflections on time and eternity. And some other subjects, moral and divine. With an appendix concerning the first day of the year.* (7th edn., 1752).

Note: Where the title has been inferred beyond reasonable doubt from a cryptic reference, this is indicated by square brackets; where the title is only suggested as the most probable, this is indicated by square brackets and an initial question mark. Bibliographic information is drawn from *The Eighteenth-Century Short Title Catalogue* (*ESTC*), and the publication date given is in most instances the date from the London edition or impression in the *ESTC* closest prior to the time of Newton's reading. Where the edition is not specifically identified, the date supplied is of the first edition, or the first to appear in the *ESTC*.

BIBLIOGRAPHY

1. MANUSCRIPTS

Angus Library, Regent's Park College, Oxford

John Ryland, Jun., 'An Account of the Rise and Progress of the Two Society's at Mr. Rylands and at Mrs. Trinder's Boarding School in Northampton', 1768–70.

John Ryland, Jun., 'The Experience of Jo/n R.l..d jun^r as wrote by himself in a Letter to Thos R..t dated Feb^y: 1770'.

Bodleian Library, University of Oxford

Wilberforce Papers
  Correspondence between Newton and William Wilberforce, 1794–1804.
  Letter from Thomas Robinson of Leicester to Newton, 1790.
Additional Wilberforce Papers
  MS autobiography of William Wilberforce.
  Correspondence between Newton and William Wilberforce, 1785–1803.
  Letters from Newton to Barbara Wilberforce, William Wilberforce of Wimbledon, Charles Middleton, Charles Grant, Hannah More.
MSS Willis, 98–100.
  Browne Willis, 'Parochial History of the Newport Pagnell Hundreds', *c*.1732, with additional notes *c*.1755 and later.

Borthwick Institute of Historical Research, York

Letter from Thomas Secker, Abp. of Canterbury, to John Gilbert, Abp. of York, 1758 (Bp. C&P, vii/175).
Letters from Lord Dartmouth to Henry Drummond, Abp. of York, 1764 (Bp. C&P, viii/290).
Institution Act Book, 1755–68.

Bristol Baptist College

Letters from Newton to John Ryland, Jun., 1771–1803.

British Library, London

Letters from Newton to William Cowper, 1767–81 (Eg. MS 3662).

Bibliography

Christ Church, Oxford

'Parochial Returns to Bishop Wake's Questionnaires of 1706, 1709, and 1712' (Wake MSS 275–6).

Cowper and Newton Museum, Olney, Buckinghamshire

Local History
  'Olney Workhouse Book Bought 1746', and another similar book recording the disbursements of the Overseers, 1746–82.
  Thomas Bainbridge, 'A Survey, Valuation and Plans of the Estates of the Right Honourable The Earl of Dartmouth situate at Olney, Warrington and Bradwell Abbey, in the County of Buckingham', 1796.
Newton MSS
  Family Bible, with autograph notes and family history on flyleaf.
  'Observations Critical and Explanatory, on all the Greek Words of ye New Testament', 1760–2, 2 vols., autograph MSS.
  'A List of the Children', 1765, notebook containing records of his meetings for children at Olney.
  Sermon and lecture notes, 29 notebooks, c.1765–85, some containing autograph diary entries, partly in shorthand.
  Notebook containing records of meetings of the Eclectic Society, 1789–95.
  Newton's autograph diary 1793–1807, entries written in an interleaved copy of his *Letters to a Wife* (1793), 2 vols.
  'Mr. Newton's account of Mr. Cowper in a Funeral Sermon', notes by Hannah Jowett, 1800.
Letters
  Letters from Newton to Josiah Jones, 1762, 1771; Joshua Symmonds, 1769–85; William Ward, 1796–8.
  Other letters from Newton to his wife, Anne Cave, Alexander Clunie, William Cowper, Richard Hansard and his wife, Elizabeth Kingsley, Hannah Wilberforce.
  Letters to Newton from William Cowper, 1776, 1780, 1788; and Joshua Symmonds, 1781.

Dr Williams's Library, London

Letters from Newton to David Jennings, 1750–60.
Letter from Newton to William Symonds, 1772.
'History of Dissenting Churches of the Congregationalist, Presbyterian and Antipaedobaptist Denominations in England and Wales' [1774] (Meen MSS).
'Biographical Collections, vol. 3' (Wilson MSS).

Bibliography

Emmanuel College, Cambridge
Letter from Newton to George Dyer, 1796.

Firestone Library, Princeton University
John Newton Collection
  Letters from Newton to William Cowper, 1780; and Thomas
    Haweis, 1763–4.
  Other letters from Newton to Robert Hall, Ebenezer Maitland,
    Dr Benamor, Hannah More, Thomas Robinson, Charles
    Grant, Josiah Jones, Joshua Symmonds, Revd Stevenson, Mrs
    Henry William Weber.
  Newton's notebook containing records of the meetings of the
    Eclectic Society, 1787–9.
  Miscellaneous poems and hymns by Newton; including
    transcripts of hymns by John Byrom, sent by Newton to
    Thomas Haweis.
John Wild Autograph Collection
  Letter from Newton to unidentified correspondent at Leicester,
    1782.
Hannay Collection
  Letters from William Cowper to Newton and his wife, 1780–3,
    1790.
  Letters from William Cowper to Matthew Powley, 1782.
  An unidentified commonplace book, c.1830, with cuttings from
    original letters by Newton, Cowper, Wilberforce, *et al.*
  Letter from William Bull to unidentified correspondent, 1811?
  Letters to Newton from William Hayley, 1803; Harriet Hesketh,
    1794–5; Mary Unwin, 1780, 1787. Other letters to Newton
    from John Johnson and William Unwin.
Hannay Collection, Box 9
  Letters from Newton to Cowper, 1767–98; John Thornton,
    1773–1802; and John Johnson, 1798–1800.
  Other letters from Newton to Samuel Greatheed, Mrs Hamilton,
    Mr Lucas, Hannah More, Mr and Mrs Nelson, Matthew
    Powley, John Ryland, Jun., Mary Unwin, Mrs Wathen, George
    West, Elizabeth Cunningham.
  Letter from James Stillingfleet to Matthew Powley, 1790.
  'Summary Account of Mrs [Susanna] Powley's Views and
    Experience of Divine Things in her Sickness in 1784', 23
    December 1784.
General MSS [bound]
  Correspondence between Newton and Cowper, 1771–97.
  Newton's autograph diary, 1751–6.

Bibliography

Newton's autograph diary, 1773–1805.
General MSS [misc.]
Letter from Newton to Mrs Cowell, 1784.
Kenneth Povey Collection
Letters from Newton to Caleb Warhurst and William Cowper.
Letter to Newton from William Unwin, 1767.
William Cowper Collection
Letters from Newton to William Cowper and Hannah More.
Robert H. Taylor Collection
Letter to Newton from William Cowper, 1785.
Letter from Newton to Revd Bowman, 1783.

Guildhall Library, London

Miscellaneous Items Relating to the Revd John Newton.
Letters from Newton to the Mitchell family, 1792, 1798; and Thomas Scott, 1779–80.
Parish Records for St Mary Woolnoth: Banns Books, 1759–1823 (some sermon notes by Newton in second volume);Lists of Preachers, 1789–1889; Vestry Minute Book, 1776–1817; 'The Unprinted Parish Registers of the United Parishes of St. Mary Woolchurch Haw and St. Mary Woolnoth, London', transcribed, typed, and indexed by Clifford R. Webb from MSS at the Guildhall Library, London, 1973.
Diocesan Records: Episcopal Visitation Books, vols. 44–50; London Diocese Books, 1770–c.1812, 1766–1810.

Historical Society of Pennsylvania, Philadelphia

Letters from Newton to Alexander Clunie, Mrs Walter Taylor, Josiah Jones, Mrs Dawson, H[annah] More, Peggy Swepston, Mrs Clurch, Capt. Clurch, Mr Mayer, William Ward, Lady Hesketh, Thomas Robinson, Mr Crawford, Mrs West.

Lambeth Palace Library, London

Ecclesiastical Records
Fulham Papers, Returns to Articles of Enquiry for St Mary Woolnoth (Osbaldeston 6, fo. 119, 1763; Porteus 28/53–1790).
Newton MSS
Newton's autograph diary, 'Miscellaneous Thoughts & Enquiries on an Important Subject', June 1758.
Newton's autograph diary for 1767, written in *The Complete pocket-book . . . for 1767*.
Newton's travel diaries for 1791–4, 1800, 1803.

340

Bibliography

Sermon and lecture notes, 3 notebooks, c.1771–3.
MS of Newton's *Letters to a Wife* (1793).
Sermons by John Laton of Chatham, transcribed by Newton, 1760–1.
Letters
  Correspondence between Newton and his wife, 1745–87; and William Bull, 1773–1804; and John Thornton, 1778–86.
  Letters from Newton to his wife's family: George Catlett, 1757; John Catlett, 1749–61; James and Elizabeth Cunningham, 1753–83; Elizabeth Catlett, 1779–88.
  Letters from Newton to Mrs Eversfield, Capt. R. Hunter, Hannah Wilberforce, George Whitefield, James Stillingfleet, Samuel Brewer, Mrs Trinder, Mary Unwin, Revd J. Mayer, Mrs E. Crabb, Miss J. Hunter, Revd J. Martin, Revd D. Williamson, Robert Hawker, Thomas Haweis.
  Letters to Newton from Revd T. Hartley, Mrs J. Thomason, Henry Venn, Capt. James Scott, Joseph Manesty, Martin Madan, Richard Conyers, I. Bennet, J. Raban, Charles Simeon, Samuel Teedon, John Berridge, the Dowager Countess of Elgin, Revd S. Webster, Claudius Buchanan, John Johnson, Harriet Hesketh, Mrs E. Harvey, Zachary Macaulay, M. Smith, Revd Aulay Macaulay, Thomas Robinson, R. Stockton, William Carey, H. R. Van Lier, J. Bull, T. Bryan.
  Letters of Mary Newton to Elizabeth Cunningham, Elizabeth Catlett, William Bull, Mrs E. Crabb; letters to Mary Newton from J. Raban and A. Glover.
  Correspondence and Papers of William Bull, 1750–1831.

Library Company of Philadelphia
Letter from Newton to Don Joseph Correa de Serra, 1793.

Lincolnshire Record Office, Lincoln
Diocesan Records: Libri Cleri for archdeaconry of Buckingham, 1763–84; Specula of diocese, c.1663–1792; Episcopal Register 39, beginning 9 December 1761.

Manuscripts in the possession of Miss Catherine Bull of Newport Pagnell
Letter from William Cowper to William Bull, 1782.
Letter from Newton to Thomas Haweis, 1780.

Mills Memorial Library, McMaster University, Hamilton, Canada
Unfinished memoir of William Cowper by Newton, 1800.

Bibliography

New York Public Library
Berg Collection
Robert Southey's notes on the life of Newton (1 fo.).

Public Record Office, Chancery Lane, London
Independent Church Meeting Book, Old Gravel Lane, Wapping (RG4/4304).
Probate of Newton's Will, 1803; codicil, 1804 (PROB. 11/1474).

Ridley Hall, Cambridge
Letters from Newton to John Thornton, 1773–8.

Southern Methodist University, Dallas, Texas
Letter from Newton to John Wesley, 18 April 1765.

University Library, University of Birmingham
CMS Archive
Correspondence between Newton and his wife, 1774–6; and letters from him to the family of Henry Venn.
Charles Hole's research notes and draft MS of a life of Newton.

University Library, University of Cambridge (Add. 7674, 7826)
Correspondence between Newton and John Thornton and his wife, 1770–1803.
Letters from John Thornton to William Richardson, 1776, 1777.

2. PRINTED PRIMARY SOURCES

(a) John Newton: Works, Letters and Early Biographies
The Aged Pilgrim's Triumph Over Sin and the Grave . . . a Series of Letters by the Rev. John Newton to Some of His Most Intimate Friends [Walter Taylor, William Cadogan, *et al.*] (1825).
BUNYAN, JOHN, *The Pilgrim's Progress*, [pt. 1], 3rd edn., with notes by John Newton and others (1789).
The Christian Character Exemplified, From the Papers of Mrs Margaret Magdalen A——S, Late Wife of Mr Frederick Charles A——S, of Goodman's Fields, ed. John Newton (Edinburgh, 1803).
The Christian Correspondent . . . Letters Written by the Rev. John Newton to Captain Alexr. Clunie (Hull, 1790).
The Correspondence of the Late Rev. John Newton with a Dissenting Minister [Samuel Palmer] *on Various Subjects and Occasions* (1809).

Bibliography

Historical Manuscripts Commission. XV Report, Appendix, Part 1, The Manuscripts of the Earl of Dartmouth, iii (1896) [containing correspondence of John Newton].

The Journal of a Slave Trader (John Newton): 1750–1754, ed. Bernard Martin and Mark Spurrell (1962).

Letters and Conversational Remarks of the Rev. John Newton, ed. John Campbell (1808).

Letters by the Rev. John Newton . . . with Biographical Sketches, ed. Josiah Bull (1869).

The Life and Writings of Mrs. Dawson . . . with nine unpublished letters from the Rev. John Newton (Kirkby Lonsdale, 1828).

Memoirs of the Life and Correspondence of Mrs Hannah More [including correspondence with John Newton], ed. William Roberts, 2nd edn., 4 vols. (1834).

Memoirs of the Life of the Late Rev. William Grimshaw . . . by John Newton . . . in Six Letters to the Rev. Henry Foster (1799; 1825).

One Hundred and Twenty Nine Letters from the Rev. John Newton to the Rev. William Bull (1847).

The Original Letters of the Reverend John Newton, A.M. [sic] *to the Rev. W. Barlass* (1819).

RYTHER, JOHN, *The Sea-Man's Preacher,* rev. edn., ed. Samuel Palmer, with a preface by John Newton (1803).

Sixty-Eight Letters from the Rev. John Newton to a Clergyman [James Coffin] *and his Family* (1845).

Twenty-Five Letters of the Rev. John Newton [to Robert and Josiah Jones] (Edinburgh, 1840).

The Works of the Rev. John Newton, 6 vols. (1808–9).

(b) Other Principal Sources and Contemporary Works

An Account of the Life, and Dealings of God with Silas Told, Late Preacher of the Gospel . . . Written by Himself (1786).

An Account of the Society for Promoting Religious Knowledge Among the Poor (1769).

Apologia Secunda: Or, a Supplementary Apology for Conformity. Two Epistles, Humbly Addressed to the Awakened Clergy. By a Layman. (1785).

The Arminian Magazine, 1–20 (1778–97).

Autobiography of William Jay, ed. George Redford and John Angell James (1st edn. 1854; repr., Edinburgh, 1974).

AVELING, THOMAS W., *Memorials of the Clayton Family* (1867).

BATEMAN, JOSIAH, *The Life of the Right Rev. Daniel Wilson,* 2 vols. (1860).

BEDDOME, BENJAMIN, *Hymns Adapted to Public Worship, or, Family Devotion* (1818).

BENNET, BENJAMIN, *The Christian Oratory*, 3rd edn. (1732).

BERRIDGE, JOHN, *Works of the Rev. John Berridge*, ed. Richard Whittingham (1838).

The Bible Preacher; or Closet Companion . . . Sermons . . . by the Late Rev. Henry Foster, ed. S. Piggot (1824).

Buckinghamshire Posse Comitatus 1798, ed. F. W. Beckett, Buckinghamshire Record Society, 22 (n.p., 1985).

BULL, JOSIAH, *John Newton of Olney* (1869).

—— *Memorials of the Rev. William Bull* (1864).

BURNET, GILBERT, *A Discourse of the Pastoral Care*, 5th edn. (1766).

—— *Conclusion of Bishop Burnet's History of His Own Life and Times* (1734).

Calendar of the Correspondence of Philip Doddridge, ed. G. F. Nuttall (1979).

CECIL, RICHARD, *Memoirs of the Rev. John Newton* (1827).

—— *Works of the Rev. Richard Cecil*, 3rd edn. (1827).

Conclusion of Bishop Burnet's History of His Own Life and Times (1734).

COWPER, WILLIAM, *Letters and Prose Writings of William Cowper*, 5 vols., ed. James King and Charles Ryskamp (Oxford, 1979–86).

—— *The Poems of William Cowper*, i. *1748–1782*, ed. John D. Baird and Charles Ryskamp (Oxford, 1980).

—— *The Poetical Works of William Cowper*, ed. H. F. Cary (1864).

CRISP, TOBIAS, *Christ Alone Exalted; the Complete Works of Tobias Crisp*, ed. John Gill, new 7th edn. (1832).

CULROSS, JAMES, *The Three Rylands* (1897).

DAWBARN, ROBERT (ed.), *History of a Forgotten Sect of Baptized Believers heretofore Known as 'Johnsonians'* (n.d.).

DEFOE, DANIEL, *A Tour Through the Whole Island of Great Britain*, 7th edn., 4 vols. (1769).

DODDRIDGE, PHILIP, *The Rise and Progress of Religion in the Soul*, new edn. (1816).

—— *Some Remarkable Passages in the Life of Colonel James Gardiner* (1747).

EDWARDS, JONATHAN, *Freedom of Will*, ed. Paul Ramsey, i, *Works of Jonathan Edwards*, ed. J. E. Smith (New Haven, 1957).

—— *On Revival* [*A Narrative of Surprising Conversions; The Distinguishing Marks of a Work of the Spirit of God; An Account of the Revival of Religion in Northampton 1740–1742*], new edn. (Edinburgh, 1965).

—— *Treatise Concerning the Religious Affections* (1st edn., 1746; repr., Edinburgh, 1986).

Bibliography

[ENFIELD, WILLIAM], *The Monthly Review*, 71 (1784), 426–9; 77 (1787), 211–13 [reviews of Newton's writings].

The Evangelical Magazine, 1–112 (1793–1905).

Familiar Letter of Reproof and Humiliation to the Rev. Thomas Towle . . . on his . . . Conduct Respecting the Publisher and Publication of . . . the New Spiritual Magazine . . . by a Clergyman of the Established Church [1785].

FLAVEL, JOHN, *Navigation Spiritualized: or, a New Compass for Seamen* (1682; 5th edn. 1708).

GAMBOLD, JOHN, *A Collection of Hymns of the Children of God in all Ages* (1754).

GIBSON, EDMUND, *Codex Juris Ecclesiastici Anglicani*, 2nd edn. (Oxford, 1761).

GILL, JOHN, *The Cause of God and Truth*, new edn. (1855).

—— *The Doctrines of God's Everlasting Love to His Elect, and Their Eternal Union with Christ . . . In a Letter to Dr. Abraham Taylor* (1732).

The Gospel Magazine, 1–7 (1766–73); ns 1–10 (1774–83).

HALYBURTON, THOMAS, *An Essay Concerning the Nature of Faith* (Edinburgh, 1714).

—— *A Modest Enquiry Whether Regeneration or Justification Has the Precedency in Order of Nature* (Edinburgh, 1714).

HART, J, *Hymns, etc., Composed on Various Subjects, with a Preface Containing a Brief Summary Account of the Author's Experience and the Great Things that God Hath Done for his Soul* (1759).

HAWEIS, THOMAS, *Carmina Christo; Hymns to the Saviour* (Bath, 1792).

—— *An Impartial and Succinct History of the Rise, Declension and Revival of the Church of Christ, from the Birth of Our Saviour to the Present Time* (1800).

HUSSEY, JOSEPH, *God's Operations of Grace but No Offers of Grace* (1707).

JERRAM, J., *Memoirs and a Selection from the Letters of . . . Charles Jerram* (1855).

'Life of the Rev. Samuel Brewer', *Evangelical Magazine*, 5 (1797), 5–18.

MADAN, MARTIN, *Collection of Psalm and Hymn Tunes Never Published before* (1769).

MANNERS, NICHOLAS, *The Life and Experience of Nicholas Manners* (York, 1785).

—— *Strictures on Omicron's Ninth Letter; the Subject of Which is Election and Perseverance* (Warrington, 1778).

MATHER, COTTON, *Magnalia Christi Americana* (1702).

[MAYO, HENRY], *An Apology and a Shield for Protestant Dissenters, In*

Bibliography

These Times of Instability and Misrepresentation. Four Letters to the Rev. Mr. John Newton . . . by a Dissenting Minister (1784).

'Memoir of the Late Rev. John Newton', *Evangelical Magazine*, 16 (1808), 49–60, 97–112.

'Memoir of the Late Rev. John Ryland, D.D.', *Baptist Magazine*, 18 (1826), 1–9.

MILNER, ISAAC, *Account of the Life and Character of the Rev. Joseph Milner*, new edn. (1804).

MILNER, JOSEPH, *The History of the Church of Christ*, 5 vols. (1794–7), 3rd edn., ed. Isaac Milner [vol. v, with additions by Isaac Milner] (1812).

Miscellaneous Collection of Satirical Pieces in Prose and Verse, Respecting Master Tommy Dishclout, B.D., and Some of His Learned Friends, Which Have Appeared at Different Times in the Various Magazines . . . by an Enemy to Acts of Injustice [1785?].

MYLES, WILLIAM, *A Chronological History of the People Called Methodists* (1803).

The New Spiritual Magazine, 1–3 (1783–5).

OWEN, JOHN, *A Practical Exposition on the 130th Psalm* (1669).

PALMER, SAMUEL, *The Protestant-Dissenter's Catechism* (1773).

PEARSON, HUGH, *Memoirs of the Life and Writings of the Rev. Claudius Buchanan* (1819).

PRATT, JOHN H., *The Thought of the Evangelical Leaders: Notes of the Discussions of the Eclectic Society* (1856; repr. Edinburgh, 1978).

PRATT, JOSIAH, *The Life, Character, and Remains of the Rev. Richard Cecil*, 5th edn. (1816).

Private Journals and Literary Remains of John Byrom, ed. Richard Parkinson, 2 vols. (Manchester, 1854–7).

The Protestant Dissenters Magazine, 1–6 (1794–9).

The Register of the Parish of Olney, Co. Bucks, 1665 to 1812, 2 vols., transcribed by O. Ratcliff [Olney, 1909].

RIPPON, JOHN, *The Baptist Annual Register for 1790, 1791, 1792, and Part of 1793* (1793).

—— *A Selection of Hymns From the Best Authors* (1827).

ROGERS, WOODES, *Cruising Voyage Round the World* (1712).

ROMAINE, WILLIAM, *A Practical Comment upon the 107th Psalm*, 5th edn. (1767).

—— *An Essay on Psalmody* (1775).

—— *Treatises upon the Life, Walk and Triumph of Faith*, new edn. in one vol. (1911).

RYLAND, JOHN, JUN. *Compendious View of the Principal Truths of the Glorious Gospel of Christ* (1769).

—— *The Life and Death of the Reverend Andrew Fuller* (1816).

—— *Pastoral Memorials of the Rev. John Ryland*, 2 vols. (1826).

—— *Serious Essays on the Truths of the Glorious Gospel, and the Various Branches of Vital Experience* (1771).

—— *Serious Remarks on the Different Representations of Evangelical Doctrine* (Bristol, 1817).

SCOTT, JOHN, *The Life of the Rev. Thomas Scott*, 6th edn. (1824).

SCOTT, THOMAS, *The Force of Truth: An Authentic Narrative* (1st edn., 1779; repr., Edinburgh, 1984).

—— *Letters and Papers of the Late Rev. Thomas Scott*, ed. John Scott (1824).

SEYMOUR, A. C. H., *The Life and Times of Selina Countess of Huntingdon*, 2 vols. (1840).

SMALLEY, JOHN, *The Consistency of the Sinner's Inability to Comply with the Gospel; with His Inexcusable Guilt in Not Complying with It, Illustrated and Confirmed: in Two Discourses on John VIth, 44th* (Hartford, 1769).

The Theological Miscellany, 1–6 (1784–9).

'The True Travels, Adventures and Observations of Captain John Smith', in *A Collection of Voyages and Travels*, 6 vols., ed. Awnsham and John Churchill (1732).

To the Beneficed Clergy of the Diocese of London, the Humble Address of their (as yet uninfected) Parishioners, printed notice (1759).

TOULMIN, JOSHUA, 'A Review of the Life and Writings of the Rev. David Jennings, D.D.', *Protestant Dissenters Magazine*, 5 (Mar. 1798), 81–9 (Apr. 1798), 121–7.

The Transcript of the Registers of the United Parishes of St. Mary Woolnoth and St. Mary Woolchurch Haw . . . 1538–1760, transcribed by J. M. S. Brooke and A. W. C. Hallen (1886).

A True and Particular Account of a Surprising and Wonderful Noise that was Heard in the Steeple of the Church at Olney . . . [1768].

VENN, HENRY, *The Complete Duty of Man*, new edn. (1841).

VENN, JOHN, *Life and a Selection from the Letters of the Late Rev. Henry Venn*, ed. Henry Venn, 2nd edn. (1835).

WALLIN, BENJAMIN, Preface to *Evangelical Hymns and Songs* (1750).

WATTS, ISAAC, *Hymns and Spiritual Songs*, 17th edn. (1751).

WESLEY, JOHN, *The Bicentennial Edition of the Works of John Wesley*, ed. R. P. Heitzenrater and Frank Baker (multi-volume work in progress) (Oxford, 1975–83; Nashville, 1983–).

—— *Letters of the Rev. John Wesley*, 8 vols., ed. John Telford (1931).

—— *Journal of the Rev. John Wesley*, 8 vols., ed. Nehemiah Curnock (1909–16).

—— *The Works of John Wesley*, ed. Thomas Jackson, 14 vols. (1872).

WHITEFIELD, GEORGE, *Journals* (Edinburgh, 1960).

Bibliography

WHITEFIELD GEORGE, *Works of the Revd. George Whitefield*, ed. John
Gillies, 6 vols. (1771).

WILBERFORCE, ROBERT ISAAC, and WILBERFORCE, ROBERT (eds.), *The
Correspondence of William Wilberforce*, 2 vols. (1840).

—— *The Life of William Wilberforce*, 5 vols. (1838).

WILLIS, BROWNE, *History and Antiquities of Buckingham* (1755).

3. SECONDARY SOURCES

ABBEY, CHARLES J., *The English Church and its Bishops, 1700–1800*, 2
vols. (1887).

—— and OVERTON, JOHN H., *The English Church in the Eighteenth
Century*, 2 vols. (1878).

ADEY, LIONEL, *Hymns and the Christian 'Myth'* (Vancouver, 1986).

—— *Class and Idol in the English Hymn* (Vancouver, 1988).

ALTHOLZ, JOSEPH L., *Religious Press in Britain, 1760–1900*, Contributions to the Study of Religion, 22, ed. H. W. Bowden (New York,
1989).

ANDERSON, HOWARD, DAGHLIAN, PHILIP B., and EHRENPREIS, IRVING
(eds.), *Familiar Letter in the Eighteenth Century* (Lawrence, Kan.,
1966).

ANSTEY, ROGER, *The Atlantic Slave Trade and British Abolition* (1975).

ARNOLD, RICHARD (ed.), *English Hymns of the Eighteenth Century: An
Anthology* (New York, 1991).

BAKER, FRANK, *Representative Verse of Charles Wesley* (1962).

—— *William Grimshaw, 1708–1763* (1963).

—— *John Wesley and the Church of England* (1970).

—— Introduction to *Letters I: 1721–1739*, ed. Frank Baker, vol. xxv
in *The Works of John Wesley*, ed. Richard P. Heitzenrater and Frank
Baker (Oxford, 1980), 1–140.

BALLEINE, G. R., *A History of the Evangelical Party in the Church of
England*, new edn. (1951).

BARTH, ROBERT J, *The Symbolic Imagination* (Princeton, 1977).

BAXTER, RICHARD, *The Reformed Pastor*, new edn. (1862).

—— *The Saints' Everlasting Rest*, new edn. (1960).

BEBBINGTON, DAVID W., *Evangelicalism in Modern Britain: A History
from the 1730s to the 1980s* (1989).

BELDEN, ALBERT, *George Whitefield: The Awakener*, 2nd edn. (1953).

BENSON, LOUIS F., *The English Hymn: Its Development and Use in
Worship* (New York, 1915).

—— *The Hymnody of the Christian Church*. Stone Lectures, 1926 (New
York, 1927).

BETT, HENRY, *The Hymns of Methodism*, 3rd edn. (1945).

348

BOGUE, DAVID, and BENNETT, JAMES, *History of Dissenters*, 4 vols. (1812).

BOLAM, C. G., GORING, JEREMY, SHORT, H. L., and THOMAS, ROGER, *The English Presbyterians* (1968).

BOUYER, LOUIS, *et al.* (eds.), *A History of Christian Spirituality*, 3 vols. (Tunbridge Wells, Kent, 1968).

BRANTLEY, RICHARD E., *Wordsworth's 'Natural Methodism'* (New Haven, 1975).

—— *Locke, Wesley, and the Method of English Romanticism, 1700–1830* (Gainesville, Fla., 1984).

BRIGDEN, T. E., 'Notes and Queries', *Proceedings of the Wesley Historical Society*, 3 (1901), 118.

BROAD, JOHN (ed.), *Buckinghamshire Dissent and Parish Life, 1669–1712* (Aylesbury, 1993).

BROWN, FORD K., *The Fathers of the Victorians: The Age of Wilberforce, 1780–1840* (Cambridge, 1961).

BROWN, JOHN, *John Bunyan* (1928).

BROWN, RAYMOND, *English Baptists of the Eighteenth Century*, History of the English Baptists, 2, ed. B. R. White (1986).

BULL, FREDERICK WILLIAM, *A History of Newport Pagnell* (Kettering, 1900).

BUNYAN, JOHN, *Grace Abounding to the Chief of Sinners* (1666; Oxford, 1962; Welwyn, 1983).

CAIRNS, WILLIAM T., 'John Newton: A Vindication', in *The Religion of Dr Johnson and Other Essays* (1946), 24–57.

CALDWELL, PATRICIA, *The Puritan Conversion Narrative* (Cambridge, 1983).

Calendar of State Papers, Domestic Series, of the Reign of Charles I (1635–6), ed. John Bruce (1866).

Calendar of State Papers, Domestic Series, of the Reign of Charles II (1672), ed. F. H. Blackburne Daniell (1899).

CALVIN, JOHN, *The Institutes of the Christian Religion*, ed. John T. McNeill, trans. Ford Lewis Battles, 2 vols., Library of Christian Classics, 22 (Philadelphia, 1954).

CARUS, WILLIAM, *Memoirs of the Life of the Rev. Charles Simeon*, 3rd edn. (1848).

CECIL, LORD DAVID, *The Stricken Deer: The Life of Cowper*, new edn. (1943).

CHAMPION, L. G., 'The Letters of John Newton to John Ryland', *Baptist Quarterly*, 27 (1977), 157–63.

CLIFFORD, ALAN C., *Atonement and Justification: English Evangelical Theology, 1640–1790, An Evaluation* (Oxford, 1990).

COLERIDGE, SAMUEL TAYLOR, *Biographia Literaria*, vol. i of *The*

Bibliography

Collected Works of Samuel Taylor Coleridge, no. 7, Bolligen Series, 75 (1983).

COLLINSON, PATRICK, *Elizabethan Puritan Movement*, 1st paperback edn. (Oxford, 1990).

Constitutions and Canons Ecclesiastical, 1604, with notes by J. V. Bullard (1934).

COPPEDGE, ALLAN, 'John Wesley and the Doctrine of Predestination', Ph.D. thesis (Cambridge, 1976).

COUPLAND, REGINALD, *Wilberforce*, 2nd edn. (1945).

CRAWFORD, MICHAEL, *Seasons of Grace: Colonial New England's Revival Tradition in Its British Context* (New York, 1991).

CROSSMAN, A. B., 'The Buckinghamshire Posse Comitatus 1798', *Milton Keynes Journal of Archeology and History*, 2 (1973), 20–8.

DAGHLIAN, PHILIP B. (ed.), *Essays in Eighteenth-Century Biography* (1968).

DALLIMORE, ARNOLD, *George Whitefield*, 2 vols. (Edinburgh, 1970).

DAVIE, DONALD, *Purity of Diction in English Verse* (1952).

—— *A Gathered Church: The Literature of the English Dissenting Interest, 1700–1930* (1978).

—— Introduction to *The New Oxford Book of Christian Verse*, ed. Donald Davie (Oxford, 1981).

—— *Dissentient Voice* (Notre Dame, Ind., 1982).

—— *The Eighteenth-Century Hymn in England* (Cambridge, 1993).

DAVIES, G. C. B., *The Early Cornish Evangelicals* (1951).

DAVIES, RUPERT, and RUPP, GORDON (eds.), *A History of the Methodist Church in Great Britain*, i (1965).

DELANY, PAUL, *British Autobiography in the Seventeenth Century* (1969).

DEMARAY, DONALD E, *The Innovation of John Newton (1725–1807): Synergism of Word and Music in Eighteenth Century Evangelism*, Texts and Studies in Religion, 36 (Lewiston, NY, 1988) [published version of the following].

—— 'John Newton (1725–1807)', Ph.D. thesis (Edinburgh, 1952).

DREYER, F. D., 'Faith and Experience in the Thought of John Wesley', *American Historical Review*, 87 (1983), 12–30.

EDWARDS, BRIAN HERBERT, *Through Many Dangers* (Welwyn, 1975).

ELLA, GEORGE MELVYN, *Paradise and Poetry: An In-Depth Study of William Cowper's Poetic Mind* (Olney, 1989).

—— *William Cowper: Poet of Paradise* (Darlington, 1993).

ELLIOTT-BINNS, L. E., *The Early Evangelicals: A Religious and a Social Study* (1953).

ENGELL, JAMES, *The Creative Imagination: Enlightenment to Romanticism* (Cambridge, Mass., 1981).

Bibliography

ERB, PETER C. (ed.), *Pietists: Selected Writings* (1983).

FORSYTH, P. T., *Positive Preaching and the Modern Mind* (1907).

FRYE, NORTHROP, *The Great Code: The Bible and Literature* (1982).

—— 'Towards Defining an Age of Sensibility', *Journal of English Literary History*, 23 (1956), 144–52.

GARNETT, JANE, and MATTHEW, COLIN (eds.), *Revival and Religion since 1700: Essays for John Walsh* (1993).

GILBERT, ALAN D, *Religion and Society in Industrial England* (1976).

GILL, FREDERICK, *The Romantic Movement and Methodism* (1937).

GORDON, GRANT, 'John Newton: A Study of a Pastoral Correspondent', Th.M. thesis (Princeton Theological Seminary, 1987).

—— 'The Call of Dr John Ryland Jr', *Baptist Quarterly*, 34 (1992), 214–17.

GORDON, JAMES, *Evangelical Spirituality from the Wesleys to John Stott* (1991).

GUEST, HARRIET, *A Form of Sound Words: The Religious Poetry of Christopher Smart* (Oxford, 1989).

GUNTER, STEPHEN W., *The Limits of 'Love Divine': John Wesley's Response to Antinomianism and Enthusiasm* (Nashville, 1989).

HALLER, WILLIAM, *The Rise of Puritanism* (New York, 1938).

HARTLEY, LODWICK, 'Cowper and the Evangelicals: Notes on Early Biographical Interpretations' *PMLA* 65 (1950), 719–31.

—— *William Cowper: The Continuing Evaluation* (Chapel Hill, NC, 1960).

HAYDEN, ROGER, 'Evangelical Calvinism Among Eighteenth-Century British Baptists', Ph.D. thesis (Keele, 1991).

HAYKIN, MICHAEL A. G., 'Anglican and Baptist: A View from the Eighteenth Century', *Prolegomena*, 2 (1990), 21–8.

—— ' "A Habitation of God, Through the Spirit": John Sutcliff (1752–1814) and the Revitalization of the Calvinistic Baptists in the late Eighteenth Century', *Baptist Quarterly*, 34 (1992), 304–19.

—— 'John Sutcliff and the Concert of Prayer', *Reformation and Revival*, 1 (1992), 65–88.

—— *One Heart and One Soul: John Sutcliff of Olney, His Friends and His Times* (Darlington, 1994).

HILDEBRANDT, F., BECKERLEGGE, O. A., and DALE, J., 'Introduction', in John Wesley (ed.), *A Collection of Hymns for the use of the People called Methodists*, ed. Hildebrandt, Beckerlegge, and Dale, Oxford Edition of the Works of John Wesley, vii (Oxford 1983), 1–69.

HENNELL, MICHAEL, *John Venn and the Clapham Sect* (1958).

HENRY, MATTHEW, *The Communicant's Companion: or, Instructions and Helps for the Right Receiving of the Lord's Supper* (1715).

HEWETT, MAURICE F., 'John Gibbs, 1627–1699', *Baptist Quarterly*, 3 (1926–7), 315–22.

HILL, CHRISTOPHER, *A Turbulent, Seditious, and Factious People: John Bunyan and His Church, 1628–1688* (Oxford, 1988).

History of the Congregational Church at Olney (Olney, 1929).

HOLE, CHARLES, *The Early History of the Church Missionary Society* (1896).

HOLIFIELD, E. BROOKS, *The Covenant Sealed: The Development of Puritan Sacramental Theology in Old and New England, 1570–1720* (New Haven, 1974).

HOLMES, URBAN T. III., *A History of Christian Spirituality: An Analytical Introduction* (San Francisco, 1980).

HOYLES, JOHN, *The Waning of the Rennaissance 1640–1740: Studies in the Thought and Poetry of Henry More, John Norris and Isaac Watts*, International Archives of the History of Ideas, 39 (The Hague, 1971).

—— *The Edges of Augustanism: The Aesthetics of Spirituality in Thomas Ken, John Byrom and William Law*, International Archives of the History of Ideas, 53 (The Hague, 1972).

HUTTON, J. E., *History of the Moravian Church* (1909).

HYLSON-SMITH, KENNETH, *Evangelicals in the Church of England, 1734–1984* (Edinburgh, 1988).

JARVIS, RUPERT C., *Customs Letter-Books of the Port of Liverpool, 1711–1813* (Manchester, 1954).

JAY, ELIZABETH, *The Religion of the Heart* (Oxford, 1979).

JONES, R. TUDOR, *Congregationalism in England, 1662–1962* (1962).

KING, JAMES, *William Cowper* (Durham, NC, 1986).

KOLPAS, SIDNEY, 'The Quest for James Coffin', *Book Collector*, 39 (1990), 220–34.

LANGFORD, PAUL, *A Polite and Commercial People: England, 1727–1783* (Oxford, 1989).

LAWTON, GEORGE, *Within the Rock of Ages: Life and Work of Augustus Montague Toplady* (Cambridge, 1983).

LEAVER, ROBIN, 'Olney Hymns 1779: 1. The Book and its Origins', *Churchman*, 93/4 (1979), 327–9.

—— 'Olney Hymns 1779: 2. Hymns and their Use', *Churchman*, 94/1 (1980), 58–66.

—— 'Olney Hymns: A Documentary Footnote', *Churchman*, 97/3 (1983), 244–5.

LECKY WILLIAM E. H., *History of England in the Eighteenth Century*, 7 vols. (1st edn. 1897–9; repr., 1921).

LINDSTRÖM, HARALD, *Wesley and Sanctification: A Study in the Doctrine of Salvation* (1946).

Bibliography

LIPSCOMB, GEORGE, *History and Antiquities of the County of Buckingham*, iv (1847).

LOANE, MARCUS, *Oxford and the Evangelical Succession* (1951).

LOVEGROVE, DERYCK, 'Idealism and Association in Early Nineteenth Century Dissent', in *Voluntary Religion*, Studies in Church History, 23, ed. W. J. Shiels and Diana Wood (Oxford, 1986), 303–17.

LOWANCE, MASON I., JR., *The Language of Canaan* (Cambridge, Mass., 1980).

McLACHLAN, H., *English Education under the Test Acts* (Manchester, 1931).

McLOUGHLIN, WILLIAM, *Revivals, Awakenings, and Reform: An Essay on Religion and Social Change in America, 1607–1977*, Chicago History of American Religion, ed. Martin E. Marty (Chicago, 1978).

MANNING, BERNARD L., *The Hymns of Wesley and Watts: Five Informal Papers* (1942).

MARSHALL, MADELEINE FORELL, and TODD, JANET, *English Congregational Hymns in the Eighteenth Century* (Lexington, Ken., 1982).

MARTIN, BERNARD, *The Ancient Mariner and the Authentic Narrative* (1949).

—— *John Newton* (1950).

—— *John Newton and the Slave Trade* (1961).

—— 'New Light on William Cowper', *English*, 7 (1950–1), 67–8.

—— 'Some Dissenting Friends of John Newton', *Congregationalist Quarterly*, 29 (1951), 133–44, 236–45.

MARTIN, ROGER, *Evangelicals United: Ecumenical Stirrings in Pre-Victorian Britain, 1795–1830*, Studies in Evangelicalism, 4 (1983).

MATHER, F. C., 'Georgian Churchmanship Reconsidered: Some Variations in Anglican Public Worship 1714–1830', *Journal of Ecclesiastical History*, 36 (1985), 255–83.

MAURICE, H., *An Impartial Account of Mr. John Mason of Water-Stratford, and his Sentiments* (1695).

MIDDLETON, JOHN WHITE, *Ecclesiastical Memoir of the First Four Decades of the Reign of George the Third* (1822).

MILLER, HUGH, *First Impressions of England and Its People* (1847).

'Mr. Thomas Trinder', Biographical notice xxix in *Biographies: Northamptonshire*, ed. John Taylor (Northampton, 1901).

MYERS, ROBERT MANSON, 'Fifty Sermons on Handel's Messiah', *Harvard Theological Review* 39/4 (Oct. 1946), 217–41.

NAYLOR, PETER, *Picking up a Pin for the Lord: English Particular Baptists from 1688 to the Early Nineteenth Century* (1992).

NOLL, MARK, BEBBINGTON, DAVID, and RAWLYK, GEORGE (eds.), *Evangelicalism: Comparative Studies of Popular Protestantism in North America, the British Isles, and Beyond, 1700–1990* (New York, 1994).

NUTTALL, GEOFFREY, F., 'Northamptonshire and *The Modern Question*: A Turning-Point in Eighteenth-Century Dissent', *Journal of Theological Studies*, NS 16 (1965), 101–23.

—— 'Methodism and the Older Dissent', *United Reformed Church Historical Society Journal*, 2 (1981), 259–74.

—— 'Baptists and Independents in Olney to the Time of John Newton', *Baptist Quarterly*, 30 (1983), 26–37.

O'BRIEN, SUSAN, 'A Transatlantic Community of Saints: The Great Awakening and the First Evangelical Network, 1735–1755', *American Historical Review*, 91 (1986), 811–32.

'O for a Closer Walk—a Note on its Original Tune', *Hymn Society of Great Britain and Ireland: Bulletin*. 8/5 (Winter, 1974), 87.

OLLARD, S. L., *The Six Students of St. Edmund Hall Expelled from the University of Oxford in 1768* (Oxford, 1911).

OLNEY, JAMES, *Metaphors of Self: The Meaning of Autobiography* (Princeton, 1972).

—— (ed.), *Autobiography: Essays Theoretical and Critical* (Princeton, 1980).

OVERTON, JOHN HENRY, *The Evangelical Revival in the Eighteenth Century* (1886).

—— *William Law . . . A Sketch of His Life, Character, and Opinions* (1881).

OVERTON, JOHN and RELTON, FREDERIC, *The English Church from the Accession of George I to the End of the Eighteenth Century* (1906).

OWEN, J., *Memoirs of Thomas Jones* (1851).

OWEN, JOHN, *Works*, ed. W. H. Goold, 16 vols. (modern repr., Edinburgh, 1965–8).

PARKER, J. I., *Among God's Giants: Aspects of Puritan Christianity* (Eastbourne, Sussex, 1991).

PAGE, WILLIAM (ed.), *Victoria History of London*, i (1909).

—— (ed.), *Victoria History of the Counties of England: Buckinghamshire*, iv (1927).

PARKER, M. PAULINE, 'The Hymn as a Literary Form', *Eighteenth-Century Studies*, 8 (1975), 392–419.

PARKINSON, F. M., 'Notes on Methodism in Liverpool', *Proceedings of the Wesley Historical Society*, 1 (1898), 104–8; 2 (1899), 65–8.

PATTISON, MARK, 'Tendencies of Religious Thought in England, 1688–1750', in *Essays and Reviews*, 2nd edn. (1860), 254–329.

PETERSON, LINDA H., 'Newman's *Apologia pro vita sua* and the Traditions of the English Spiritual Autobiography', *PMLA*, 100 (1985), 300–14.

PODMORE, C. J., 'The Bishops and the Brethren: Anglican Attitudes to the Moravians in the Mid-Eighteenth Century', *Journal of Ecclesiastical History*, 41 (1990), 622–46.

—— (ed.), *Fetter Lane Moravian Congregation, London, 1742–1992* (1992).

POLLOCK, JOHN, *Wilberforce* (1977).

—— *Amazing Grace* (1981).

PORTER, ROY, *English Society in the Eighteenth Century*, rev. edn. (Harmondsworth, 1990).

POURRAT, PIERRE, *Christian Spirituality*, 3 vols. (Tunbridge Wells, 1922–7).

POVEY, KENNETH, 'Handlist of Manuscripts in the Cowper and Newton Musuem, Olney, Bucks', *Transactions of the Cambridge Bibliographical Society*, 4 (1965), 107–27.

QUINLAN, M. J., *William Cowper: A Critical Life* (Minneapolis, 1953).

RACK, H. D., 'Survival and Revival: John Bennet, Methodism, and the Old Dissent', in *Protestant Evangelicalism: Britain, Ireland, Germany and America, c.1750–c.1950*, Studies in Church History, subsidia, 7, ed. K. Robbins (Oxford, 1990), 1–23.

—— *Reasonable Enthusiast: John Wesley and the Rise of Methodism* (1989).

RATCLIFF, OLIVER, *History and Antiquities of the Newport Hundreds* (Olney, 1990).

—— and BROWN, HERBERT, *Olney: Past and Present* (Olney, 1893).

RAWLYK, GEORGE, and NOLL, MARK (eds.), *Amazing Grace: Evangelicalism in Australia, Britain, Canada, and the United States* (Montreal, 1994).

REYNOLDS, JOHN, *The Evangelicals at Oxford, 1735–1871* (Oxford, 1975).

RIVERS, ISABEL, 'Strangers and Pilgrims: Sources and Patterns of Methodist Narrative', in J. D. Hilson, M. M. B. Jones, and J. R. Watson (eds.), *Augustan Worlds* (Leicester, 1978), 189–203.

—— (ed.), *Books and their Readers in Eighteenth-Century England* (Leicester, 1982).

—— *Reason, Grace, and Sentiment: A Study of the Language of Religion and Ethics in England, 1660–1780*, i. *Whichcote to Wesley* (Cambridge, 1991).

ROBBINS, KEITH (ed.), *Protestant Evangelicalism: Britain, Ireland, Germany, and America, c.1750–c.1950: Essays in Honour of W. R. Ward* (Oxford, 1990).

ROBINSON, H. WHEELER, 'A Baptist Student—John Collett Ryland', *Baptist Quarterly*, 3 (1926), 25–33.

ROBISON, OLIN C., 'The Particular Baptists in England, 1760–1820', D.Phil. thesis (Oxford, 1963).

ROSMAN, DOREEN M., *Evangelicals and Culture* (1984).

ROUTLEY, ERIK, *Christian Hymns Observed* (Princeton, 1982).

RUPP, GORDON, 'Introductory Essay', in Davies and Rupp (eds.), *A History of the Methodist Church in Great Britain*, i (1965).

—— *Religion in England, 1688–1791*, in Henry Chadwick and Owen Chadwick (eds.), Oxford History of the Christian Church, (Oxford, 1986).

RUSSELL, NORMA, *A Bibliography of William Cowper to 1837*, Oxford Bibliographical Society Publications, NS 12 (Oxford, 1963).

RYLE, J. C., *Christian Leaders of the Eighteenth Century* (1st edn., 1885; repr., Edinburgh, 1978).

SANGSTER, P. E., 'The Life of Rowland Hill (1744–1833) and his Position in the Evangelical Revival', D.Phil. thesis (Oxford, 1964).

SEELEY, MARY, *Later Evangelical Fathers* (1879).

SMYTH, CHARLES, *Simeon and Church Order: A Study of the Origins of the Evangelical Revival in Cambridge in the Eighteenth Century* (Cambridge, 1940).

—— 'The Evangelical Movement in Perspective', *Cambridge Historical Journal*, 7 (1943), 160–74.

SOUTHEY, ROBERT, *The Life and Works of William Cowper*, 15 vols. (1835–7).

SPACKS, PATRICIA MEYER, 'Forgotten Genres', *Modern Language Studies*, 18/1 (1988), 47–57.

STAUFFER, DONALD A., *The Art of Biography in Eighteenth-Century England* (Princeton, 1941).

STEPHEN, JAMES, *Essays in Ecclesiastical Biography* (1849; new edn., 1875).

STEWART, KEITH, 'Towards Defining an Aesthetic for the Familiar Letter in Eighteenth-Century England', *Prose Studies*, 5 (1982), 179–92.

STOCK, EUGENE, *History of the Church Missionary Society*, 3 vols. and suppl. (1899–1916).

STOEFFLER, F. ERNEST, *The Rise of Evangelical Pietism*, Studies in the History of Religions, 9 (Leiden, 1971).

STOUT, HARRY S., *The Divine Dramatist: George Whitefield and the Rise of Modern Evangelicalism* (Grand Rapids, Mich., 1991).

SYKES, H. NORMAN, *Church and State in England in the Eighteenth Century* (Cambridge, 1934).

THEIN, ADELAID E., 'The Religion of John Newton', *Philological Quarterly*, 21 (1942), 146–70.

THOMSON, R. W., 'John Newton and His Baptist Friends', *Baptist Quarterly*, 9 (1939), 368–71.

Bibliography

TODD, JANET, 'The Preacher as Prophet: John Newton's Evangelical Hymns', *The Hymn* (1980), 149–53, 158.

TOLLEY, CHRISTOPHER, 'The Legacy of Evangelicalism in the Lives and Writings of Certain Descendants of the Clapham Sect', D.Phil. thesis (Oxford, 1980).

TOON, PETER, *The Emergence of Hyper-Calvinism in English Non-Conformity, 1689–1765* (1967).

TOWLSON, CLIFFORD W., *Moravian and Methodist* (1957).

TYERMAN, LUKE, *Life and Times of the Rev. John Wesley*, 3rd edn., 3 vols. (1876).

—— *Life of the Rev. George Whitefield*, 2 vols. (1876).

VIRGIN, PETER, *The Church in an Age of Negligence* (Cambridge, 1989).

VON ROHR, JOHN, *The Covenant of Grace in Puritan Thought*, American Academy of Religion Studies in Religion, 45, ed. Charley Hardwick and James O. Duke (Atlanta, 1986).

WADDINGTON, JOHN, *Congregational History, 1700–1800* (1876).

WAKEFIELD, GORDON, *Puritan Devotion* (1957).

WALLACE, DEWEY D., JR., *Puritans and Predestination: Grace in English Protestant Theology, 1525–1695* (Chapel Hill, NC, 1982).

Walsh, John, 'The Yorkshire Evangelicals in the Eighteenth Century: With Special Reference to Methodism', Ph.D. thesis (Cambridge, 1956).

—— 'The Magdalene Evangelicals', *Church Quarterly Review* 159 (1958), 499–511.

—— 'Joseph Milner's Evangelical Church History', *Journal of Ecclesiastical History*, 10 (1959), 174–87.

—— 'The Origins of the Evangelical Revival', in G. V. Bennet and John Walsh (eds.), *Essays in Modern English Church History* (1966), 132–62.

—— 'Methodism and the Mob in the Eighteenth Century', in G. J. Cumming and David Baker (eds.), *Popular Practice and Belief*, Studies in Church History, 8 (Cambridge, 1972), 267–76.

—— 'The Cambridge Methodists', in *Christian Spirituality: Essays in Honour of Gordon Rupp* (1973).

—— 'The Anglican Evangelicals in the Eighteenth Century', in Marcel Simon (ed.), *Aspects de L'Anglicanisme* (Paris, 1974), 87–102.

—— 'Religious Societies: Methodist and Evangelical, 1738–1800', in W. J. Shiels and Diana Wood (eds.), *Voluntary Religion*, Studies in Church History, 23 (Oxford, 1986), 279–302.

WALSH, JOHN, HAYDON, COLIN, and TAYLOR, STEPHEN (eds.), *The Church of England, c.1689–c.1833: From Toleration to Tractarianism* (Cambridge, 1993).

Bibliography

WARD, W. REGINALD, 'The Relations of Enlightenment and Religious Revival in Central Europe and in the English-Speaking World', in Derek Baker (ed.), *Reform and Reformation: England and the Continent, c.1500–c.1750*, Studies in Church History, 2 (Oxford, 1979), 281–305.

—— Introduction to *Journals and Diaries I*, ed. W. Reginald Ward and Richard P. Heitzenrater, vol. xviii in *The Works of John Wesley*, ed. Richard P. Heitzenrater and Frank Baker (Nashville, 1988), 1–119.

—— *The Protestant Evangelical Awakening* (Cambridge, 1992).

WATKINS, OWEN C, *The Puritan Experience* (1972).

WATSON, J. R., 'Cowper's Olney Hymns', *Essays and Studies*, NS 38 (1985), 45–65.

WATTS, MICHAEL R., *The Dissenters*, i. *From the Reformation to the French Revolution* (Oxford, 1978).

WEBER, MAX, *The Protestant Ethic and the Spirit of Capitalism*, trans. Talcott Parsons (New York, 1958).

WELCH, EDWIN (ed.), *Two Calvinistic Chapels, 1743–1811* (1975).

WESTERKAMP, MARILYN J., *The Triumph of the Laity: Scots–Irish Piety and the Great Awakening, 1625–1760* (New York, 1988).

WHITLEY, W. T., *The Baptists of North-west England, 1649–1913* (1913).

—— *The Baptists of London, 1612–1928* [1928].

WILLMER, HADDON, 'Evangelicalism, 1785–1835', Hulsean Prize Essay (Cambridge, 1962).

WILSON, WALTER, *The History and Antiquities of Dissenting Churches and Meeting Houses in London*, 4 vols. (1808–14).

WOOD, A. SKEVINGTON, 'John Newton's Church History', *Evangelical Quarterly*, 23 (1951), 51–70.

—— 'The Influence of Thomas Haweis on John Newton', *Journal of Ecclesiastical History*, 4 (1953), 187–202.

—— *Thomas Haweis, 1734–1820* (1957).

—— *The Inextinguishable Blaze* (1960).

WORCESTER, J. F., *The Worcester Family: or the Descendants of Rev. William Worcester* (Lynn, Mass., 1856).

WRIGHT, THOMAS, *Town of Cowper* (1893).

—— 'Olney Men, 7', *Olney Advertiser* (13 November 1909).

—— *Romance of the Lace Pillow* (Olney, 1919).

—— *The Life of William Cowper*, 2nd edn. (1921).

WÜRZBACH, NATASCHA (ed.), *The Novel in Letters: Epistolary Fiction in the Early English Novel, 1678–1740* (1969).

INDEX

Index

Index

Greek Orthodoxy, *see* Eastern
 Orthodoxy
Green, John 104–5
Grimshaw, William 46, 52, 85, 95,
 109, 137, 140
Gunter, Stephen 132, 137
Guyon, Mme 238
Guyse, John 70

Hale, Matthew 333
Hall, Joseph 123
Hall, Robert, Jun. 146, 149
Hall, Robert, Sen. 142–3, 147, 155
Halyburton, Thomas 80, 150–1, 155,
 156, 333
Hammond, William 260
Handel, George Frideric 162, 265
Hart, Joseph 270
Hartley, Lodwick 3
Haweis, Thomas 4, 32–3, 41, 47, 96,
 99–104, 112–13, 116–17, 239,
 247, 258, 265, 293, 317–18
Hawker, Robert 162
Hawksmoor, Nicholas 306
Hayward, Samuel 22, 70, 72
Henry, Matthew 226, 334
Hensemen, William 176
Herbert, George 273, 286
Hervey, James 21, 55, 66, 117, 122,
 128–30, 133, 134, 184, 333, 334
Hesketh, Lady Harriot 171
high Calvinism, *see under* Calvinism
Hill, Richard 122
Hill, Rowland 122, 300
Hooker, Richard 88
Hopkins, John 264
Horneck, Anthony 336
Howe, John 333
Hoyles, John 284, 286–7
Huguenots 174
Huntingdon, Countess of 86, 96, 138,
 184–5, 298–300, 303–4, 326
Hussey, Joseph 144–5, 147, 152
hymns 64–5, 138–9, 188, 193, 197,
 198, 199, 201, 202, 237, 257–88,
 329, 331
hyper-Calvinism, *see under* Calvinism
hypothetical universalism 121–4

Ignatius Loyola, St 219, 234
inability, moral and natural 153–4, 165
Independents 37, 51, 53–4, 69–70, 71,
 85, 98–9, 108, 110–11, 121, 130,

132, 144–5, 178–81, 184–5, 205,
 215, 217–18, 298, 302–5, 315,
 316, 319, 323
Ingham, Benjamin 85

James, John 174
Janeway, James 197
Jay, William 167, 311–12
Jennings, David 54, 63, 67–70, 91–2
Jerram, Charles 295
John Climacus, St 274
Johnson, John 76–7, 142
Johnson, Samuel 285
Johnson, Wolsey 177, 184
Jones, Robert 157
Jones, Thomas, of Clifton Reynes
 157–8, 242
Jones, Thomas, of Creaton 109
Jones, Thomas, of St Saviour's,
 Southwark 96
Joss, Torial 298
Josselin, Ralph 175
justification 15, 42, 57, 60, 116–17,
 124–5, 134–5, 137, 138–9, 144,
 148, 150, 151, 155, 164, 230, 231,
 253, 314, 328

Keene, Edmund 89, 104
Kempis, Thomas à 19, 332
Kent, Joseph 176
Knight, Mr 101

Lambe, Sir John 173–4
latitude, latitudinarianism 79, 128,
 133, 140–1, 156, 328, 330
La Trobe, Benjamin 301, 313
Laud, William 174–5
Law, William 59–60, 239, 245, 286–7
Leaver, Robin 265–6
Lecky, William 5
lectureships, London 291–5
legalism 122, 124, 231, 330
 see also moralism
Leighton, Robert 80, 335
letters, *see* familiar letter, genre
Liverpool 20–2, 61, 68, 73–4, 76–9,
 82, 83–4, 88, 92, 97–9, 101–2,
 106–8, 111–13, 116, 126–7,
 129–32, 139, 161, 212, 218, 225,
 226, 239, 258
Locke, John 139, 330
Lollards 240

Index

Index